# COCOA® PROGRAMMING FOR MAC® OS X

## FOURTH EDITION

# Cocoa® Programming for Mac® OS X

## FOURTH EDITION

**Aaron Hillegass**
**Adam Preble**

**✦✦Addison-Wesley**

Upper Saddle River, NJ • Boston • Indianapolis • San Francisco
New York • Toronto • Montreal • London • Munich • Paris • Madrid
Capetown • Sydney • Tokyo • Singapore • Mexico City

The publisher offers excellent discounts on this book when ordered in quantity for bulk purchases or special sales, which may include electronic versions and/or custom covers and content particular to your business, training goals, marketing focus, and branding interests. For more information, please contact:

U.S. Corporate and Government Sales
(800) 382-3419
corpsales@pearsontechgroup.com

For sales outside the United States, please contact:

International Sales
international@pearson.com

Visit us on the Web: informit.com/aw

*Library of Congress Cataloging-in-Publication Data*
Hillegass, Aaron.
    Cocoa programming for Mac OS X / Aaron Hillegass, Adam Preble.—4th ed.
        p.   cm.
    Includes index.
    ISBN 978-0-321-77408-8 (pbk. : alk. paper)
    1. Cocoa (Application development environment)  2. Operating systems
(Computers)  3. Mac OS.  4. Macintosh (Computer)—Programming.  I. Preble, Adam. II. Title.

    QA76.76.O63H57145 2012
    005.26'8—dc23

                                                              2011034459

ISBN-13: 978-0-321-77408-8
ISBN-10:    0-321-77408-6

Text printed in the United States on recycled paper at RR Donnelley in Crawfordsville, Indiana.
First printing, November 2011

*For Aaron's sons, Walden and Otto*

*and*

*For Adam's daughter, Aimee*

# CONTENTS

# PREFACE

If you are developing applications for the Mac, or are hoping to do so, this book is just the resource you need. Does it cover everything you will ever want to know about programming for the Mac? Of course not. But it does cover probably 80% of what you need to know. You can find the remaining 20%—the 20% that is unique to you—in Apple's online documentation.

This book, then, acts as a foundation. It covers the Objective-C language and the major design patterns of Cocoa. It will also get you started with the two most commonly used developer tools: Xcode and Instruments. After reading this book, you will be able to understand and utilize Apple's online documentation.

There is a lot of code in this book. Through that code, we will introduce you to the idioms of the Cocoa community. Our hope is that by presenting exemplary code, we can help you to become more than a Cocoa developer—a stylish Cocoa developer.

This fourth edition includes technologies introduced in Mac OS X 10.6 and 10.7. These include Xcode 4, ARC, blocks, view-based table views, and the Mac App Store. We have also devoted one chapter to the basics of iOS development.

This book is written for programmers who already know some C programming and something about objects. If you don't know C or objects, you should first read *Objective-C Programming: The Big Nerd Ranch Guide*. You are not expected to have any experience with Mac programming. This hands-on book assumes that you have access to Mac OS X and the developer tools. Xcode 4.2, Apple's IDE, is available for free. If you are a member of the paid Mac or iOS Developer Programs, Xcode can also be downloaded from the Apple Developer Connection Web site (http://developer.apple.com/). Enrollment in these programs enables you to submit your applications to the Mac and iOS App Stores, respectively.

We have tried to make this book as useful for you as possible, if not indispensable. That said, we'd love to hear from you at cocoabook@bignerdranch.com if you have any suggestions for improving it.

—Aaron Hillegass and Adam Preble

# ACKNOWLEDGMENTS

Creating this book required the efforts of many people. We want to thank them for their help. Their contributions have made this a better book than we could have ever written alone.

Thanks to the students who took the Cocoa programming course at the Big Nerd Ranch. They helped us work the kinks out of the exercises and explanations that appear here. Their curiosity inspired us to make the book more comprehensive, and their patience made it possible.

Thank you to all the readers of the first three editions, who made such great suggestions on our forums (http://forums.bignerdranch.com/).

Thank you to all the instructors at the Ranch, who made great additions and caught many of our most egregious errors.

A final shout out to the people at Addison-Wesley, who took our manuscript and made it into a book. They put the book on trucks and convinced bookstores to put it on the shelves. Without their help, it would still be just a stack of paper.

# Chapter 1
# COCOA: WHAT IS IT?

## A Little History

The story of Cocoa starts with a delightful bit of history. Once upon a time, two guys named Steve started a company called Apple Computer in their garage. The company grew rapidly, so they hired an experienced executive named John Sculley to be its CEO. After a few conflicts, John Sculley moved Steve Jobs to a position where he had no control over the company at all. Steve Jobs left to form another computer company, called NeXT Computer.

NeXT hired a small team of brilliant engineers. This small team developed a computer, an operating system, a printer, a factory, and a set of development tools. Each piece was years ahead of competing technologies, and the masses were excited and amazed. Unfortunately, the excited masses did not buy either the computer or the printer. In 1993, the factory was closed, and NeXT Computer, Inc., became NeXT Software, Inc.

The operating system and the development tools continued to sell under the name NeXTSTEP. While the average computer user had never heard of NeXTSTEP, it was very popular with several groups: scientists, investment banks, and intelligence agencies. These were people who developed new applications every week, and they found that NeXTSTEP enabled them to implement their ideas faster than any other technology.

What was this operating system? NeXT decided to use Unix as the core of NeXTSTEP. It relied on the source code for BSD Unix from the University of California at Berkeley. Why Unix? Unix crashed much less frequently than Microsoft Windows or Mac OS and came with powerful, reliable networking capabilities.

Apple has made the source code to the Unix part of Mac OS X available under the name Darwin. A community of developers continues to work to improve Darwin. You can learn more about Darwin at www.macosforge.org.

NeXT then wrote a *window server* for the operating system. A window server takes events from the user and forwards them to the applications. The application then sends drawing commands back to the window server to update what the user sees. One of the nifty things about the NeXT window server is that the drawing code that goes to the window server is the same drawing code that would be sent to the printer. Thus, a programmer has to write the drawing code only once, and it can then be used for display on the screen or printing. In the NeXTSTEP days, programmers were writing code that generated PostScript. With Mac OS X, programmers are writing code that uses the Core Graphics framework (also known as Quartz). Quartz can composite those graphics onto the screen, send them to the printer, or generate PDF data. The Portable Document Format is an open standard for vector graphics created by the Adobe Corporation.

If you have used Unix machines before, you are probably familiar with the X window server. The window server for Mac OS X is completely different but fulfills the same function as the X window server: It gets events from the user, forwards them to the applications, and puts data from the applications onto the screen.

NeXTSTEP came with a set of libraries and tools to enable programmers to deal with the window manager in an elegant manner. The libraries were called frameworks. In 1993, the frameworks and tools were revised and renamed OpenStep, which was itself later renamed Cocoa.

As shown in Figure 1.1, the window server and your application are Unix processes. Cocoa enables your application to receive events from the window server and draw to the screen.

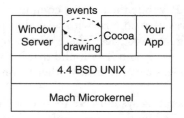

**Figure 1.1**   Where Is Cocoa?

Programming with the frameworks is done in a language called *Objective-C*. Like C++, Objective-C is a C programming language extension that made it object-oriented. Unlike C++, Objective-C is weakly typed and extremely powerful. With power comes responsibility: Objective-C also allows programmers to make ridiculous errors. Objective-C is a very simple addition to C, and you will find it very easy to learn.

Programmers loved OpenStep. It enabled them to experiment more easily with new ideas. In fact, Tim Berners-Lee developed the first Web browser and the first Web server on NeXTSTEP. Securities analysts could code and test new financial models much more quickly. Colleges could develop the applications that made their research possible. We don't know what the intelligence community was using it for, but they bought thousands of copies of OpenStep. Because the OpenStep development tools were so useful, they were ported to Solaris and Windows NT, and the NeXTSTEP operating system was ported to most of the popular CPUs of the day: Intel, Motorola, Hewlett-Packard's PA-RISC, and SPARC. (Oddly enough, OpenStep didn't run on a Mac until the first version of Mac OS X Server, known as Rhapsody, shipped in 1999.)

For many years, Apple Computer had been working to develop an operating system with many of the features of NeXTSTEP. This effort was known as Copland. Project Copland gradually spun out of control, and Apple finally decided to pull the plug and buy the next version of Mac OS from another company. After surveying the existing operating systems, Apple selected NeXTSTEP. Because NeXT was small, Apple simply bought the whole company in December 1996.

NeXTSTEP became Mac OS X. It is Unix underneath, and you can get all the standard Unix programs (such as the Apache Web server) on Mac OS X. It is extremely stable and the user interface is spectacular.

In 2008, the iOS SDK, as it would eventually be called, was announced. Apple's incredibly successful App Store has brought an audience of millions to iOS developers, many of whom are also Cocoa developers on the Mac. Cocoa Touch is built on top of the very same foundations as Cocoa, and indeed many of the classes are identical. More important, the principles and design patterns are essentially unchanged. In 2010, just ahead of Mac OS X Lion, Apple introduced the Mac App Store, bringing the same ease of distribution to Mac developers.

You, the developer, are going to love Mac OS X because Cocoa will enable you to write full-featured applications in a radically more efficient and elegant manner.

# Tools

You *will* love Cocoa but perhaps not immediately. First, you will learn the basics. Let's start with the tools that you will use.

All the tools for Cocoa development come as part of the Mac OS X Developer Tools, and you get them for free with Mac OS X. Although the Developer Tools will add about a dozen handy applications to your system, you will use one application primarily: Xcode. Behind the scenes, either the LLVM (Low Level Virtual Machine) or the GNU C compiler (gcc) will be used to compile your code, and the GNU debugger (gdb) or the LLDB (Low Level Debugger) will help you find your errors.

*Xcode* tracks all the resources that will go into an application: code, images, sounds, and so on. You will edit your code in Xcode, and Xcode can compile and launch your application. Xcode can also be used to invoke and control the debugger. We strongly recommend using Xcode 4.2 or greater when trying the exercises in this book. While many of the concepts covered can be applied in the Xcode 3 and even earlier, the style of memory management used (ARC) requires the Xcode 4.2 compiler.

Inside Xcode, you will use the *Interface Builder* editor as a GUI builder. It edits XIB files, allowing you to lay out windows and add widgets to those windows. It is, however, much more. Interface Builder allows the developer to create objects and edit their attributes. Most of those objects are UI elements such as buttons and text fields, but some will be instances of classes that you create.

You will also use *Instruments* to profile your application's CPU, memory, and filesystem usage. Instruments can also be used to debug memory-management issues. Instruments is built on top of dtrace, which makes it possible to create new instruments.

# Language

This book uses Objective-C for all the examples. Objective-C is a simple and elegant extension to C, and mastering it will take about two hours if you already know C and an object-oriented language such as Java or C++.

It is possible to develop Cocoa applications in Ruby or Python. This book will not cover that technique, but there is plenty of information on the Web. To understand that information, you will still need a working knowledge Objective-C.

With Mac OS 10.5, Objective-C underwent a major revision. All the code in this book is Objective-C 2.0, and almost all of the code in this book uses ARC for memory management. We will discuss memory management in further detail in Chapter 4.

The Objective-C code will be compiled by the LLVM compiler. The compiler allows you to freely mix C, C++, and Objective-C code in a single file.

The debugger, gdb or lldb, will be used to set breakpoints and browse variables at runtime. Objective-C gives you a lot of freedom to do dumb things; you will be glad to have a decent debugger.

# Objects, Classes, Methods, and Messages

All Cocoa programming is done using object-oriented concepts. This section very briefly reviews terms used in object-oriented programming. If you have not done any object-oriented programming before, we recommend that you read *The Objective-C Language*. The PDF file for the book is on the Apple Web site, The URL is http://developer.apple.com/library/mac/documentaion/Cocoa/Conceptual/ObjectiveC/ObjC.pdf.

What is an object? An *object* is like a C struct: It takes up memory and has variables inside it. The variables in an object are called *instance variables*. So when dealing with objects, the first questions we typically ask are: How do you allocate space for one? What instance variables does the object have? How do you destroy the object when you are done with it?

Some of the instance variables of an object will be pointers to other objects. These pointers enable one object to "know about" another.

*Classes* are structures that can create objects. Classes specify the variables that the object has and are responsible for allocating memory for the object. We say that the object is an *instance* of the class that created it (Figure 1.2).

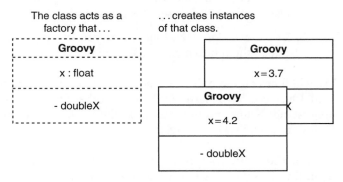

**Figure 1.2**   Classes Create Instances

An object is better than a struct because an object can have functions associated with it. We call the functions *methods*. To call a method, you send the object a *message* (Figure 1.3).

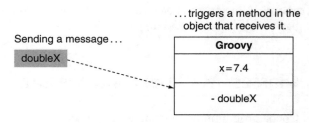

**Figure 1.3**    Messages Trigger Methods

# Frameworks

A *framework* is a collection of classes that are intended to be used together. That is, the classes are compiled together into a reusable library of code. Any related resources are put into a directory with the library. The directory is renamed with the extension .framework. You can find the built-in frameworks for your machine in /System/Library/Frameworks. Cocoa is made up of three frameworks:

1. *Foundation*: Every object-oriented programming language needs the standard value, collection, and utility classes. Strings, dates, lists, threads, and timers are in the Foundation framework.

2. *AppKit*: All things related to the user interface are in the AppKit framework. These include windows, buttons, text fields, events, and drawing classes. You will also see this framework called the *ApplicationKit*.

3. *Core Data*: Core Data makes it easy to save your objects to a file and then reload them into memory. We say that it is a *persistence* framework.

We will focus on these three frameworks because they are the most commonly used. Once you have mastered these, the other frameworks will be easier to understand. Numerous other frameworks handle such duties as encryption, QuickTime, and CD burning.

You can also create your own frameworks from the classes that you create. Typically, if a set of classes is used in several applications, you will want to turn them into a framework.

# How to Read This Book

This book acts as the guide through activities to help you understand Cocoa programming. Often, we will ask you to do something and explain the details or theory afterward. If you are confused, read a little more. Usually, the help you seek will be only a paragraph or two away.

If you are still stumped, you can get help on the Web site for this book: www.bignerdranch.com/books. Errata, hints, and examples are listed there as well. Also, all the solutions for the exercises can be downloaded from there. You can also post questions about the book and concepts discussed in the book on the Big Nerd Ranch forums (http://forums.bignerdranch.com/).

Each chapter will guide you through the process of adding features to an application. This is not, however, a cookbook. This book teaches ideas, and the exercises show these ideas in action. Don't be afraid to experiment.

There are about 300 classes in the Cocoa frameworks. All are documented in the online reference (accessed through Xcode's `Help` menu). Cocoa programmers spend a lot of time browsing through these pages. But until you understand a lot about Cocoa, it is hard to find the right starting place in your search for answers. As this book introduces you to a new class, look it up in the reference. You may not understand everything you find there, but browsing through the reference will give you some appreciation for the richness of the frameworks. When you reach the end of this book, the reference will become your guide.

Most of the time, Cocoa fulfills the following promise: Common things are easy, and uncommon things are possible. If you find yourself writing many lines of code to do something rather ordinary, you are probably on the wrong track.

# Typographical Conventions

To make the book easier to comprehend, we've used several typographical conventions.

In Objective-C, class names are always capitalized. In this book, we've also made them appear in a monospaced bold font. In Objective-C, method names start with a lowercase letter. Method names will also appear in a monospaced bold font. For example, you might see "The class **NSObject** has the method **dealloc**."

Other literals, including instance variable names that you would see in code, will appear in a regular monospaced font. Also, filenames will appear in this same font. Thus, you might see "In MyClass.m, set the variable favoriteColor to nil."

Code samples in this book appear in the regular monospaced font. New portions, which you will need to type yourself, will appear in bold.

## Common Mistakes

Having watched many, many people work through this material, we've seen the same mistakes made hundreds of times. Two mistakes are particularly common: capitalization mistakes and forgotten connections.

Capitalization mistakes happen because C and Objective-C are case-sensitive languages—the compiler does not consider Foo and foo to be the same thing. If you are having trouble making something compile, check to make sure that you have typed all the letters in the correct case.

When creating an application, you will use the Interface Builder editor to connect objects together. Forgotten connections usually allow your application to build and run but result in aberrant behavior. If your application is misbehaving, go back to Interface Builder and check your connections.

It is easy to miss some warnings the first time a file is compiled. Because Xcode does incremental compiles, you may not see those warnings again unless you clean and rebuild the project. If you are stuck, cleaning and rebuilding is certainly worth a try.

## How to Learn

All sorts of people come to our class: the bright and the not so bright, the motivated and the lazy, the experienced and the novice. Inevitably, the people who get the most from the class share one characteristic: They remain focused on the topic at hand.

The first trick to maintaining focus is to get enough sleep: ten hours of sleep each night while you are studying new ideas. Before dismissing this idea, try it. You will wake up refreshed and ready to learn. *Caffeine is not a substitute for sleep.*

The second trick is to stop thinking about yourself. While learning something new, many students will think, "Damn, this is hard for me. I wonder if I am stupid." Because stupidity is such an unthinkably terrible thing in our culture, the students will then spend hours constructing arguments that explain why they are intelligent yet are having difficulties. The moment you start down this path, you have lost your focus.

Aaron used to have a boss named Rock. Rock had earned a degree in astrophysics from Cal Tech and had never had a job that used his knowledge of the heavens. He was once asked if he regretted getting the degree. "Actually, my degree in astrophysics has proved to be very valuable," he said. "Some things in this world are just hard. When I am struggling with something, I sometimes think 'Damn, this is hard for me. I wonder if I am stupid,' and then I remember that I have a degree in astrophysics from Cal Tech; I must not be stupid."

Before going any further, assure yourself that you are not stupid and that some things are just hard. Armed with this silly affirmation and a well-rested mind, you are ready to conquer Cocoa.

## Chapter 2
# LET'S GET STARTED

Many books would start off by giving you a lot of philosophy. This would be a waste of precious paper at this point. Instead, we are going to guide you through writing your first Cocoa application. Upon finishing, you will be excited and confused…and ready for the philosophy.

Our first project will be a random number generator application. It will have two buttons: Seed random number generator using time and Generate random number. A text field will display the generated number. This simple example involves taking user input and generating output. At times, the description of what you are doing and why will seem, well, terse. Don't worry—we will explore all this in more detail throughout this book. For now, just play along.

Figure 2.1 shows what the completed application will look like.

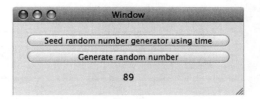

**Figure 2.1** Completed Application

# In Xcode

Assuming that you have installed the Developer Tools, you will find Xcode in /Developer/Applications/. You will be using the application a lot, so drag it to the dock at the bottom of your screen. Launch Xcode. (If you have never run Xcode before, you may get a Welcome page. Just take all the defaults and click through.)

As mentioned earlier, Xcode will keep track of all the resources that go into your application. All these resources will be kept in a directory called the *project directory*. The first step in developing a new application is to create a new project directory with the default skeleton of an application.

## Create a New Project

Under the File menu, choose New, then New Project.... When the panel appears (see Figure 2.2), choose the type of project you would like to create: Cocoa Application. Note that many other types of projects are available as well.

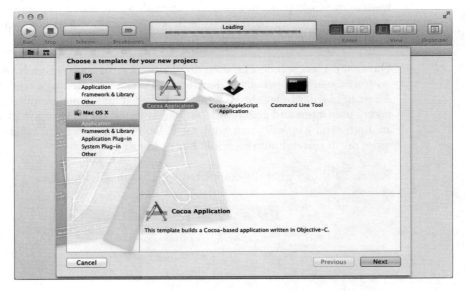

**Figure 2.2**    Choose Project Type

In this book, we will discuss the following major types of projects:

*Application:* A program that creates windows.

*Tool:* A program that does not have a graphical user interface. Typically, a tool is a command-line utility or a daemon that runs in the background.

*Bundle or framework:* A directory of resources that can be used in an application or tool. A bundle (also called a *plug-in*) is dynamically loaded at runtime. An application typically links against a framework at compile time.

For the project name, type in Random, as in Figure 2.3. Application names are typically capitalized. Set the Class Prefix to Random and uncheck Create

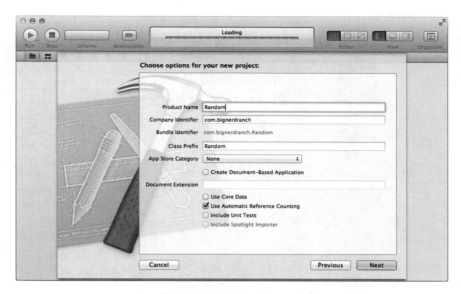

**Figure 2.3**   Name Project

Document-Based Application, Use Core Data, and Include Unit Tests. Make sure that Use Automatic Reference Counting is checked. We will use this setting in every new project in this book.

Next, you will pick the directory in which your project directory will be created. By default, your project directory will be created inside your home directory. Uncheck Create local git repository for this project. Click the Create button.

A project directory will be created for you, with the skeleton of an application inside it. You will extend this skeleton into the source for a complete application and then compile the source into a working application.

Looking at the new project in Xcode, you will see an outline view on the left side of the window. Each item in the outline view represents a file in your project. This is the project tab of the navigator; other navigator tabs show such information as compiler errors or find results. For now, you will be dealing with editing files, so expand the item that says Random to see the files that will be compiled into an application.

The skeleton of a project that was created for you will compile and run. It has a menu and a window. Click on the Run toolbar item to build and run the project, as shown in Figure 2.4.

While the application is launching, you will see a bouncing icon in the dock. The name of your application will then appear in the menu. This means that your

Choose

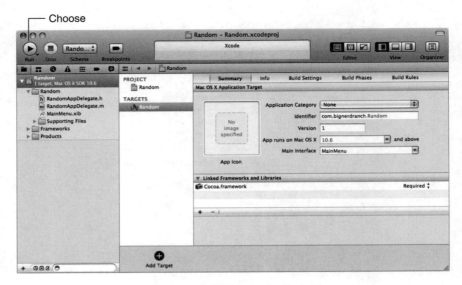

**Figure 2.4**   Skeleton of a Project

application is now active. The window for your application may be hidden by another window. If you do not see your window, choose **Hide Others** from the Random menu. You should see an empty window, as shown in Figure 2.5.

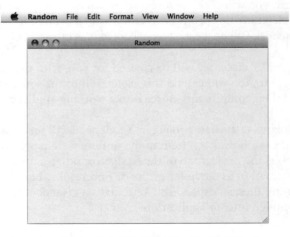

**Figure 2.5**   Running the Project

Although it doesn't do much, your application is already fully functional. Even printing works. There is exactly one line of code in the application. Let's look at it now; quit Random and return to Xcode.

## The main Function

Expand Supporting Files and select main.m by single-clicking on it. The code will appear in the editor (Figure 2.6). If you double-click on the filename, it will open in a new window. Because we deal with many files in a day, this tends to overwhelm us rather quickly, so we use the single-window style.

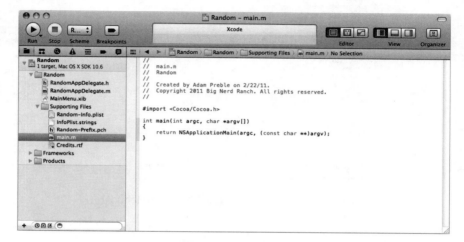

**Figure 2.6**    main() Function

You will almost never modify main.m in an application project. The default **main()** simply calls **NSApplicationMain()**, which loads and runs the objects that make up your application. In the next section, we will learn how **NSApplicationMain()** knows which objects to load.

# In Interface Builder

In the project navigator under Random, you will find a file called MainMenu.xib. Click on it to open it in the Interface Builder editor. Next, click the Utilities view toggle in the toolbar to show the right-side panel (Figure 2.7).

Interface Builder allows you to create and edit user interface objects, such as windows and buttons, for use in your application. You can also create instances of your custom classes and make connections between those instances and the standard user interface objects. When users interact with the user interface objects, the connections you have made between them and your custom classes will cause your code to be executed. Interface Builder saves these objects and their connections to a XIB (pronounced "zib") file.

Menu for your app            Inspector panel           Utilities view toggle

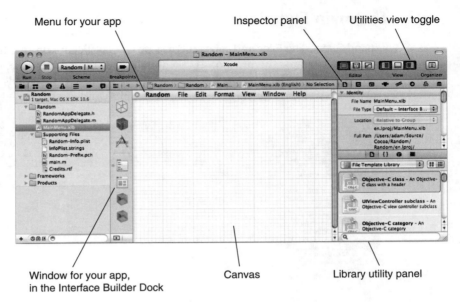

Window for your app,           Canvas         Library utility panel
in the Interface Builder Dock

**Figure 2.7**    MainMenu.xib

## The Utility Area

The utility area has two panels: the Inspector and the Library. The Inspector panel contains settings for the currently selected file or Interface Builder object. The Library panel contains file templates, snippets, objects, and media that can be used in your project. User interface widgets can be dragged from the object library into your interface. For example, if you want a button, you can drag it from the object library area.

## The Blank Window

Click on the window icon in the Interface Builder dock. The blank window that appears represents an instance of the **NSWindow** class that is inside your XIB file (Figure 2.8).

As you drop objects from the library onto the window, they will be added to the XIB file. After you have created instances of these objects and edited their attributes, saving the XIB file is like "freeze-drying" (or *archiving*) the objects into the file. When our Random application runs, **NSRunApplication()** *unarchives* the objects we created in the XIB and brings them back to life. A more complex application would likely have several XIB files that are loaded as needed.

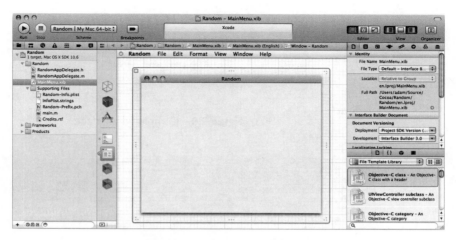

**Figure 2.8**  NSWindow Instance

Once your application has loaded the objects, it simply waits for the user to do something. When the user clicks or types, your code will be called automatically. If you have never written an application with a graphical user interface before, this change will be startling to you: The user is in control, and your code simply reacts to what the user does.

### For the More Curious: XIBs and NIBs

A XIB file is an XML representation of user interface objects and their connections. When you build your application, the XIB file is compiled into a NIB file. The XIB file is easier to work with, particularly for source control, but the NIB file is smaller and easier to parse, which is why the file that ships with your application is a NIB. Generally speaking, you will manipulate only XIB files, and your application will use only NIB files, but most developers use the words XIB and NIB interchangeably. (*Trivia:* "NIB" stands for "NeXT Interface Builder"; "NS" stands for "NeXTSTEP.")

## Lay Out the Interface

We are going to walk you through it, but keep in mind that your goal is to create a user interface that looks like Figure 2.9.

Select Cocoa in the library selector bar. Drag a button from the Library window (as shown in Figure 2.10) and drop it onto the blank window. (To make it easier

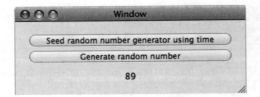

**Figure 2.9**   Completed Interface

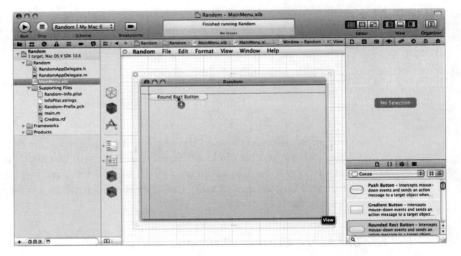

**Figure 2.10**   Dragging a Button

to find, you can either select the Cocoa -> Controls group in the pop-up at the top of the Library panel or type button in the search field.)

Double-click on the button to change its title to Seed random number generator using time.

Copy and paste the button. Relabel the new button Generate random number. Drag out a Label text field (as shown in Figure 2.11) and drop it onto the window.

To make the text field as wide as the buttons, drag the left and right sides of the text field toward the sides of the window. (You may notice that blue lines appear when you are close to the edge of the window. These guides are intended to help you conform to Apple's GUI guidelines.)

Make the window smaller by dragging the transparent handles surrounding it.

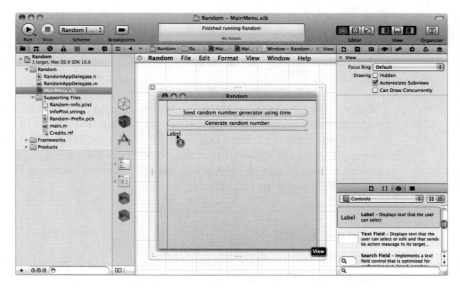

**Figure 2.11**   Dragging a Text Field

To make the text field center its contents, you will need to use the Attributes Inspector. Select the text field, and select the Attributes Inspector tab at the top of the inspector panel. Click on the center-justify button (Figure 2.12).

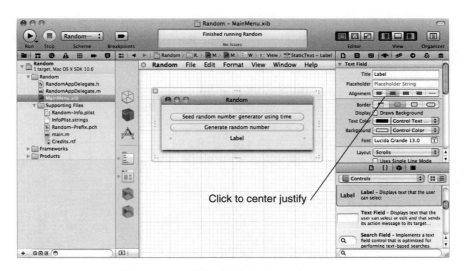

**Figure 2.12**   Text Field Attributes Inspector

# The Dock

In your XIB file, some objects, such as buttons, are visible, and others (like your custom controller objects), are invisible. The icons that represent the invisible objects appear in the *dock*.

The dock contains icons representing the main menu and the window. First Responder is a fictional object, but it is a very useful fiction. It will be fully explained in Chapter 21. File's Owner in this XIB is the **NSApplication** object for your application. The **NSApplication** object takes events from the event queue and forwards them to the appropriate window. We will discuss the meaning of File's Owner in depth in Chapter 12.

# Create a Class

In Objective-C, every class is defined by two files: a header file and an implementation file. The header file, also known as the interface file, declares the instance variables and methods your class will have. The implementation file defines what those methods do.

In Xcode, use the File->New->New File... menu item to create a new Cocoa -> Objective-C class. Name the class RandomController and set it to be a subclass of **NSObject**. (Figure 2.13).

The files RandomController.h and RandomController.m will appear in your project. If they don't appear in the Random group, drag them there (Figure 2.14).

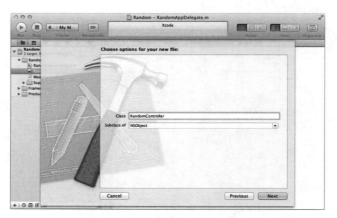

**Figure 2.13**   Create a New Class

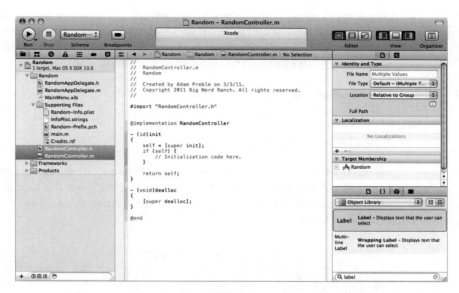

**Figure 2.14**    RandomController.h and .m in the Random Group

In RandomController.h, you will add instance variables and methods to your class. Instance variables that are pointers to other objects are called *outlets*. Methods that can be triggered by user interface objects are called *actions*.

Edit RandomController.h to look like this:

```
#import <Foundation/Foundation.h>

@interface RandomController : NSObject {
    IBOutlet NSTextField *textField;
}
- (IBAction)seed:(id)sender;
- (IBAction)generate:(id)sender;
@end
```

What can an Objective-C programmer tell from this file?

1. **RandomController** is a subclass of **NSObject**.

2. **RandomController** has one instance variable: textField is a pointer to an instance of the class **NSTextField**.

3. **RandomController** has two methods: **seed:** and **generate:** are action methods.

By convention, the names of methods and instance variables start with lowercase letters. If the name would be multiple words in English, each new word after the first one is capitalized—for example, `favoriteColor`. Also by convention, class names start with capital letters—for example, **RandomController.**

Save RandomController.h.

## Create an Instance

Next, you will create an instance of the class **RandomController** in your XIB file. Select MainMenu.xib to return to Interface Builder. From the Library panel, drag a blue Object (under Cocoa -> Objects & Controllers), and drop it onto the Interface Builder dock (Figure 2.15).

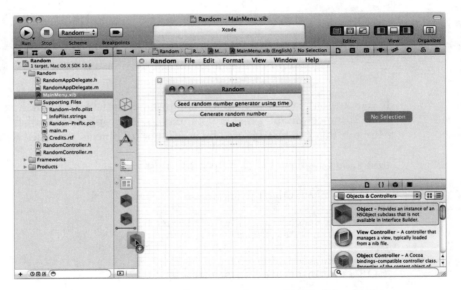

**Figure 2.15**   Drag an Object onto the Interface Builder dock.

In the Identity Inspector, set its class to **RandomController** (Figure 2.16). (Your actions and outlets should appear in the Connections Inspector. If they do not, check RandomController.h. You have a mistake in it, or it hasn't been saved.)

## Make Connections

A lot of object-oriented programming has to do with which objects need to know about which other objects. Now you are going to introduce some objects to each

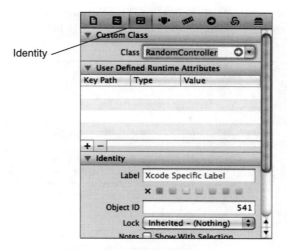

Identity

**Figure 2.16**  Setting the Class

other. Cocoa programmers would say, "We are now going to set the outlets of our objects." To introduce one object to another, you will Control-drag from *the object that needs to know* to the *object it needs to know about*. The object diagram in Figure 2.17 shows which objects need to be connected in your example.

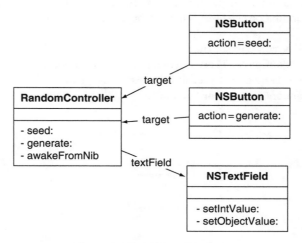

**Figure 2.17**  Object Diagram

You will set **RandomController**'s textField instance variable to point to the **NSTextField** object on the window that currently says Label. Right-click (or Control-click if you have a one-button mouse) on the icon that represents your instance of **RandomController**. The Connection panel will then appear. Drag from the circle beside `textField` to the text field that says Label (Figure 2.18).

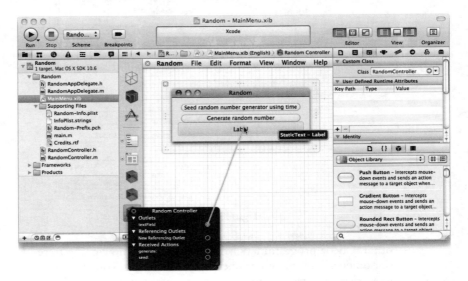

**Figure 2.18** Set the textField Outlet

This step is all about pointers: You have to just set the pointer `textField` in your **RandomController** object to point to the text field.

Now you will set the Seed button's `target` outlet to point to your instance of **RandomController**. Furthermore, you want the button to trigger **RandomController**'s `seed:` method. Control-drag from the button to your instance of **RandomController**. When the panel appears, select **seed:** (Figure 2.19).

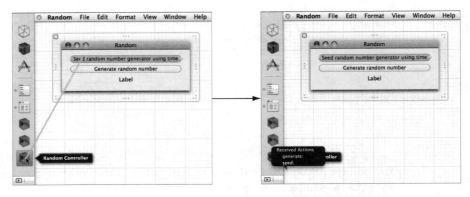

**Figure 2.19** Set the Target and Action of the Seed Button

Similarly, you will set the Generate button's `target` outlet to point to your instance of **RandomController** and set its action to the **generate:** method. Control-drag from the button to **RandomController**. Choose **generate:** in the Received Actions panel (Figure 2.20).

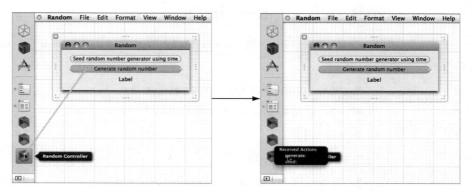

**Figure 2.20**    Set the Target and Action of the Generate Button

# A Look at Objective-C

If this is the first time that you are seeing Objective-C code, you may be alarmed to discover that it looks quite different from C++ or Java code. The syntax may be different, but the underlying concepts are the same. For example, a class in Java would be declared like this:

```
import com.megacorp.Bar;
import com.megacorp.Baz;

public class Rex extends Bar implements Baz {
...methods and instance variables...
}
```

This says, "The class **Rex** inherits from the class **Bar** and implements the methods declared in the **Baz** interface."

The analogous class in Objective-C would be declared like this:

```
#import <megacorp/Bar.h>
#import <megacorp/Baz.h>

@interface Rex : Bar <Baz> {
...instance variables...
}
...methods...
@end
```

If you know Java, Objective-C really isn't so strange. Note that like Java, Objective-C allows only single inheritance; that is, a class has only one superclass.

## Types and Constants in Objective-C

Objective-C programmers use a few types that are not found in the rest of the C world.

- id is a pointer to any type of object.
- BOOL is the same as char but is used as a Boolean value.
- YES is 1.
- NO is 0.
- IBOutlet is a macro that evaluates to nothing. Ignore it. (IBOutlet is a hint to Interface Builder when it reads the declaration of a class from a .h file.)
- IBAction is the same as void. It also acts as a hint to Interface Builder.
- nil is the same as NULL. We use nil instead of NULL for pointers to objects.

## Look at the Header File

Click on RandomController.h. Study it for a moment. It declares **RandomController** to be a subclass of **NSObject**. Instance variables are declared inside the braces.

```
#import <Foundation/Foundation.h>

@interface RandomController : NSObject
{
    IBOutlet NSTextField *textField;
}
- (IBAction)generate:(id)sender;
- (IBAction)seed:(id)sender;
@end
```

#import is similar to the C preprocessor's #include. However, #import ensures that the file is included only once. You are importing <Foundation/Foundation.h> because that includes the declaration of **NSObject**, which is the superclass of **RandomController**.

Note that the declaration of the class starts with @interface. The @ symbol is not used in the C programming language. To minimize conflicts between C code and Objective-C code, Objective-C keywords are prefixed by @. Here are a few other Objective-C keywords: @end, @implementation, @class, @selector, @protocol, @property, and @synthesize.

## Edit the Implementation File

Now look at RandomController.m. It contains the implementations of the methods. You can find it in the project navigator, or you can use Xcode's Navigate -> Jump to Next Counterpart command, Control-Command-UpArrow, which flips the editor between corresponding .h and .m files. You can also enable the Assistant Editor in the toolbar, which automatically shows the counterpart for the selected file beside it.

In C++ or Java, you might implement a method something like this:

```
public void increment(Object sender) {
    count++;
    textField.setIntValue(count);
}
```

In English, you would say, "**increment** is a public instance method that takes one argument that is an object. The method doesn't return anything. The method increments the count instance variable and then sends the message **setIntValue()** to the textField object with count as an argument."

In Objective-C, the analogous method would look like this:

```
- (void)increment:(id)sender
{
    count++;
    [textField setIntValue:count];
}
```

Objective-C is a very simple language. It has no visibility specifiers: All methods are public, and all instance variables are protected. (In fact, there are visibility specifiers for instance variables, but they are rarely used. The default is protected, and that works nicely.)

In Chapter 3, we will explore Objective-C in all its beauty. For now, just copy the following methods. You can safely remove the **init** and **dealloc** methods Xcode has created for you.

```
#import "RandomController.h"

@implementation RandomController

- (IBAction)generate:(id)sender
{
    // Generate a number between 1 and 100 inclusive
    int generated;
    generated = (int)(random() % 100) + 1;

    NSLog(@"generated = %d", generated);

    // Ask the text field to change what it is displaying
    [textField setIntValue:generated];
}

- (IBAction)seed:(id)sender
{
    // Seed the random number generator with the time
    srandom((unsigned)time(NULL));
    [textField setStringValue:@"Generator seeded"];
}

@end
```

(Remember that IBAction is the same as void. Neither method returns anything.)

Because Objective-C is C with a few extensions, you can call functions, such as **random()** and **srandom()** from the standard C and Unix libraries.

## Build and Run

Your application is now finished. Click Run in the toolbar to run your application again.

If your code has an error, Xcode's status display will show that the build has failed. Select the Issue navigator to see a list of build issues. If you click on an issue, the erroneous line of code will be highlighted in the editor. In Figure 2.21, the programmer has forgotten a semicolon. The compiler is smart about certain types of errors; in this case, a callout is shown with a proposed solution to the problem. Press Return to apply the proposed solution.

Once your application is running, click the buttons and see the generated random numbers. Congratulations—you have a working Cocoa application.

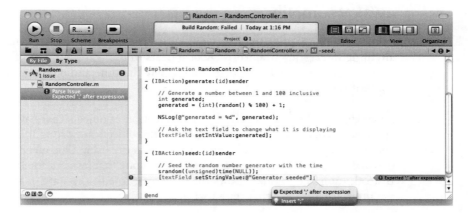

**Figure 2.21**   Compiling

Did you see the log statement on the console? When things go badly, the Cocoa classes will log to the console, so you will want to keep an eye on the console while testing your application. The console is part of the **Debug Area**. You can control console visibility by using the **Debug Area** toggle on the toolbar. By default, Xcode is configured to show the console only when log output is generated and to hide it when the program exits. You can configure Xcode to always show the log in the **Behaviors** tab of the Preferences panel, as shown in Figure 2.22.

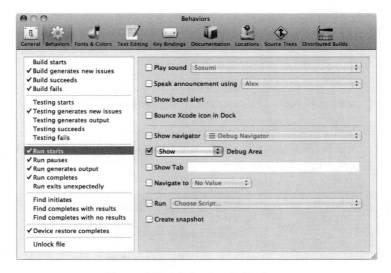

**Figure 2.22**   Behaviors in Preferences

# awakeFromNib

Note that your application is flawed: When the application starts, instead of anything interesting, the word Label appears in the text field. Let's fix that problem. You will make the text field display the time and date that the application started.

As we discussed earlier, a NIB file is a collection of objects that have been archived. When the program is launched, the objects are brought back to life before the application handles any events from the user. This mechanism is a bit unusual; most GUI builders generate source code that lays out the user interface. Instead, Interface Builder allows the developer to edit the state of the objects in the interface and save that state to a file.

After being brought to life but before any events are handled, all objects are automatically sent the message **awakeFromNib**. You will add an **awakeFromNib** method that will initialize the text field's value.

Add the **awakeFromNib** method to RandomController.m. For now, just type it in. You will understand it later on. Briefly, you are creating an instance of **NSDate** that represents the current time. Then you are telling the text field to set its value to the new calendar date object:

```
- (void)awakeFromNib
{
    NSDate *now;
    now = [NSDate date];
    [textField setObjectValue:now];
}
```

The order in which the methods appear in the file is not important. Just make sure that you add them after @implementation and before @end.

You will never have to call **awakeFromNib**; it gets called automatically. Simply run your application again. You should now see the date and time when the app runs (Figure 2.23).

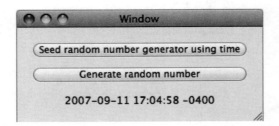

**Figure 2.23**   Completed Application

In Cocoa, a lot of things, such as **awakeFromNib**, get called automatically. Some of the confusion that you may experience as you read this book will come from trying to figure out which methods you have to call and which will get called for you automatically. We'll try to make the distinction clear.

# Documentation

Before this chapter wraps up, you should know where to find the documentation, as it may prove handy if you get stuck while doing an exercise later in the book. The easiest way to get to the documentation is by choosing Documentation and API Reference from Xcode's Help menu (Figure 2.24).

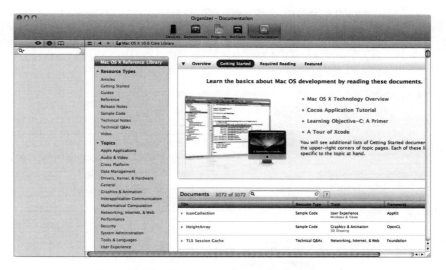

**Figure 2.24**   Documentation and API Reference

If you Option-click on a method, class, or function name, Xcode will show a quick-help pop-over from which you can go to the full documentation for that term. Also, the Quick Help Inspector in the utility area displays quick help for the term under the cursor, or the selected object in Interface Builder.

# What Have You Done?

You have now gone through the steps involved in creating a simple Cocoa application:

- Create a new project.
- Lay out an interface.

- Create custom classes.
- Connect the interface to your custom class or classes.
- Add code to the custom classes.
- Compile.
- Test.

# Chronology of an Application

Let's briefly discuss the chronology of an application: When the process is started, it runs the **NSApplicationMain** function, which creates an instance of **NSApplication**. The application object reads the main NIB file and unarchives the objects inside. The objects are all sent the message **awakeFromNib**. Then the application object checks for events. The timeline for these events appears in Figure 2.25.

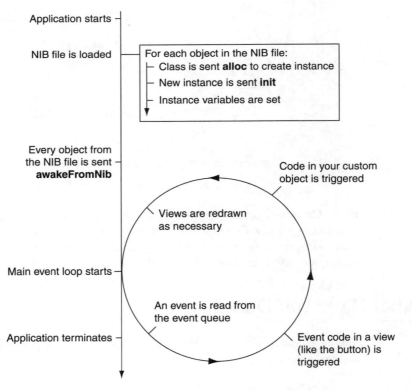

**Figure 2.25**    A Timeline

When it receives an event from the keyboard mouse, the window server puts the event data into the event queue for the appropriate application, as shown in Figure 2.26.The application object reads the event data from its queue and forwards it to a user interface object, such as a button, and your code gets triggered. If your code changes the data in a view, the view is redisplayed. Then the application object checks its event queue for another event. This process of checking for events and reacting to them constitutes the *main event loop*.

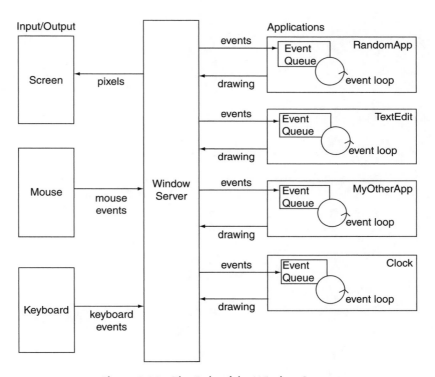

**Figure 2.26**    The Role of the Window Server

When the user chooses Quit from the menu, NSApp is sent the **terminate:** message. This ends the process, and all your objects are destroyed.

Puzzled? Excited? Move on to the next chapter so we can fill in some blanks.

# Chapter 3
# OBJECTIVE-C

Once upon a time, a man named Brad Cox decided that it was time for the world to move toward a more modular programming style. C was a popular and powerful language. Smalltalk was an elegant untyped object-oriented language. Starting with C, Brad Cox added Smalltalk-like classes and message-sending mechanisms. He called the result *Objective-C*. Objective-C is a very simple extension of the C language. In fact, it was originally just a C preprocessor and a library.

Objective-C is not a proprietary language. Rather, it is an open standard that has been included in the Free Software Foundation's GNU C compiler (gcc) for many years. More recently, Apple has become heavily involved in the clang/LLVM (Low Level Virtual Machine) open source compiler projects, which are much faster and more versatile than gcc. In Xcode projects, LLVM is the default compiler.

Cocoa was developed using Objective-C, and most Cocoa programming is done in Objective-C. Teaching C and basic object-oriented concepts could consume an entire book. This chapter assumes that you already know a little C and something about objects and introduces you to the basics of Objective-C. If you fit the profile, you will find learning Objective-C to be easy. If you do not, our own *Objective-C Programming: The Big Nerd Ranch Guide* or Apple's *The Objective-C Language* offer more gentle introductions.

## Creating and Using Instances

Chapter 1 mentioned that classes are used to create objects, that the objects have methods, and that you can send messages to the objects to trigger these methods. In this section, you will learn how to create an object and send messages to it.

As an example, we will use the class **NSMutableArray**. You can create a new instance of **NSMutableArray** by sending the message **alloc** to the **NSMutableArray** class like this:

```
[NSMutableArray alloc];
```

This method returns a pointer to the space that was allocated for the object. You could hold onto that pointer in a variable like this:

```
NSMutableArray *foo;
foo = [NSMutableArray alloc];
```

While working with Objective-C, it is important to remember that foo is just a pointer. In this case, it points to an object.

Before using the object that foo points to, you would need to make sure that it is fully initialized. The **init** method will handle this task, so you might write code like this:

```
NSMutableArray *foo;
foo = [NSMutableArray alloc];
[foo init];
```

Take a long look at the last line; it sends the message **init** to the object that foo points to. We would say, "foo is the receiver of the message **init**." Note that a message send consists of a receiver (the object foo points to) and a message (**init**) wrapped in brackets. You can also send messages to *classes*, as demonstrated by sending the message **alloc** to the class **NSMutableArray**.

The method **init** returns the newly initialized object. As a consequence, you will always nest the message sends like this:

```
NSMutableArray *foo;
foo = [[NSMutableArray alloc] init];
```

What about destroying the object when we no longer need it? We will talk about this in the next chapter.

Some methods take arguments. If a method takes an argument, the method name (called a *selector*) will end with a colon. For example, to add objects to the end of the array, you use the **addObject:** method (assume that bar is a pointer to another object):

```
[foo addObject:bar];
```

If you have multiple arguments, the selector will have multiple parts. For example, to add an object at a particular index, you could use the following:

```
[foo insertObject:bar atIndex:5];
```

Note that **insertObject:atIndex:** is one selector, not two. It will trigger one method with two arguments. This outcome seems strange to most C and Java programmers but should be familiar to Smalltalk programmers. The syntax also makes your code easier to read. For example, it is not uncommon to see a C++ method call like this:

```
if (x.intersectsArc(35.0, 19.0, 23.0, 90.0, 120.0))
```

It is much easier to guess the meaning of the following code:

```
if ([x intersectsArcWithRadius:35.0
              centeredAtX:19.0
                        Y:23.0
                fromAngle:90.0
                  toAngle:120.0])
```

If it seems odd right now, just use it for a while. Most programmers grow to appreciate the Objective-C messaging syntax.

You are now at a point where you can read simple Objective-C code, so it is time to write a program that will create an instance of **NSMutableArray** and fill it with ten instances of **NSNumber**.

# Using Existing Classes

If it isn't running, start Xcode. Close any projects that you were working on. Under the File menu, choose New -> New Project…. When the panel pops up, choose to create a Command Line Tool (Figure 3.1).

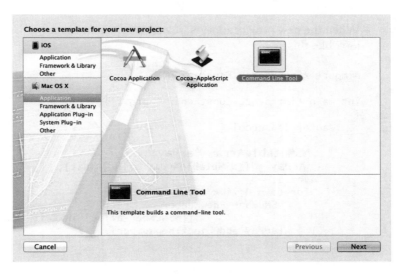

**Figure 3.1**    Choose Project Type

A *command-line tool* has no graphical user interface and typically runs on the command line or in the background as a daemon. Unlike in an application project, you will always alter the **main** function of a command-line tool.

Name the project lottery (Figure 3.2). Unlike the names of applications, most tool names are lowercase. Set the Type to Foundation.

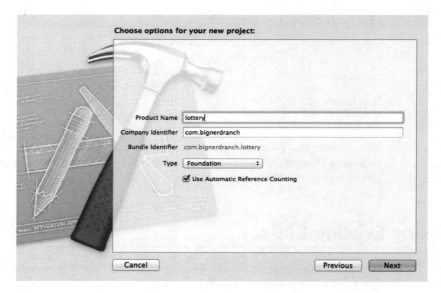

**Figure 3.2**   Name Project

When the new project appears, select main.m in the lottery group. Edit main.m to look like this:

```
#import <Foundation/Foundation.h>

int main (int argc, const char * argv[])
{
    @autoreleasepool {

        NSMutableArray *array;
         array = [[NSMutableArray alloc] init];
        int i;
        for (i = 0; i < 10; i++) {
            NSNumber *newNumber =
                        [[NSNumber alloc] initWithInt:(i * 3)];
            [array addObject:newNumber];
        }
```

```
        for ( i = 0; i < 10; i++) {
            NSNumber *numberToPrint = [array objectAtIndex:i];
            NSLog(@"The number at index %d is %@",  i, numberToPrint);
        }

    }
    return 0;
}
```

Here is the play-by-play for the code:

```
#import <Foundation/Foundation.h>
```

You are including the headers for all the classes in the Foundation framework. The headers are precompiled, so this approach is not as computationally intensive as it sounds.

```
int main (int argc, const char *argv[])
```

The **main** function is declared just as it would be in any Unix C program.

```
@autoreleasepool {
```

This code defines an autorelease pool for the code enclosed by the braces. We will discuss the importance of autorelease pools in the next chapter.

```
NSMutableArray *array;
```

One variable is declared here: `array` is a pointer to an instance of **NSMutableArray**. Note that no array exists yet. You have simply declared a pointer that will refer to the array once it is created.

```
array = [[NSMutableArray alloc] init];
```

Here, you are creating the instance of **NSMutableArray** and making the `array` variable point to it.

```
for (i = 0; i < 10; i++) {
    NSNumber *newNumber = [[NSNumber alloc] initWithInt:(i*3)];
    [array addObject:newNumber];
}
```

Inside the `for` loop, you have created a local variable called `newNumber` and set it to point to a new instance of **NSNumber**. Then you have added that object to the array.

The array does not make copies of the **NSNumber** objects. Instead, it simply keeps a list of pointers to the **NSNumber** objects. Objective-C programmers make very few copies of objects, because it is seldom necessary.

```
for ( i = 0; i < 10; i++) {
    NSNumber *numberToPrint = [array objectAtIndex:i];
    NSLog(@"The number at index %d is %@", i, numberToPrint);
}
```

Here, you are printing the contents of the array to the console. **NSLog** is a function much like the C function **printf()**; it takes a format string and a comma-separated list of variables to be substituted into the format string. When displaying the string, **NSLog** prefixes the generated string with the name of the application and a time stamp.

In **printf**, for example, you would use **%x** to display an integer in hexadecimal form. With **NSLog**, we have all the tokens from **printf** and the token **%@** to display an object. The object gets sent the message **description**, and the string it returns replaces **%@** in the string. We will discuss the **description** method in detail soon.

All the tokens recognized by **NSLog()** are listed in Table 3.1.

**Table 3.1**  Possible Tokens in Objective-C Format Strings

| Symbol | Displays |
| --- | --- |
| %@ | id |
| %d, %D, %i | long |
| %u, %U | unsigned long |
| %hi | short |
| %hu | unsigned short |
| %qi | long long |
| %qu | unsigned long long |
| %x, %X | unsigned long printed as hexadecimal |
| %o, %O | unsigned long printed as octal |
| %f, %e, %E, %g, %G | double |
| %c | unsigned char as ASCII character |
| %C | unichar as Unicode character |
| %s | char * (a null-terminated C string of ASCII characters) |
| %S | unichar * (a null-terminated C string of Unicode characters) |
| %p | void * (an address printed in hexadecimal with a leading 0x) |
| %% | a % character |

**Note:** If the @ symbol before the quotes in @"The number at index %d is %@" looks a little strange, remember that Objective-C is the C language with a couple of extensions. One of the extensions is that strings are instances of the class **NSString**. In C, strings are just pointers to a buffer of characters that ends in the null character. Both C strings and instances of **NSString** can be used in the same file. To differentiate between constant C strings and constant **NSString**s, you must put @ before the opening quote of a constant **NSString**.

```
// C string
char *foo;
// NSString
NSString *bar;
foo = "this is a C string";
bar = @"this is an NSString";
```

You will use mostly **NSString** in Cocoa programming. Wherever a string is needed, the classes in the frameworks expect an **NSString**. However, if you already have a bunch of C functions that expect C strings, you will find yourself using **char** * frequently.

You can convert between C strings and **NSString**s:

```
const char *foo = "Blah blah";
NSString *bar;
// Create an NSString from a C string
bar = [NSString stringWithUTF8String:foo];

// Create a C string from an NSString
foo = [bar UTF8String];
```

Because **NSString** can hold Unicode strings, you will need to deal with the multibyte characters correctly in your C strings, and this can be quite difficult and time consuming. (Besides the multibyte problem, you will have to wrestle with the fact that some languages read from right to left.) Whenever possible, you should use **NSString** instead of C strings.

---

Our **main()** function ends by returning 0, indiciating that no error occurred:

```
    return 0;
}
```

Run the completed command-line tool (Figure 3.3). (If your console doesn't appear, use the View -> Show Debug Area menu item and ensure that the console, the right half, is enabled.)

## Sending Messages to nil

In most object-oriented languages, your program will crash if you send a message to null. In applications written in those languages, you will see many

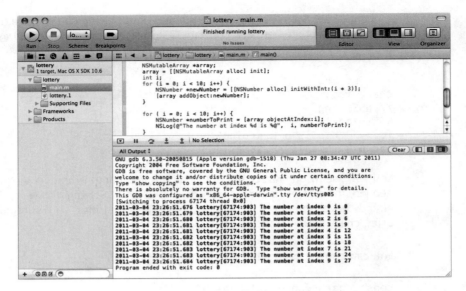

**Figure 3.3**   Completed Execution

checks for `null` before sending a message. In Java, for example, you frequently see the following:

```
if (foo != null) {
    foo.doThatThingYouDo();
}
```

In Objective-C, it is okay to send a message to `nil`. The message is simply discarded, which eliminates the need for these sorts of checks. For example, this code will build and run without an error:

```
id foo;
foo = nil;
int bar = [foo count];
```

This approach is different from how most languages work, but you will get used to it.

You may find yourself asking over and over, "Argg! Why isn't this method getting called?" Chances are that the pointer you are using, convinced that it is not `nil`, is in fact `nil`.

In the preceding example, what is `bar` set to? Zero. If `bar` were a pointer, it would be set to `nil` (`zero` for pointers). For other types, the value is less predictable.

# NSObject, NSArray, NSMutableArray, and NSString

You have now used these standard Cocoa objects: **NSObject**, **NSMutableArray**, and **NSString**. (All classes that come with Cocoa have names with the NS prefix. Classes that you will create will *not* start with NS.) These classes are all part of the Foundation framework. Figure 3.4 shows an inheritance diagram for these classes.

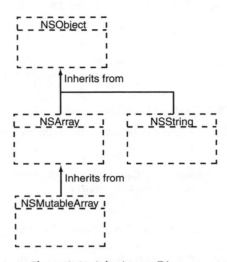

**Figure 3.4**   Inheritance Diagram

Let's go through a few of the commonly used methods on these classes. For a complete listing, you can access the online documentation in Xcode's Help menu.

## *NSObject*

**NSObject** is the root of the entire Objective-C class hierarchy. Some commonly used methods on **NSObject** are described next.

```
- (id)init
```

Initializes the receiver after memory for it has been allocated. An **init** message is generally coupled with an **alloc** message in the same line of code:

```
TheClass *newObject = [[TheClass alloc] init];
```

```
- (NSString *)description
```

Returns an **NSString** that describes the receiver. The debugger's print object command ("po") invokes this method. A good **description** method will often make debugging easier. Also, if you use %@ in a format string, the object that should be substituted in is sent the message **description**. The value returned by the **description** method is put into the log string. For example, the line in your main function

```
NSLog(@"The number at index %d is %@", i, numberToPrint);
```

is equivalent to

```
NSLog(@"The number at index %d is %@", i,
                        [numberToPrint description]);
```

```
- (BOOL)isEqual:(id)anObject
```

Returns YES if the receiver and anObject are equal and NO otherwise. You might use it like this:

```
if ([myObject isEqual:anotherObject]) {
    NSLog(@"They are equal.");
}
```

But what does equal really mean? In **NSObject**, this method is defined to return YES if and only if the receiver and anObject are the same object—that is, if both are pointers to the same memory location.

Clearly, this is not always the "equal" that you would hope for, so this method is overridden by many classes to implement a more appropriate idea of equality. For example, **NSString** overrides the method to compare the characters in the receiver and anObject. If the two strings have the same characters in the same order, they are considered equal.

Thus, if x and y are **NSStrings**, there is a big difference between these two expressions:

```
x == y
```

and

```
[x isEqual:y]
```

The first expression compares the two pointers. The second expression compares the characters in the strings. Note, however, that if x and y are instances of a class that has not overridden **NSObject**'s **isEqual:** method, the two expressions are equivalent.

## *NSArray*

An **NSArray** is a list of pointers to other objects. It is indexed by integers. Thus, if there are *n* objects in the array, the objects are indexed by the integers 0 through *n* – 1. You cannot put a nil in an **NSArray**. (This means that there are no "holes" in an **NSArray**, which may confuse some programmers who are used to Java's Object[].) **NSArray** inherits from **NSObject**.

An **NSArray** is created with all the objects that will ever be in it. You can neither add nor remove objects from an instance of **NSArray**. We say that **NSArray** is *immutable*. (Its mutable subclass, **NSMutableArray**, will be discussed next.) Immutability is nice in some cases. Because it is immutable, a horde of objects can share one **NSArray** without worrying that one object in the horde might change it. **NSString** and **NSNumber** are also immutable. Instead of changing a string or number, you will simply create another one with the new value. (In the case of **NSString**, there is also the class **NSMutableString** that allows its instances to be altered.)

A single array can hold objects of many different classes. Arrays cannot, however, hold C primitive types, such as int or float.

Here are some commonly used methods implemented by **NSArray**:

- (unsigned)count

Returns the number of objects currently in the array.

- (id)objectAtIndex:(unsigned)i

Returns the object located at index i. If i is beyond the end of the array, you will get an error at runtime.

- (id)lastObject

Returns the object in the array with the highest index value. If the array is empty, nil is returned.

- (BOOL)containsObject:(id)anObject

Returns YES if anObject is present in the array. This method determines whether an object is present in the array by sending an **isEqual:** message to each of the array's objects and passing anObject as the parameter.

- (unsigned)indexOfObject:(id)anObject

Searches the receiver for anObject and returns the lowest index whose corresponding array value is equal to anObject. Objects are considered equal if **isEqual:** returns YES. If none of the objects in the array are equal to anObject, **indexOfObject:** returns NSNotFound.

## NSMutableArray

**NSMutableArray** inherits from **NSArray** but extends it with the ability to add and remove objects. To create a mutable array from an immutable one, use **NSArray**'s **mutableCopy** method.

Here are some commonly used methods implemented by **NSMutableArray**:

```
- (void)addObject:(id)anObject
```

Inserts anObject at the end of the receiver. You are not allowed to add nil to the array.

```
- (void)addObjectsFromArray:(NSArray *)otherArray
```

Adds the objects contained in otherArray to the end of the receiver's array of objects.

```
- (void)insertObject:(id)anObject atIndex:(unsigned)index
```

Inserts anObject into the receiver at index, which cannot be greater than the number of elements in the array. If index is already occupied, the objects at index and beyond are shifted up one slot to make room. You will get an error if anObject is nil or if index is greater than the number of elements in the array.

```
- (void)removeAllObjects
```

Empties the receiver of all its elements.

```
- (void)removeObject:(id)anObject
```

Removes all occurrences of anObject in the array. Matches are determined on the basis of anObject's response to the **isEqual:** message.

```
- (void)removeObjectAtIndex:(unsigned)index
```

Removes the object at index and moves all elements beyond index down one slot to fill the gap. You will get an error if index is beyond the end of the array.

As mentioned earlier, you cannot add nil to an array. Sometimes, you will want to put an object into an array to represent nothingness. The **NSNull** class exists for exactly this purpose. There is exactly one instance of **NSNull**, so if you want to put a placeholder for nothing into an array, use **NSNull** like this:

```
[myArray addObject:[NSNull null]];
```

## *NSString*

An **NSString** is a buffer of Unicode characters. In Cocoa, all manipulations involving character strings are done with **NSString**. As a convenience, the Objective-C language also supports the @"..." construct to create a string object constant from a 7-bit ASCII encoding:

```
NSString *temp = @"this is a constant string";
```

**NSString** inherits from **NSObject**. Here are some commonly used methods implemented by **NSString**:

- (id)initWithFormat:(NSString *)format, ...

Works like **sprintf**. Here, format is a string containing tokens, such as %d. The additional arguments are substituted for the tokens:

```
int x = 5;
char *y = "abc";
id z = @"123";
NSString *aString = [[NSString alloc] initWithFormat:
            @"The int %d, the C String %s, and the NSString %@",
            x, y, z];
```

- (NSUInteger)length

Returns the number of characters in the receiver.

- (NSString *)stringByAppendingString:(NSString *)aString

Returns a string object made by appending aString to the receiver. The following code snippet, for example, would produce the string "Error: unable to read file."

```
NSString *errorTag = @"Error: ";
NSString *errorString = @"unable to read file.";
NSString *errorMessage;
errorMessage = [errorTag stringByAppendingString:errorString];
```

- (NSComparisonResult)compare:(NSString *)otherString

Compares the receiver and otherString and returns NSOrderedAscending if the receiver is alphabetically prior to otherString, NSOrderedDescending if otherString is comes before the receiver, or NSOrderedSame if the receiver and otherString are equal.

- (NSComparisonResult)caseInsensitiveCompare:(NSString *)
otherString

Like **compare:**, except the comparison ignores letter case.

## "Inherits from" versus "Uses" or "Knows About"

Beginning Cocoa programmers are often eager to create subclasses of **NSString** and **NSMutableArray**. Don't. Stylish Objective-C programmers almost never do. Instead, they use **NSString** and **NSMutableArray** as parts of larger objects, a technique known as composition. For example, a **BankAccount** class *could* be a subclass of **NSMutableArray**. After all, isn't a bank account simply a collection of transactions? The beginner would follow this path. In contrast, the old hand would create a class **BankAccount** that inherited from **NSObject** and has an instance variable called transactions that would point to an **NSMutableArray**.

It is important to keep track of the difference between "uses" and "is a subclass of." The beginner would say, "**BankAccount** inherits from **NSMutableArray**." The old hand would say, "**BankAccount** uses **NSMutableArray**." In the common idioms of Objective-C, "uses" is much more common than "is a subclass of."

You will find it much easier to use a class than to subclass one. Subclassing involves more code and requires a deeper understanding of the superclass. By using composition instead of inheritance, Cocoa developers can take advantage of very powerful classes without really understanding how they work.

In a strongly typed language, such as C++, inheritance is crucial. In an untyped language, such as Objective-C, inheritance is just a hack that saves the developer some typing. There are only two inheritance diagrams in this entire book. All the other diagrams are object diagrams that indicate which objects know about which other objects. This is much more important information to a Cocoa programmer.

# Creating Your Own Classes

Where I live, the state government has decided that the uneducated have entirely too much money: You can play the lottery every week. Let's imagine that a lottery entry has two numbers between 1 and 100, inclusive. You will write a program that will make up lottery entries for the next ten weeks. Each **LotteryEntry** object will have a date and two random integers (Figure 3.5).

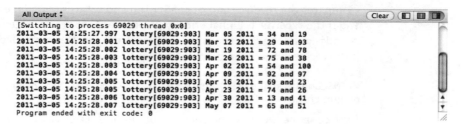

**Figure 3.5**   Completed Program

Besides learning how to create classes, you will build a tool that will certainly make you fabulously wealthy.

## Creating the LotteryEntry Class

In Xcode, create a new file. Select **Objective-C class** as the type. Name the class **LotteryEntry**, and set it to be a subclass of **NSObject** (Figure 3.6).

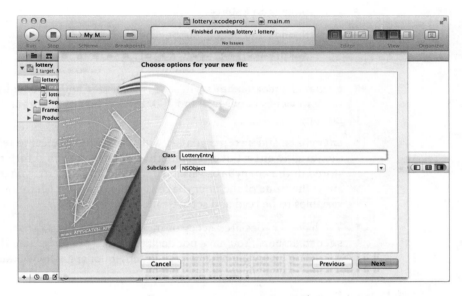

**Figure 3.6**   New LotteryEntry Class

Note that you are also causing LotteryEntry.h to be created. Drag both files into the lottery group if they are not already there.

### *LotteryEntry.h*

Edit the LotteryEntry.h file to look like this:

```
#import <Foundation/Foundation.h>

@interface LotteryEntry : NSObject {
    NSDate *entryDate;
    int firstNumber;
    int secondNumber;
}
```

```
- (void)prepareRandomNumbers;
- (void)setEntryDate:(NSDate *)date;
- (NSDate *)entryDate;
- (int)firstNumber;
- (int)secondNumber;
@end
```

You have created a header file for a new class called **LotteryEntry** that inherits from **NSObject**. It has three instance variables:

- entryDate is an **NSDate**.

- firstNumber and secondNumber are both ints.

You have declared five methods in the new class:

- **prepareRandomNumbers** will set firstNumber and secondNumber to random values between 1 and 100. It takes no arguments and returns nothing.

- **entryDate** and **setEntryDate:** will allow other objects to read and set the variable entryDate. The method **entryDate** will return the value stored in the entryDate variable. The method **setEntryDate:** will allow the value of the entryDate variable to be set. Methods that allow variables to be read and set are called *accessor methods*.

- You have also declared accessor methods for reading firstNumber and secondNumber. (You have not declared accessors for setting these variables; you are going to set them directly in **prepareRandomNumbers**.)

## LotteryEntry.m

Edit LotteryEntry.m to look like this:

```
#import "LotteryEntry.h"

@implementation LotteryEntry

- (void)prepareRandomNumbers
{
    firstNumber = ((int)random() % 100) + 1;
    secondNumber = ((int)random() % 100) + 1;
}

- (void)setEntryDate:(NSDate *)date
{
    entryDate = date;
}
```

```
- (NSDate *)entryDate
{
    return entryDate;
}

- (int)firstNumber
{
    return firstNumber;
}

- (int)secondNumber
{
    return secondNumber;
}
@end
```

Here is the play-by-play for each method:

> **prepareRandomNumbers** uses the standard **random** function to generate a pseudorandom number. You use the mod operator (%) and add 1 to get the number in the range 1–100.
>
> **setEntryDate:** sets the pointer `entryDate` to a new value.
>
> **entryDate**, **firstNumber**, and **secondNumber** return the values of variables.

## Changing main.m

Now let's look at `main.m`. Many of the lines have stayed the same, but several have changed. The most important change is that we are using **LotteryEntry** objects instead of **NSNumber** objects.

Here is the heavily commented code. (You don't have to type in the comments.)

```
#import <Foundation/Foundation.h>
#import "LotteryEntry.h"

int main (int argc, const char *argv[]) {

    @autoreleasepool {

        // Create the date object
        NSDate *now = [[NSDate alloc] init];
        NSCalendar *cal = [NSCalendar currentCalendar];
        NSDateComponents *weekComponents =
            [[NSDateComponents alloc] init];
```

```
    // Seed the random number generator
    srandom((unsigned)time(NULL));
    NSMutableArray *array;
    array = [[NSMutableArray alloc] init];

    int i;
    for (i = 0; i < 10; i++) {

        [weekComponents setWeek:i];

        // Create a date/time object that is 'i' weeks from now
        NSDate *iWeeksFromNow;
        iWeeksFromNow = [cal dateByAddingComponents:weekComponents
                                             toDate:now
                                            options:0];

        // Create a new instance of LotteryEntry
        LotteryEntry *newEntry = [[LotteryEntry alloc] init];
        [newEntry prepareRandomNumbers];
        [newEntry setEntryDate:iWeeksFromNow];

        // Add the LotteryEntry object to the array
        [array addObject:newEntry];

    }

    for (LotteryEntry *entryToPrint in array) {
        // Display its contents
        NSLog(@"%@", entryToPrint);
    }
  }
  return 0;
}
```

Note the second loop. Here you are using Objective-C's mechanism for enumerating over the members of a collection.

This program will create an array of LotteryEntry objects, as shown in Figure 3.7.

## Implementing a description Method

Build and run your application. You should see something like Figure 3.8.

Hmm. Not quite what we hoped for. After all, the program is supposed to reveal the dates and the numbers you should play on those dates, and you can't see either. (You are seeing the default **description** method as defined in **NSObject**.) Next, you will make the **LotteryEntry** objects display themselves in a more meaningful manner.

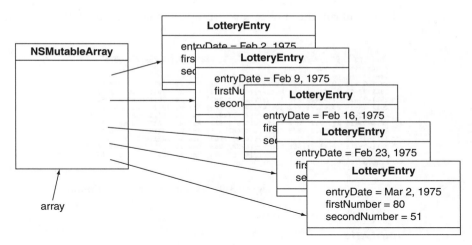

**Figure 3.7**  Object Diagram

```
All Output ‡                                                    Clear  □ ▥ ▣
[Switching to process 68946 thread 0x0]
2011-03-05 14:17:15.347 lottery[68946:903] <LotteryEntry: 0x100110e80>
2011-03-05 14:17:15.347 lottery[68946:903] <LotteryEntry: 0x1001110b0>
2011-03-05 14:17:15.348 lottery[68946:903] <LotteryEntry: 0x100111120>
2011-03-05 14:17:15.348 lottery[68946:903] <LotteryEntry: 0x100111170>
2011-03-05 14:17:15.349 lottery[68946:903] <LotteryEntry: 0x1001111c0>
2011-03-05 14:17:15.349 lottery[68946:903] <LotteryEntry: 0x100111210>
2011-03-05 14:17:15.349 lottery[68946:903] <LotteryEntry: 0x100111100>
2011-03-05 14:17:15.350 lottery[68946:903] <LotteryEntry: 0x1001112f0>
2011-03-05 14:17:15.350 lottery[68946:903] <LotteryEntry: 0x100111340>
2011-03-05 14:17:15.350 lottery[68946:903] <LotteryEntry: 0x100111390>
Program ended with exit code: 0
```

**Figure 3.8**  Completed Execution

Add a **description** method to LotteryEntry.m:

```
- (NSString *)description
{
    NSDateFormatter *df = [[NSDateFormatter alloc] init];
    [df setTimeStyle:NSDateFormatterNoStyle];
    [df setDateStyle:NSDateFormatterMediumStyle];
    NSString *result;
    result = [[NSString alloc] initWithFormat:@"%@ = %d and %d",
            [df stringFromDate:entryDate],
            firstNumber, secondNumber];
    return result;
}
```

Build and run the application. Now you should see the dates and numbers:

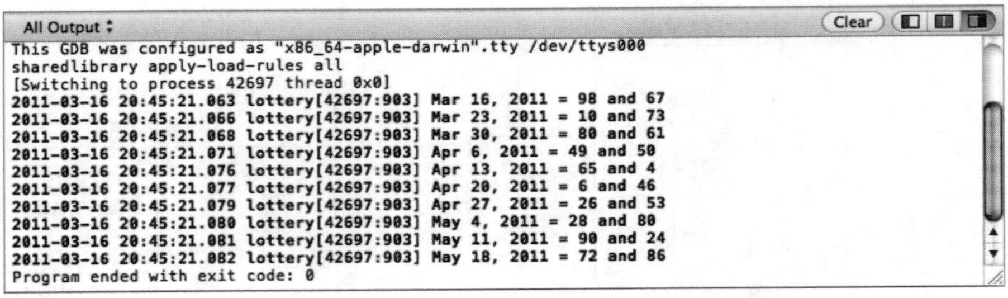

```
All Output ⛋                                                    Clear ⬚ ⬚ ⬚
This GDB was configured as "x86_64-apple-darwin".tty /dev/ttys000
sharedlibrary apply-load-rules all
[Switching to process 42697 thread 0x0]
2011-03-16 20:45:21.063 lottery[42697:903] Mar 16, 2011 = 98 and 67
2011-03-16 20:45:21.066 lottery[42697:903] Mar 23, 2011 = 10 and 73
2011-03-16 20:45:21.068 lottery[42697:903] Mar 30, 2011 = 80 and 61
2011-03-16 20:45:21.071 lottery[42697:903] Apr 6, 2011 = 49 and 50
2011-03-16 20:45:21.076 lottery[42697:903] Apr 13, 2011 = 65 and 4
2011-03-16 20:45:21.077 lottery[42697:903] Apr 20, 2011 = 6 and 46
2011-03-16 20:45:21.079 lottery[42697:903] Apr 27, 2011 = 26 and 53
2011-03-16 20:45:21.080 lottery[42697:903] May 4, 2011 = 28 and 80
2011-03-16 20:45:21.081 lottery[42697:903] May 11, 2011 = 90 and 24
2011-03-16 20:45:21.082 lottery[42697:903] May 18, 2011 = 72 and 86
Program ended with exit code: 0
```

**Figure 3.9**   Execution with Description

## NSDate

Before moving on to any new ideas, let's examine **NSDate** in some depth. Instances of **NSDate** represent a single point in time and are basically immutable: You can't change the day or time once it is created. Because **NSDate** is immutable, many objects often share a single date object. There is seldom any need to create a copy of an **NSDate** object.

Here are some of the commonly used methods implemented by **NSDate**:

+ (id)date

Creates and returns a date initialized to the current date and time.

This is a *class method*. In the interface file, implementation file, and documentation, class methods are recognizable because they start with + instead of –. A class method is triggered by sending a message to the class instead of an instance. This one, for example, could be used as follows:

```
NSDate *now;
now = [NSDate date];
```

- (id)dateByAddingTimeInterval:(NSTimeInterval)interval

Creates and returns a date initialized to the date represented by the receiver *plus* the given interval.

- (NSTimeInterval)timeIntervalSinceDate:(NSDate *)anotherDate

Returns the interval in seconds between the receiver and anotherDate. If the receiver is earlier than anotherDate, the return value is negative. **NSTimeInterval** is the same as double.

CREATING YOUR OWN CLASSES

```
+ (NSTimeInterval)timeIntervalSinceReferenceDate
```

Returns the interval in seconds between the first instant of January 1, 2001 GMT and the receiver's time.

```
- (NSComparisonResult)compare:(NSDate *)otherDate
```

Returns NSOrderedAscending if the receiver is earlier than otherDate, NSOrderedDescending if otherDate is earlier, or NSOrderedSame if the receiver and otherDate are equal.

## Writing Initializers

Notice the following lines in your **main** function:

```
newEntry = [[LotteryEntry alloc] init];
[newEntry prepareRandomNumbers];
```

You are creating a new instance and then immediately calling **prepareRandom-Numbers** to initialize firstNumber and secondNumber. This is something that should be handled by the initializer, so you are going to override the **init** method in your **LotteryEntry** class.

In the LotteryEntry.m file, change the method **prepareRandomNumbers** into an **init** method:

```
- (id)init
{
    self = [super init];
    if (self)
    {
        firstNumber = ((int)random() % 100) + 1;
        secondNumber = ((int)random() % 100) + 1;
    }
    return self;
}
```

The **init** method calls the superclass's initializer at the beginning, initializes its own variables, and then returns self, a pointer to the object itself (the object that is running this method). (If you are a Java or C++ programmer, self is the same as the this pointer.)

Now delete the following line in main.m:

```
[newEntry prepareRandomNumbers];
```

In LotteryEntry.h, delete the following declaration:

```
- (void)prepareRandomNumbers;
```

Build and run your program to reassure yourself that it still works.

Take another look at our **init** method. Why do we bother to assign the return value of the superclass's initializer to self and then test the value of self? The answer is that the initializers of some Cocoa classes will return nil if initialization was impossible. In order to handle these cases gracefully, we must both test the return value of [super init] and return the appropriate value for self from our initiailizer.

This pattern is debated among some Objective-C programmers. Some say that it is unnecessary, since most classes' initializers don't fail, and most classes' initializers don't return a different value for self. We believe it best to be in the habit of assigning to self and testing that value. The effort required is minimal compared to the debugging headaches that await you if you make an incorrect assumption about the superclass's behavior.

## Initializers with Arguments

Look at the same place in main.m. It should now look like this:

```
LotteryEntry *newEntry = [[LotteryEntry alloc] init];
[newEntry setEntryDate:iWeeksFromNow];
```

It might be nicer if you could supply the date as an argument to the initializer. Change those lines to look like this:

```
LotteryEntry *newEntry = [[LotteryEntry alloc]
                                initWithEntryDate:iWeeksFromNow];
```

You may see a compiler error; ignore it, as we are about to fix the problem.

Next, declare the method in LotteryEntry.h:

```
- (id)initWithEntryDate:(NSDate *)theDate;
```

Now, change (and rename) the **init** method in LotteryEntry.m:

```
- (id)initWithEntryDate:(NSDate *)theDate
{
    self = [super init];
    if (self)
```

```
    {
        entryDate = theDate;
        firstNumber = ((int)random() % 100) + 1;
        secondNumber = ((int)random() % 100) + 1;
    }
    return self;
}
```

Build and run your program. It should work correctly.

However, your class **LotteryEntry** has a problem. You are going to e-mail the class to your friend Rex. Rex plans to use the class **LotteryEntry** in his program but might not realize that you have written **initWithEntryDate:**. If he made this mistake, he might write the following lines of code:

```
NSDate *today = [NSDate date];
LotteryEntry *bigWin = [[LotteryEntry alloc] init];
[bigWin setEntryDate:today];
```

This code will not create an error. Instead, it will simply go up the inheritance tree until it finds **NSObject**'s **init** method. The problem is that `firstNumber` and `secondNumber` will not get initialized properly—both will be zero.

To protect Rex from his own ignorance, you will override **init** to call your initializer with a default date:

```
- (id)init
{
    return [self initWithEntryDate:[NSDate date]];
}
```

Add this method to your LotteryEntry.m file.

Note that **initWithEntryDate:** still does all the work. Because a class can have multiple initializers, we call the one that does the work the *designated initializer*. If a class has several initializers, the designated initializer typically takes the most arguments. You should clearly document which of your initializers is the designated initializer. Note that the designated initializer for **NSObject** is **init**.

> **Conventions for Creating Initializers (rules that Cocoa programmers try to follow regarding initializers):**
>
> - You do not have to create any initializer in your class if the superclass's initializers are sufficient.
>
> - If you decide to create an initializer, you must override the superclass's designated initializer.

- If you create multiple initializers, only one does the work—the designated initializer. All other initializers call the designated initializer.

- The designated initializer of your class will call its superclass's designated initializer.

The day will come when you will create a class that must, must, must have some argument supplied. Override the superclass's designated initializer to throw an exception:

```
- (id)init
{
    @throw [NSException exceptionWithName:@"BNRBadInitCall"
                reason:@"Initialize Lawsuit with initWithDefendant:"
                userInfo:nil];
    return nil;
}
```

# The Debugger

The Free Software Foundation developed the compiler (gcc) and the debugger (gdb) that come with Apple's developer tools. Apple has made significant improvements to both over the years. This section discusses the processes of setting breakpoints, invoking the debugger, and browsing the values of variables.

While browsing code, you may have noticed a gray margin to the left of your code. If you click in that margin, a breakpoint will be added at the corresponding line. Add a breakpoint in main.m at the following line (Figure 3.10):

```
[array addObject:newEntry];
```

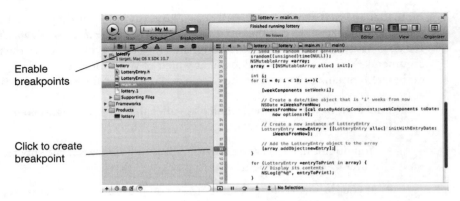

**Figure 3.10**   Creating a Breakpoint

When you run the program, Xcode will start the program in the debugger if you have any breakpoints. To test this, run it now. The debugger will take a few seconds to get started, and then it will run your program until it hits the breakpoint.

When your application is running, the debugger bar will be shown below the editor area. The debugger bar contains a button to toggle visibility of the full debugger area, including the variables view and console, as well as buttons to control the execution of your program and information about the current thread and function.

Xcode's default behavior is to show the full debugger area when a breakpoint is hit. If you do not see the debugger area at the bottom of the window, use the debugger area view toggle in the debugger bar (or toolbar), or the View->Show Debugger Area menu item.

You should also see the Debug navigator on the left, which shows the threads in our application and frames on the stack for each thread. Because the breakpoint is in **main()**, the stack is not very deep. In the variables view on the left in the debugger area, you can see the variables and their values (Figure 3.11).

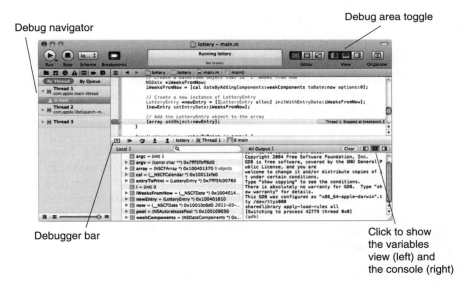

**Figure 3.11**    Stopped at a Breakpoint

Note that the variable i is currently 0.

Return your attention to the debugger bar. Four of the buttons above the variables view are for pausing (or continuing) and stepping over, into, and out of functions. Click the `Continue` button to execute another iteration of the loop. Click the `Step-Over` button to walk through the code line by line.

The gdb debugger, being a Unix thing, was designed to be run from a terminal. When execution is paused, the gdb terminal will appear in the Console panel.

In the debug console, you have full access to all of gdb's capabilities. One very handy feature is "print-object" (po). If a variable is a pointer to an object, when you po it, the object is sent the message **description**, and the result is printed in the console. Try printing the `newEntry` variable.

```
po newEntry
```

You should see the result of your **description** method (Figure 3.12).

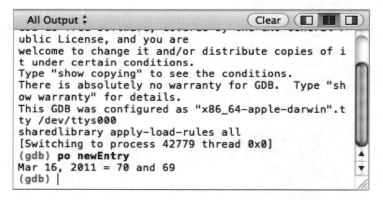

**Figure 3.12**   Using the gdb Console

Exceptions are raised when something goes very wrong. To make the debugger stop whenever an exception is thrown, you will want to add an exception breakpoint. Click the Add button at the bottom of the breakpoint navigator and select Add Exception Breakpoint.... Set the exception type to Objective-C and click Done (Figure 3.13). Disable the existing breakpoint in `main()` by clicking on the blue breakpoint icon in the breakpoint navigator. The breakpoint will be dimmed when it is disabled.

You can test this exception breakpoint by asking for an index that is not in an array. Immediately after the array is created, ask it what its first object is:

```
array = [[NSMutableArray alloc] init];
NSLog(@"first item = %@", [array objectAtIndex:0]);
```

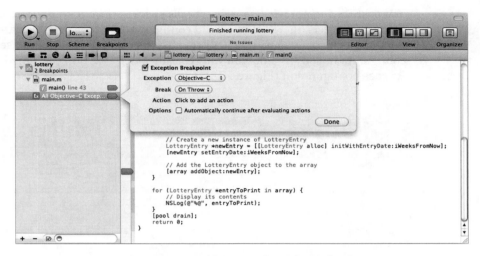

**Figure 3.13**    Adding an Exception Breakpoint

Rebuild and restart the program. It should stop when the exception is raised.

One of the challenging things about debugging Cocoa programs is that they will often limp along in a broken state for quite a while. Using the macro **NSAssert()**, you can get the program to throw an exception as soon as the train leaves the track. For example, in **setEntryDate:**, you might want an exception thrown if the argument is nil. Add a call to **NSAssert()**:

```
- (id)initWithEntryDate:(NSDate *)theDate
{
    self = [super init];
    if (self) {
        NSAssert(theDate != nil, @"Argument must be non-nil");
        entryDate = theDate;
        firstNumber = ((int)random() % 100) + 1;
        secondNumber = ((int)random() % 100) + 1;
    }
    return self;
}
```

Build it and run it. Your code, being correct, will not throw an exception. So change the assertion to something incorrect:

```
NSAssert(theDate == nil, @"Argument must be non-nil");
```

Now build and run your application. Note that a message, including the name of the class and method, is logged and an exception is thrown. Wise use of **NSAssert()** can help you hunt down bugs much more quickly.

You probably do not need your assert calls checked in your completed product. On most projects, there are two build configurations: Debug and Release. In the Debug version, you will want all your asserts checked. In the Release configuration, you will not. You will typically block assertion checking in the Release configuration (Figure 3.14).

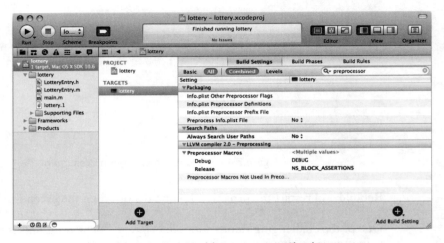

**Figure 3.14**    Disabling Assertion Checking

To do this, bring up the build settings by selecting the lottery project in the project navigator (topmost item). Then select the lottery target, change to the Build Settings tab, and find the Preprocessor Macros item. A quick way to find it is to use the search field at the top of the Build Settings panel. The Preprocessor Macros item will have one item beneath it for each build configuration: Debug and Release. Set the Release item value to NS_BLOCK_ASSERTIONS.

Now, if you build and run the Release configuration, you'll see that your assertion is not getting checked. (Before going on, fix your assertion: It should ensure that dates are *not* nil.)

You can change your current build configuration to Release by opening the scheme editor (in the Product menu, click Edit Scheme...). Select the Run action; on the Info panel, change Build Configuration to Release. Now when you build and run your application, it will be built using the Release configuration. Note that the default build configuration for the Archive action is Release. We will discuss build configurations in more detail in Chapter 37.

**NSAssert()** works only inside Objective-C methods. If you need to check an assertion in a C function, use **NSCAssert()**.

That's enough to get you started with the debugger. For more in-depth information, refer to the documentation from the Free Software Foundation (www.gnu.org/).

# What Have You Done?

You have written a simple program in Objective-C, including a `main()` function that created several objects. Some of these objects were instances of `LotteryEntry`, a class that you created. The program logged some information to the console.

At this point, you have a fairly complete understanding of Objective-C. Objective-C is not a complex language. The rest of the book is concerned with the frameworks that make up Cocoa. From now on, you will be creating event-driven applications, not command-line tools.

# Meet the Static Analyzer

One of the handiest tools in Xcode is the static analyzer. The static analyzer uses Apple's LLVM compiler technology to analyze your code and find bugs. Traditionally, developers have relied on compiler warnings for hints on potential trouble areas in their code. The static analyzer goes much deeper, looking past syntax and tracing how values are used within your code.

Because of the default compiler settings and our careful typing, you should find, if you run the analyzer now, that our application has no issues as it stands. Let's modify our project settings so that we can better see the static analyzer at work.

As we did before, open the project's build settings by selecting the project in the project navigator on the left. Then select the lottery target. In the Build Settings tab, find the setting for Objective-C Automatic Reference Counting. Change its value to No (Figure 3.15).

Now analyze the lottery application. In the Product menu, click Analyze. In the issues navigator, you will see several issues found by the static analyzer; select one and drill down in the tree to examine the analyzer's thought process (Figure 3.16).

In this case, the static analyzer has found a number of memory-related problems in our program because we disabled a feature called automatic reference counting, which we will discuss in the next chapter. This is one of the more

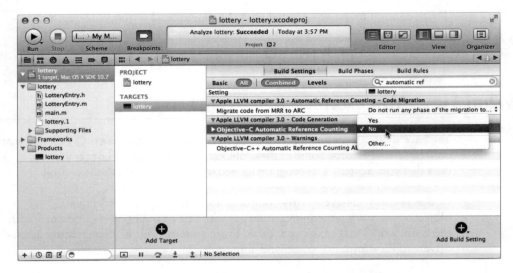

**Figure 3.15**  Disable Automatic Reference Counting

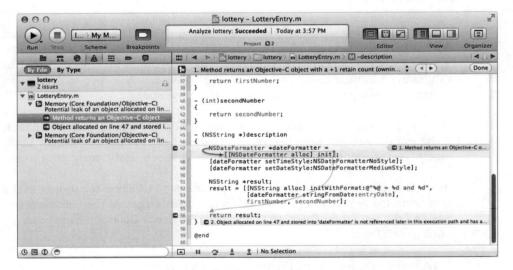

**Figure 3.16**  The Static Analyzer at Work

useful aspects of the static analyzer: It knows the rules for retain-count memory management in Objective-C, and it can also identify other dangerous patterns in your code.

Leave automatic reference counting disabled for now.

# For the More Curious: How Does Messaging Work?

As mentioned earlier, an object is like a C struct. **NSObject** declares an instance variable called isa. Because **NSObject** is the root of the entire class inheritance tree, every object has an isa pointer to the class structure that created the object (Figure 3.17). The class structure includes the names and types of the instance variables for the class. It also has the implementation of the class's methods. The class structure has a pointer to the class structure for its superclass.

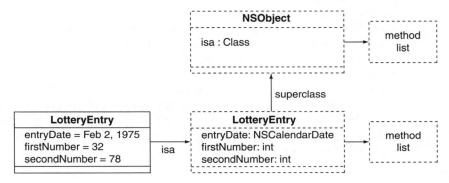

**Figure 3.17**    Each Object Has a Pointer to Its Class

The methods are indexed by the selector. The selector is of type SEL. Although SEL is defined to be char *, it is most useful to think of it as an int. Each method name is mapped to a unique int. For example, the method name **addObject:** might map to the number 12. When you look up methods, you will use the selector, not the string @"addObject:".

As part of the Objective-C data structures, a table maps the names of methods to their selectors. Figure 3.18 shows an example.

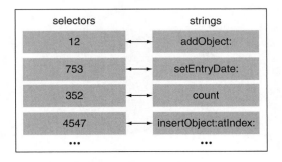

**Figure 3.18**    The Selector Table

At compile time, the compiler looks up the selectors wherever it sees a message send. Thus,

```
[myObject addObject:yourObject];
```

becomes (assuming that the selector for **addObject:** is 12)

```
objc_msgSend(myObject, 12, yourObject);
```

Here, **objc_msgSend()** looks at myObject's isa pointer to get to its class structure and looks for the method associated with 12. If it does not find the method, it follows the pointer to the superclass. If the superclass does not have a method for 12, it continues searching up the tree. If it reaches the top of the tree without finding a method, the function throws an exception.

Clearly, this is a very dynamic way of handling messages. These class structures can be changed at runtime. In particular, using the **NSBundle** class makes it relatively easy to add classes and methods to your program while it is running. This very powerful technique has been used to create applications that can be extended by other developers.

# Challenge

Use **NSDateFormatter**'s **setDateFormat:** to customize the format string on the date objects in your **LotteryEntry** class.

## Chapter 4

# MEMORY MANAGEMENT

Let's say that two instances of **Person** each have a favoriteColor that is a pointer to a color object. If two people have the same favoriteColor, the objects will have pointers to the same color object. As the people age, their favorite color might change. Eventually, the color object might be no one's favorite (Figure 4.1).

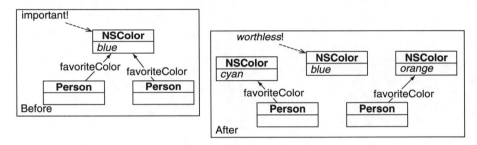

**Figure 4.1** The Problem

We do not want this orphaned color to be taking up room in the memory of our program. We want the memory deallocated so that we can put new objects in that memory, but we must be sure that the color is not deallocated while any objects are pointing to it.

This is a relatively tricky problem. Apple has come up with three solutions:

1. The first is manual reference counting, or retain counts: Every object has a retain count, which should represent the number of other objects that have pointers to it. If the color is the favorite of two people, the retain count of that color should be 2. When the retain count of an object goes to zero, it is deallocated.

2. Then, in Mac OS 10.5, Apple introduced garbage collection for Objec-tive-C. The garbage collector babysits the entire object graph, looking for objects that can't be reached from the variables that are in scope. The unreachable objects are automatically deallocated.

**3.** The new solution, introduced in Mac OS 10.7 and iOS 5, is automatic reference counting, more commonly known as ARC. ARC relies on the original retain-count mechanism but with a twist: The compiler manages the bookkeeping of retain counts for you.

What are the trade-offs? Manual reference counting is, after all, *manual* and requires some work on your part: You need to explicitly retain objects that you want to keep around and explicity release them when you are no longer interested in them. If not used carefully, the retain-count mechanism allows for a dastardly problem: Object A retains Object B, B retains A. Together, they are an island of memory that will never go away, because they are retaining each other. This is known as a retain cycle. Figure 4.2 is an example of a common form that retain cycles take.

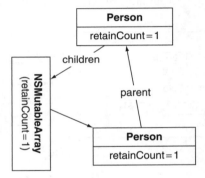

**Figure 4.2**    An Island of Garbage

The garbage collector sounds good on the surface but has a performance cost: It requires CPU time to scan through the objects, looking for garbage. This can sometimes result in poorer or uneven performance. For example, in an application that requires smooth performance, such as an action game, or an application that plays back video being rendered in real time, the garbage collector can cause hiccups in the processing while it is doing a scan. Additionally, the garbage collector cannot manage memory that you allocate manually, such as with **malloc()**, without special treatment. Garbage-collected code cannot run on versions of Mac OS X prior to 10.5, nor will it be portable to iOS, which does not support garbage collection (likely for the performance reasons discussed earlier).

ARC provides the best of both worlds: You get the speed and efficiency of manual reference counting, along with the freedom from memory-management concerns that garbage collection allows. ARC isn't perfect, however. It doesn't magically fix the problem of retain cycles and, like garbage collection, doesn't manage manually allocated memory.

ARC is enabled by default in Xcode's project templates. Although we'll take advantage of ARC for the rest of this book, we'll pretend for most of this chapter that ARC doesn't exist, so we can learn how retain counts work. It's important to have a firm grasp on the rules surrounding retain counts in order to work effectively in the ARC environment. If you want to write code for versions of Mac OS X prior to 10.6 or iOS prior to 4.0, you'll need to know how to use retain counts.

# Living with Manual Reference Counting

Retain counts are a pretty simple concept. Every object in Objective-C has a retain count. The retain count is an integer. When an object is created by the **alloc** method, the retain count is set to 1. When the retain count becomes zero, the object is deallocated. You increment the retain count by sending the message **retain** to the object. You decrement the retain count by sending the message **release** to the object.

An object's retain count should represent how many other objects have references to it. When the retain count becomes zero, this indicates that no one cares about it any more. It is deallocated so that the memory it was occupying can be reused.

A commonly used analogy is that of the dog and the leash. Each person who wants to ensure that the dog will stay around retains the dog by attaching a leash to its collar. Many people can retain the dog; as long as at least one person is retaining the dog, the dog will not go free. When zero people are retaining the dog, it will be deallocated. The retain count of an object, then, is the number of "leashes" on that object (Figure 4.3).

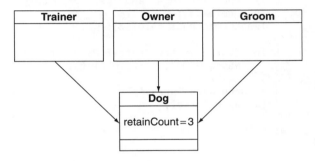

**Figure 4.3**   Objects Retain Each Other

The retain-count system gives the developer a lot of control over how and when objects are deallocated, but it requires that you meticulously retain and release objects. If you release an object too many times, it will be deallocated prematurely, and your program will crash. If you retain an object too many times, it will never get deallocated, and you will waste memory.

Fortunately, some simple rules govern when you should retain and release objects. These rules take the guesswork out of memory management with retain counts. In fact, once you are clear on these rules, it will be very clear in most cases when to retain and when to release. We'll cover the rules later in this chapter.

## Leak-Free Lottery

We didn't give any thought to memory management in the lottery exercise we started in the previous chapter. Let's open that project and fix it. Note that if you did not disable automatic reference counting at the end of the Chapter 3 be sure to make that build setting change now.

Open `lottery.m`. In **main()**, we had created an instance of **NSDate**:

```
NSDate *now = [[NSDate alloc] init];
```

After this line, now has a retain count of 1 because it was just allocated. Whenever we create a new instance of an object, we are taking responsibility for releasing it. Here's how we would release now:

```
[now release];
```

We had also created instances of **NSMutableArray** and **NSDateComponents**. Open `main.m` and release these objects once we are done with them:

```
    }
    // Done with 'now' and 'weekComponents'
    [now release];
    [weekComponents release];

    for (LotteryEntry *entryToPrint in array) {
        NSLog(@"%@", entryToPrint);
    }
    // Done with 'array'
    [array release];
    }
    return 0;
}
```

Now the objects will be properly deallocated before the process ends.

What about the **LotteryEntry** instances we added to the array?

```
// Create a new instance of LotteryEntry
LotteryEntry *newEntry = [[LotteryEntry alloc]
                          initWithEntryDate:iWeeksFromNow];
// Add the LotteryEntry object to the array
[array addObject:newEntry];
```

An array does not make a copy of an object when it is added. Instead, the array stores a pointer to the object and sends it the message **retain**. When the array is deallocated, the objects in the array are sent the message **release**. (Also, if an object is removed from an array, it is sent **release**.)

Let's quickly go over the life of the **LotteryEntry** object in your application:

1. When the entry object is created, it has a retain count of 1.

2. When the entry object is added to the array, its retain count is incremented to 2.

3. When the array is deallocated, it releases the entry. This decrements the retain count to 1.

So the **LotteryEntry** object is being leaked (it is never deallocated). In this example, the process ends an instant later, and the operating system reclaims all the memory. Thus, the lack of deallocation is not a big deal. However, in a program that ran a long time, such a memory leak would be a bad thing. To practice being tidy Objective-C programmers, let's fix the code by releasing the object after we add it to the array.

The revised loop should look like this:

```
    LotteryEntry *newEntry = [[LotteryEntry alloc]
                              initWithEntryDate:iWeeksFromNow];
    [array addObject:newEntry];
    [newEntry release];
}
```

We would say that "array now has ownership of newEntry."

Perhaps you are beginning to think more critically about object ownership and lifetime. Consider **LotteryEntry**'s instance variable, entryDate. What guarantee does **LotteryEntry** have that the **NSDate** instance will not be deallocated out from under it?

Right now, it has no guarantee. That's why it's very common for objects to retain objects they hold references to. This is called a strong reference. In some situations, a weak reference (nonretaining) is more appropriate; this is generally used to avoid creating a retain cycle. For example, a parent object generally retains its children (perhaps indirectly via an array), but the child will not retain its parent.

Open `LotteryEntry.m` and modify the initializer to retain `entryDate`:

```
- (id)initWithEntryDate:(NSDate *)theDate
{
    self = [super init];
    if (self) {
        entryDate = [theDate retain];
        firstNumber = ((int)random() % 100) + 1;
        secondNumber = ((int)random() % 100) + 1;
    }
    return self;
}
```

Now that it has a strong reference to entryDate, LotteryEntry must release it when it no longer needs it. The perfect place to relinquish ownership is **dealloc**.

## dealloc

When an object with a retain count of 1 is sent **release**, the **dealloc** method will be called. An object's **dealloc** method must release any objects that it was retaining and then call the superclass's **dealloc** method. Add a **dealloc** method to LotteryEntry.m:

```
- (void)dealloc
{
    NSLog(@"deallocating %@", self);
    [entryDate release];
    [super dealloc];
}
```

Note that we always call [super dealloc] at the *end* of an implementation of **dealloc**.

Build and run your app. It should work fine, and you should see that the entries are being properly deallocated (Figure 4.4).

There is, however, still a memory leak.

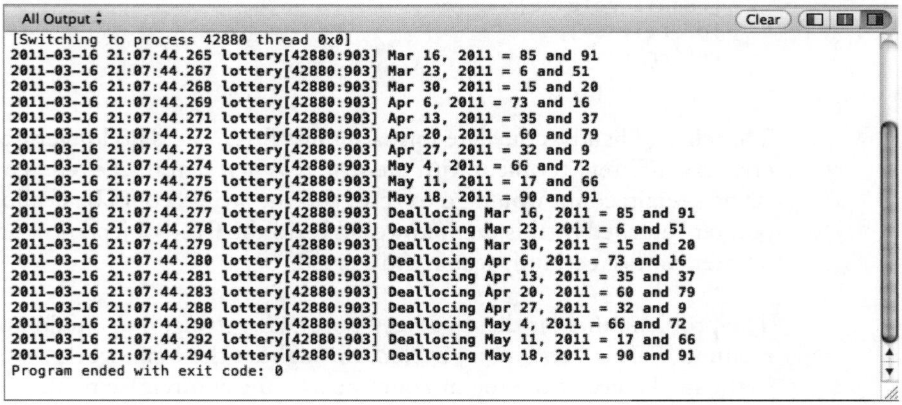

**Figure 4.4**    Running without the Garbage Collector

## Autoreleasing Objects

In the previous chapter, you created a **description** method that looks like this:

```
- (NSString *)description
{
    NSDateFormatter *df = [[NSDateFormatter alloc] init];
    [df setTimeStyle:NSDateFormatterNoStyle];
    [df setDateStyle:NSDateFormatterMediumStyle];
    NSString *result;
    result = [[NSString alloc] initWithFormat:@"%@ = %d and %d",
            [df stringFromDate:entryDate],
            firstNumber, secondNumber];
    return result;
}
```

This code works perfectly well but results in an annoying memory leak. When the method returns, df and result both have a retain count of 1.

We might attempt to fix this leak with something like this:

```
- (NSString *)description
{
    NSDateFormatter *df = [[NSDateFormatter alloc] init];
    [df setTimeStyle:NSDateFormatterNoStyle];
    [df setDateStyle:NSDateFormatterMediumStyle];
    NSString *result;
    result = [[NSString alloc] initWithFormat:@"%@ = %d and %d",
            [df stringFromDate:entryDate],
            firstNumber, secondNumber];
```

```
    [result release];
    [df release];
    return result;
}
```

This change handles the date formatter just fine, as it is no longer needed, but creates a different problem with the string. When sent the **release** message, the string's retain count would go to zero, and the string would be deallocated. The pointer returned by this method would be to the freed object, now an invalid pointer, almost certainly leading to a crash.

The problem, then, is that you need to return a string, but you do not want to retain it. This is a common problem throughout the frameworks, which leads us to the final piece of the retain-count puzzle: the autorelease pool.

Autorelease pools simplify releasing objects. You can add an object to the current autorelease pool simply by sending it the message **autorelease**. Adding an object to an autorelease pool marks it to be sent a **release** message at some point in the future.

The release message is sent once the pool is drained. In a Cocoa application, an autorelease pool is created before every event is handled and is drained after the event has been handled. Thus, unless the objects in the autorelease pool are being retained, they will be destroyed as soon as the event has been handled.

In the case of the lottery project, a command-line tool, there is no event loop, and so the autorelease pool has been created explicitly. This hints at another aspect of autorelease pools: They can be nested to reduce peak memory consumption, for example, in a large loop. The topmost pool is the pool to which autoreleased objects will be sent.

Note that if you **autorelease** an object *n* times, it will be sent **release** *n* times once the pool is drained.

## *Autoreleased Objects Are Useful*

One correct solution to our problem is then to autorelease the string before we return it:

```
- (NSString *)description
{
    NSDateFormatter *df = [[NSDateFormatter alloc] init];
    [df setTimeStyle:NSDateFormatterNoStyle];
    [df setDateStyle:NSDateFormatterMediumStyle];
    NSString *result;
```

```
    result = [[NSString alloc] initWithFormat:@"%@ = %d and %d",
            [df stringFromDate:entryDate],
            firstNumber, secondNumber];
    [result autorelease];
    [df release];
    return result;
}
```

You can think of autoreleasing as an alternative to directly releasing an object. Sometimes, Objective-C programmers autorelease objects out of necessity, such as in this case, when returning an object from a method; other times, it is more a matter of convenience.

Because you will frequently need objects that you are not retaining, many classes have class methods that return autoreleased objects. **NSString**, for example, has **stringWithFormat:**. The simplest correct solution then would be:

```
- (NSString *)description
{
    NSDateFormatter *df = [[NSDateFormatter alloc] init];
    [df setTimeStyle:NSDateFormatterNoStyle];
    [df setDateStyle:NSDateFormatterMediumStyle];
    NSString *result;
    result = [NSString stringWithFormat:@"%@ = %d and %d",
            [df stringFromDate:entryDate],
            firstNumber, secondNumber];
    [df release];
    return result;
}
```

## *Autoreleased Objects Are Convenient*

Recall that an autoreleased object won't be released until the pool is drained (usually when the current cycle of the event loop ends). This behavior makes it perfect for providing an intermediate result. For example, if you had an array of **NSString** objects, you could create a string with all the elements in uppercase and concatenated together, like this:

```
- (NSString *)concatenatedAndAllCaps
{
    int i;
    NSString *sum = @"";
    NSString *upper;

    for (i=0; i < [myArray count]; i++) {
      upper = [[myArray objectAtIndex:i] uppercaseString];
      sum = [NSString stringWithFormat:@"%@%@", sum, upper];
    }
    return sum;
}
```

With this method, if you have 13 strings in the array, 26 autoreleased strings will be created (13 by **uppercaseString** and 13 by **stringWithFormat:**; the initial constant string is a special case and doesn't count). One of the resulting strings is returned and may be retained by the object that asked for it. The other 25 strings are deallocated automatically at the end of the event loop. (Note that you would probably get better performance in this example by appending the uppercased string to an **NSMutableString** instead of creating a new string and adding it to the autorelease pool each time through the loop.)

## The Retain-Count Rules

Now that you are familiar with **retain**, **release**, and **autorelease**, you are ready for the rules.

In these rules, we use the word "you" to mean "an instance of whatever class you are currently working on." It is a useful form of empathy: You imagine that you are the object you are writing. So, for example, "If you retain the string, it will not be deallocated" really means "If an instance of the class that you are currently working on retains the string, it will not be deallocated."

Here, then, are the rules. (Implementation details are in parentheses.)

- If you create an object by using a method whose name starts with **alloc** or **new** or contains **copy**, you have taken ownership of it. (That is, assume that the new object has a retain count of 1 and is not in the autorelease pool.) You have a responsibility to release the object when you no longer need it. Some of the common methods that convey ownership are **alloc** (which is always followed by an **init** method), **copy**, and **mutableCopy**.

- An object created through any other means, such as a convenience method, is not owned by you. (That is, assume that it has a retain count of 1 and is already in the autorelease pool and thus doomed unless it is retained before the autorelease pool is drained.)

- If you don't own an object and want to ensure its continued existence, take ownership by sending it the message **retain**. (This increments the retain count.)

- When you own an object and no longer need it, send it the message **release** or **autorelease**. (The message **release** decrements the retain count immediately; **autorelease** causes the message **release** to get sent when the autorelease pool is drained.)

- As long as it has at least one owner, an object will continue to exist. (When its retain count goes to zero, it is sent the message **dealloc**.)

One of the tricks to understanding memory management is to think locally. The **LotteryEntry** class does not need to know anything about other objects that also care about its entryDate. As long as a **LotteryEntry** instance retains objects it wants to keep, you won't have any problems. Programmers new to the language sometimes make the mistake of trying to keep tabs on objects throughout an application. Don't do this. If you follow these rules and always think local to a class, you never have to worry what the rest of an application is doing with an object.

# Accessor Methods

An object has instance variables. Other objects cannot access these variables directly. To enable other objects to read and set an instance variable, an object will usually have a pair of accessor methods.

For example, if a class **Rex** has an instance variable named fido, the class will probably have at least two other methods: **fido** and **setFido:**. The **fido** method enables other objects to read the fido variable; the **setFido:** method enables other objects to set the fido variable.

If you have a nonpointer type, the accessor methods are quite simple. For example, if your class has an instance variable called foo of type int, you would create the following accessor methods:

```
- (int)foo
{
    return foo;
}
- (void)setFoo:(int)x
{
    foo = x;
}
```

These methods will allow other objects to get and set the value of foo.

Matters become more complicated if foo is a pointer to an object. In the "setter" method, you need to make sure that the new value is retained and the old value released, as shown in Figure 4.5. If you assume that foo is a pointer to an **NSDate**, there are three common idioms in setter methods. All three work correctly, and you can probably find some experienced Cocoa programmers who will argue the superiority of any one of them. Each has trade-offs.

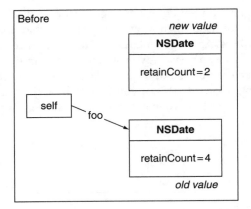

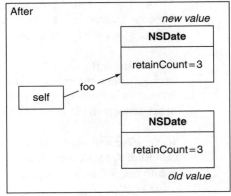

**Figure 4.5**    Before and After setFoo:

The first idiom is "Retain, Then Release":

```
- (void)setFoo:(NSDate *)x
{
    [x retain];
    [foo release];
    foo = x;
}
```

Here, it is important to retain before releasing. Suppose that you reverse the order. If x and foo are both pointers to the same object that happens to have a retain count of 1, the release would cause the object to be deallocated before it was retained. *Trade-off:* If they are the same value, this method performs an unnecessary retain and release.

The second idiom is "Check Before Change":

```
- (void)setFoo:(NSDate *)x
{
    if (foo != x) {
      [foo release];
      foo = [x retain];
    }
}
```

Here, you are not setting the variable unless a different value is passed in. *Trade-off:* An extra `if` statement is necessary.

The final idiom is "Autorelease Old Value":

```
- (void)setFoo:(NSDate *)x
{
    [foo autorelease];
    foo = [x retain];
}
```

Here, you autorelease the old value. *Trade-off:* An error in retain counts will result in a crash one event loop after the error. This behavior makes the bug harder to track down. In the first two idioms, your crash will happen closer to your error. Also, **autorelease** carries some performance overhead.

You have read the trade-offs and can make your own decision on which to use. In this book, we will use "Retain, Then Release."

The "getter" method for an object is the same as that for a nonpointer type:

```
- (NSDate *)foo
{
    return foo;
}
```

Most Java programmers would name this method **getFoo**. Don't. Objective-C programmers call this method **foo**. In the common idioms of Objective-C, a method prefixed with **get** takes an address where data can be copied. For example, if you have an **NSColor** object and you want its red, green, blue, and alpha components, you would call **getRed:green:blue:alpha:** as follows:

```
float r, g, b, a;

[myFavoriteColor getRed:&r green:&g blue:&b alpha:&a];
```

(For readers who might be a bit rusty with their C, & returns the address where the variable holds its data.)

If you used your accessor methods to read the variables, your **description** method would look like this:

```
- (NSString *)description
{
    return [NSString stringWithFormat:@"%@ = %d and %d",
        [self entryDate], [self firstNumber], [self secondNumber]];
}
```

OO purists would argue that this is the most correct implementation of the **description** method.

Change **setEntryDate:** in LotteryEntry.m to correctly retain the new value and release the old:

```
- (void)setEntryDate:(NSDate *)date
{
    [date retain];
    [entryDate release];
    entryDate = date;
}
```

Congratulations! You have now completed converting the lottery project to a retain-counted application. Run the static analyzer on the application (Product -> Analyze); you should have zero issues.

# Living with ARC

Although manual reference counting is fairly simple, it can be difficult to execute perfectly. At best, this leads to minor leaks but more typically results in crashes. At the end of Chapter 3, we saw that the static analyzer was able to find Objective-C memory errors in our code. Some clever engineers at Apple asked, "If we can find memory errors, why don't we go ahead and fix them?" ARC is the result.

ARC is a compiler feature, based on the same technology that powers the static analyzer. When you compile your application, your use of Objective-C object pointers (references) is examined by the compiler, which then applies the same rules we described earlier in this chapter, retaining, releasing, and autoreleasing to ensure that the objects live as long as necessary and are deallocated when they are no longer needed.

Essentially, this means that all the memory-related changes we made to the lottery project were unnecessary under ARC. In fact, when using ARC, it is an error to call **retain**, **release**, or **autorelease**. With ARC, you will think less about retain counts and focus more on object relationships. Relationships are defined by references, which are simply object pointers. There are two types of references: strong and weak.

## Strong References

By default, references are strong. If you assign an object to a strong reference, ARC assumes that you want that object to stick around and retains it implicitly. If that reference is changed to a new value, the old object is released and the new object retained, just like the **setEntryDate:** setter we wrote in the previous section. Thus, the same setter can be rewritten as follows, without any memory concerns:

```
- (void)setEntryDate:(NSDate *)date
{
    entryDate = date;
}
```

ARC will take care of releasing any strong references in **dealloc** for you. You can still implement **dealloc** to take care of any other cleanup tasks.

## Weak References

Weak references are similar to the old manual reference-counted pointers: There is no implicit retain; the pointer value is simply changed in memory. Such references have long been an area ripe for causing crashes, however. If the pointer is not retained, the object can be deallocated, leaving a bad pointer to cause a crash when it is used. ARC addresses this by automatically setting weak references to nil when the object they point to has been deallocated. This is known as a "zeroing weak reference."

When would you want to use a weak pointer? Recall the retain-cycle issue we touched on before, where two objects are retaining each other and thus are never deallocated. In ARC, this is referred to as a strong reference cycle. By using weak references strategically, we can avoid these cycles altogether. Consider the following class definition:

```
@interface Person : NSObject {
    Person *parent; // Bad! This causes a strong reference cycle!
    NSMutableArray *children;
}
@end
```

Because references are strong by default, a class like this would quickly result in a strong reference cycle. **Person** has a strong reference to both parent and children; the children array has strong references to objects it contains. We can use the __weak qualifier to fix this problem and make parent a weak reference:

```
@interface Person : NSObject {
    __weak Person *parent; // Good! No strong reference cycle.
    NSMutableArray *children;
}
@end
```

This pattern is commonly used in Objective-C: The parent-to-child relationship is strong, whereas the child-to-parent relationship is weak.

Note that only classes compiled with ARC can have weak references made to them. An exception will be thrown if you try to make an assignment to a __weak variable and the class does not support weak references. You can use the __unsafe_unretained qualifier in place of __weak in cases like this. The object will not be retained, but this reference will not be set to nil when the object is deallocated.

## ARC Odds and Ends

- ARC code is able to work with manually reference-counted code without modification. In fact, it is possible to use ARC on a per file basis. It is important, however, that manually reference-counted code adhere to the rules discussed earlier in this chapter.

- Xcode provides a migration tool to convert existing projects to ARC. This tool can be found in the Edit menu, under Refactor -> Convert to Objective-C Automatic Reference Counting.

- Although ARC code can run on Mac OS X 10.6 and iOS 4, weak references are not supported on those platforms.

- Although Objective-C can be intermixed with plain C in most cases, ARC does not allow C structures to contain object pointers.

- Property names may not begin with new.

- Under ARC it is an error to call retain, release, autorelease, or dealloc (such as with [super dealloc]). Additionally, you cannot override retain, release, or autorelease.

# Chapter 5
# TARGET/ACTION

Once upon a time, there was a company called Taligent. Taligent was created by IBM and Apple to develop a set of tools and libraries like Cocoa. About the time Taligent reached the peak of its mindshare, Aaron met one of its engineers at a trade show and asked him to create a simple application: A window would appear with a button, and when the button was clicked, the words "Hello, World!" would appear in a text field. The engineer created a project and started subclassing madly, subclassing the window and the button and the event handler. Then he started generating code: dozens of lines to get the button and the text field onto the window. After 45 minutes, Aaron had to leave. The app still did not work. That day, Aaron knew that the company was doomed. A couple of years later, Taligent quietly closed its doors forever.

Most C++ and Java tools work on the same principles as the Taligent tools. The developer subclasses many of the standard classes and generates many lines of code to get controls to appear on windows. Most of these tools work.

While writing an application that uses the AppKit framework, you will seldom subclass the classes that represent windows, buttons, or events. Instead, you will create objects that will work with the existing classes. Also, you will not create code to get controls on windows. Instead, the XIB file will contain all this information. The resulting application will have significantly fewer lines of code. At first, this outcome may be alarming. In the long run, most programmers find it delightfully elegant.

To understand the AppKit framework, a good place to start is with the class **NSControl**. **NSButton**, **NSSlider**, **NSTextView**, and **NSColorWell** are all subclasses of **NSControl**. A control has a *target* and an *action*. The target is simply a pointer to another object. The action is a message (a selector) to send to the target. Recall that you set the target and action for two buttons in Chapter 2. There you set your **Foo** object to be the target of both buttons, and you set the action on one to **seed:** (Figure 5.1) and the action on the other to **generate:**.

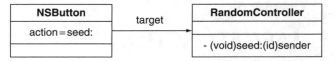

**Figure 5.1**    A Button Has a Target and an Action

When the user interacts with the control, it sends the `action` message to its `target`. For example, when the button is clicked, the button sends the `target` its `action` message (Figure 5.2).

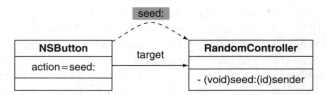

**Figure 5.2**    The Button Sends a Message

The `action` methods take one argument: the sender. This enables the receiver to know which control sent the message. Often, you will call back to the sender to get more information. For example, a check box will send its `action` message when it is turned on and when it is turned off. After getting the `action` message, the receiver might call back to the button to find out whether it is currently on or off:

```
- (IBAction)toggleFoo:(id)sender
{
    BOOL isOn = [sender state];
    ...
}
```

To better understand **NSControl**, you should become acquainted with its ancestors: **NSControl** inherits from **NSView**, which inherits from **NSResponder**, which inherits from **NSObject**. Each member of the family tree adds some capabilities (Figure 5.3).

At the top of the class hierachy is **NSObject**. All classes inherit from **NSObject**, and this is where they get the basic methods: **retain**, **release**, **dealloc**, and **init**. **NSResponder** is a subclass of **NSObject**. Responders have the ability to handle events with such methods as **mouseDown:** and **keyDown:**. **NSView** is a subclass of **NSResponder** and has a place on a window, where it draws itself. You can create subclasses of **NSView** to display graphs and allow the user to drag and drop data. **NSControl** inherits from **NSView** and adds the `target` and the `action`.

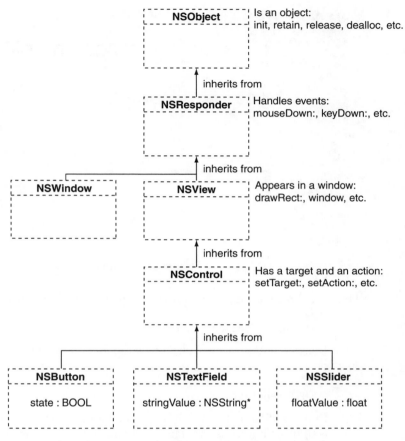

**Figure 5.3**   Inheritance Diagram for NSControl

# Some Commonly Used Subclasses of NSControl

Before using some controls, let's take a brief look at the three most commonly used controls: **NSButton**, **NSSlider**, and **NSTextField**.

## NSButton

Instances of **NSButton** can have appearances: oval, square, check box. They can also have various behaviors when clicked: toggle (like a check box) or momentarily on (like most other buttons). Buttons can have icons and sounds associated with them. Figure 5.4 shows the Attributes Inspector for an **NSButton** in Interface Builder.

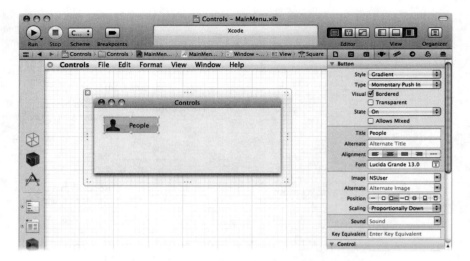

**Figure 5.4**    Button Inspector

Here are three messages that you will frequently send to buttons.

    - (void)setEnabled:(BOOL)yn

Enabled buttons can be clicked by the user. Disabled buttons are grayed out.

    - (NSInteger)state

Returns NSOnState (which is 1) if the button is on, or NSOffState (which is 0) if the button is off. This method allows you to see whether a check box is checked or unchecked.

    - (void)setState:(NSInteger)aState

This method turns the button on or off. It allows you to check or uncheck a check box programmatically. Set the state to NSOnState to check the check box and to NSOffState to uncheck it.

## NSSlider

Instances of **NSSlider** can be vertical or horizontal. They can send the action to the target continuously while being changed, or they can wait to send the action until the user releases the mouse button. A slider can have markers, and it can prevent users from choosing values between the markers (Figure 5.5). Circular sliders are also possible.

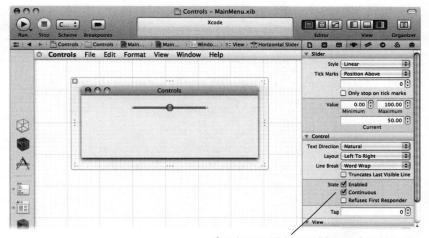

Continuous sliders send an action message as the user moves the slider. Noncontinuous sliders send an action message only when the user releases the mouse button.

**Figure 5.5**  Slider Inspector

Here are two methods of **NSSlider** that you will use frequently:

- (void)setFloatValue:(float)x

Moves the slider to x.

- (float)floatValue

Returns the current value of the slider.

# NSTextField

An instance of **NSTextField** can allow a user to type a single line of text. Text fields may or may not be editable. Uneditable text fields are commonly used as labels on a window. Compared to buttons and sliders, text fields are relatively complex. We will plumb the depths of the mysteries surrounding text fields in later chapters. Figure 5.6 shows the Attributes information panel for an **NSTextField** in Interface Builder.

Text fields have a placeholder string. When the text field is empty, the placeholder string is displayed in gray.

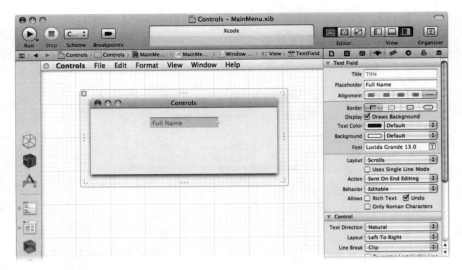

**Figure 5.6**    Text Field Inspector

**NSSecureTextField** is a subclass of **NSTextField** and is used for such things as passwords. As the user types, bullets appear instead of the typed characters. You cannot copy or cut from an **NSSecureTextField**.

Here are a few of the most commonly used **NSTextField** methods:

```
- (NSString *)stringValue
```

```
- (void)setStringValue:(NSString *)aString
```

Allow you to get and set the string data being displayed in the text field.

```
- (NSObject *)objectValue
```

```
- (void)setObjectValue:(NSObject *)obj
```

Allow you to get and set the data being displayed in the text field as an arbitrary object type. This behavior is helpful if you are using a formatter. **NSFormatter**s are responsible for converting a string into another type, and vice versa. If no formatter is present, these methods use the **description** method.

For example, you might use a text field to allow the user to type in a date. As the programmer, you don't want the string that the user typed in; you want an instance of **NSDate**. By attaching an **NSDateFormatter**, you ensure that the text field's **objectValue** method will return an **NSDate**. Also, when you call **setObjectValue:** with an **NSDate**, the **NSDateFormatter** will format it as a string for the user. (You will create a custom formatter class in Chapter 26.)

Figure 5.7 shows some other controls you might want to play with. Drag them out, inspect them, and see how they act when you compile and run the app.

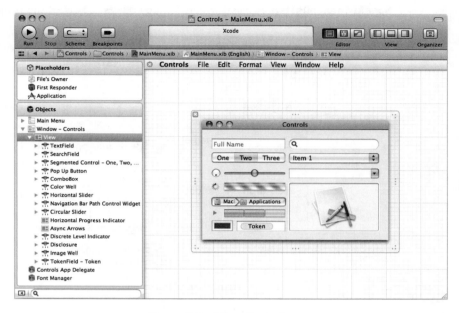

**Figure 5.7**    Some Controls

# Start the SpeakLine Example

As a simple example of using controls, you will build an application that enables users to type in a line of text and hear it spoken by the Mac OS X speech synthesizer. The app will look like Figure 5.8 when you are done with this chapter.

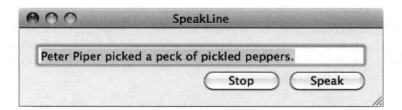

**Figure 5.8**    Completed Application

Figure 5.9 presents a diagram of the objects that you will create and their pointers to one another. Note that all the classes that start with NS are part of the Cocoa frameworks and thus already exist. Your code will be in the **SpeakLineAppDelegate** class, which Xcode creates as part of the project template.

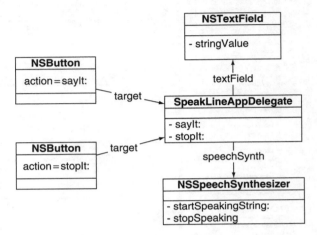

**Figure 5.9**   Object Diagram

In Xcode, create a new project. Name the project SpeakLine and set the Class Prefix to SpeakLine. A new project will appear.

# Lay Out the XIB File

Click on MainMenu.xib to open it in Interface Builder. Click the window icon in Interface Builder's dock to open it. With the window selected, uncheck Resize in the Attributes Inspector. We will still be able to resize the window in the editor, but the user will not.

Next, drag out a text field and two buttons from the Library panel. Double-click on the text field to change the text to read "Peter Piper picked a peck of pickled peppers" (or some other text that will amuse you when it is spoken by the machine). Change the labels on the buttons to read Speak and Stop. The result should look like Figure 5.8.

The **SpeakLineAppDelegate** class, which Xcode created as part of our project, will be the target of the two buttons. Each control will trigger a different action method.

With MainMenu.xib still selected, enable the **Assistant Editor**, using the toolbar button (Figure 5.10). The Assistant Editor shows a counterpart to the currently selected file. The counterpart for MainMenu.xib is the application delegate header file, SpeakLineAppDelegate.h. If you do not see SpeakLineAppDelegate.h in the Assistant Editor, select **Automatic** in the leftmost segment of the jump bar at the top of the Assistant Editor.

Click for Assistant Editor

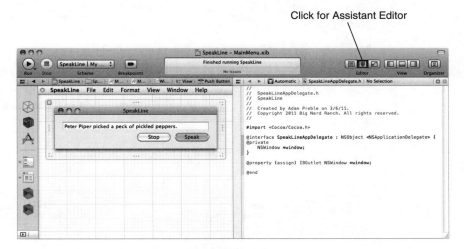

**Figure 5.10**   Enable the Assistant Editor

In Chapter 2 we learned how to create outlets and actions and how to create connections between user interface objects by using Interface Builder. We could type out all the outlets and actions for this project as before. Instead, we will use the Assistant Editor to make our task much easier.

## Making Connections in Interface Builder

Making a connection is analogous to introducing people. You say, "Mrs. Robinson, this is Dr. Pepper." If it is important that Dr. Pepper also know Mrs. Robinson, you would continue, "Dr. Pepper, this is Mrs. Robinson." With objects in Interface Builder, you will drag from *the object that needs to know* to the object that *it needs to know about*. You might also drag the other way to create a connection in the opposite direction, if necessary.

For example, when a user clicks the **Stop** button, the button needs to send a message to your **SpeakLineAppDelegate**, so the button needs to know about the **SpeakLineAppDelegate**. For this reason, you will Control-drag from the button to the **SpeakLineAppDelegate**. However, instead of dragging to the blue object in the Interface Builder dock as we did before, we will Control-drag from the button *to the interface definition area* within the Assistant Editor, as shown in Figure 5.11. In the pop-over that appears, set the Connection to Action, enter

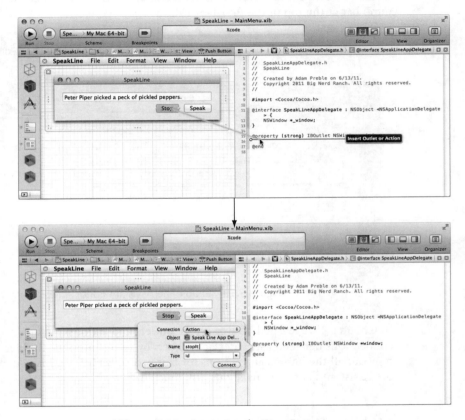

**Figure 5.11**   Set Action for Stop Button

**stopIt:** for the Name, and click Connect. An IBAction line will appear at the insertion point.

Now Control-drag from the Speak button to the SpeakLineAppDelegate.h interface again in order to create an action named **sayIt:**.

In order to synthesize the speech for the line of text, the **SpeakLineAppDelegate** will need to ask the text field for the line of text. Thus, the **SpeakLineAppDelegate** needs to have a pointer to the text field. This time, Control-drag from the text field to just below the `window` outlet in `SpeakLineAppDelegate.h`. Set the Connection to Outlet, name it `textField`, and click Connect, as shown in Figure 5.12.

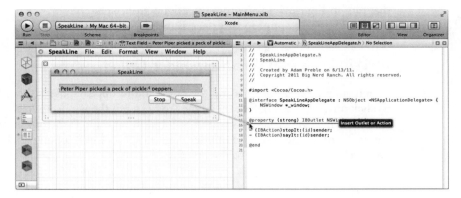

**Figure 5.12**    Control-drag to Create the textField Outlet

Xcode will create a new `@property` line. A property is like a setter and getter in one, however in this case there is no clear instance variable backing the property. In fact, the complier will automatically create an instance variable named `_textField`. How do we know this? Look for the `@synthesize` line in `SpeakLineAppDelegate.m`. We will learn more about properties in Chapter 7.

Note that if we were using the Connection panel instead of the Assistant Editor to create an outlet connection, we would be dragging *from* **SpeakLineAppDelegate** *to* the text field.

`SpeakLineAppDelegate.h` should now look like this:

```
#import <Cocoa/Cocoa.h>

@interface SpeakLineAppDelegate : NSObject <NSApplicationDelegate>

@property (assign) IBOutlet NSWindow *window;
@property (weak) IBOutlet NSTextField *textField;

- (IBAction)stopIt:(id)sender;
- (IBAction)sayIt:(id)sender;

@end
```

If you look at `SpeakLineAppDelegate.m`, you will find that Xcode has created stubs for the **sayIt:** and **stopIt:** actions.

At this point, you have set all but one of the connections shown in the object diagram in Figure 5.9. The missing connection, `speechSynth`, will be done programmatically—not in Interface Builder.

### NSWindow's initialFirstResponder Outlet

When your application runs and the new window appears, users should not have to click on a text field before they type. You can tell the window which view should be receiving keyboard events when the window appears. Control-click on the window icon in the Interface Builder dock to get its Connection panel. Drag from `initialFirstResponder` to the text field.

# Implementing the SpeakLineAppDelegate Class

Now you need to write some code, so select the `SpeakLineAppDelegate.h` file. Add an instance variable named `speechSynth` of type **NSSpeechSynthesizer**:

```
#import <Cocoa/Cocoa.h>

@interface SpeakLineAppDelegate : NSObject <NSApplicationDelegate>
{
    NSSpeechSynthesizer *_speechSynth;
}

@property (assign) IBOutlet NSWindow *window;
@property (weak) IBOutlet NSTextField *textField;

- (IBAction)sayIt:(id)sender;
- (IBAction)stopIt:(id)sender;

@end
```

Note that because we are not setting the `speechSynth` variable in the XIB file, we don't flag it as IBOutlet.

Open the `SpeakLineAppDelegate.m` file. This is where you will make the methods do something:

```
#import "SpeakLineAppDelegate.h"

@implementation SpeakLineAppDelegate
```

```objc
@synthesize window = _window;
@synthesize textField = _textField;

- (id)init
{
    self = [super init];
    if (self) {
        // Logs can help the beginner understand what
        // is happening and hunt down bugs.
        NSLog(@"init");

        // Create a new instance of NSSpeechSynthesizer
        // with the default voice.
        _speechSynth = [[NSSpeechSynthesizer alloc]
                                        initWithVoice:nil];
    }
    return self;
}

- (IBAction)sayIt:(id)sender
{
    NSString *string = [_textField stringValue];

    // Is the string zero-length?
    if ([string length] == 0) {
        NSLog(@"string from %@ is of zero-length", _textField);
        return;
    }
    [_speechSynth startSpeakingString:string];
    NSLog(@"Have started to say: %@", string);
}

- (IBAction)stopIt:(id)sender
{
    NSLog(@"stopping");
    [_speechSynth stopSpeaking];
}
@end
```

Your application is done. Build it and run it. You should be able to start the recitation of the text in the text field and stop it in mid-sentence.

*Final note*: A menu item (an instance of **NSMenuItem**) also has a target and an action. Everything we've talked about in this chapter applies to menu items.

# For the More Curious: Setting the Target Programmatically

Note that the action of a control is a selector. **NSControl** includes the following method:

```
- (void)setAction:(SEL)aSelector
```

But how would you get a selector? The Objective-C compiler directive @selector will tell the compiler to look up the selector for you. For example, to set the action of a button to the method **drawMickey:**, you could do the following:

```
SEL mySelector;
mySelector = @selector(drawMickey:);
[myButton setAction:mySelector];
```

At compile time, @selector(drawMickey:) will be replaced by the selector for **drawMickey:**.

If you needed to find a selector for an **NSString** at runtime, you could use the function **NSSelectorFromString()**:

```
SEL mySelector;
mySelector = NSSelectorFromString(@"drawMickey:");
[myButton setTarget:someObjectWithADrawMickeyMethod];
[myButton setAction:mySelector];
```

# Challenge

This exercise is an important challenge you should do before moving on. Although it is easy to follow the instructions, you will eventually want to create your own applications. Here is where you can start to develop some independence. Feel free to refer back to the earlier examples for guidance.

Create another application that will present the user with the window shown in Figure 5.13. This application can have only one window open, so it is not a document-based application.

When the user types in a string and clicks the button, change the message text to display the input string and the number of characters it has (Figure 5.14).

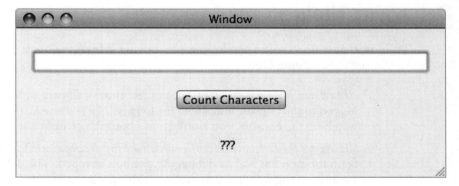

**Figure 5.13**    Before Input

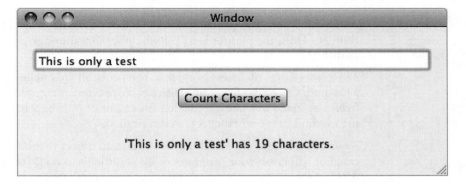

**Figure 5.14**    After Input

It is important to know how to use the Cocoa classes in your application. For this exercise, you should recognize that the **NSTextField** class has the following methods:

```
- (NSString *)stringValue;
- (void)setStringValue:(NSString *)aString;
```

You will also find it useful to know about the following methods of the class **NSString**:

```
- (NSUInteger)length;
+ (NSString *)stringWithFormat:(NSString *),...;
```

You will create a controller object with two outlets and one action. (This is hard, and you are not stupid. Good luck!)

# Debugging Hints

Now that you are writing code, not just copying it from the book, you are ready for some debugging hints.

*Always watch the console.* If a Cocoa object throws an exception, it will be logged to the console and the event loop will be restarted. If you aren't watching the console, you won't know about the error at all.

*Always use the Debug build configuration during development.* The Release configuration has had its debugging symbols stripped. The debugger will act a bit strangely when it is dealing with a program with no debugging symbols.

Here are some common problems and common fixes:

*Nothing happens.* You probably forgot to make a connection in Interface Builder. Thus, the pointer is nil. Remember that messages sent to nil do nothing.

*Made connection, still nothing happens.* You probably misspelled the name of a method. Objective-C is case sensitive, so setFoo: is completely different from setfoo:. Try putting in a log statement or putting a breakpoint on the method to see whether it is getting called.

*Application crashes.* If you send a message to an object that has been deallocated, it will crash your program. (This is difficult to do if you are using ARC or the garbage collector.) Hunting these crashers can be difficult; after all, the problem object has already been deallocated. One way to hunt them down is to ask the frameworks to turn your objects into "zombies" instead of deallocating them. When you send a message to a zombie, it throws a descriptive exception that says something like, "You tried to send the message -count to a freed instance of the class Fido." This will stop the debugger on that line.

To turn on zombies, open the Product menu and select Edit Scheme.... Select the Run (application name).app action and switch to the Diagnostics tab. Check Enable Zombie Objects.

*No objects are being freed, it still crashes.* Check the type of your arguments. For example, this is a great way to crash your app:

```
int x = 5;
NSLog(@"x is %@", x);
```

See the problem? x is an int, but %@ specifies an object.

*Interface Builder won't let me make a connection.* A .h file is messed up. A missing semicolon? A variable declared to be **NSTabView** instead of **NSTableView**? Look carefully.

# Chapter 6
# HELPER OBJECTS

Once upon a time, there was a man with no name. Knight Industries decided that if this man were given guns and wheels and booster rockets, he would be the perfect crime-fighting tool. First, they thought, "Let's subclass him and override everything we need to add the guns and wheels and booster rockets." The problem was that to subclass Michael Knight, you would need to know an awful lot about his guts so that you could wire them to guns and booster rockets. So instead, they created a helper object, the Knight Industries 2000, or "KITT the super car."

Note how this is different from the RoboCop approach. RoboCop was a man subclassed and extended. The whole RoboCop project involved dozens of surgeons who extended the man's brain into a fighting machine. This is the approach taken with many object-oriented frameworks.

While approaching the perimeter of an arms dealer's compound, Michael Knight would speak to KITT over his watch-radio. "KITT," he would say, "I need to get to the other side of that wall." KITT would then blast a big hole in the wall with a small rocket. After destroying the wall, Kitt would return control to Michael, who would stroll through the rubble.

Many objects in the Cocoa framework are extended in much the same way. That is, an existing object needs to be extended for your purpose. Instead of subclassing the table view, you simply supply it with a helper object. For example, when a table view is about to display itself, it will turn to the helper object to ask such things as, "How many rows of data am I displaying?" and "What should be displayed in the first column, second row?"

Thus, to extend an existing Cocoa class, you will frequently create a helper object. This chapter focuses on creating helper objects and connecting them to the standard Cocoa objects.

# Delegates

In the SpeakLine application, the use of your interface would be more obvious if the Stop button remained disabled unless the speech synthesizer were speaking and if the Speak button were enabled only when the speech synthesizer was silent. Thus, the **SpeakLineAppDelegate** should enable the button when it starts the speech synthesizer and then disable the button when the speech synthesizer stops.

Many classes in the Cocoa framework have an instance variable called `delegate`. You can set the `delegate` outlet to point to a helper object. In the documentation for the class, the `delegate` methods are clearly described. For example, the **NSSpeechSynthesizer** class has the following `delegate` methods:

```
- (void)speechSynthesizer:(NSSpeechSynthesizer *)sender
        didFinishSpeaking:(BOOL)finishedSpeaking;

- (void)speechSynthesizer:(NSSpeechSynthesizer *)sender
            willSpeakWord:(NSRange)characterRange
                 ofString:(NSString *)string;

- (void)speechSynthesizer:(NSSpeechSynthesizer *)sender
         willSpeakPhoneme:(short)phonemeOpcode;
```

The Apple programmer who wrote **NSSpeechSynthesizer** put these hooks in. He is Michael Knight. You are KITT.

Of the three messages that the speech synthesizer sends to its `delegate`, you care about only the first one: **speechSynthesizer:didFinishSpeaking:**.

In your application, you will make the **SpeakLineAppDelegate** the delegate of the speech synthesizer and implement **speechSynthesizer:didFinish-Speaking:**. The method will be called automatically when the utterance is complete. The new object diagram is shown in Figure 6.1.

Note that you do not have to implement any of the other `delegate` methods. The implemented methods will be called; the unimplemented ones will be ignored. Also note that the first argument is always the object that is sending the message—in this case, the speech synthesizer.

In SpeechLineAppDelegate.h, change the **SpeechLineAppDelegate** class declaration:

```
@interface SpeakLineAppDelegate : NSObject
    <NSApplicationDelegate, NSSpeechSynthesizerDelegate> {
```

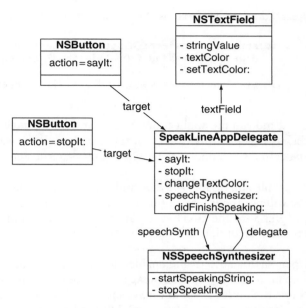

**Figure 6.1**    New SpeakLine Object Diagram

This change tells the compiler that **SpeakLineAppDelegate** conforms to the **NSSpeechSynthesizerDelegate** protocol. We will cover protocols in Chapter 10.

Now, in SpeakLineAppDelegate.m, set the delegate outlet of the speech synthesizer:

```
- (id)init
{
    self = [super init];
    if (self) {
        // Logs can help the beginner understand what
        // is happening and hunt down bugs.
        NSLog(@"init");

        // Create a new instance of NSSpeechSynthesizer
        // with the default voice.
        _speechSynth = [[NSSpeechSynthesizer alloc]
                                    initWithVoice:nil];

        [_speechSynth setDelegate:self];
    }
    return self;
}
```

Next, add the `delegate` method. For now, just log a message:

```
- (void)speechSynthesizer:(NSSpeechSynthesizer *)sender
        didFinishSpeaking:(BOOL)finishedSpeaking
{
    NSLog(@"finishedSpeaking = %d", finishedSpeaking);
}
```

Build and run the application. Note that the `delegate` method is called if you click the Stop button or if the utterance plays all the way to the end. (`finished-Speaking` is YES only if the utterance plays to the end.)

To enable and disable the Stop and Start buttons, you will need outlets for them. We will use the Interface Builder editor and the Assistant Editor as we did in Chapter 5 for the `textField` outlet to create and connect `startButton` and `stopButton` outlets in `SpeakLineAppDelegate.h`.

Open `MainMenu.xib` and enable the Assistant Editor. Control-drag from the Stop button to the **SpeakLineAppDelegate** class interface to create a new outlet. Name the outlet `stopButton`, as shown in Figure 6.2. Also, Control-drag from the Speak button to create a `speakButton` outlet.

The Stop button should be disabled when it first appears on screen, so select the button and disable it in the Attributes `Inspector` as shown in Figure 6.3. Save the NIB file.

In Xcode, edit the `SpeakLineAppDelegate.m` file to properly enable and disable the button. In **sayIt:**, enable the button:

```
- (IBAction)sayIt:(id)sender
{
    NSString *string = [_textField stringValue];

    // Is the string zero-length?
    if ([string length] == 0) {
        NSLog(@"string from %@ is of zero-length", _textField);
        return;
    }
    [_speechSynth startSpeakingString:string];
    NSLog(@"Have started to say: %@", string);

    [_stopButton setEnabled:YES];
    [_speakButton setEnabled:NO];
}
```

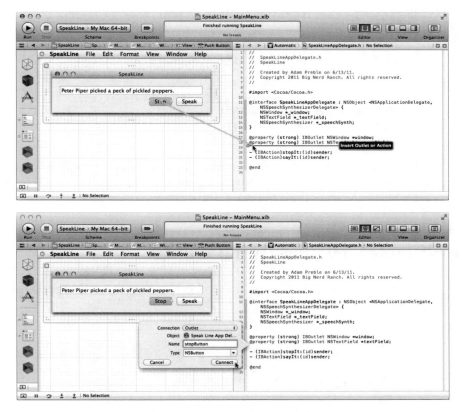

**Figure 6.2**  Set stopButton Outlet

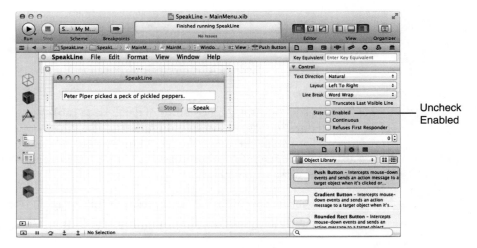

**Figure 6.3**  Disable Stop Button

In **speechSynthesizer:didFinishSpeaking:**, reset the buttons to their initial states:

```
- (void)speechSynthesizer:(NSSpeechSynthesizer *)sender
       didFinishSpeaking:(BOOL)finishedSpeaking
{
    NSLog(@"finishedSpeaking = %d", finishedSpeaking);
    [_stopButton setEnabled:NO];
    [_speakButton setEnabled:YES];
}
```

Build and run the application. You should see that the Stop button is enabled only when the synthesizer is generating speech. The Speak button should be enabled only when the synthesizer is silent.

# The NSTableView and Its dataSource

Next, you will add a table view that will enable the user to change the voice, as shown in Figure 6.4.

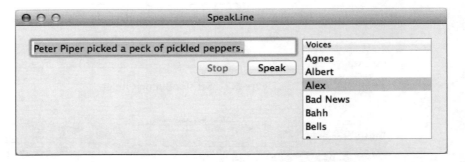

**Figure 6.4**    *Completed Application*

A table view is used for displaying columns of data. An **NSTableView** has a helper object called a dataSource, as shown in Figure 6.5. The table view expects its data source to have some methods. We say, "The data source must conform to the NSTableDataSource informal protocol." This is a fancy way of saying that it must implement these two methods:

```
- (NSInteger)numberOfRowsInTableView:(NSTableView *)aTableView;
```

The dataSource will reply with the number of rows that will be displayed.

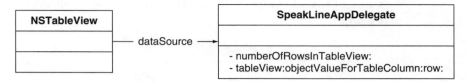

**Figure 6.5**    NSTableView's dataSource

```
- (id)tableView:(NSTableView *)aTableView
   objectValueForTableColumn:(NSTableColumn *)aTableColumn
                        row:(NSInteger)rowIndex;
```

The dataSource will reply with the object that should be displayed in the row rowIndex of the column aTableColumn.

If you have editable cells in your table view and are using a cell-based table view (as we are in this exercise), you will need to implement one more method:

```
- (void)tableView:(NSTableView *)aTableView
   setObjectValue:(id)anObject
   forTableColumn:(NSTableColumn *)aTableColumn
               row:(NSInteger)rowIndex;
```

The dataSource takes the input that the user put into row rowIndex of aTableColumn. You do not have to implement this method if your table view is not editable.

Note that you are taking a very passive position in getting data to appear. Your data source will wait until the table view asks for the data. When they first work with **NSTableView** (or **NSBrowser** or **NSOutlineView**, which work in a very similar manner), most programmers want to boss the table view around and tell it, "You will display 7 in the third row in the fifth column." It doesn't work that way. When it is ready to display the third row and the fifth column, the table view will ask its dataSource for the object to display. Your class is its servant.

How, then, will you get the table view to fetch updated information? You will tell the table view to **reloadData**. It will then reload all the cells that the user can see.

## SpeakLineAppDelegate Interface File

You are going to make your instance of **SpeakLineAppDelegate** become the dataSource of the table view. This involves two steps: implementing the two methods listed earlier and setting the table view's dataSource outlet to the instance of **SpeakLineAppDelegate**. Figure 6.6 provides a diagram of where you are going.

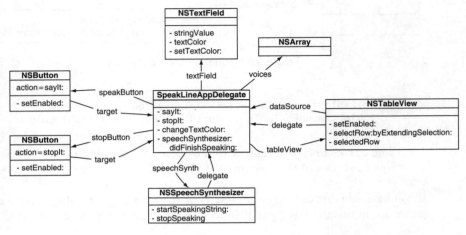

**Figure 6.6** Object Diagram

First, add the declaration of a new instance variable to SpeakLineAppDelegate.h:

```
#import <Cocoa/Cocoa.h>

@interface SpeakLineAppDelegate : NSObject
  <NSApplicationDelegate, NSSpeechSynthesizerDelegate> {
    NSArray *_voices;
    NSSpeechSynthesizer *_speechSynth;
}
```

Save the file. In SpeakLineAppDelegate.m, change the **init** method to initialize _voices:

```
- (id)init
{
    self = [super init];
    if (self) {

        // Create a new instance of NSSpeechSynthesizer
        // with the default voice.
        _speechSynth = [[NSSpeechSynthesizer alloc]
                                    initWithVoice:nil];
```

```
        [_speechSynth setDelegate:self];

        _voices = [NSSpeechSynthesizer availableVoices];
    }
    return self;
}
```

# Lay Out the User Interface

Open MainMenu.xib and select the window icon in the dock to show the window. You will edit the window to look like Figure 6.7.

**Figure 6.7**   Completed Interface

Make the window wider and drag an **NSTableView** onto the window (Figure 6.8).

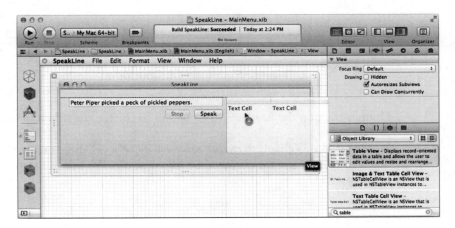

**Figure 6.8**   Drop a Table View on the Window

Select the table view so you can look at its attributes in the Inspector. (This may be a bit challenging. The table view is inside the scroll view, and the table view column is inside the table view. Experiment with clicks and double-clicks. You will know that you have selected the table view when the title of the last section of the jump bar is Table View.

In the Inspector, set the Content Type to Cell Based, make the table view have only one column, and disable column selection (Figure 6.9).

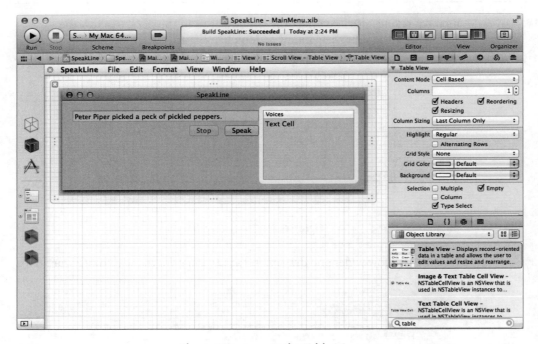

**Figure 6.9**    Inspect the Table View

Double-click on the header of the column to change the title to Voices.

Note that in this chapter's exercise, we are using a cell-based table view, as it is much simpler to use for trivial tables like this one. We will use view-based tables in Chapter 11.

# Make Connections

First, you will set the `dataSource` outlet of the **NSTableView** to be the **Speak-LineAppDelegate**. Select the **NSTableView**. Control-click in the table view to bring up the Connections panel. Drag from the `dataSource` outlet to the **SpeakLineAppDelegate** (Figure 6.10).

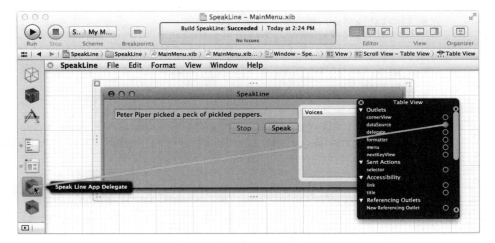

**Figure 6.10**   Set the NS tableView's dataSource Outlet

If you do not see `dataSource` in the Inspector, you have selected **NSScrollView**, not **NSTableView** inside it. The scroll view is the object that takes care of scrolling and the scroll bars. You will learn more about scroll views in Chapter 17. For now, just click in the interior of the table view until the title of the Connection panel says **NSTableView**.

Also, set the **SpeakLineAppDelegate** to be the `delegate` of the table view.

Now use the Assistant Editor to create an outlet called `tableView` on **SpeakLineAppDelegate** and connect it to the table view. Make sure that you have the table view selected and Control-drag to the class declaration in the header file, as done in Chapter 5.

# Edit SpeakLineAppDelegate.m

Implement the data source methods in `SpeakLineAppDelegate.m`:

```
- (NSInteger)numberOfRowsInTableView:(NSTableView *)tv
{
    return (NSInteger)[_voices count];
}

- (id)tableView:(NSTableView *)tv
        objectValueForTableColumn:(NSTableColumn *)tableColumn
                            row:(NSInteger)row
{
    NSString *v = [_voices objectAtIndex:row];
    return v;
}
```

The identifer for a voice is a long string such as `com.apple.speech.synthe-sis.voice.Fred`. If you want just the name `Fred`, replace the last method with this one:

```
- (id)tableView:(NSTableView *)tv
    objectValueForTableColumn:(NSTableColumn *)tableColumn
                        row:(NSInteger)row
{
    NSString *v = [_voices objectAtIndex:row];
    NSDictionary *dict = [NSSpeechSynthesizer attributesForVoice:v];
    return [dict objectForKey:NSVoiceName];
}
```

(The screenshots in this chapter assume that you've done the pretty version.)

Next, build and run the application. Now you get a list of the possible voices, but selecting a voice doesn't do anything yet.

Besides having a `dataSource` outlet, a table view has a `delegate` outlet. The delegate is informed whenever the selection changes. In `SpeakLineAppDelegate.m`, implement **tableViewSelectionDidChange:**. (The class **NSNotification** will be introduced later in this book. For now, just note that you are passed a notification object as an argument to this delegate method.)

```
- (void)tableViewSelectionDidChange:(NSNotification *)notification
{
    NSInteger row = [_tableView selectedRow];
    if (row == -1) {
        return;
    }
```

```
    NSString *selectedVoice = [_voices objectAtIndex:row];
    [_speechSynth setVoice:selectedVoice];
    NSLog(@"new voice = %@", selectedVoice);
}
```

The speech synthesizer will not allow you to change the voice while it is speaking, so you should prevent the user from changing the selected row. The table view should be enabled and disabled with `speakButton`:

```
- (IBAction)sayIt:(id)sender
{
    NSString *string = [_textField stringValue];
    if ([string length] == 0) {
        return;
    }

    [_speechSynth startSpeakingString:string];
    NSLog(@"Have started to say: %@", string);
    [_stopButton setEnabled:YES];
    [_startButton setEnabled:NO];
    [_tableView setEnabled:NO];
}
- (void)speechSynthesizer:(NSSpeechSynthesizer *)sender
        didFinishSpeaking:(BOOL)complete
{
    NSLog(@"complete = %d", complete);
    [_stopButton setEnabled:NO];
    [_startButton setEnabled:YES];
    [_tableView setEnabled:YES];
}
```

Your users will want to see that the default voice is selected in table view when the application starts. Create a new method, **awakeFromNib**, and within it select the appropriate row and scroll to it, if necessary:

```
- (void)awakeFromNib
{
    // When the table view appears on screen, the default voice
    // should be selected
    NSString *defaultVoice = [NSSpeechSynthesizer defaultVoice];
    NSInteger defaultRow = [_voices indexOfObject:defaultVoice];
    NSIndexSet *indices = [NSIndexSet indexSetWithIndex:defaultRow];
    [_tableView selectRowIndexes:indices byExtendingSelection:NO];
    [_tableView scrollRowToVisible:defaultRow];
}
```

Build and run the application. If the speech synthesizer is speaking, you will not be able to change the voice, as the table view should be disabled. If the speech synthesizer is not speaking, you should be able to change the voice.

## Common Errors in Implementing a Delegate

There are two very common errors that people make when implementing a delegate:

- *Misspelling the name of the method*: The method will not be called, and you will not get any error or warning from the compiler. The best way to avoid this problem is to copy and paste the declaration of the method from the documentation or the header file.

- *Forgetting to set the delegate outlet*: You will not get any error or warning from the compiler if you make this error.

## Many Objects Have Delegates

Delegation is a commonly used design pattern in Cocoa. Here are some of the classes in the AppKit framework having `delegate` outlets:

```
NSAlert
NSAnimation
NSApplication
NSBrowser
NSDatePicker
NSDrawer
NSFontManager
NSImage
NSLayoutManager
NSMatrix
NSMenu
NSPathControl
NSRuleEditor
NSSavePanel
NSSound
NSSpeechRecognizer
NSSpeechSynthesizer
NSSplitView
NSTabView
NSTableView
NSText
NSTextField
NSTextStorage
NSTextView
NSTokenField
NSToolbar
NSWindow
```

# For the More Curious: How Delegates Work

The delegate doesn't have to implement all the methods, but if the object does implement a delegate method, it will get called. In many languages, this sort of thing would be impossible. How is it achieved in Objective-C?

**NSObject** has the the following method:

```
- (BOOL)respondsToSelector:(SEL)aSelector
```

Because every object inherits (directly or indirectly) from **NSObject**, every object has this method. It returns YES if the object has a method called aSelector. Note that aSelector is a SEL, not an **NSString**.

Imagine for a moment that you are the engineer who has to write **NSTableView**. You are writing the code that will change the selection from one row to another. You think to yourself, "I should check with the delegate." To do so, you add a snippet of code that looks like this:

```
// About to change to row "rowIndex"

// Set the default behavior
BOOL ok = YES;

// Check whether the delegate implements the method
if ([delegate respondsToSelector:
                            @selector(tableView:shouldSelectRow:)])
{
    // Execute the method
    ok = [delegate tableView:self shouldSelectRow:rowIndex];
}

// Use the return value
if (ok)
{
    ...actually change the selection...
}
```

Note that the delegate is sent the message only if it has implemented the method. If the delegate doesn't implement the message, the default behavior happens. (In reality, the result from **respondsToSelector:** is usually cached by the object with the delegate outlet. This makes performance considerably faster than would be implied by the code.)

After writing this method, you would carefully make note of its existence in the documentation for your class.

If you wanted to see the checks for the existence of the delegate methods, you could override **respondsToSelector:** in your delegate object:

```
- (BOOL)respondsToSelector:(SEL)aSelector
{
    NSString *methodName = NSStringFromSelector(aSelector);
    NSLog(@"respondsToSelector:%@", methodName);
    return [super respondsToSelector:aSelector];
}
```

You might want try adding this method to AppController.m now.

# Challenge: Make a Delegate

Create a new application with one window. Make an object that is a delegate of the window. As the user resizes the window, make sure that the window always remains twice as tall as it is wide.

Here is the signature of the delegate method you will implement:

```
- (NSSize)windowWillResize:(NSWindow *)sender
                    toSize:(NSSize)frameSize;
```

The first argument is the window being resized. The second argument is a C struct that contains the size that the user has asked for:

```
typedef struct _NSSize {
    float width;
    float height;
} NSSize;
```

Here is how you create an NSSize that is 200 points wide and 100 points tall:

```
NSSize mySize = NSMakeSize(200.0, 100.0);
NSLog(@"mySize is %f wide and %f tall", mySize.width, mySize.height);
```

You can set the intial size of the window in the Size Inspector in Interface Builder.

# Challenge: Make a Data Source

Make a to-do list application. The user will type tasks into the text field. When the user clicks the Add button, you will add the string to a mutable array, and the new task will appear at the end of the list (Figure 6.11).

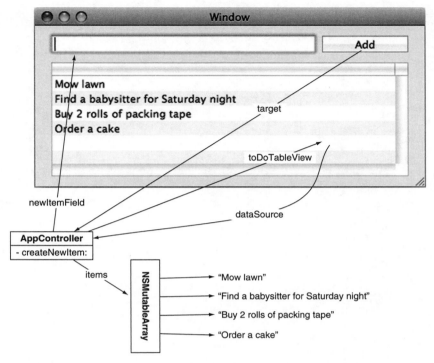

**Figure 6.11**   Diagram of Challenge

When a new string is added to the array, you will need to send the message **reloadData** to the table view before you will see it.

You get extra points for making the table view editable. (*Hint:* **NSMutableArray** has a method **-replaceObjectAtIndex:withObject:**)

# Chapter 7

# KEY-VALUE CODING AND KEY-VALUE OBSERVING

Key-value coding (or KVC) is a mechanism that allows you to set and get the value of a variable by its name. The name is just a string, but we refer to that name as a *key*. So, for example, imagine that you have a class called **Student** that has an instance variable called firstName of type NSString:

```
@interface Student : NSObject
{
    NSString *firstName;
}
...
@ends
```

If you had an instance of **Student**, you could set its firstName like this:

```
Student *s = [[Student alloc] init];
[s setValue:@"Larry" forKey:@"firstName"];
```

You could read the value of its firstName like this:

```
NSString *x = [s valueForKey:@"firstName"];
```

The methods **setValue:forKey:** and **valueForKey:** are defined in **NSObject**. We know: This doesn't look like rocket science, but it turns out that the ability to read and set a variable by its name is really powerful. The rest of this chapter will be a simple example that should illustrate some of that power.

## Key-Value Coding

In Xcode, create a new project of type Cocoa Application. Name the project KvcFun and set the Class Prefix to KvcFun.

Open KvcFunAppDelegate.h, and add an instance variable called fido of type int:

```
@interface KvcFunAppDelegate : NSObject <NSApplicationDelegate> {
    int fido;
}
@property (assign) IBOutlet NSWindow *window;
@end
```

In KvcFunAppDelegate.m, you are going to create an **init** method that sets and reads fido using key-value coding. This is a bit silly because it is going to be a long-winded way to get a simple result. This is designed to be illustrative rather than practical.

What makes the method so long-winded is that the key-value coding methods work with objects, so instead of passing an int, you will need to create an **NSNumber**. Add this method to KvcFunAppDelegate.m:

```
- (id)init
{
    self = [super init];
    if (self) {
        [self setValue:[NSNumber numberWithInt:5]
                forKey:@"fido"];
        NSNumber *n = [self valueForKey:@"fido"];
        NSLog(@"fido = %@", n);
    }
    return self;
}
```

The key-value coding mechanism will automatically convert the **NSNumber** to an int before using it to set the value of fido. Build and run the application, but don't expect much. When the blank window appears, fido = 5 will be logged to the console.

If you have accessor methods for getting and setting fido, they will be used. You must, however, give them the correct names. The getter must be called **fido** and the setter must be called **setFido:**. Note that this is more than a just a convention; if you give your accessors nonstandard names, they will not get called by the key-value coding methods. Add **fido** and **setFido:** to KvcFunApp-Delegate.m:

```
- (int)fido
{
    NSLog(@"-fido is returning %d", fido);
    return fido;
}
```

```
- (void)setFido:(int)x
{
    NSLog(@"-setFido: is called with %d", x);
    fido = x;
}
```

Declare these methods in KvcFunAppDelegate.h:

```
- (int)fido;
- (void)setFido:(int)x;
```

Build and run the application. Note that your accessor methods are being called.

# Bindings

Many graphical objects in Cocoa have *bindings*. When you bind a key, such as fido, to an attribute of a graphical object, such as its value or its font color, the view will automatically keep those in sync. You are going to add a slider, bind its value to fido, and see how it uses key-value coding to keep them in sync.

Open MainMenu.xib. Drop a slider on the window. In the Attributes Inspector, make the slider Continuous (Figure 7.1).

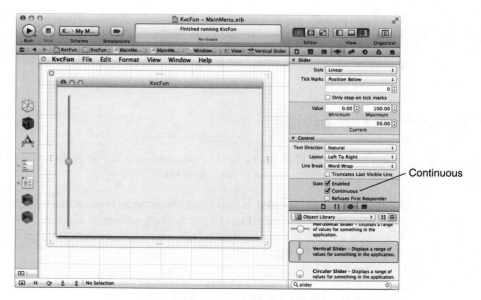

**Figure 7.1**    Make Slider Continuous

In the Bindings Inspector, bind the value of the slider to the fido key of the instance of **KvcFunAppDelegate** (Figure 7.2).

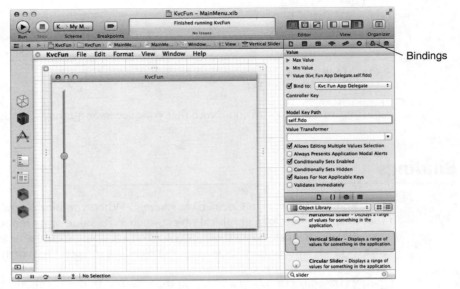

**Figure 7.2**    Bind Value of Slider to fido

Build and run the application. Note that the slider uses **valueForKey:** to get its initial value (which triggers your **fido** method). As you move the slider, it calls **setValue:forKey:** to update the value of fido (which triggers your **setFido:** method).

# Key-Value Observing

What happens if fido is changed by something other than the slider? How would the slider know that it has a new value?

When the slider is created, it tells the **KvcFunAppDelegate** that it is observing its fido key. Whenever the value of fido is changed by the accessor methods or by key-value coding, the **KvcFunAppDelegate** sends a message to the slider notifying it that fido has changed.

In MainMenu.xib again, add a Label text field to the window, and bind its value to **KvcFunAppDelegate**'s fido key (Figure 7.3).

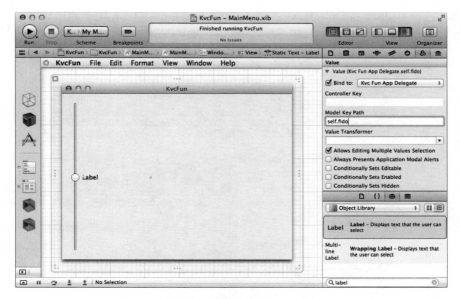

**Figure 7.3**    Bind Value of Label to fido

Build and run the app. Note that when you move the slider, **setFido:** is called. This notifies the text field that fido has changed. The text field uses **valueForKey:** to get the new value of fido. Thus, you see the **fido** method getting called.

## Making Keys Observable

The previous section mentioned that when you use accessors or key-value coding to change the value for a key, the observers are automatically notified of the change. What happens if you change the variable directly?

Open KvcFunAppDelegate.h and declare a new action method:

```
- (IBAction)incrementFido:(id)sender;
```

In KvcFunAppDelegate.m, implement the method:

```
- (IBAction)incrementFido:(id)sender
{
    fido++;
    NSLog(@"fido is now %d", fido);
}
```

Open `MainMenu.xib`. Add a button to the window, label it Increment Fido, and Control-drag from the button to the instance **KvcFunAppDelegate**. The button should trigger the **incrementFido:** action (Figure 7.4).

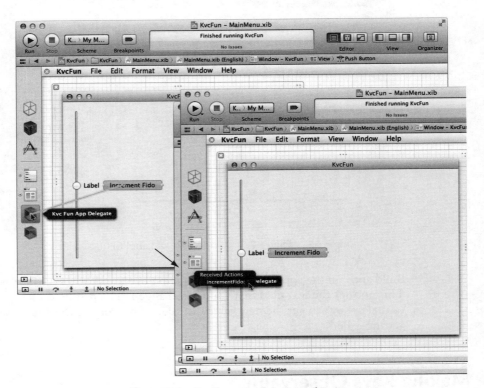

**Figure 7.4**    Set Target and Action of Button

You would hope that when the button is clicked, the slider would move and the text field would update itself. Sadly, neither happens. Try building and running the application.

If you are going to change the variable directly, you will need to explicitly trigger the notification of the observers. Change the **incrementFido:** method:

```
- (IBAction)incrementFido:(id)sender
{
    [self willChangeValueForKey:@"fido"];
    fido++;
    NSLog(@"fido is now %d", fido);
    [self didChangeValueForKey:@"fido"];
}
```

Build and run the application now; the Increment Fido button should work correctly.

There are two other solutions that would work. First, you could use key-value coding:

```
- (IBAction)incrementFido:(id)sender
{
    NSNumber *n = [self valueForKey:@"fido"];
    NSNumber *npp = [NSNumber numberWithInt:[n intValue] + 1];
    [self setValue:npp forKey:@"fido"];
}
```

Or you could use the accessor method to change fido:

```
- (IBAction)incrementFido:(id)sender
{
    [self setFido:[self fido] + 1];
}
```

Type this version in. Then build and run it.

Figure 7.5 is an object diagram of what you have done. Note that we are going to be using half-arrows to represent bindings.

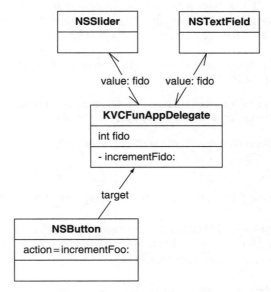

**Figure 7.5**   Object Diagram

# Properties

As you can guess, we spend a lot of time calling accessor methods, so much so that Objective-C gives programmers the option of calling accessors by using dot notation. If you have a pointer `rover` to an object with a getter method **rex**, you can call it like this:

```
NSLog(@"Rover's rex is %@", rover.rex);
```

To call **setRex:**, you could do this:

```
rover.rex = [NSDate date];
```

Objective-C programmers have varying opinions about whether dot notation is a good addition to the language. Some consider it syntactic sugar, a feature that can (dangerously) disguise message sends, which do not behave the same as, say, assigning values in a structure. Others think that those dangers are outweighed by the brevity it brings to the language. For clarity, we won't be using it in this book.

What about writing the accessor methods? If your object has 12 instance variables, do you need to write 12 setters and 12 getters?

Properties provide a very elegant way to eliminate a lot of this code. In the KvcFunAppDelegate.h file, replace the declaration of the **fido** and **setFido:** methods with the declaration of a *property*:

```
@interface KvcFunAppDelegate : NSObject <NSApplicationDelegate> {
    int fido;
}
@property (assign) IBOutlet NSWindow *window;
@property (readwrite, assign) int fido;

- (IBAction)incrementFido:(id)sender;

@end
```

This one line is equivalent to declaring **setFido:** and **fido** methods.

In KvcFunAppDelegate.m, you can use @synthesize to implement the accessor methods. Delete your **fido** and **setFido:** methods from KvcFunAppDelegate.m, and replace them with this line:

```
@synthesize fido;
```

Note that everything still works. (Naturally, you won't see the log statements anymore.) The `@synthesize` directive implements the accessor methods for `fido` as they are described in `KvcFunAppDelegate.h`.

## Attributes of a Property

In general, the declaration of a property looks like this:

```
@property (attributes) type name;
```

The attributes can include `readwrite` or `readonly`. The default is `readwrite`. A property marked `readonly` gets no setter method.

To describe how the setter method should work, the attributes can also include one of the following: `assign`, `strong`, `weak`, `copy`. Let's look at each in turn:

- `assign` (the default) makes a simple assignment happen. This attribute is most commonly used for scalar, nonpointer types, such as integers and floating-point values.

- `strong` says that this property is a strong reference. It keeps the object being pointed to from being deallocated while this pointer is set. It is specific to ARC code; if you are not using ARC, the `retain` attribute is equivalent.

- `weak` denotes a weak reference. It is similar to `assign`, except that once the object being pointed to is deallocated, this property will be set to `nil`. It is supported only by code compiled with ARC.

- `copy` makes a copy of the new value and assigns the variable to the copy. This attribute is often used for properties that are strings and other classes with mutable subclasses.

Attributes can also include `nonatomic`. If your application is multithreaded, it is sometimes important that your setter methods be *atomic*. That is, the execution of the setter method from one thread will not conflict with the execution of the same setter method on another thread. By default, the `@synthesize` call will generate accessors with this property. This involves using a lock to ensure that only one thread at a time is executing the setter. Creating and using the locks introduces some overhead. If you know that the accessors for a property don't need to be atomic, you can eliminate the overhead by adding `nonatomic` to the attributes.

If a property name exactly matches the corresponding instance variable name, you can simply `@synthesize` that name:

```
@synthesize fido;
```

If, however, you prefer to use a prefix with your instance variables (Xcode likes to use an underscore prefix), you can specify the instance variable name by using this technique:

```
@synthesize fido = _fido;
```

## For the More Curious: Key Paths

Objects are often arranged in a network. For example, a person might have a spouse who has a scooter that has a model name (Figure 7.6).

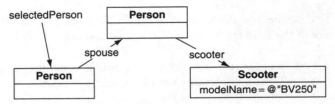

**Figure 7.6**   Objects Are a Directed Graph

To get the selected person's spouse's scooter's model name, you can use a key path:

```
NSString *mn;
mn = [selectedPerson valueForKeyPath:@"spouse.scooter.modelName"];
```

We'd say that spouse and scooter are relationships of the **Person** class and that modelName is an attribute of the **Scooter** class.

There are also operators that you can include in key paths. For example, if you have an array of **Person** objects, you could get their average expectedRaise by using key paths:

```
NSNumber *theAverage;
theAverage = [employees valueForKeyPath:@"@avg.expectedRaise"];
```

Here are some commonly used operators:

```
@avg
@count
@max
@min
@sum
```

Now that you know about key paths, we can discuss how to create bindings programmatically. If you had a text field in which you wanted to show the average expected raise of the arranged objects of an array controller, you could create a binding like this:

```
[textField bind:@"value"
      toObject:employeeController
   withKeyPath:@"arrangedObjects.@avg.expectedRaise"
       options:nil];
```

Of course, it is usually easier to create a binding in Interface Builder.

Use the **unbind:** method to remove the binding:

```
[textField unbind:@"value"];
```

# For the More Curious: Key-Value Observing

How did the text field become an observer of the fido key in the **KvcFunApp-Delegate** object? When it wakes up from being on the NIB, it adds itself as an observer. If you wanted to become an observer of this key, your line of code might look something like this:

```
[theAppDelegate addObserver:self
                 forKeyPath:@"fido"
                    options:NSKeyValueChangeOldKey
                    context:somePointer];
```

This method is defined in **NSObject**. It is how you say, "Hey! Send me a message whenever fido changes." The options and context determine what extra data is sent along with that message when fido changes. The method that is triggered looks like this:

```
- (void)observeValueForKeyPath:(NSString *)keyPath
                      ofObject:(id)object
                        change:(NSDictionary *)change
                       context:(void *)context
{
...
}
```

The keyPath, in this case, would be @"fido"; the object would be the **KvcFunAppDelegate**; context would be the pointer somePointer that was supplied as the context when you became an observer; change is a dictionary (a collection of key-value pairs) that can hold the old value of fido and/or the new value.

# Chapter 8
# NSArrayController

In the object-oriented programming community, a very common design pattern is *Model-View-Controller*. This design pattern says that each class you write should fall into exactly one of the following groups.

1. *Model* classes describe your data. For example, if you write banking systems, you would probably create a model class called **SavingsAccount** that would have a list of transactions and a current balance. The best model classes include nothing about the user interface and can be used in several applications.

2. *View* classes are part of the GUI. For example, **NSSlider** is a view class. The best views are general-purpose classes and can be used in several applications.

3. *Controller* classes are usually application-specific and are responsible for controlling the flow of the application. The user needs to see the data, so a controller object reads the model from a file or a database and then displays the model by using view classes. When the user makes changes, the view objects inform the controller, which subsequently updates the model objects. The controller also saves the data to the filesystem or database.

Until Mac OS X 10.3, Cocoa programmers wrote in their controller objects a lot of code that simply moved data from the model objects into the view objects and back again. To make common sorts of controller classes easier to write, Apple introduced **NSController** and bindings.

**NSController** is an abstract class (Figure 8.1). **NSObjectController**, a subclass of **NSController**, displays the information, or content of an object. **NSArrayController** is a controller that has an array of data objects as its content. In this exercise, we will use an **NSArrayController**.

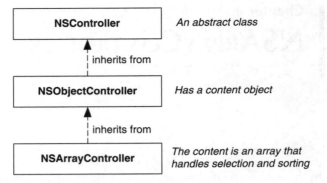

**Figure 8.1**    Controller Classes

# Starting the RaiseMan Application

Over the next few chapters, you will create a full-featured application for keeping track of employees and the raise that each person will receive this year. As this book progresses, you will add file saving, undo, user preferences, and printing capabilities. After this chapter, the application will look like Figure 8.2.

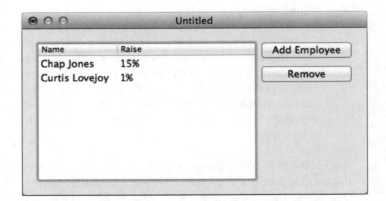

**Figure 8.2**    Completed Application

(Yes, experienced Cocoa programmers, you could create an application like this using Core Data, but we want you to see how it is done manually. Then, Core Data will not seem so magical.)

Create a new project in Xcode. Choose Cocoa Application for the type. Name the project RaiseMan, set the Class Prefix to RM, and enable Create Document-Based

Application. Set the document extension to `rsmn`, and disable Use Core Data and Include Unit Tests (Figure 8.3).

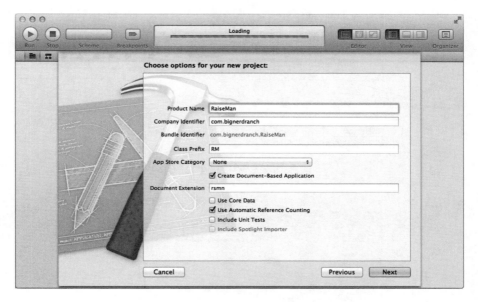

**Figure 8.3**   New Document-Based Project

What is a *document-based* application? It is an application in which several documents can be open simultaneously. TextEdit, for example, is a document-based application. System Preferences, on the other hand, is not a document-based application. You will learn more about document architecture in Chapter 10.

The object diagram for this application is shown in Figure 8.4. The table columns are connected to the **NSArrayController** by bindings rather than by outlets. This is a cell-based table view; we will discuss view-based table views in Chapter 11.

Note that the class **RMDocument** has already been created for you. **RMDocument** is a subclass of **NSDocument**. The document object is responsible for reading and writing files. In this exercise, we will use an **NSArrayController** and bindings to construct our simple interface, so we won't be adding any code to **RMDocument** just yet.

To create a new **Person** class, choose the File -> New -> New File... menu item. When presented with the possibilities, choose Objective-C class. Name the class `Person` and set it to be a subclass of **NSObject**, as shown in Figure 8.5.

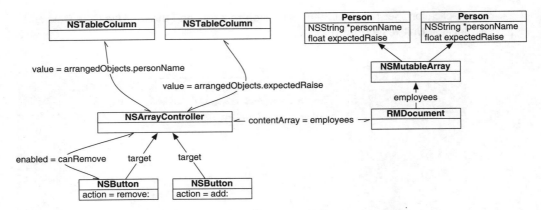

**Figure 8.4**    Object Diagram

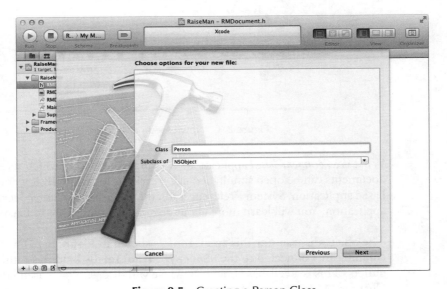

**Figure 8.5**    Creating a Person Class

Edit the Person.h file to declare two properties:

```
#import <Foundation/Foundation.h>

@interface Person : NSObject {
    NSString *personName;
    float expectedRaise;
}
@property (readwrite, copy) NSString *personName;
@property (readwrite) float expectedRaise;
@end
```

Now edit Person.m to synthesize these properties and to modify the overriding **init**:

```
#import "Person.h"

@implementation Person

@synthesize personName;
@synthesize expectedRaise;

- (id)init
{
    self = [super init];
    if (self) {
        expectedRaise = 0.05;
        personName = @"New Person";
    }
    return self;
}

@end
```

Note that **Person** is a model class—it has no information about the user interface. As such, this class doesn't need to know about all the Cocoa frameworks. Thus, instead of importing Cocoa/Cocoa.h, we are importing Foundation/Foundation.h. Either would work, but importing the smaller framework is more stylish. It indicates, for example, that this class could be reused in a command-line tool or an iOS application.

Declare the employees array (which will contain instances of the **Person** class) in RMDocument.h:

```
@interface RMDocument : NSDocument {
    NSMutableArray *employees;
}
- (void)setEmployees:(NSMutableArray *)a;
@end
```

Now in RMDocument.m, modify init to instantiate the employees array. Create the **setEmployees:** method. Leave the rest of the template methods in place for now.

```
- (id)init
{
    self = [super init];
    if (self) {
        employees = [[NSMutableArray alloc] init];
    }
    return self;
}
```

```
- (void)setEmployees:(NSMutableArray *)a
{
    // This is an unusual setter method.  We are going to add a lot
    // of smarts to it in the next chapter.
    if (a == employees)
        return;

    employees = a;
}
```

# RMDocument.xib

Click on RMDocument.xib to open it in the Interface Builder editor.

Delete the text field that says Your document contents here. Drop a table view and two buttons onto the window. Relabel and arrange them as shown in Figure 8.6. Use the Attributes Inspector to make sure that the table view's Content Mode is set to Cell Based.

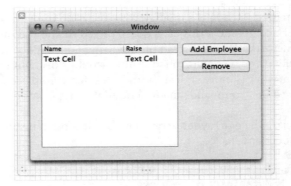

**Figure 8.6**   Document Window

Drag out an **NSArrayController** (from Cocoa->Objects & Controllers) and drop it into the editor area. An **NSArrayController** icon will appear in the Interface Builder dock.

Ensure that the array controller is selected in the dock. Open the Attributes Inspector for the **NSArrayController** instance; under Object Controller, set the Class Name to **Person**. Add the keys personName and expectedRaise as shown in Figure 8.7.

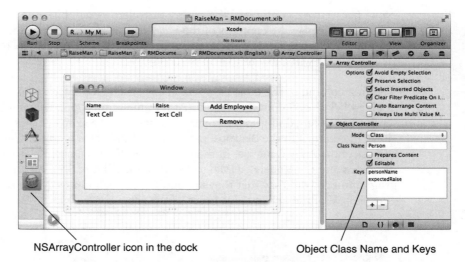

NSArrayController icon in the dock                    Object Class Name and Keys

**Figure 8.7**   Configure NSArrayController's Class Name and Keys

With the array controller still selected, change to the **Bindings Inspector** (its icon resembles a knot). Find the **Content Array** binding in the list and expand it. Check **Bind to;** in the pop-up; select **File's Owner.** Leave the **Controller Key** blank and enter `employees` for the **Model Key Path** (Figure 8.8). Cocoa programmers would say that they are binding the **Content Array** of the array controller to the `employees` array of File's Owner (which is the instance of **RMDocument**).

Bindings Inspector

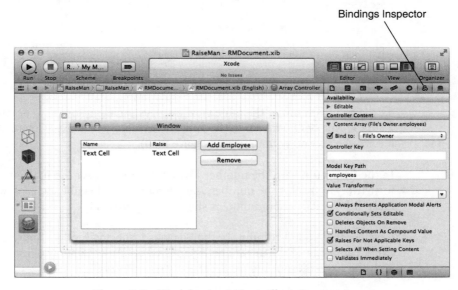

**Figure 8.8**   Bind the Array Controller's Content Array

Now that we have configured the array controller, we will bind the table-view columns to display the contents of the array controller. In Chapter 6, we implemented the **NSTableViewDataSource** protocol to populate the table view; bindings will allow us to skip that code.

The first column of the table view will display each employee's name. Click and double-click the column to select it. (At no time in this book will you bind a scroll view or cell; doing so is a common mistake, so keep an eye on the jump bar above the editor.) In the Bindings Inspector, find the Value binding. Check Bind to and select the Array Controller in the pop-up. Set the Controller Key to arrangedObjects and the Model Key Path to personName (Figure 8.9). Again, Cocoa programmers would say that they are binding the column's value to the personName of the arrangedObjects of the array controller.

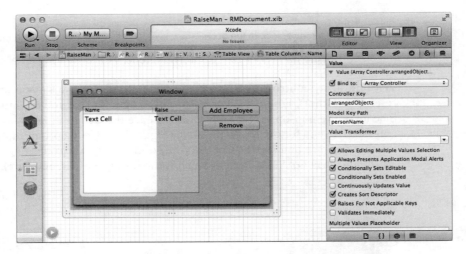

**Figure 8.9**    Bind the First Column to the Array Controller

The second column of the table view displays each employee's expected raise. Find the Number Formatter in the Library (in Library->Cocoa->Controls) and drag it onto the second column's cell (Figure 8.10).

In the Inspector, with the number formatter selected, set the formatter (a 10.4+ formatter) to display the number as a percentage and enable Lenient, which will make it less picky about input, as shown in Figure 8.11.

Reselect the second column. In the Bindings Inspector, bind value to the expectedRaise of the arrangedObjects of the Array Controller, just as you did with the first column (Figure 8.12).

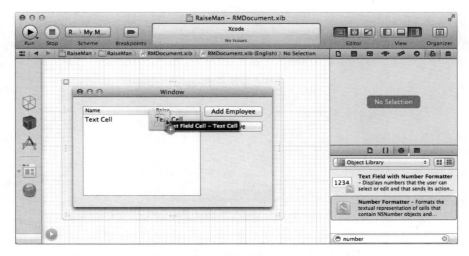

**Figure 8.10**    Add a Number Formatter

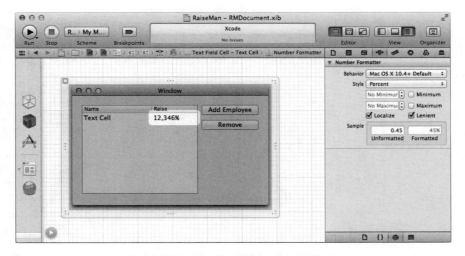

**Figure 8.11**    Number Formatter Attributes

Control-drag from the Add Employee button to the array controller to set the target of the button. Set the action to **add:**.

Control-drag to make the array controller become the target of the Remove button. Set the action to **remove:**. Also, in the Bindings Inspector, bind the button's enabled binding to the canRemove attribute of the **NSArrayController**, as shown in Figure 8.13.

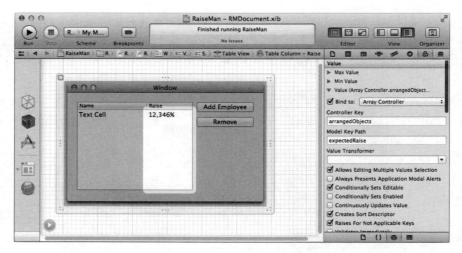

**Figure 8.12** Bind the Second Column to arrangedObjects.expectedRaise

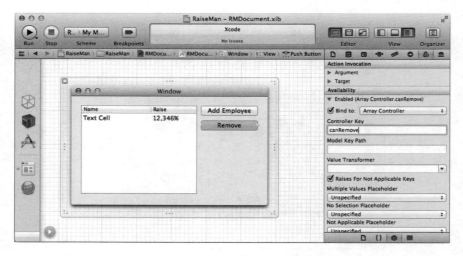

**Figure 8.13** Binding the Enabled Attribute of the Remove Button

The user will also want to remove the selected employees by pressing the delete key on his or her keyboard. Select the Remove button; in the Attributes Inspector, set the keyboard equivalent to the Delete key (Figure 8.14). To set the key equivalent, click in the text field and then type the key you wish to associate with this button. Xcode will record the keystroke used and display it in the text field. To remove a key equivalent, click the X button at the right-hand side of the text field.

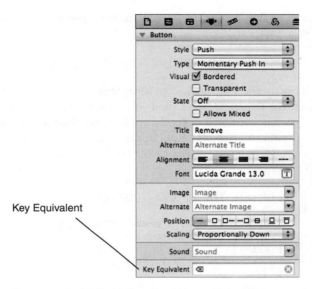

Key Equivalent

**Figure 8.14**   Make Delete Key Trigger Delete Button

Build and run your application. You should be able to create and delete **Person** objects. You should also be able to edit the attributes of the **Person** objects using the table view. Finally, you should be able to open multiple untitled documents. (No, you can't save those documents to a file. Soon, Grasshopper.)

# Key-Value Coding and nil

Note that our example contains very little code. You described what should be displayed in each of the columns in Interface Builder, but there is no code that calls the accessor methods of your **Person** class. How does this work? Key-value coding. Key-value coding makes generic, reusable classes like **NSArrayController** possible.

The key-value coding methods will automatically coerce the type for you. For example, when the user types in a new expected raise, the formatter creates an instance of **NSNumber**. The key-value coding method **setValue:forKey:** automatically converts that into a `float` before calling **setExpectedRaise:**. This behavior is extremely convenient.

There is, however, a problem with converting an NSDecimalNumber * into a `float`: Pointers can be `nil`, but `floats` cannot. If **setValue:forKey:** is passed a nil value that needs to be converted into a nonpointer type, it will call its own method:

```
- (void)setNilValueForKey:(NSString *)s
```

This method, as defined in **NSObject**, throws an exception. Thus, if the user left the Expected Raise field empty, your object would throw an exception. Typically, you will override **setNilValueForKey:** so that it sets the instance variable to a default value. In this case, you are going to override this method in your **Person** class and set expectedRaise to 0.0. Add the following method to Person.m:

```
- (void)setNilValueForKey:(NSString *)key
{
    if ([key isEqual:@"expectedRaise"]) {
        [self setExpectedRaise:0.0];
    } else {
        [super setNilValueForKey:key];
    }
}
```

# Add Sorting

While the application is running, click on the column headers and note that sorting works (badly). In particular, the **compare:** method is ordering the names. This **compare:** method is very strongly case sensitive. For example, Z will come before a. Let's change the method used for sorting.

Open RMDocument.xib. You can set the sorting criteria in the Attributes Inspector for each column. Users will be able to choose on which attribute the data will be sorted, by clicking on the header of the column containing that attribute.

Select the column that displays personName. In the Inspector, set the sort key to be personName and the selector to be **caseInsensitiveCompare:**, as shown in Figure 8.15.

The **caseInsensitiveCompare:** method is part of **NSString**. For example, you might do this:

```
NSString *x = @"Piaggio";
NSString *y = @"Italjet";
NSComparisonResult result = [x caseInsensitiveCompare:y];
```

```
// Would x come first in the dictionary?
if (result == NSOrderedAscending)  {
    ...
}
```

NSComparisonResult is just an integer. NSOrderedAscending is −1.
NSOrderedSame is 0. NSOrderedDescending is 1.

Build and run your application. Click on the header of the column to sort the
data. Click again to see the data in reverse order.

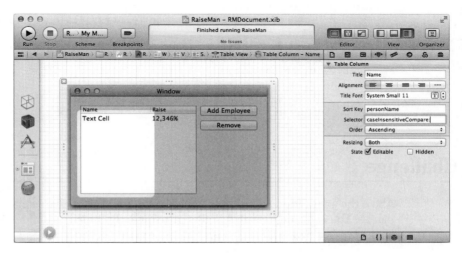

**Figure 8.15**    Sorting on personName

# For the More Curious: Sorting without NSArrayController

In Chapter 6, you populated a table view by implementing the dataSource
methods explicitly. You might have wondered then how you could implement
this sorting behavior in your own application.

The information that you added to the columns of the table is packed into an
array of **NSSortDescriptor** objects. A sort descriptor includes the key, a selector,
and an indicator of whether data should be sorted into ascending or descending
order. If you have an **NSMutableArray** of objects, you can use the following
method to sort it:

```
- (void)sortUsingDescriptors:(NSArray *)sortDescriptors
```

An optional table-view dataSource method is triggered when the user clicks on the header of a column with a sort descriptor:

```
- (void)tableView:(NSTableView *)tableView
    sortDescriptorsDidChange:(NSArray *)oldDescriptors
```

Thus, if you have a mutable array that holds the information for a table view, you can implement the method like this:

```
- (void)tableView:(NSTableView *)tableView
          sortDescriptorsDidChange:(NSArray *)oldDescriptors
{
    NSArray *newDescriptors = [tableView sortDescriptors];
    [myArray sortUsingDescriptors:newDescriptors];
    [tableView reloadData];
}
```

And voila!, sorting in your application.

# Challenge 1

Make the application sort people based on the number of characters in their names. You can complete this challenge using only Interface Builder—the trick is to use a key path. (*Hint:* Strings have a **length** method.)

# Challenge 2

In the first edition of this book, readers created the RaiseMan application without using **NSArrayController** or the bindings mechanism. (These features were added in Mac OS X 10.3.) To do so, readers used the ideas from previous chapters. The challenge, then, is to rewrite the RaiseMan application without using **NSArrayController** or the bindings mechanism. Bindings often seem rather magical, and it is good to know how to do things without resorting to magic.

Be sure to start afresh with a new project—in the next chapter, we will build on your existing project.

The **Person** class will stay exactly the same. In RMDocument.xib, you will set the identifier of each column to be the name of the variable that you would like

displayed (use the `Attributes Inspector` in Interface Builder). Then, the
**RMDocument** class will be the dataSource of the table view and the `target` of the
Create New Employee and Delete buttons. **RMDocument** will have an array of
**Person** objects that it displays. To get you started, here is RMDocument.h:

```
#import <Cocoa/Cocoa.h>
@class Person;

@interface RMDocument : NSDocument
{
    NSMutableArray *employees;
    IBOutlet NSTableView *tableView;
}
- (IBAction)createEmployee:(id)sender;
- (IBAction)deleteSelectedEmployees:(id)sender;
@end
```

Here are the interesting parts of RMDocument.m:

```
- (id)init
{
    self = [super init];
    if (self) {
        employees = [NSMutableArray array];
    }
    return self;
}

#pragma mark Action methods

- (IBAction)deleteSelectedEmployees:(id)sender
{
    // Which row is selected?
    NSIndexSet *rows = [tableView selectedRowIndexes];

    // Is the selection empty?
    if ([rows count] == 0) {
        NSBeep();
        return;
    }
    [employees removeObjectsAtIndexes:rows];
    [tableView reloadData];
}

- (IBAction)createEmployee:(id)sender
{
    Person *newEmployee = [[Person alloc] init];
    [employees addObject:newEmployee];
    [tableView reloadData];
}
```

```
#pragma mark Table view dataSource methods

- (NSInteger)numberOfRowsInTableView:(NSTableView *)aTableView
{
    return [employees count];
}

- (id)tableView:(NSTableView *)aTableView
        objectValueForTableColumn:(NSTableColumn *)aTableColumn
                            row:(NSInteger)rowIndex
{
    // What is the identifier for the column?
    NSString *identifier = [aTableColumn identifier];

    // What person?
    Person *person = [employees objectAtIndex:rowIndex];

    // What is the value of the attribute named identifier?
    return [person valueForKey:identifier];
}

- (void)tableView:(NSTableView *)aTableView
    setObjectValue:(id)anObject
    forTableColumn:(NSTableColumn *)aTableColumn
            row:(NSInteger)rowIndex
{
    NSString *identifier = [aTableColumn identifier];
    Person *person = [employees objectAtIndex:rowIndex];

    // Set the value for the attribute named identifier
    [person setValue:anObject forKey:identifier];
}
```

Once you have it working, be sure to add sorting!

# Chapter 9
# NSUndoManager

Using **NSUndoManager**, you can add undo capabilities to your applications in a very elegant manner. As objects are added, deleted, and edited, the undo manager keeps track of all messages that must be sent to undo these changes. As you invoke the undo mechanism, the undo manager keeps track of all messages that must be sent to redo *those* changes. This mechanism works by utilizing two stacks of **NSInvocation** objects.

This is a pretty heavy topic to cover so early in a book. (Sometimes when we think about undo, our heads start to swim a bit.) However, undo interacts with the document architecture. If we tackle this work now, you will see in the next chapter how the document architecture is supposed to work.

## NSInvocation

As you might imagine, it is handy to be able to package up a message (including the selector, the receiver, and all arguments) as an object that can be invoked at your leisure. Such an object is an instance of **NSInvocation**.

One exceedingly convenient use for invocations is in message forwarding. When an object is sent a message that it does not understand, before raising an exception, the message-sending system checks whether the object has implemented the following method:

```
- (void)forwardInvocation:(NSInvocation *)x
```

If the object has such a method, the message sent is packed up as an **NSInvocation** and **forwardInvocation:** is called.

# How the NSUndoManager Works

Suppose that the user opens a new RaiseMan document and makes three edits:

1. Inserts a new record
2. Changes the name from `New Employee` to `Rex Fido`
3. Changes the raise from 0 to 20

As each edit is performed, your controller will add an invocation that would undo that edit to the undo stack. For the sake of simplifying the prose, let's say, "The *inverse* of the edit gets added to the undo stack."

Figure 9.1 shows what the undo stack would look like after these three edits.

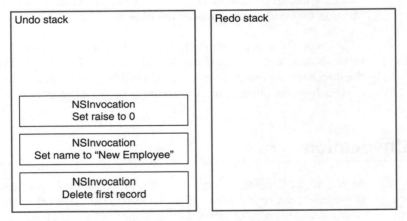

**Figure 9.1**   The Undo Stack

If the user now chooses the Undo menu item, the first invocation is taken off the stack and invoked. This would change the person's raise back to zero. If the user chooses the Undo menu item again, the person's name would change back to `New Employee`.

Each time an item is popped off the undo stack and invoked, the inverse of the undo operation must be added to the redo stack. Thus, after undoing the two operations described, the undo and redo stacks should look like Figure 9.2.

The undo manager is quite clever: When the user is doing edits, the undo invocations go onto the undo stack. When the user is undoing edits, the undo invocations go onto the redo stack. When the user is redoing edits, the undo invocations go onto the undo stack. These tasks are handled automatically

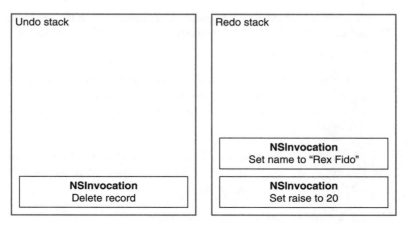

**Figure 9.2**    The Revised Undo Stack

for you; your only job is to give the undo manager the inverse invocations that need to be added.

Now suppose that you are writing a method called **makeItHotter** and that the inverse of this method is called **makeItColder**. Here is how you would enable the undo:

```
- (void)makeItHotter
{
    temperature = temperature + 10;
    [[undoManager prepareWithInvocationTarget:self] makeItColder];
    [self showTheChangesToTheTemperature];
}
```

As you might guess, the **prepareWithInvocationTarget:** method notes the target and returns the undo manager itself. Then, the undo manager cleverly overrides **forwardInvocation:** such that it adds the invocation for **makeItColder:** to the undo stack.

To complete the example, you would implement **makeItColder:**

```
- (void)makeItColder
{
    temperature = temperature - 10;
    [[undoManager prepareWithInvocationTarget:self] makeItHotter];
    [self showTheChangesToTheTemperature];
}
```

Note that we have again registered the inverse with the undo manager. If **makeItColder** is invoked as a result of an undo, this inverse will go onto the redo stack.

The invocations on either stack are grouped. By default, all invocations added to a stack during a single event are grouped together. Thus, if one user action causes changes in several objects, all the changes are undone by a single click of the Undo menu item.

The undo manager can also change the label on the Undo and Redo menu items. For example, "Undo Insert" is more descriptive than just "Undo." To set the label, use the following code:

```
[undoManager setActionName:@"Insert"];
```

How do you get an undo manager? You can create one explicitly, but note that each instance of **NSDocument** already has its own undo manager.

# Adding Undo to RaiseMan

Let's give users the ability to undo the effects of clicking the Add New Employee and Delete buttons, as well as the ability to undo the changes they make to **Person** objects in the table. The necessary code will go into your **RMDocument** class.

## Key-Value Coding and To-Many Relationships

When designing a class, think of your instance variables as having one of four possible purposes:

1. *Simple attributes*. Example: Each student has a first name. Simple attributes are typically numbers or instances of **NSString**, **NSDate**, or **NSData**.

2. *To-one relationships*. Example: Each student has a school. It is like a simple attribute, but the type is a complex object, not a simple one. To-one relationships are implemented using pointers: An instance of **Student** has a pointer to an instance of **School**.

3. *Ordered to-many relationships*. Example: Each playlist has a list of songs. The songs are in a particular order. This is typically implemented using an **NSMutableArray**.

**4.** *Unordered to-many relationships.* Example: Each department has a bunch of employees. You can display the employees in a particular order (such as sorted by last name), but that ordering is not inherent in the relationship. This is typically implemented using an **NSMutableSet**.

Earlier, we discussed how we could set simple attributes and to-one relationships using key-value coding. Remember that when setting or getting a value for **fido**, KVC will use the accessors if they exist. Similarly, we can create accessors for ordered and unordered to-many relationships.

Let's say, for example, that an instance of **Playlist** has an **NSMutableArray** of **Song** objects. If you want to use key-value coding to manipulate that array you will ask the playlist for its **mutableArrayValueForKey:**. You will get back a proxy object.

That proxy object knows that it represents the array that holds the songs.

```
id arrayProxy = [playlist mutableArrayValueForKey:@"songs"];
int songCount = [arrayProxy count];
```

In this example, when asked for the **count**, the proxy object will ask the **Playlist** object if it has a **countOfSongs** method. If **Playlist** does, it will call the method and return the result. If there is no such method, **Playlist** will get the array of songs and ask the array for its **count** (Figure 9.3). Note, then, that naming the method **countOfSongs** is not just a convention; rather, the key-value coding mechanism goes looking for a method with the right name.

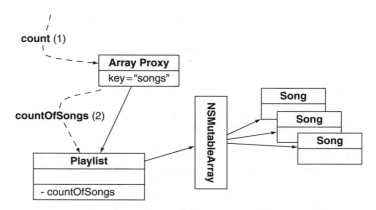

**Figure 9.3**  Key-Value Coding for Ordered Relationships

There are several cases, so here is a list:

```
id arrayProxy = [playlist mutableArrayValueForKey:@"songs"];

int x = [arrayProxy count]; // is the same as
int x = [playlist countOfSongs]; // if countOfSongs exists

id y = [arrayProxy objectAtIndex:5] // is the same as
id y = [playlist objectInSongsAtIndex:5]; // if the method exists

[arrayProxy insertObject:p atIndex:4] // is the same as
[playlist insertObject:p inSongsAtIndex:4]; // if the method exists

[arrayProxy removeObjectAtIndex:3] // is the same as
[playlist removeObjectFromSongsAtIndex:3] // if the method exists
```

There is a similar set of calls for unordered to-many relationships (Figure 9.4).

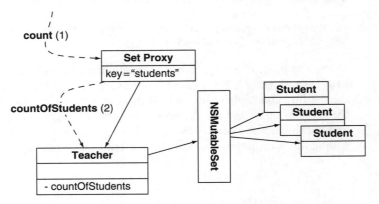

**Figure 9.4**   Key-Value Coding for Unordered Relationships

```
id setProxy = [teacher mutableSetValueForKey:@`students"];

int x = [setProxy count]; // is the same as
int x = [teacher countOfStudents]; // if countOfStudents exists

[setProxy addObject:newStudent]; // is the same as
[teacher addStudentsObject:newStudent]; // if the method exists

[setProxy removeObject:expelledStudent]; // is the same as
[teacher removeStudentsObject:expelledStudent]; // if the method exists
```

Because we have bound the `contentArray` of the array controller to the
`employees` array of the **RMDocument** object, the array controller will use
key-value coding to add and remove **Person** objects. You will take advantage of

this to add undo invocations to the undo stack when people are added and removed.

Before we declare these methods in the header file, we must tell the compiler that the **Person** class exists. In RMDocument.h, add:

```
#import <Cocoa/Cocoa.h>
@class Person;
```

Now declare the methods in RMDocument.h:

```
- (void)insertObject:(Person *)p inEmployeesAtIndex:(NSUInteger)index;
- (void)removeObjectFromEmployeesAtIndex:(NSUInteger)index;
```

As we will be referencing the **Person** class in the methods we add to RMDocument.m, import **Person**'s header file near the top:

```
#import "RMDocument.h"
#import "Person.h"
```

Now add the method implementations to RMDocument.m:

```
- (void)insertObject:(Person *)p inEmployeesAtIndex:(NSUInteger)index
{
    NSLog(@"adding %@ to %@", p, employees);
    // Add the inverse of this operation to the undo stack
    NSUndoManager *undo = [self undoManager];
    [[undo prepareWithInvocationTarget:self]
                        removeObjectFromEmployeesAtIndex:index];
    if (![undo isUndoing]) {
        [undo setActionName:@"Add Person"];
    }

    // Add the Person to the array
    [employees insertObject:p atIndex:index];
}

- (void)removeObjectFromEmployeesAtIndex:(NSUInteger)index
{
    Person *p = [employees objectAtIndex:index];
    NSLog(@"removing %@ from %@", p, employees);
    // Add the inverse of this operation to the undo stack
    NSUndoManager *undo = [self undoManager];
    [[undo prepareWithInvocationTarget:self] insertObject:p
                                inEmployeesAtIndex:index];
    if (![undo isUndoing]) {
        [undo setActionName:@"Remove Person"];
    }

    [employees removeObjectAtIndex:index];
}
```

These methods will be called automatically when the **NSArrayController** wishes to insert or remove **Person** objects (for example, when the Add Employee and Remove buttons send it **insert:** and **remove:** messages).

At this point, you have made it possible to undo deletions and insertions. Undoing edits will be a little trickier. Before tackling this task, build and run your application. Test the undo capabilities that you have at this point. Note that redo also works.

# Key-Value Observing

In Chapter 7, we discussed key-value coding. To review, key-value coding is a way to read and change a value by name. *Key-value observing* allows you to be informed when these sorts of changes occur.

To enable undo capabilities for edits, you will want your document object to be informed of changes to the keys `expectedRaise` and `personName` for all its **Person** objects.

A method in **NSObject** allows you to register to be informed of these changes:

```
- (void)addObserver:(NSObject *)observer
        forKeyPath:(NSString *)keyPath
          options:(NSKeyValueObservingOptions)options
          context:(void *)context;
```

You supply the object that should be informed as `observer` and the `keyPath` for which you wish to be informed about changes. The `options` variable defines what you would like to have included when you are informed about the changes. For example, you can be told about the old value (before the change) and the new value (after the change). The `context` variable is a pointer to data that you would like sent with the rest of the information.

When a change occurs, the observer is sent the following message:

```
- (void)observeValueForKeyPath:(NSString *)keyPath
                ofObject:(id)object
                  change:(NSDictionary *)change
                 context:(void *)context;
```

The observer is told which key path changed in which object. Here, `change` is a dictionary that (depending on the options you asked for when you registered as an observer) may contain the old value and/or the new value. Of course, this method is sent the `context` pointer supplied when the method was registered as an observer.

### *Using the Context Pointer Defensively*

Because any object observing key-value changes must implement a method with this specific selector (**observeValueForKeyPath:ofObject:change:context:**), it is possible to mistakenly intercept notifications intended for another class.

Consider the case of a fictional class **Maple**, which is a subclass of a fictional class **Tree**. Both classes observe the key path season independently. Unless the developer takes precautions, **Maple** will receive its key-value-observing (KVO) messages *and* those intended for **Tree**, because **Maple** has effectively overridden the KVO method. To fix this, **Maple** must correctly identify observation messages intended for itself versus those intended for its superclass. If the message is not intended for that specific class, Maple should pass the message on to its superclass.

The solution to this problem is to use a class-specific pointer value as the context argument. We will use this approach in the following steps of this exercise as a demonstration, although it is not necessary within the conditions of this specific exercise.

# Undo for Edits

The first step is to register your document object to observe changes to its **Person** objects. Add the following static variable and methods near the top of RMDocument.m:

```
// RMDocumentKVOContext enables this class to differentiate
// between its KVO messages and those intended for a superclass.
static void *RMDocumentKVOContext;

- (void)startObservingPerson:(Person *)person
{
    [person addObserver:self
            forKeyPath:@"personName"
              options:NSKeyValueObservingOptionOld
              context:&RMDocumentKVOContext];

    [person addObserver:self
            forKeyPath:@"expectedRaise"
              options:NSKeyValueObservingOptionOld
              context:&RMDocumentKVOContext];
}

- (void)stopObservingPerson:(Person *)person
{
    [person removeObserver:self
            forKeyPath:@"personName"
              context:&RMDocumentKVOContext];
```

```
        [person removeObserver:self
                  forKeyPath:@"expectedRaise"
                     context:&RMDocumentKVOContext];
}
```

Call these methods every time a **Person** enters or leaves the document:

```
- (void)insertObject:(Person *)p inEmployeesAtIndex:(NSUInteger)index
{
    // Add the inverse of this operation to the undo stack
    NSUndoManager *undo = [self undoManager];
    [[undo prepareWithInvocationTarget:self]
        removeObjectFromEmployeesAtIndex:index];
    if (![undo isUndoing]) {
        [undo setActionName:@"Add Person"];
    }

    // Add the Person to the array
    [self startObservingPerson:p];
    [employees insertObject:p atIndex:index];
}

- (void)removeObjectFromEmployeesAtIndex:(NSUInteger)index
{
    Person *p = [employees objectAtIndex:index];
    // Add the inverse of this operation to the undo stack
    NSUndoManager *undo = [self undoManager];
    [[undo prepareWithInvocationTarget:self] insertObject:p
                                      inEmployeesAtIndex:index];
    if (![undo isUndoing]) {
        [undo setActionName:@"Remove Person"];
    }
    [self stopObservingPerson:p];
    [employees removeObjectAtIndex:index];
}

- (void)setEmployees:(NSMutableArray *)a
{
    for (Person *person in employees) {
        [self stopObservingPerson:person];
    }

    employees = a;

    for (Person *person in employees) {
        [self startObservingPerson:person];
    }
}
```

Now, implement the method that does edits and is its own inverse:

```
- (void)changeKeyPath:(NSString *)keyPath
             ofObject:(id)obj
              toValue:(id)newValue
```

```
{
    // setValue:forKeyPath: will cause the key-value observing method
    // to be called, which takes care of the undo stuff
    [obj setValue:newValue forKeyPath:keyPath];
}
```

Implement the method that will be called whenever a **Person** object is edited by either the user or the **changeKeyPath:ofObject:toValue:** method. Note that this method puts a call to **changeKeyPath:ofObject:toValue:** on the undo stack with the old value for the changed key:

```
- (void)observeValueForKeyPath:(NSString *)keyPath
                      ofObject:(id)object
                        change:(NSDictionary *)change
                       context:(void *)context
{
    if (context != &RMDocumentKVOContext)
    {
        // If the context does not match, this message
        // must be intended for our superclass.
        [super observeValueForKeyPath:keyPath
                             ofObject:object
                               change:change
                              context:context];
        return;
    }

    NSUndoManager *undo = [self undoManager];
    id oldValue = [change objectForKey:NSKeyValueChangeOldKey];

    // NSNull objects are used to represent nil in a dictionary
    if (oldValue == [NSNull null]) {
        oldValue = nil;
    }
    NSLog(@"oldValue = %@", oldValue);
    [[undo prepareWithInvocationTarget:self] changeKeyPath:keyPath
                                                  ofObject:object
                                                   toValue:oldValue];
    [undo setActionName:@"Edit"];
}
```

That should do it. Once you build and run your application, undo and redo should work flawlessly.

In testing your application, you may encounter an error: The document could not be autosaved. Now that you are interacting with the undo system, AppKit is noticing that your document has unsaved changes and is trying to autosave the document. You will learn how to save your document to a file in the next chapter.

# Begin Editing on Insert

Your app is coming along nicely, but your users will complain, "Why do I have to double-click to start editing after an insert? It is obvious that I am going to immediately change the name of the new person. Can't you start the editing as part of the insert?"

Oddly, this is a little tricky to do. So, here is the code snippet you need. First, RMDocument.h is going to need an `action` and two instance variables:

```
@interface RMDocument : NSDocument
{
    NSMutableArray *employees;
    IBOutlet NSTableView *tableView;
    IBOutlet NSArrayController *employeeController;
}
- (IBAction)createEmployee:(id)sender;
```

Save that file. Open RMDocument.xib and Control-drag from the Add Employee button to the File's Owner (which is the instance of **RMDocument**). Set its `action` to **createEmployee:**

Control-click on the File's Owner. Drag to connect the `tableView` outlet to the table view and the `employeeController` outlet to the array controller (Figure 9.5).

**Figure 9.5**   Setting the tableView Outlets

Now, in RMDocument.m, add the **createEmployee:** method:

```
- (IBAction)createEmployee:(id)sender
{
    NSWindow *w = [tableView window];

    // Try to end any editing that is taking place
    BOOL editingEnded = [w makeFirstResponder:w];
    if (!editingEnded) {
        NSLog(@"Unable to end editing");
        return;
    }
    NSUndoManager *undo = [self undoManager];

    // Has an edit occurred already in this event?
    if ([undo groupingLevel] > 0) {
        // Close the last group
        [undo endUndoGrouping];
        // Open a new group
        [undo beginUndoGrouping];
    }
    // Create the object
    Person *p = [employeeController newObject];

    // Add it to the content array of 'employeeController'
    [employeeController addObject:p];

    // Re-sort (in case the user has sorted a column)
    [employeeController rearrangeObjects];

    // Get the sorted array
    NSArray *a = [employeeController arrangedObjects];

    // Find the object just added
    NSUInteger row = [a indexOfObjectIdenticalTo:p];
    NSLog(@"starting edit of %@ in row %lu", p, row);

    // Begin the edit in the first column
    [tableView editColumn:0
                      row:row
                withEvent:nil
                   select:YES];
}
```

We don't really expect you to understand every line of that code now, but browse through the method and try to get the gist. Build and run the application.

# For the More Curious: Windows and the Undo Manager

A view can add edits to the undo manager. **NSTextView**, for example, can put each edit that a person makes to the text onto the undo manager. How does the text view know which undo manager to use? First, it asks its `delegate`. **NSTextView** delegates can implement this method:

```
- (NSUndoManager *)undoManagerForTextView:(NSTextView *)tv;
```

Next, it asks its window. **NSWindow** has a method for this purpose:

```
- (NSUndoManager *)undoManager;
```

The window's `delegate` can supply an undo manager for the window by implementing the following method:

```
- (NSUndoManager *)windowWillReturnUndoManager:(NSWindow *) window;
```

The undo/redo menu items reflect the state of the undo manager for the key window (Figure 9.6). (The key window is what most users call the "active window." Cocoa developers call it *key* because it is the one that will get the keyboard events if the user types.)

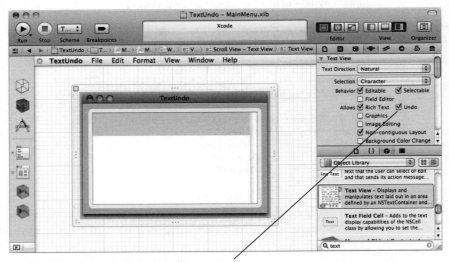

To add edits to the window's undo manager

**Figure 9.6**  NSTextView Inspector

# Chapter 10

# Archiving

While an object-oriented program is running, a complex graph of objects is being created. It is often necessary to represent this graph of objects as a stream of bytes, a process called *archiving* (Figure 10.1). This stream of bytes can then be sent across a network connection or written into a file. For example, when creating a NIB from the XIB file you edited in the Interface Builder editor, the compiler is archiving objects into a file. (Instead of "archiving," a Java programmer would call this process "serialization.")

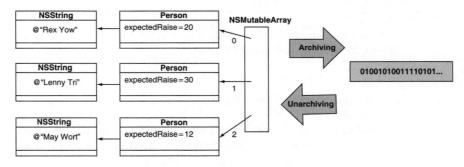

**Figure 10.1**   Archiving

When you need to recreate the graph of objects from the stream of bytes, you will *unarchive* it. When your application starts up, it unarchives the objects from the NIB file that was created by the compiler.

Although objects have both instance variables and methods, only the instance variables and the name of the class go into the archive. In other words, only data, not code, goes into the archive. As a result, if one application archives an object and another application unarchives the same object, both applications must have the code for the class as linked in. In the NIB file, for example, you have used classes like **NSWindow** and **NSButton** from the AppKit framework. If you do not link your application against the AppKit framework, it will be unable to create the instances of **NSWindow** and **NSButton** that it finds in the NIB file.

There was once a shampoo ad that said, "I told two friends, and they told two friends, and they told two friends, and so on, and so on, and so on." The implication was that as long as you told your friends about the shampoo, everyone who matters would eventually wind up using the shampoo. Object archiving works in much the same way. You archive a root object, it archives the objects to which it is attached, they archive the objects to which they are attached, and so on, and so on, and so on. Eventually, every object that matters will be in the archive.

Archiving involves two steps. First, you need to teach your objects how to archive themselves. Second, you need to cause the archiving to occur.

The Objective-C language has a construct called a *protocol*, which is identical to the Java construct called an *interface*. That is, a protocol is a list of method declarations. When you create a class that implements a protocol, it promises to implement all the methods declared in the protocol.

# NSCoder and NSCoding

One protocol is called **NSCoding**. If your class implements **NSCoding**, it promises to implement the following methods:

```
- (id)initWithCoder:(NSCoder *)coder;
- (void)encodeWithCoder:(NSCoder *)coder;
```

An **NSCoder** is an abstraction of a stream of bytes. You can write your data to a coder or read your data from a coder. The **initWithCoder:** method in your object will read data from the coder and save that data to its instance variables. The **encodeWithCoder:** method in your object will read its instance variables and write those values to the coder. In this chapter, you will implement both methods in your **Person** class.

**NSCoder** is an *abstract class*. You won't ever create instances of an abstract class. Instead, an abstract class has some capabilities that are intended to be inherited by subclasses. You will create instances of the concrete subclasses. Namely, you will use **NSKeyedUnarchiver** to read objects from a stream of data, and you will use **NSKeyedArchiver** to write objects to the stream of data.

## Encoding

**NSCoder** has many methods, but most programmers find themselves using just a few of them repeatedly. Here are the methods most commonly used when you are encoding data onto the coder:

```
- (void)encodeObject:(id)anObject forKey:(NSString *)aKey
```

This method writes anObject to the coder and associates it with the key aKey. This will cause anObject's **encodeWithCoder:** method to be called (and they told two friends, and they told two friends...).

For each of the common C primitive types (such as int and float), **NSCoder** has an encode method:

```
- (void)encodeBool:(BOOL)boolv forKey:(NSString *)key
```

```
- (void)encodeDouble:(double)realv forKey:(NSString *)key
```

```
- (void)encodeFloat:(float)realv forKey:(NSString *)key
```

```
- (void)encodeInt:(int)intv forKey:(NSString *)key
```

To add encoding to your **Person** class, add the following method to Person.m:

```
- (void)encodeWithCoder:(NSCoder *)coder
{
    [coder encodeObject:personName forKey:@"personName"];
    [coder encodeFloat:expectedRaise forKey:@"expectedRaise"];
}
```

If you looked at the documentation for **NSString**, you would see that it implements the **NSCoding** protocol. Thus, the personName knows how to encode itself.

All the commonly used AppKit and Foundation classes implement the **NSCoding** protocol, with the notable exception of **NSObject**. Because it inherits from **NSObject**, **Person** doesn't call [super encodeWithCoder:coder]. If **Person**'s superclass *had* implemented the **NSCoding** protocol, the method would have looked like this:

```
- (void)encodeWithCoder:(NSCoder *)coder
{
    [super encodeWithCoder:coder];
    [coder encodeObject:personName forKey:@"personName"];
    [coder encodeFloat:expectedRaise forKey:@"expectedRaise"];
}
```

The call to the superclass's **encodeWithCoder:** method would give the superclass a chance to write its variables onto the coder. Thus, each class in the hierarchy writes only its instance variables (and not its superclass's instance variables) onto the coder.

## Decoding

When decoding data from the coder, you will use the analogous decoding methods:

- (id)decodeObjectForKey:(NSString *)aKey

- (BOOL)decodeBoolForKey:(NSString *)key

- (double)decodeDoubleForKey:(NSString *)key

- (float)decodeFloatForKey:(NSString *)key

- (int)decodeIntForKey:(NSString *)key

If, for some reason, the stream does not include the data for a key, you will get zero for the result. For example, if the object did not write out data for the key foo when the stream was first written, the coder will return 0.0 if it is later asked to decode a float for the key foo. If asked to decode an object for the key foo, the coder will return nil.

To add decoding to your **Person** class, add the following method to your Person.m file:

```
- (id)initWithCoder:(NSCoder *)coder
{
    self = [super init];
    if (self) {
        personName = [coder decodeObjectForKey:@"personName"];
        expectedRaise = [coder decodeFloatForKey:@"expectedRaise"];
    }
    return self;
}
```

Once again, you did not call the superclass's implementation of **initWithCoder:**, because **NSObject** doesn't have one. If **Person**'s superclass *had* implemented the **NSCoding** protocol, the method would have looked like this:

```
- (id)initWithCoder:(NSCoder *)coder
{
    self = [super initWithCoder:coder];
    if (self) {
        personName = [coder decodeObjectForKey:@"personName"];
        expectedRaise = [coder decodeFloatForKey:@"expectedRaise"];
    }
    return self;
}
```

The attentive reader may now be saying, "Chapter 3 said that the designated initializer does all the work and calls the superclass's designated initializer. It said that all other initializers call the designated initializer. But **Person** has an **init** method, which is its designated initializer, and this new initializer doesn't call it." You are right: **initWithCoder:** is an exception to initializer rules.

You have now implemented the methods in the **NSCoding** protocol. To declare your **Person** class as implementing the **NSCoding** protocol, you will edit the Person.h file. Change the declaration of your class to look like this:

```
@interface Person : NSObject <NSCoding> {
```

Now try to compile the project. Fix any errors. You could run the application at this point, if you like. However, although you have taught **Person** objects to encode themselves, you haven't asked them to do so. Thus, you will see no change in the behavior of your application.

# The Document Architecture

Applications that deal with multiple documents have a lot in common. All can create new documents, open existing documents, save or print open documents, and remind the user to save edited documents when he or she tries to close a window or quit the application. Apple supplies three classes that take care of most of the details for you: **NSDocumentController**, **NSDocument**, and **NSWindowController**. Together, these three classes constitute the *document architecture*.

The purpose of the document architecture relates to the Model-View-Controller design pattern discussed in Chapter 8. In RaiseMan, your subclass of **NSDocument** (with the help of **NSArrayController**) acts as the controller. It will have a pointer to the model objects, and will be responsible for the following duties:

- Saving the model data to a file
- Loading the model data from a file
- Displaying the model data in the views
- Taking user input from the views and updating the model

## Info.plist and NSDocumentController

When it builds an application, Xcode includes a file called Info.plist. (Later in this chapter, you will change Info.plist.) When the application is launched, it reads from Info.plist, which tells it what type of files it works with. If it finds that it is a document-based application, it creates an instance of **NSDocumentController** (Figure 10.2). You will seldom have to deal with the document controller; it lurks in the background and takes care of a bunch of details for you. For example, when you choose the New or Save All menu item, the document controller handles the request. If you need to send messages to the document controller, you could get to it like this:

```
NSDocumentController *dc;
dc = [NSDocumentController sharedDocumentController];
```

The document controller has an array of document objects—one for each open document.

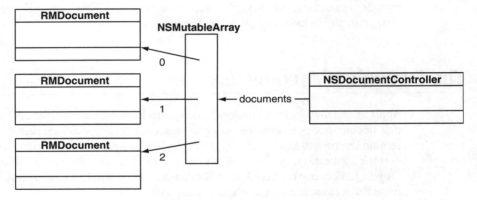

**Figure 10.2** Document Controller

# NSDocument

The document objects are instances of a subclass of **NSDocument**. In your RaiseMan application, for example, the document objects are instances of **RMDocument**. For many applications, you can simply extend **NSDocument** to do what you want; you don't have to worry about **NSDocumentController** or **NSWindowController** at all.

## Saving

The menu items Save, Save As…, Save All, and Close are all different, but all deal with the same problem: getting the model into a file or file wrapper. (A file wrapper is a directory that looks like a file to the user.) To handle these menu items, your **NSDocument** subclass must implement one of three methods:

```
- (NSData *)dataOfType:(NSString *)aType
                error:(NSError **)e
```

Your document object supplies the model to go into the file as an **NSData** object. **NSData**, essentially a buffer of bytes, is the easiest and most popular way to implement saving in a document-based application. Return nil if you are unable to create the data object, and the user will get an alert sheet indicating that the save attempt failed. Note that you are passed the type, which allows you to save the document in one of several possible formats. For example, if you wrote a graphics program, you might allow the user to save the image as a gif or a jpg file. When you are creating the data object, aType indicates the format that the user has requested for saving the document. If you are dealing with only one type of data, you may simply ignore aType. To signal that you were unable to save the data, return nil and create an **NSError** object that describes what went wrong.

```
- (NSFileWrapper *)fileWrapperOfType:(NSString *)aType
                              error:(NSError **)e
```

Your document object returns the model as an **NSFileWrapper** object. It will be written to the filesystem in the location chosen by the user. To signal that you were unable to create the file wrapper, return nil and create an **NSError** object that describes what went wrong.

```
- (BOOL)writeToURL:(NSURL *)absoluteURL
            ofType:(NSString *)typeName
             error:(NSError **)outError;
```

Your document object is given the URL and the type and is responsible for storing the data into the URL. (The URL is typically just a file on the filesystem.) Return YES if the save is successful and NO if the save fails. Return NO signal that you were unable to write the data to the URL, and create an **NSError** object that describes what went wrong.

**NSError** can be a bit confusing. The idea is that if the method is unable for some reason, to do its job, the method creates an **NSError** and puts a pointer to that error in the supplied address. For example, to read an **NSData** from a file, you would supply an address where the pointer to the error would be placed:

```
NSError *e;
NSData *d = [NSData dataWithContentsOfFile:@"/tmp/x.txt"
                              options:0
                                error:&error];
// Did the read fail?
if (d == nil) {
    NSLog(@"Read failed: %@", [error localizedDescription]);
}
```

Thus, **NSData** will either return a data object or create an error object.

In these save and load methods, you will be responsible for creating an **NSError** if the methods fail.

## *Loading*

The Open..., Open Recent, and Revert To Saved menu items, although different, all deal with the same basic problem: getting the model from a file or file wrapper. To handle these menu items, your **NSDocument** subclass must implement one of three methods:

```
- (BOOL)readFromData:(NSData *)data
            ofType:(NSString *)typeName
             error:(NSError **)outError
```

Your document is passed an **NSData** object that holds the contents of the file that the user is trying to open. Return YES if you successfully create a model from the data. If you return NO, the user will get an Alert panel that should explain why it was unable to parse the file. The contents of the Alert panel will be determined by the **NSError** object you give it.

```
- (BOOL)readFromFileWrapper:(NSFileWrapper *)fileWrapper
                    ofType:(NSString *)typeName
                     error:(NSError **)outError;
```

Your document reads the data from an **NSFileWrapper** object.

```
- (BOOL)readFromURL:(NSURL *)absoluteURL
            ofType:(NSString *)typeName
             error:(NSError **)outError;
```

Your document object is passed a URL (usually just a path to a file on the filesystem). The document reads the data from the file.

After implementing one save method and one load method, your document will know how to read from and write to files. When opening a file, the document will read the document file before reading the NIB file. As a consequence, you will not be able to send messages to the user interface objects immediately after loading the file (because they won't exist yet). To solve this problem, after the NIB file is read, your document object is sent the following method:

```
- (void)windowControllerDidLoadNib:(NSWindowController *)x;
```

In your **NSDocument** subclass, you will implement this method to update the user interface objects.

If the user chooses Revert To Saved from the menu, the model is loaded, but **windowControllerDidLoadNib:** is not called. You will, therefore, also have to update the user interface objects in the method that loads the data, just in case it was a revert operation. One common way to deal with this possibility is to check one of the outlets set in the NIB file. If it is `nil`, the NIB file has not been loaded, and there is no need to update the user interface.

## NSWindowController

The final class in the document architecture that we might discuss would be **NSWindowController**, but you will not initially need to worry about it. For each window that a document opens, it will typically create an instance of **NSWindowController**. As most applications have only one window per document, the default behavior of the window controller is usually perfect. Nevertheless, you might want to create a custom subclass of **NSWindowController** in the following situations:

- You need to have more than one window on the same document. For example, in a CAD program you might have a window of text that describes the solid and another window that shows a rendering of the solid.

- You want to put the user interface controller logic and model controller logic into separate classes.

- You want to create a window without a corresponding **NSDocument** object. You will do this in Chapter 12.

# Saving and NSKeyedArchiver

Now that you have taught your object to encode and decode itself, you will use it to add saving and loading to your application. When it is time to save your people to a file, your **RMDocument** class will be asked to create an instance of **NSData**. Once your object has created and returned an **NSData** object, it will be automatically written to a file.

To create an **NSData** object, you will use the **NSKeyedArchiver** class. **NSKeyedArchiver** has the following class method:

```
+ (NSData *)archivedDataWithRootObject:(id)rootObject
```

This method archives the objects into the **NSData** object's buffer of bytes.

Once again, we return to the idea of "I told two friends, and they told two friends." When you encode an object, it will encode its objects, and they will encode their objects, and so on, and so on, and so on. What you will encode, then, is the employees array. It will encode the **Person** objects to which it has references. Each **Person** object (because you implemented **encodeWithCoder:**) will, in turn, encode the personName string and the expectedRaise float.

To add saving capabilities to your application, edit the method **dataOfType:error:** in RMDocument.m so that it looks like this:

```
- (NSData *)dataOfType:(NSString *)aType
              error:(NSError **)outError
{
    // End editing
    [[tableView window] endEditingFor:nil];

    // Create an NSData object from the employees array
    return [NSKeyedArchiver archivedDataWithRootObject:employees];
}
```

Note that we just ignored the error argument. There will be no errors.

# Loading and NSKeyedUnarchiver

Now you will add the ability to load files to your application. Once again, **NSDocument** has taken care of most of the details for you.

To do the unarchiving, you will use **NSKeyedUnarchiver**, which has the following handy method:

```
+ (id)unarchiveObjectWithData:(NSData *)data
```

In RMDocument.m, edit your **readFromData:ofType:error:** method to look like this:

```
- (BOOL)readFromData:(NSData *)data
             ofType:(NSString *)typeName
              error:(NSError **)outError
{
    NSLog(@"About to read data of type %@", typeName);
    NSMutableArray *newArray = nil;
    @try {
        newArray = [NSKeyedUnarchiver unarchiveObjectWithData:data];
    }
```

```
    @catch (NSException *e) {
        NSLog(@"exception = %@", e);
        if (outError) {
            NSDictionary *d = [NSDictionary
                dictionaryWithObject:@"The data is corrupted."
                                forKey:NSLocalizedFailureReasonErrorKey];
            *outError = [NSError errorWithDomain:NSOSStatusErrorDomain
                                            code:unimpErr
                                        userInfo:d];
        }
        return NO;
    }
    [self setEmployees:newArray];
    return YES;
}
```

You could update the user interface after the XIB file is loaded, but **NSArray-Controller** will handle it for you: the **windowControllerDidLoadNib:** method doesn't need to do anything. Leave it here for now because you will add to it in Chapter 13:

```
- (void)windowControllerDidLoadNib:(NSWindowController *)aController
{
    [super windowControllerDidLoadNib:aController];

}
```

Note that your document is asked which XIB file to load when a document is opened or created. This method also needs no changing:

```
- (NSString *)windowNibName
{
    return @"RMDocument";
}
```

The window is automatically marked as edited when you make an edit, because you have properly enabled the undo mechanism. When you register your changes with the undo manager for this document, it will automatically mark the document as edited.

At this point, your application can read and write to files. Compile your application and try it out. Everything should work correctly, but all your files will show up as Document Type files and have a generic document icon. Let's look at how to define our application's document type more fully.

# Setting the Extension and Icon for the File Type

RaiseMan files already have the extension .rsmn, which we configured when we created the project. But .rsmn files need an icon. Find an .icns file and copy it into your project. A fine icon is found at /Developer/Examples/TextEdit/txt.icns. Drag it from the Finder into the Supporting Files group inside the Project Navigator view of Xcode (Figure 10.3).

**Figure 10.3**    Drag Icon into Project

Xcode will bring up a sheet. Make sure that you check Copy items into destination group's folder (Figure 10.4). This will copy the icon file into your project directory.

To set the document type information, select the RaiseMan target in the Project Navigator. Under the Info tab, find the Document Types heading and expand the existing document type. Set the name to be RaiseMan Doc, the Icon to txt, and the identifier to com.bignerdranch.raiseman-doc.

Next, configure an exported UTI for RaiseMan documents. A UTI describes the type of data contained in the file; we will cover UTIs in more detail later in this chapter.

Exported UTIs are found immediately below the Document Types heading in the target info. If there is not already a blank exported UTI, add one by using the Add button. Set the Description, Identifier, Icon, and Extensions to be identical to

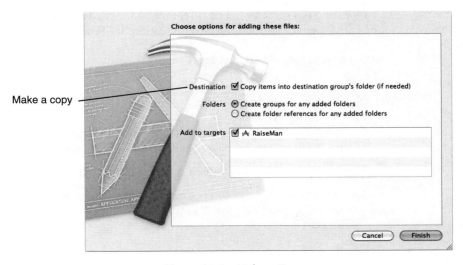

**Figure 10.4** Make a Copy

the settings you made in the Document Type. For Conforms To, type `public.data` (Figure 10.5).

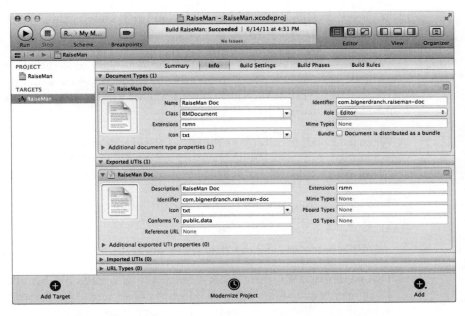

**Figure 10.5** Configuring the Document Type and Exported UTI

Build and run your application. You should be able to save data to a file and read it in again. In Finder, the `txt.icns` icon will be used as the icon for your `.rsmn` files.

An application is a directory. The directory contains the NIB files, images, sounds, and executable code for the application. In Terminal, try the following:

```
> cd /Applications/TextEdit.app/Contents
> ls
```

You will see three interesting things.

1. The `Info.plist` file, which includes the information about the application, its file types, and associated icons. Finder uses this information.

2. The `MacOS/` directory, which contains the executable code.

3. The `Resources/` directory, which has the images, sounds, and NIB files that the application uses. You will see localized resources for several different languages.

# For the More Curious: Preventing Infinite Loops

The astute reader may be wondering: "If object A causes object B to be encoded, and object B causes object C to be encoded, and then object C causes object A to be encoded again, couldn't it just go around and around in an infinite loop?" It would, but **NSKeyedArchiver** was designed with this possibility in mind.

When an object is encoded, a unique token is also put onto the stream. Once archived, the object is added to the table of encoded objects under that token. When told to encode the same object again **NSKeyedArchiver** simply puts a token in the stream.

When it decodes an object from the stream **NSKeyedUnarchiver** puts both the object and its token in a table. If it finds a token with no associated data, the unarchiver knows to look up the object in the table instead of creating a new instance.

This idea led to the method in **NSCoder** that often confuses developers when they read the documentation:

```
- (void)encodeConditionalObject:(id)anObject forKey:(NSString *)aKey
```

This method is used when object A has a pointer to object B, but object A doesn't really care if B is archived. However, if *another* object *has* archived B, A would like the token for B put into the stream. If no other object has archived B, it will be treated like `nil`.

For example, if you were writing an **encodeWithCoder:** method for an **Engine** object (Figure 10.6), it might have an instance variable called `car` that is a pointer to the **Car** object that it is part of. If you are archiving only the **Engine**, you wouldn't want the entire **Car** archived. But if you were archiving the entire **Car**, you would want the car pointer set. In this case, you would make the **Engine** object encode the car pointer conditionally.

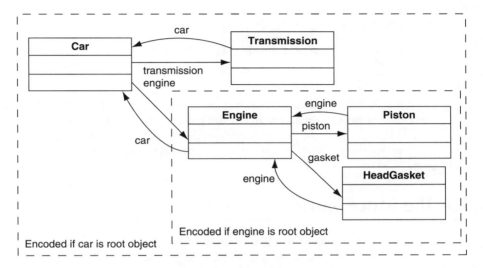

**Figure 10.6**   Conditional Encoding Example

# For the More Curious: Creating a Protocol

Creating your own protocol is very simple. Here is a protocol with two methods. The protocol would typically be in a file called Foo.h:

```
@protocol Foo
- (void)fido:(int)x;
- (float)rex;
@end
```

With Objective-C 2.0, **@optional** was added to the protocol grammar. Now you can indicate which methods in a protocol are required and which are optional:

```
@protocol Foo
- (void)fido:(int)x;
- (float)rex;
@optional
- (int)rover;
- (void)spot:(int)x;
@end
```

In this example, **fido:** and **rex** are required; **rover** and **spot:** are optional.

If you had a class that wanted to implement the **Foo** protocol and the **NSCoding** protocol, the class would look like this:

```
#import "Spunky.h"
#import "Foo.h"

@interface ZsaZsa : Spunky <Foo, NSCoding>
...etc...
@end
```

A class doesn't have to redeclare any method it inherits from its superclass, nor does it have to redeclare any of the methods from the protocols it implements. Thus, in our example, the interface file for the class **ZsaZsa** is not required to list any of the methods in **Spunky** or **Foo** or **NSCoding**.

# For the More Curious: Automatic Document Saving

In Mac OS X Lion Apple introduced automatic document-saving support to Cocoa. With automatic document saving, your users will no longer need to be concerned with manually saving their documents. By monitoring the change count (described later), Cocoa will cue your document to archive itself at appropriate times. When the user does manually save the document, a new version will be created. The user can then browse past versions by using an interface similar to Time Machine. Untitled documents (documents not explicitly saved by the user) will even be preserved between runs of your application.

In order to support automatic document saving, your **NSDocument** subclass must opt in by overriding the class method **autosavesInPlace** to return YES:

```
+ (BOOL)autosavesInPlace {
    return YES;
}
```

If your document saves its data quickly, opting in is probably an easy choice. Otherwise, autosaving in place may not be appropriate for your application, as it will cause the interface to block until the save is completed. Refer to Apple's *Mac OS X Application Programming Guide* for a more in-depth discussion.

The Cocoa application template in Xcode enables this feature; **NSDocument**'s implementation of this method returns NO.

# For the More Curious: Document-Based Applications without Undo

The **NSUndoManager** for your application knows when unsaved edits have occurred. Also, the window is automatically marked as edited. But what if you've written an application and are not registering your changes with the undo manager?

**NSDocument** keeps track of how many changes have been made. It has a method for this purpose:

```
- (void)updateChangeCount:(NSDocumentChangeType)change;
```

The NSDocumentChangeType can be one of the following: NSChangeDone, NSChangeUndone, or NSChangeCleared. NSChangeDone increments the change count, NSChangeUndone decrements the change count, and NSChangeCleared sets the change count to 0. The window is marked as dirty unless the change count is 0.

# Universal Type Identifiers

One of the enduring problems in working with computers is embodied in the question: What does this data represent? On the Mac, this question gets asked in several places: when a file is opened from the Finder, when data is copied off the pasteboard, when a file is indexed by Spotlight, and when a file is viewed through Quicklook. Thus far, there have been several anwers: file extensions, creator codes, MIME types.

Apple has decided that the long-term solution to the problem is universal type identifiers (UTIs). A UTI is a string that identifies the type of data. This data may be in a file or in a memory buffer. UTIs are organized hierarchically. For example, the UTI public.image conforms to public.data.

Your application tells Mac OS X what UTIs your application can read and write, including new, custom UTI, by setting values in its Info.plist. The Info.plist is an XML file that has a dictionary of key-value pairs. Exported UTIs are stored in the key UTExportedTypeDeclarations. The steps you followed earlier to add an exported UTI created this key. The pasteboard, which we will cover in Chapter 21, also uses UTIs to identify data types.

There is a large set of system-defined UTIs. You can find the entire list in Apple's documentation.

# Chapter 11

# BASIC CORE DATA

At this point, you've implemented an application that keeps track of an array of objects, takes care of undo, and handles saving and loading from a file. As you can imagine, there are an awful lot of applications like the one you just wrote.

Apple decided to make this type of application extremely easy to write:

- **NSArrayController** will hold on to an array of objects.

- Bindings will eliminate much of the glue code that would be necessary to keep the model objects in sync with the views.

- **NSManagedObjectContext** will observe the instance variables of your data objects and will take care of undo for you and loading and saving the data.

So, the punchline is: Using Core Data and bindings, the RaiseMan application that you have written can be created with no code at all. In this section, you are going to write a simple Core Data application (not unlike RaiseMan) that has no code.

## NSManagedObjectModel

In order to know how to save and load the data in your objects, the system needs to know something about that data: What are the names of the attributes of your object? What are their types? To supply this information, you will create a managed object model. Xcode has an editor that will make it easy for you to describe your data-bearing objects in a `.xcdatamodeld` file. At runtime, this file will be read in, and an instance of **NSManagedObjectModel** will be created.

The model uses terminology that is a little different from what we are used to. Instead of "class," the model uses the term *entity*. Instead of "instance variable," the model uses the word *property*.

In the model are two kinds of properties: *attributes* and *relationships*. An attribute holds a simple data type: a string, a date, or a number. We will talk about relationships in Chapter 32.

The RaiseMan application used a subclass of **NSDocument** named **RMDocument**. In this application, you will have a subclass of **NSPersistentDocument** called **MyDocument**. **NSPersistentDocument**, a subclass of **NSDocument**, automatically reads in the model and creates an **NSManagedObjectContext**. **NSPersistent-Document** will eliminate the need for many lines of code.

Start Xcode and create a new project of type Cocoa Application. Name the project CarLot, set the Class Prefix to My, and the Document Extension to carlot. Enable both Create Document-Based Application and Use Core Data. Imagine that you own several used-car lots. This application will enable you to keep track of the cars that you wish to sell. When the application is done, it will look like Figure 11.1.

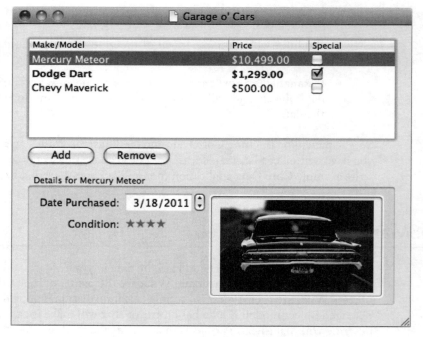

**Figure 11.1**   Completed Application

In the new project, open MyDocument.xcdatamodeld. Click the Add Entity button at the bottom left of the editor to create a new entity. Name the entity Car.

With the **Car** entity still selected, click the button at the bottom of the Attributes editor. Add six attributes and give them the following names and types:

| Name | Type |
|------|------|
| condition | Int 16 |
| datePurchased | Date |
| makeModel | String |
| onSpecial | Boolean |
| photo | Transformable |
| price | Decimal |

Figure 11.2 shows what car looks like in the modeler. We could put a lot of other things in the model, but that is enough for this exercise.

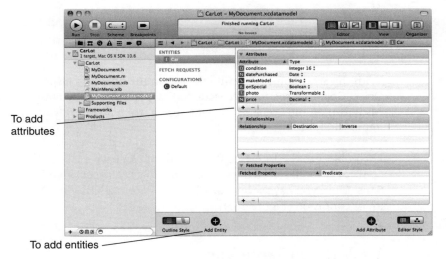

To add attributes

To add entities

**Figure 11.2**   Completed Model

# Interface

Open MyDocument.xib. Delete the text field that says Your document contents here. Drag an array controller onto the Interface Builder dock. The array controller will be using the document object's **NSManagedObjectContext** to fetch and store data. Use the Bindings Inspector to bind the array controller's managedObjectContext to the File's Owner's managedObjectContext (Figure 11.3).

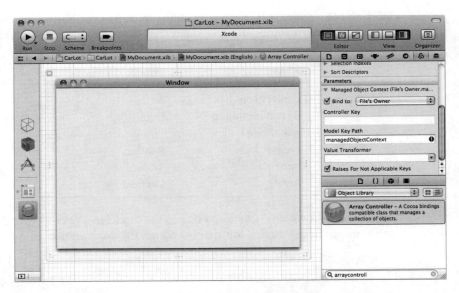

**Figure 11.3**    Give the Array Controller a Managed Object Context

With the array controller still selected, in the Attributes Inspector under the Object Controller section, set Mode to Entity Name and the entity name to **Car**. Also, turn on the Prepares Content option, so that the array controller will fetch immediately after it is created.

Each object in the Interface Builder editor can have a label. With the **NSArray-Controller** still selected, change to the Identity Inspector and set its Label to Cars. Once you have several array controllers in a XIB, the labels will eliminate a lot of confusion (Figure 11.4).

## View-Based Table Views

In Mac OS X 10.7, Apple introduced view-based table views, which are similar to iOS table views. Prior to 10.7, Cocoa developers used cell-based table views, which are very fast and lightweight, but customization tends to be very involved. View-based table views, on the other hand, make customizing the appearance of your table view cells rather simple: You can use Xcode's Interface Builder for this purpose.

Drag out a table view (from Cocoa->Data Views). In the Attributes Inspector, set the Content Mode to be View Based and give it three columns. Name the columns Make/Model, Price, and Special.

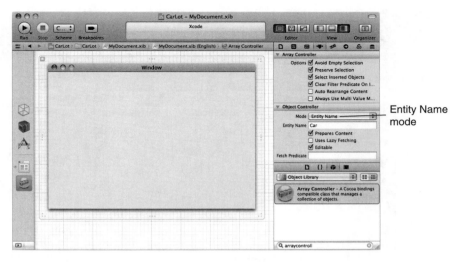

Entity Name
mode

**Figure 11.4**    Inspect the Attributes of the Cars Array Controller

Use the object hierarchy view (expanded dock view) to select the Table Cell View
in the first column and delete it—it is a child of the Table Column. Now drag an
Image & Text Table Cell View from the Library onto the first column. Each
column should now contain a Table Cell View (**NSTableCellView**), and within it
a Static Text (**NSTextField**). The first column's cell view contains an image view
as well (Figure 11.5).

Now drop a number formatter (from Cocoa->Controls) onto the **NSTextField**
in the Price column (Figure 11.6). In the Attributes Inspector, use the 10.4+
formatter, and set the style to Currency.

The third column will be populated by check boxes, so select the **NSTextField**
in the third column's cell view and delete it. Make sure that you have selected
and deleted the Static Text - Table View Cell, and not the Table Cell View itself.
This will take two clicks directly on the cell.

Now drop a Check Box (from Cocoa->Data Views)—not the Check Box Cell—in
place of the text field in the third column. Select the check box and clear its title
(Figure 11.7).

Below the table view, drop an **NSDatePicker**, two buttons, an **NSImageView**
(which is called Image Well in the Library), and an **NSLevelIndicator** onto the
window. Label the buttons *Add* and *Remove*. Put label text fields next to the date

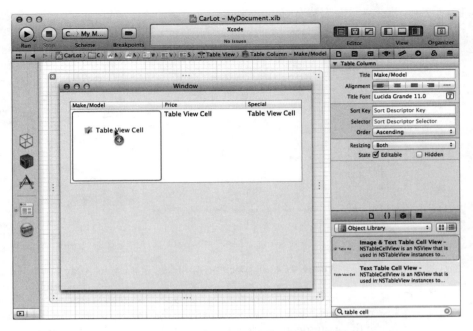

**Figure 11.5**  Drop an Image & Text Table Cell View

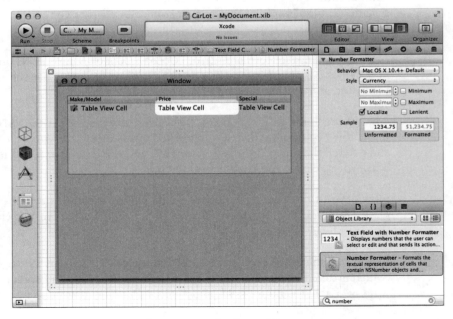

**Figure 11.6**  Configure Formatter

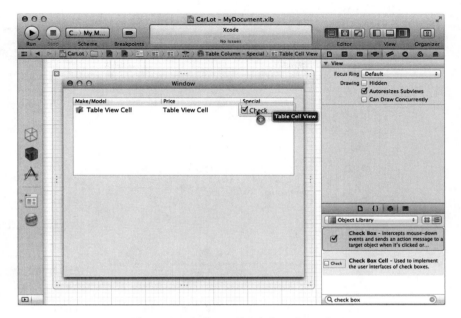

**Figure 11.7**    Drop Check Box Control

picker and the level indicator. The labels should be *Date Purchased* and *Condition*. Make the **NSImageView** editable by using the Attributes Inspector (Figure 11.8).

In the Attributes Inspector of the **NSLevelIndicator**, set its max to 5 and its min to 0. Set its style to Rating mode (to get the stars). Also, make the level indicator editable (Figure 11.8).

Select the date picker, the image view, the two labels, and the level indicator. Using the Editor -> Embed -> Box menu item, wrap them in a box (Figure 11.9).

## Connections and Bindings

Now you are going to do a bunch of bindings. We will walk you through it step-by-step. Figure 11.10 is a diagram of the bindings that you are going to create between your views and the array controller.

If you have used cell-based table views in the past, you will find the bindings on view-based table views to be much more straightforward. With view-based tables, you will bind the table's contents to the array controller; then the values of the controls you place within the cell views, not the table column, will be bound to the object value for that row. A reminder: In this book, you will never bind a scroll view or a cell.

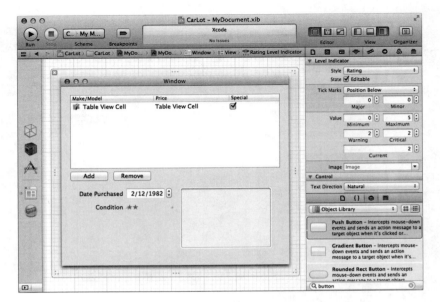

**Figure 11.8**    Attributes of the NSLevelIndicator

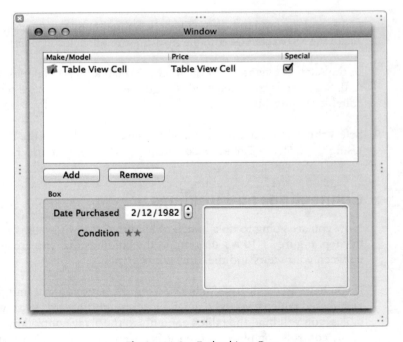

**Figure 11.9**    Embed in a Box

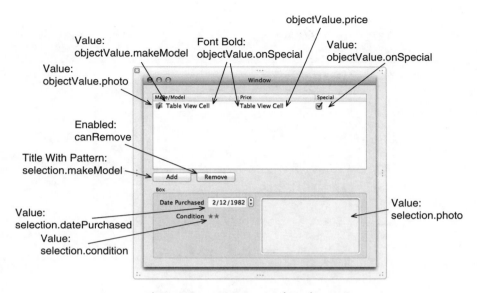

**Figure 11.10**    Summary of Bindings

Start by binding the table view's Content binding to Cars' arrangedObjects.
Leave the Model Key Path empty. Remember, Cars is the **NSArrayController**.
Next, bind the Selection Indexes to Cars' selectionIndexes. See Figure 11.11.

Now bind the value of each column's cell view control(s), as shown in the
following table.

| Binding | Bind to | Controller Key | Key Path |
|---|---|---|---|
| value of Col 0 Image View | Table Cell View | *Empty* | objectValue.photo |
| value of Col 0 Text Field | Table Cell View | *Empty* | objectValue.makeModel |
| value of Col 1 Text Field | Table Cell View | *Empty* | objectValue.price |
| value of Col 2 Check Box | Table Cell View | *Empty* | objectValue.onSpecial |

Note the pattern in the bindings. Each control's value is bound to a particular
property of the table cell view's objectValue. Recall that the table's content is
bound to the **NSArrayController**'s arranged objects. Each of those objects is an
instance of our Car entity. When the table view's contents are bound, the
objectValue property of the table cell view (**NSTableCellView**) is populated
with the entity instance for that row. Once we understand this, we can configure
very straightforward bindings, such as those in the table.

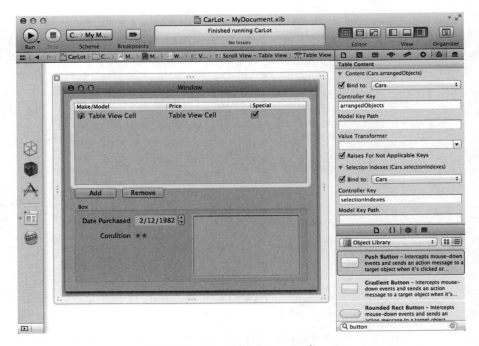

**Figure 11.11**    Table View Bindings

Before continuing, use the Attributes Inspector to set the Behavior of each Static Text Field to Editable.

Make the Add button trigger the **add:** method of the array controller (Figure 11.12).

Make the Remove button trigger the **remove:** method of the array controller.

Bind the value of the controls to the selection of the array controller as follows:

| Binding | Bind to | Controller Key | Key Path |
|---|---|---|---|
| value of date picker | Cars | selection | datePurchased |
| enabled of Remove button | Cars | canRemove | |
| value of level indicator | Cars | selection | condition |

Bind the value of the image view to Cars. Choose the controller key selection and the key path photo. Also, check the box that says Conditionally Sets Editable. See Figure 11.13.

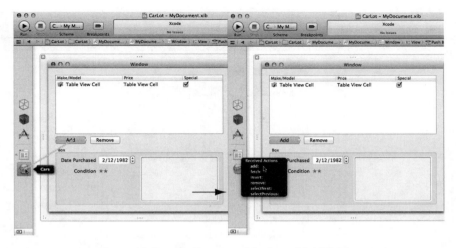

**Figure 11.12**   Set Target and Action of Add Button

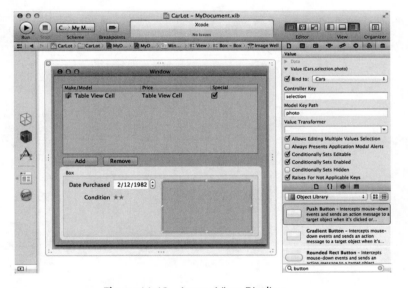

**Figure 11.13**   Image View Binding

Select the box. In the Bindings Inspector, under the Title With Pattern heading, bind Display Pattern Title1 to Cars (our custom name for the array controller). Set the Controller Key to `selection` and the Model Key Path to `makeModel`. Set the Display Pattern to `Details for %{title1}@`. Set the No Selection Placeholder to <no selection>. Set the Null Placeholder to <no Make/Model>. See Figure 11.14.

Let's also make the text of the first two columns appear in bold if the car is on special. Bind the Font Bold of the Static Text (**NSTextField**) in each of the first

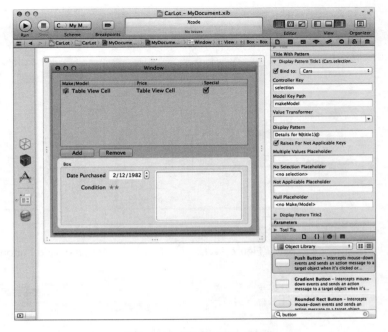

**Figure 11.14**    Box Binding

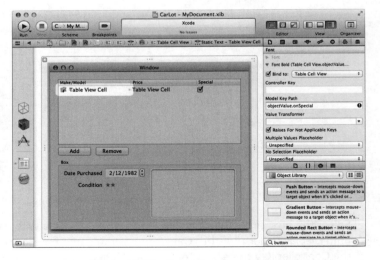

**Figure 11.15**    Specials Appear in Bold

two columns to Table Cell View. Set the Model Key Path to `objectValue.onSpecial` (Figure 11.15).

You are done. Build and run the application. Saving and loading should work. Undo should work. Magic, eh?

# How Core Data Works

Although you have written no code, many objects will be created to make this work. Figure 11.16 is a diagram of some of them.

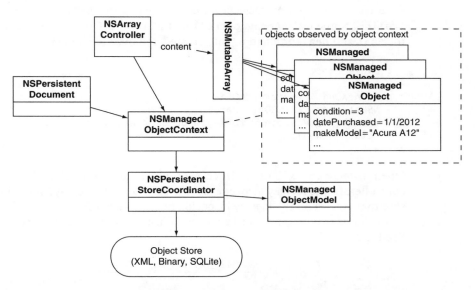

**Figure 11.16**    Overview of Core Data

So, the **NSPersistentDocument** reads in the model you created and uses it to create an instance of **NSManagedObjectModel**. In our case, the managed object model has one **NSEntityDescription** (which describes our **Car** entity). That entity description has several instances of **NSAttributeDescription**.

Once it has the model, the persistent document creates an instance of **NSPersistentStoreCoordinator** and an instance of **NSManagedObjectContext**. The **NSManagedObjectContext** fetches instances of **NSManagedObject** from the object store. While those managed objects are in memory, the managed object context observes them. Whenever the data inside the managed objects is changed, the managed object context registers the undo action with the document's **NSUndoManager**. The managed object context also knows which objects have been changed and need to be saved.

So, among the classes in the Core Data framework, you will find yourself interacting with **NSManagedObjectContext** the most. To fetch objects, you will use **NSManagedObjectContext**. To save changes to your object graph, you will use **NSManagedObjectContext**.

Given that we are probably going to add cars to the system when we purchase
them, it would be nice if the datePurchased attribute were set to the current
date. One good way to do this is to subclass **NSArrayController** and override its
**newObject** method.

Create a new file of type Objective-C class. It will be a subclass of **NSArrayController**. Name it **CarArrayController**. In CarArrayController.m, remove
the **init** and **dealloc** the template created and override **newObject**:

```
- (id)newObject
{
    id newObj = [super newObject];
    NSDate *now = [NSDate date];
    [newObj setValue:now forKey:@"datePurchased"];
    return newObj;
}
```

Open MyDocument.xib in the Interface Builder editor and select the array
controller. In the Identity Inspector, set the class to be **CarArrayController**. (Be
sure that you are in the Identity Inspector, not the Attributes Inspector; this array
controller is still holding on to an array of instances of the **Car** entity.)
See Figure 11.17.

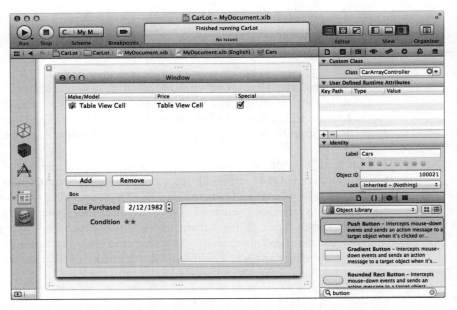

**Figure 11.17**    Change Class of Array Controller

Build and run your application. When new cars are added, their datePurchased
attribute should be initialized to the current date.

# For the More Curious: View-Based versus Cell-Based Table Views

You have now used both view-based and cell-based table views: view based in this chapter, cell based in the SpeakLine exercise. You are probably wondering why there are two types and which one you should choose.

Cell-based table views have been around since Cocoa's origins at NeXT. This type of table view uses cells for performance reasons and works very well for displaying simple data. But customization can be challenging, and incorporating animation or interactive controls, such as buttons, into cells can be extremely challenging. Cell-based table views are your only choice if you are targeting Mac OS X 10.6 or earlier.

View-based table views were introduced in Mac OS X 10.7 and offer easy, convenient customization, allowing the use of the Interface Builder editor to lay out the cell contents. Animation and interactive controls can be easily used, as the table cells are in fact views.

Bindings on cell-based table views are not as obvious but are simpler: Bind the table column only. Bindings on view-based table views are completely different but more logical: Bind the table view's contents and then bind individual controls within the cell views directly to the desired property. This has the advantage of allowing for relatively trivial compound cells (cells containing multiple controls).

# Challenge

After studying the code for **createNewEmployee:** in the RaiseMan application, make the **CarArrayController** select the Make/Model column of the table view when a new record is created. Hint: You will need to add an outlet to **CarArray-Controller**.

## Chapter 12

# NIB FILES AND NSWINDOWCONTROLLER

In RaiseMan, you are already using two NIB files: `MainMenu.nib` and `RMDocument.nib`. (Recall that the compiler converts our XIB files to NIB files during the build process.) `MainMenu.nib` is automatically loaded by **NSApplication** when the application first launches. `RMDocument.nib` is automatically loaded each time an instance of `RMDocument` is created. In this chapter, you will learn how to load NIB files by using **NSWindowController**.

Why would you want to load a NIB file? Most commonly, your application will have several windows (such as a Find panel and a Preferences panel) that are used only occasionally. By putting off loading the NIB until the window is needed, your application will launch faster. Furthermore, if the user never needs the window, your program will use less memory.

## NSPanel

In this chapter, you will create a Preferences panel. The panel will be an instance of **NSPanel**, which is a subclass of **NSWindow**. There are not that many differences between a panel and a general window, but because a panel is meant to be auxiliary (as opposed to a document window), it acts a little differently.

- A panel can become the key window without becoming the main window. For example, when bringing up a Print panel, the user can type into it (it is key), but the document the user was looking at remains the main window (that is what will be printed). **NSApplication** has a `mainWindow` outlet and a `keyWindow` outlet. Both outlets point at the same window unless a panel is involved; panels do not typically become the main window.

- If it has a `close` button, you can close a panel by pressing the Escape key. Panels do not appear in the window list in the Window menu. After all, a user who is looking for a window is probably looking for a document, not a panel.

All windows have a Boolean variable called `hidesOnDeactivate`. If it is set to YES, the window will hide itself when the application is not active. Most document windows have this variable set to NO; most auxiliary panels have it set to YES. This mechanism reduces screen clutter. You can set `hidesOnDeactivate` by using the Attributes Inspector in Interface Builder.

# Adding a Panel to the Application

The Preferences panel that you are going to add will not do anything except appear for now. In Chapter 13, however, you will learn about user defaults and will make the Preferences panel do something.

The Preferences panel will be in its own NIB file. You will create a subclass of **NSWindowController** called **PreferenceController**. An instance of **PreferenceController** will act as the controller for the Preferences panel. When creating an auxiliary panel, it is important to remember that you may want to reuse it in the next application. Creating a class to act just as a controller and a NIB that contains only the panel makes it easier to reuse the panel in another application. Hip programmers would say, "By making the application more modular, we can maximize reuse." The modularity also makes it easier to divide tasks among several programmers. A manager can say, "Rex, you are in charge of the Preferences panel. Only you may edit the NIB file and the preference controller class."

The objects on the Preferences panel will be connected to the preference controller. In particular, the preference controller will be the `target` of a color well and the check box. The Preferences panel will appear when the user clicks on the Preferences... menu item. When running, it will look like Figure 12.1.

Figure 12.2 presents a diagram of the objects that you will create and the NIB files in which they will reside.

We will start by creating **PreferenceController**; this will allow us to take advantage of Xcode's code completion later. Open the `RaiseMan` project, choose New -> New File... from the File menu, and create a new Objective-C class file that

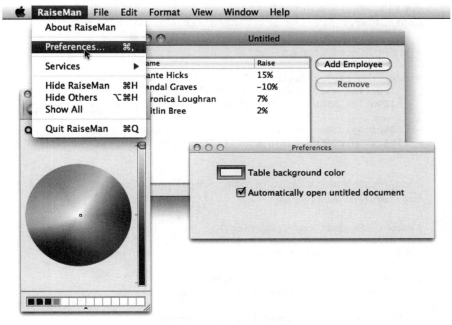

**Figure 12.1**   Completed Application

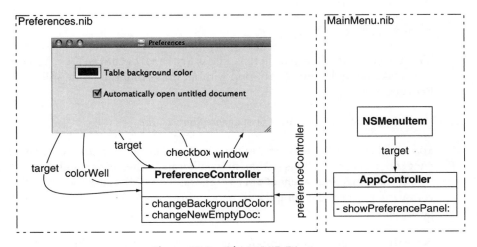

**Figure 12.2**   Object/NIB Diagram

is a subclass of **NSWindowController**. Name the subclass **Preference-Controller**. Edit PreferenceController.h to look like this:

```
#import <Cocoa/Cocoa.h>

@interface PreferenceController : NSWindowController {
    IBOutlet NSColorWell *colorWell;
    IBOutlet NSButton *checkbox;
}
- (IBAction)changeBackgroundColor:(id)sender;
- (IBAction)changeNewEmptyDoc:(id)sender;
@end
```

Next, create a new subclass of **NSObject** called **AppController**. Edit AppController.h to look like this:

```
#import <Foundation/Foundation.h>

@class PreferenceController;

@interface AppController : NSObject {
    PreferenceController *preferenceController;
}
- (IBAction)showPreferencePanel:(id)sender;

@end
```

Note the Objective-C syntax:

```
@class PreferenceController;
```

This tells the compiler that there is a class **PreferenceController**. You can then make the following declaration without importing the header file for **PreferenceController**:

```
    PreferenceController *preferenceController;
```

You could replace @class PreferenceController; with #import "PreferenceController.h". This statement would import the header, and the compiler would learn that **PreferenceController** was a class. Because the import command requires the compiler to parse more files, @class will often result in faster builds.

Note that you must always import the superclass's header file, because the compiler needs to know which instance variables are declared in the superclass. In this case, NSObject.h is imported by Foundation/Foundation.h.

# Setting Up the Menu Item

Open `MainMenu.xib`. Drag an **NSObject** from the Library (under Objects & Controllers) to the dock. In the `Identity Inspector`, set its class to **AppController** (Figure 12.3).

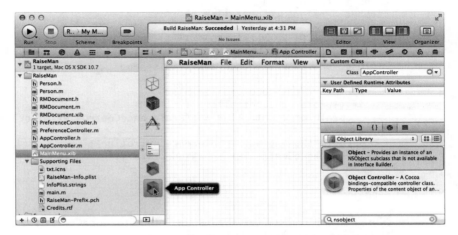

**Figure 12.3**   Create an Instance of AppController

Within the Interface Builder editor, click the application menu item `RaiseMan`. Control-drag from the Preferences… menu item to the **AppController**. Make it the `target` and set the `action` to **showPreferencePanel:** (Figure 12.4).

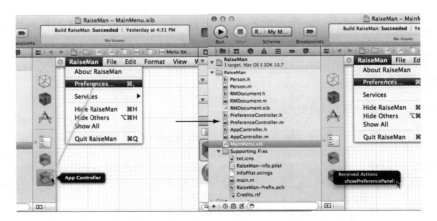

**Figure 12.4**   Set the Target of the Menu Item

## AppController.m

Now you need to write the code for **AppController**. Make the contents of AppController.m look like this:

```
#import "AppController.h"
#import "PreferenceController.h"

@implementation AppController

- (IBAction)showPreferencePanel:(id)sender
{
    // Is preferenceController nil?
    if (!preferenceController) {
        preferenceController = [[PreferenceController alloc] init];
    }
    NSLog(@"showing %@", preferenceController);
    [preferenceController showWindow:self];
}

@end
```

Note that this code creates the instance of **PreferenceController** only once. If the preferenceController variable is non-nil, it simply sends the message **showWindow:** to the existing instance.

Note also that we import PreferenceController.h into the .m file that uses it.

## Preferences.xib

In Xcode, create a new empty XIB file named Preferences.xib (Figure 12.5).

Click on Preferences.xib to open it in the editor. Bring up the Identity Inspector, select File's Owner, and set its class to **PreferenceController** (Figure 12.6).

### File's Owner

When a NIB file is loaded into an application that has been running for a while, the objects that already exist need to establish some connection to the objects read from the NIB file. File's Owner provides this connection. File's Owner is a placeholder in a NIB file for an object that will already exist when the NIB file is loaded. An object loading a NIB file will provide the owner object. The owner is put into the place that File's Owner represents. In your application, the owner will be the instance of **PreferenceController** that was created by the **AppController**.

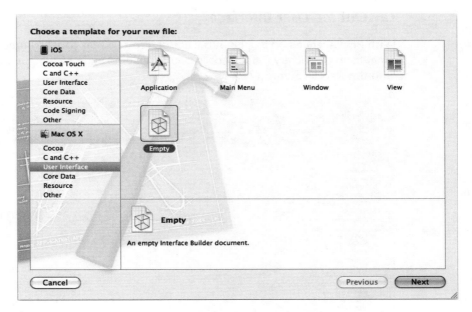

**Figure 12.5**   Create an Empty XIB File

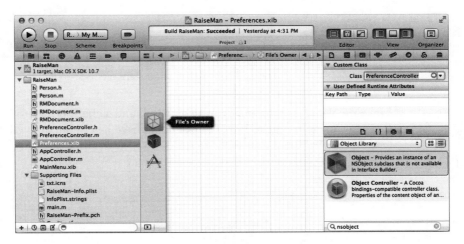

**Figure 12.6**   Set File's Owner to Be a PreferenceController

The use of File's Owner is confusing to many people. You will not instantiate
**PreferenceController** in the NIB file. Instead, you have just informed the
NIB file that the owner (which will be provided when the NIB file is loaded) is a
**PreferenceController**.

## Lay Out the User Interface

With Preferences.xib open in the editor, create a new panel by dragging a panel from the Library (under Application->Windows) and dropping it anywhere onto the screen (Figure 12.7).

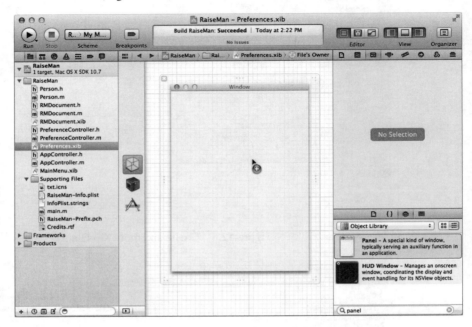

**Figure 12.7**   Create an Instance of NSPanel

Make the panel smaller and drop a color well and a check box onto it. Label them as shown in Figure 12.8. (Check boxes have labels, but you will have to drag out a label for the color well.)

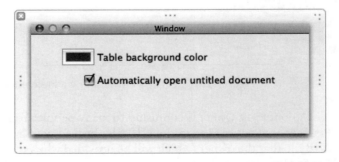

**Figure 12.8**   Completed Interface

Set the `target` of the color well to be File's Owner (your **PreferenceController**) and set the `action` to be **changeBackgroundColor:** (Figure 12.9).

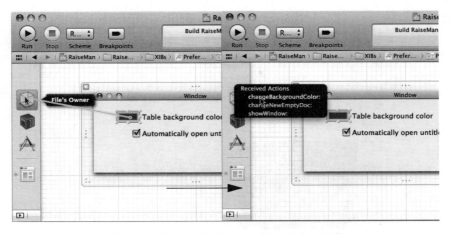

**Figure 12.9**   Set the Target of the Color Well

Also, make your **PreferenceController** be the `target` of the check box and set the `action` to be **changeNewEmptyDoc:**.

Control-click on File's Owner to bring up the connections window. Set the `colorWell` outlet of File's Owner to the color well object. Set the `checkbox` outlet of File's Owner to the check box object. See Figure 12.10.

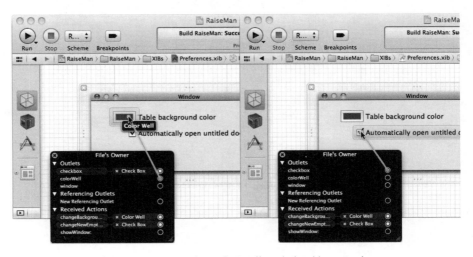

**Figure 12.10**   Set the colorWell and checkbox Outlets

Control-click File's Owner to get the connection window. Connect the window outlet to the panel (Figure 12.11).

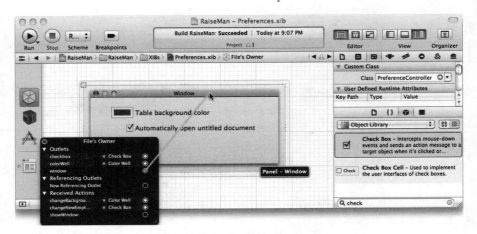

**Figure 12.11**    Set the window Outlet of File's Owner

Open the Attributes Inspector for the panel. Disable resizing. Change the title on the window to Preferences (Figure 12.12).

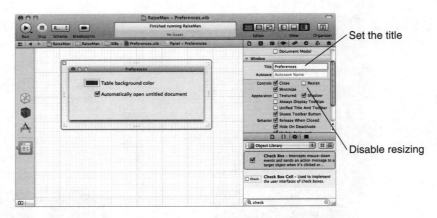

**Figure 12.12**    The New Window's Attributes

# PreferenceController.m

In Xcode, edit `PreferenceController.m` to look like this:

```
#import "PreferenceController.h"

@implementation PreferenceController

- (id)init
{
    self = [super initWithWindowNibName:@"Preferences"];
    return self;
}

- (void)windowDidLoad
{
    [super windowDidLoad];
    NSLog(@"Nib file is loaded");
}

- (IBAction)changeBackgroundColor:(id)sender
{
    NSColor *color = [colorWell color];
    NSLog(@"Color changed: %@", color);
}

- (IBAction)changeNewEmptyDoc:(id)sender
{
    NSInteger state = [checkbox state];
    NSLog(@"Checkbox changed %ld", state);
}

@end
```

Note that you set the name of the NIB file to be loaded in the **init** method. This NIB file will be loaded automatically when it is needed. The instance of **PreferenceController** will be substituted for the File's Owner in the NIB file.

After the NIB file is loaded, the **PreferenceController** will be sent **windowDidLoad**. It offers an opportunity (similar to **awakeFromNib** or **window-ControllerDidLoadNib:**) for the controller object to initialize the user interface objects that have been read from the NIB file.

When sent **showWindow:** for the first time, the **NSWindowController** automatically loads the NIB file and moves the window onto the screen and to the front. The NIB file is loaded only once. When the user closes the Preferences panel, it is moved off screen but not deallocated. The next time the user asks for the Preferences panel, it is simply moved onto the screen.

The **changeBackgroundColor:** and **checkboxChanged:** methods are quite boring right now—they simply print out a message. In the next chapter, you will change them to update the user's defaults database.

Build and run the application. The new panel should appear, and altering the check box or color well should result in a message in the console (Figure 12.13).

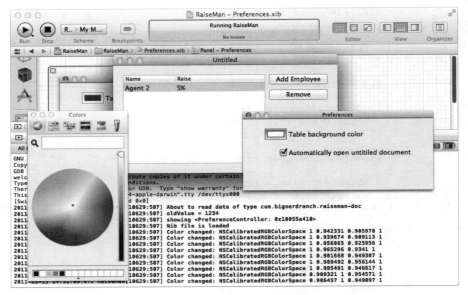

**Figure 12.13**    Completed Application

The first time a user encounters a color well, it may seem confusing. If you click the edge of the color well, the edge becomes highlighted, the Color panel appears, and the well is in `active` mode.

# For the More Curious: NSBundle

A *bundle* is a directory of resources that may be used by an application. Resources include images, sounds, compiled code, and NIB files. (Users often use the word "plug-in" instead of "bundle.") The class **NSBundle** is a very elegant way of dealing with bundles.

Your application is a bundle. In Finder, an application looks to the user like any other file, but it is really a directory filled with NIB files, compiled code, and other resources. We call this directory the *main bundle* of the application.

Some resources in a bundle can be localized. For example, you could have two versions of foo.nib, one for English speakers and one for French speakers. The bundle would have two subdirectories: English.lproj and French.lproj. You would put an appropriate version of foo.nib in each. When your application asks the bundle to load foo.nib, the bundle will automatically load the French version of foo.nib, if the user has set the preferred language to French. We will cover localization in Chapter 16.

To get the main bundle of an application, use the following code:

```
NSBundle *myBundle = [NSBundle mainBundle];
```

This is the most commonly used bundle. If you need to access resources in another directory, however, you could ask for the bundle at a certain path:

```
NSBundle *goodBundle;
goodBundle = [NSBundle bundleWithPath:@"~/Library/Application Sup-
port/MyApp/Good.bundle"];
```

Once you have an **NSBundle** object, you can ask it for its resources:

```
// Extension is optional
NSString *path = [goodBundle pathForImageResource:@"Mom"];
NSImage *momPhoto = [[NSImage alloc] initWithContentsOfFile:path];
```

A bundle may have a library of code. By asking for a class from the bundle, the bundle will link in the library and search for a class by that name:

```
Class newClass = [goodBundle classNamed:@"Rover"];
id newInstance = [[newClass alloc] init];
```

If you do not know the name of any classes in the bundle, you can simply ask for the principal class:

```
Class aClass = [goodBundle principalClass];
id anInstance = [[aClass alloc] init];
```

As you see, **NSBundle** is handy in many ways. In this section, the **NSBundle** was responsible (behind the scenes) for loading the NIB file. If you wanted to load a NIB file without an **NSWindowController**, you could do it like this:

```
BOOL successful = [NSBundle loadNibNamed:@"About" owner:someObject];
```

Note that you would supply the object that will act as the File's Owner.

# Challenge

Create a XIB file with a custom About panel. Add an outlet to **AppController** to point to the new window. Also add a **showAboutPanel:** method. Load the NIB by using **NSBundle**, and make **AppController** the File's Owner.

# Chapter 13
# USER DEFAULTS

Many applications have Preferences panels that allow the user to choose a preferred appearance or behavior. The user's choices go into the user defaults database in the user's home directory. Note that only the choices that vary from the factory defaults are saved in the user defaults database. If you go to ~/Library/Preferences, you can see your user defaults database. The files are in a binary format, but you can use *Xcode's* property list editor to browse though them.

The **NSUserDefaults** class allows your application to register the factory defaults, save the user's preferences, and read previously saved user preferences.

The color well that you dropped into the Preferences window in the previous chapter will determine the background color of the table view. When the user changes his or her preference, your application will write the new preference to the user defaults database. When your application creates a new document window, it will read from the user defaults database. As a consequence, only windows created after the change will be affected (Figure 13.1).

**Figure 13.1**   Completed Application

207

Also, have you noticed that every time you start the application, it brings up an untitled document? The Automatically open new document check box will allow the user to choose whether the untitled document should appear.

# NSDictionary and NSMutableDictionary

Before you do anything with user defaults, we need to discuss the classes **NSDictionary** (Figure 13.2) and **NSMutableDictionary**. A dictionary is a collection of key-value pairs. The keys are strings, and the values are pointers to objects.

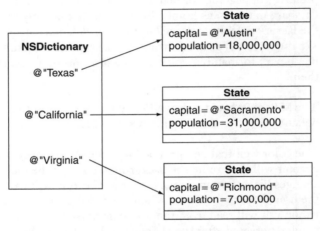

**Figure 13.2**    An Instance of NSDictionary

A string can be a key only once in a dictionary. When you want to know the value to which a key is bound, you will use the method **objectForKey:**.

```
anObject = [myDictionary objectForKey:@"foo"];
```

If the key is not in the dictionary, this method will return nil.

**NSMutableDictionary** is a subclass of **NSDictionary**. An instance of **NSDictionary** is created with all the keys and values it will ever have. You can query the object, but you cannot change it. **NSMutableDictionary**, on the other hand, allows you to add and remove keys and values.

# NSDictionary

A dictionary is implemented as a hash table, so looking up keys is very fast. Here are a few of the most commonly used methods in the class **NSDictionary**:

```
- (NSArray *)allKeys
```

Returns a new array containing the keys in the dictionary.

```
- (unsigned)count
```

Returns the number of key-value pairs in the dictionary.

```
- (id)objectForKey:(NSString *)aKey
```

Returns the value associated with aKey or returns nil if no value is associated with aKey.

A for-in loop will enumerate through the keys in a dictionary:

```
NSDictionary *dict = ...
for (NSString *key in dict) {
    NSLog(@"%@ -> %@", key, [dict objectForKey:key]);
}
```

# NSMutableDictionary

Here are some commonly used methods in the class **NSMutableDictionary**:

```
+ (id)dictionary
```

Creates an empty dictionary.

```
- (void)removeObjectForKey:(NSString *)aKey
```

Removes aKey and its associated value object from the dictionary.

```
- (void)setObject:(id)anObject forKey:(NSString *)aKey
```

Adds an entry to the dictionary, consisting of aKey and its corresponding value object anObject. The value object receives a retain message before being added to the dictionary. If aKey already exists in the receiver, the receiver's previous value object for that key is sent a release message, and anObject takes its place.

# NSUserDefaults

Every application comes with a set of defaults "from the factory." When a user edits his or her defaults, only the differences between the user's wishes and the factory defaults are stored in the user's defaults database. Thus, every time the application starts up, you need to remind it of the factory defaults. This operation is called *registering defaults*.

After registering, you will use the user defaults object to determine how the user wants the app to behave. This process is called *reading and using the defaults*. The data from the user's defaults database will be read automatically from the filesystem.

In your Preferences panel, you will allow the user to set the defaults. The changes to the defaults object will be written automatically to the filesystem. This process is known as *setting the defaults* (Figure 13.3).

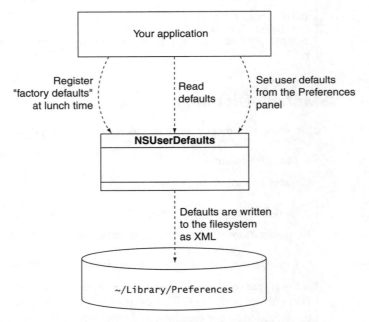

**Figure 13.3**    NSUserDefaults and the Filesystem

Here are some commonly used methods that are implemented in **NSUserDefaults**:

```
+ (NSUserDefaults *)standardUserDefaults
```
Returns the shared defaults object.

```
- (void)registerDefaults:(NSDictionary *)dictionary
```

Registers the factory defaults for the application.

```
- (void)setBool:(BOOL)value          forKey:(NSString *)defaultName
- (void)setFloat:(float)value         forKey:(NSString *)defaultName
- (void)setInteger:(NSInteger)value  forKey:(NSString *)defaultName
- (void)setObject:(id)value           forKey:(NSString *)defaultName
```

Methods for changing and saving a user's wishes.

```
- (BOOL)boolForKey:(NSString *)defaultName
- (float)floatForKey:(NSString *)defaultName
- (NSInteger)integerForKey:(NSString *)defaultName
- (id)objectForKey:(NSString *)defaultName
```

Methods for reading the defaults. If the user hasn't changed them, the factory defaults are returned.

```
- (void)removeObjectForKey:(NSString *)defaultName
```

Removes the user's preference, so the application will return to using the factory defaults.

## Precedence of Types of Defaults

So far, we have talked about two levels of precedence: What the user writes to his or her defaults database overrides the factory defaults. In fact, several more levels of precedence exist. These levels of default settings are known as *domains*. Here are the domains used by an application, from highest to lowest priority:

*Arguments*: Passed on the command line. Most people start their applications by double-clicking on an icon instead of by working from the command line, so this feature is seldom used in a production app.

*Application*: What comes from the user's defaults database.

*Global*: What the user has set for his or her entire system.

*Language:* What is set based on the user's preferred language.

*Registered defaults*: The factory defaults for the app.

# Setting Defaults

## The Identifier for the Application

What is the plist file in ~/Library/Preferences created for this application called? By default, it uses the identifier of the application that created it. You set this identifier in Chapter 10 to be com.bignerdranch.RaiseMan, so the filename will be com.bignerdranch.RaiseMan.plist.

## Create Keys for the Names of the Defaults

You will be registering, reading, and setting defaults in several classes in your application. To make sure that you always use the same name, you should declare those strings in a single file and then simply #import that file into any file where you use the names.

There are several ways to do this (for example, you could use the C preprocessor's #define command), but most Cocoa programers use global variables for this purpose. Add the following lines to your PreferenceController.h file after the #import statement:

```
extern NSString * const BNRTableBgColorKey;
extern NSString * const BNREmptyDocKey;
```

Now define these variables in PreferenceController.m. Put them after the #import lines but before @implementation:

```
NSString * const BNRTableBgColorKey = @"BNRTableBackgroundColor";
NSString * const BNREmptyDocKey = @"BNREmptyDocumentFlag";
```

Why would we declare global variables that simply contain a constant string? After all, you could just remember what the string was and type it in whenever you need it. The problem is that you might misspell the string. If the string is surrounded by quotes, the compiler will accept the misspelled string. In contrast, if you misspell the name of a global variable, the compiler will catch your error.

To keep the global variables from conflicting with another company's global variables, you have prefixed them with BNR (for Big Nerd Ranch). Global variables from Cocoa are prefixed with NS. These prefixes are important only when you start using classes and frameworks developed by third parties. (Note that class names are also global. You might prefer to prefix all your class names with BNR to keep them from conflicting with anyone else's classes.)

## Register Defaults

Each class is sent the message **initialize** before any other message. To ensure that your defaults are registered early, you will override **initialize** in AppController.m:

```
+ (void)initialize
{
    // Create a dictionary
    NSMutableDictionary *defaultValues = [NSMutableDictionary dictionary];

    // Archive the color object
    NSData *colorAsData = [NSKeyedArchiver archivedDataWithRootObject:
                                              [NSColor yellowColor]];

    // Put defaults in the dictionary
    [defaultValues setObject:colorAsData forKey:BNRTableBgColorKey];
    [defaultValues setObject:[NSNumber numberWithBool:YES]
                    forKey:BNREmptyDocKey];

    // Register the dictionary of defaults
    [[[NSUserDefaults standardUserDefaults]
                                      registerDefaults: defaultValues];
    NSLog(@"registered defaults: %@", defaultValues);
}
```

This is a class method; that is why its declaration is prefixed with a +.

Note that we had to store the color as a data object. **NSColor** objects do not know how to write themselves out as XML, so we pack them into a data object that does. One group of classes does know how to write themselves out as XML, known as the *property list* classes: **NSString**, **NSArray**, **NSDictionary**, **NSDate**, **NSData**, and **NSNumber**. A property list comprises any combination of these classes. For example, a dictionary containing arrays of dates is a property list.

# Letting the User Edit the Defaults

Next, you will alter the **PreferenceController** class so that the Preferences panel will cause the defaults database to get updated. Declare the following methods in PreferenceController.h:

```
+ (NSColor *)preferenceTableBgColor;
+ (void)setPreferenceTableBgColor:(NSColor *)color;
+ (BOOL)preferenceEmptyDoc;
+ (void)setPreferenceEmptyDoc:(BOOL)emptyDoc;
```

These class methods will make it easier for us to set and get the current default values, and will abstract away the details of how the preferences are stored.

Implement the new class methods in `PreferenceController.m`:

```
+ (NSColor *)preferenceTableBgColor
{
    NSUserDefaults *defaults = [NSUserDefaults standardUserDefaults];
    NSData *colorAsData = [defaults objectForKey:BNRTableBgColorKey];
    return [NSKeyedUnarchiver unarchiveObjectWithData:colorAsData];
}

+ (void)setPreferenceTableBgColor:(NSColor *)color
{
    NSData *colorAsData =
                 [NSKeyedArchiver archivedDataWithRootObject:color];
    [[NSUserDefaults standardUserDefaults] setObject:colorAsData
                                              forKey:BNRTableBgColorKey];
}

+ (BOOL)preferenceEmptyDoc
{
    NSUserDefaults *defaults = [NSUserDefaults standardUserDefaults];
    return [defaults boolForKey:BNREmptyDocKey];
}

+ (void)setPreferenceEmptyDoc:(BOOL)emptyDoc
{
    [[NSUserDefaults standardUserDefaults] setBool:emptyDoc
                                            forKey:BNREmptyDocKey];
}
```

Now let's modify **windowDidLoad** and the action methods to make use of the preferences:

```
- (void)windowDidLoad
{
    [super windowDidLoad];

    [colorWell setColor:
                 [PreferenceController preferenceTableBgColor]];
    [checkbox setState:
                 [PreferenceController preferenceEmptyDoc]];
}

- (IBAction)changeBackgroundColor:(id)sender
{
    NSColor *color = [colorWell color];
    [PreferenceController setPreferenceTableBgColor:color];
}
```

```
- (IBAction)changeNewEmptyDoc:(id)sender
{
    NSInteger state = [checkbox state];
    [PreferenceController setPreferenceEmptyDoc:state];
}
```

In the **windowDidLoad** method, you are reading the defaults and making the
color well and check box reflect the current settings. In **changeBackground-
Color:** and **changeNewEmptyDoc:**, you are updating the defaults database.

You should now be able to build and run your application. It will read and write to
the defaults database, so the Preferences panel will display the last color you chose
and indicate whether the check box was on or off. You have not, however, done
anything with this information yet, so the untitled document will continue to
appear, and the background of the table view will continue to be white.

# Using the Defaults

Now you are going to use the defaults. First, you will make your **AppController**
become a delegate of the **NSApplication** object and suppress the creation of an
untitled document, depending on the user defaults. Then, in **RMDocument**, you
will set the background color of the table view from the user defaults.

## Suppressing the Creation of Untitled Documents

As before, there are two steps to creating a delegate: implementing the delegate
method and setting the **delegate** outlet to point to the object (Figure 13.4).

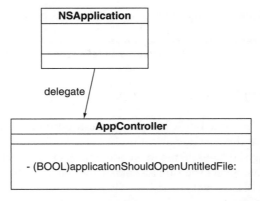

**Figure 13.4**   Delegate Suppresses Creation of Untitled Documents

Before automatically creating a new untitled document, the **NSApplication** object will send the message **applicationShouldOpenUntitledFile:** to its delegate. In AppController.m, add the following method:

```
- (BOOL)applicationShouldOpenUntitledFile:(NSApplication *)sender
{
    NSLog(@"applicationShouldOpenUntitledFile:");
    return [PreferenceController preferenceEmptyDoc];
}
```

To make your **AppController** the delegate of the **NSApplication** object, open the MainMenu.xib file, and Control-click on File's Owner (which represents the **NSApplication** object) to bring up its connection window. Drag from delegate to your **AppController**.

## Setting the Background Color on the Table View

Open RMDocument.m and import PreferenceController.h at the top. This will allow us to use the BNRTableBgColorKey constant.

```
#import "PreferenceController.h"
```

After the NIB file for a new document window has been successfully unarchived, your **RMDocument** object is sent the message **windowControllerDidLoadNib:**. At that moment, you can update the background color of the table view.

You should already have this method in RMDocument.m; just edit it to look like this:

```
- (void)windowControllerDidLoadNib:(NSWindowController *)aController
{
    [super windowControllerDidLoadNib:aController];

    [tableView setBackgroundColor:
                    [PreferenceController preferenceTableBgColor]];
}
```

Build and run your application.

Note that Mac OS X Lion's state-restoration features may make it tricky to observe the new document preference. You can disable state restoration by editing the Run scheme in Xcode. Open the Product menu and select Edit Scheme. Select the Run RaiseMan.app scheme, change to the Options pane, and check Disable state restoration (Figure 13.5).

**Figure 13.5**     Disabling State Restoration

# For the More Curious: NSUserDefaultsController

Sometimes, you will want to bind to a value from the **NSUserDefaults** object. An **NSUserDefaultsController** makes this possible. All the NIBs in your application will use a single shared instance of **NSUserDefaultsController**.

For example, if you wanted to use bindings (instead of target/action) to deal with the check box on the Preferences panel, you would bind it to the shared **NSUserDefaultsController**'s value, BNREmptyDocumentFlag (Figure 13.6).

# For the More Curious: Reading and Writing Defaults from the Command Line

The user defaults database is found in ~/Library/Preferences/. To edit it from the command line, you use a tool called *defaults*. For example, to see your defaults for Xcode, you can bring up the Terminal and enter the following command:

```
defaults read com.apple.Xcode
```

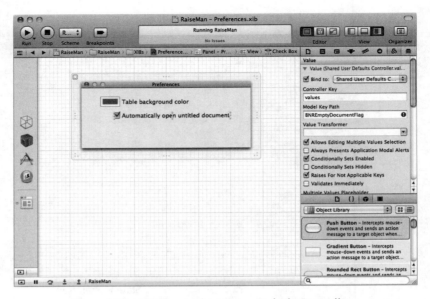

**Figure 13.6**     Binding to the NSUserDefaultsController

You should see all your defaults for Xcode. The first few lines of Aaron's look like this:

```
{
    DocViewerHasSetPrefs = YES;
    NSNavBrowserPreferedColumnContentWidth = 155;
    NSNavLastCurrentDirectoryForOpen = "~/RaiseMan";
    NSNavLastRootDirectoryForOpen = "~";
    NSNavPanelExpandedSizeForOpenMode = "{518, 400}";
    NSNavPanelFileListModeForOpenMode = 1;
```

You can also write to the defaults database. To set Xcode's default directory in the **NSOpenPanel** to the /Users directory, you could enter this:

```
defaults write com.apple.Xcode NSNavLastRootDirectoryForOpen /Users
```

Try this:

```
defaults read com.bignerdranch.RaiseMan
```

To see your global defaults, enter this:

```
defaults read NSGlobalDomain
```

# Challenge

Add to the Preferences panel a button that will remove all the user's defaults. Label the button Reset Preferences. Don't forget to update the Preferences window to reflect the new defaults.

## Chapter 14
# USING NOTIFICATIONS

A user may have several RaiseMan documents open when he or she decides that it is too hard to read them with a purple background. The user opens the Preferences panel and changes the background color but then is disappointed to find that the color of the existing windows doesn't change. When the user sends you an e-mail about this problem, you reply, "The defaults are read only when the document window is created. Just save the document, close it, and open it again." In response, the user sends you a mean e-mail. It would be better to update all the existing windows. But how many are there? Will you have to keep a list of all open documents?

## What Notifications Are and Are Not

Every running application has an instance of **NSNotificationCenter**, which functions much like a bulletin board. Objects register as interested in certain notifications ("Please write me if anyone finds a lost dog"); we call the registered object an *observer*. Other objects can then post notifications to the center ("I have found a lost dog"). That notification is subsequently forwarded to all objects that are registered as interested. We call the object that posted the notification a *poster*.

Many standard Cocoa classes post notifications: Windows send notifications that they have changed size. When the selection of a table view changes, the table view sends a notification. The notifications sent by standard Cocoa objects are listed in the online documentation.

In our example, you will register all your **RMDocument** objects as observers. Your preference controller will post a notification when the user chooses a new color. When sent the notification, the **RMDocument** objects will change the background color.

Before the **RMDocument** object is deallocated, you must remove it from the notification center's list of observers. Typically, this is done in the **dealloc** method.

(If you are using garbage collection, the instance of **RMDocument** will be automatically removed from the notification center when it is deallocated.)

# What Notifications Are Not

A notification center allows objects in an application to send notifications to other objects *in that same application*. When programmers first hear about the notification center, they sometimes think that it is a form of interprocess communications. ("I will create an observer in one application and post notifications from an object in another.")

Notifications do not travel between applications. (Look into **NSDistributedNotificationCenter** if you need to pass notifications between applications.)

# NSNotification

Notification objects are very simple. A notification is like an envelope into which the poster will place information for the observers. A notification has two important instance variables: name and object. Nearly always, object is a pointer to the object that posted the notification. (It is analogous to a return address.)

Thus, the notification also has two interesting methods:

```
- (NSString *)name
- (id)object
```

# NSNotificationCenter

The **NSNotificationCenter** is the brains of the operation. It allows you to do three things: register observer objects, post notifications, and unregister observers.

Here are some commonly used methods implemented by **NSNotificationCenter**:

```
+ (NSNotificationCenter *)defaultCenter
```

Returns the notification center.

```
- (void)addObserver:(id)anObserver
         selector:(SEL)aSelector
             name:(NSString *)notificationName
           object:(id)anObject
```

Registers anObserver to receive notifications with the name notifica-tionName and containing anObject (Figure 14.1). When a notification of the name notificationName containing the object anObject is posted, anObserver is sent an aSelector message with this notification as the argument.

If notificationName is nil, the notification center sends the observer all notifications with an object matching anObject.

If anObject is nil, the notification center sends the observer all notifications with the name notificationName.

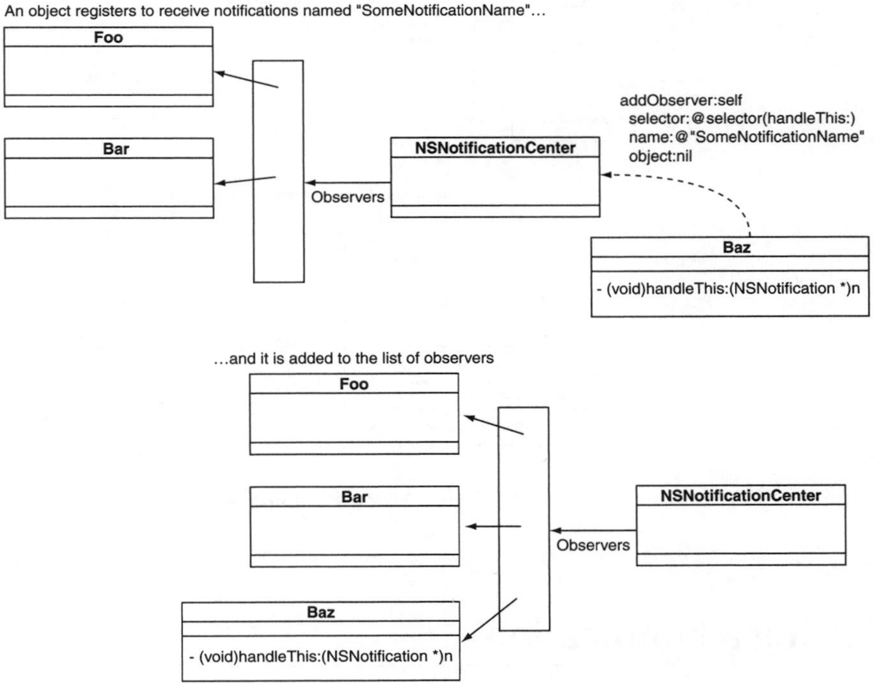

**Figure 14.1**  Registering for Notifications

The observer is *not* retained by the notification center. Note that the method takes a selector.

`- (void)postNotification:(NSNotification *)notification`

Posts a notification to the notification center (Figure 14.2).

`- (void)postNotificationName:(NSString *)aName`
                  `object:(id)anObject`

Creates and posts a notification.

`- (void)removeObserver:(id)observer`

Removes `observer` from the list of observers.

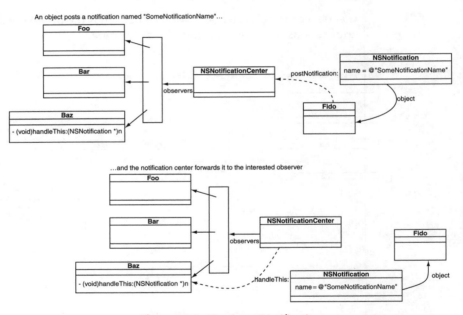

**Figure 14.2**   Posting a Notification

# Posting a Notification

Posting a notification is the easiest step, so you will start there. When it receives a **changeBackgroundColor:** message, your **PreferenceController** object will post a notification with the new color.

You are going to name the notification @"BNRColorChanged", but you are going to create a global variable for the constant. (Experienced programmers put a prefix on the notification so that it doesn't conflict with other notifications that may be flying around the application.) Open Preference-Controller.h and add the declaration with the other string constants:

```
extern NSString * const BNRColorChangedNotification;
```

In PreferenceController.m, define the constant:

```
NSString * const BNRColorChangedNotification = @"BNRColorChanged";
```

Make your **changeBackgroundColor:** method in PreferenceController.m look like this:

```
- (IBAction)changeBackgroundColor:(id)sender
{
    NSColor *color = [colorWell color];
    [PreferenceController setPreferenceTableBgColor:color];

    NSNotificationCenter *nc = [NSNotificationCenter defaultCenter];
    NSLog(@"Sending notification");
    [nc postNotificationName:BNRColorChangedNotification object:self];
}
```

# Registering as an Observer

To register as an observer, you must supply the object that is the observer, the name of the notification in which it is interested, and the message that you want sent when an interesting notification arrives. You can also specify that you are interested only in notifications with a certain object attached to them. (Remember that this is often the object that posted the notification. Thus, when you specify that you want resize notifications with a certain window attached, you are saying that you are interested only in the resizing of that particular window.)

Edit your **RMDocument** class's **init** method as follows:

```
- (id)init
{
    self = [super init];
    if (self) {
        employees = [[NSMutableArray alloc] init];

        NSNotificationCenter *nc =
                [NSNotificationCenter defaultCenter];
```

```
        [nc addObserver:self
               selector:@selector(handleColorChange:)
                   name:BNRColorChangedNotification
                 object:nil];
        NSLog(@"Registered with notification center");
    }
    return self;
}
```

Then implement **dealloc** to remove the instance of **RMDocument** from the notification center:

```
- (void)dealloc
{
    [[NSNotificationCenter defaultCenter] removeObserver:self];
}
```

# Handling the Notification When It Arrives

When the notification arrives, the method **handleColorChange:** is called. For now, just log its arrival. Add this method to your RMDocument.m file:

```
- (void)handleColorChange:(NSNotification *)note
{
    NSLog(@"Received notification: %@", note);
}
```

Build and run the application. Note that the notifications are sent and received when the color is edited in the Preferences panel.

# The userInfo Dictionary

If you wanted to include more than just the poster with the notification, you would use the userInfo dictionary. Every notification has a variable called userInfo that can be attached to an **NSDictionary** filled with other information that you want to pass to the observers. In this case, we want to add the color to the userInfo dictionary. **RMDocument** will use the color when the notification arrives. In PreferenceController.m, add a userInfo dictionary to the notification:

```
- (IBAction)changeBackgroundColor:(id)sender
{
    NSColor *color = [sender color];
```

```
    [PreferenceController setPreferenceTableBgColor:color];

    NSNotificationCenter *nc = [NSNotificationCenter defaultCenter];
    NSLog(@"Sending notification");
    NSDictionary *d = [NSDictionary dictionaryWithObject:color
                                                  forKey:@"color"];
    [nc postNotificationName:BNRColorChangedNotification
                      object:self
                    userInfo:d];
}
```

In RMDocument.m, read the color out of the userInfo dictionary:

```
- (void)handleColorChange:(NSNotification *)note
{
    NSLog(@"Received notification: %@", note);
    NSColor *color = [[note userInfo] objectForKey:@"color"];
    [tableView setBackgroundColor:color];
}
```

Open several windows and change the preferred background color. Note that all of them receive the notification and change color immediately.

# For the More Curious: Delegates and Notifications

An object that has made itself the delegate of a standard Cocoa object is probably interested in receiving notifications from that object as well. For example, if you have implemented a delegate to handle the **windowShouldClose:** delegate method for a window, that same object is likely to be interested in the NSWindow-DidResizeNotification from that same window.

If a standard Cocoa object has a delegate and posts notifications, the delegate is automatically registered as an observer for the methods it implements. If you are implementing such a delegate, how would you know what to call the method?

The naming convention is simple: Start with the name of the notification. Remove the NS from the beginning and make the first letter lowercase. Remove the Notification from the end. Add a colon. For example, to be notified that the window has posted an NSWindowDidResizeNotification, the delegate would implement the following method:

```
- (void)windowDidResize:(NSNotification *)aNotification
```

This method will be called automatically after the window resizes. You can also find this method listed in the documentation and header files for the class **NSWindow.**

# Challenge

Make your application beep when it gives up its active status. **NSApplication** posts an NSApplicationDidResignActiveNotification notification. Your **AppController** is a delegate of **NSApplication**. **NSBeep()** will cause a system beep.

# Chapter 15
# USING ALERT PANELS

Occasionally, you will want to warn the user about something by means of an Alert panel. Alert panels are easy to create. While most things in Cocoa are object oriented, showing a modal Alert panel is typically done with a C function: **NSRunAlertPanel()**. Here is the declaration:

```
NSInteger NSRunAlertPanel(NSString *title,
                          NSString *msg,
                          NSString *defaultButton,
                          NSString *alternateButton,
                          NSString *otherButton, ...);
```

The following code would result in the Alert panel shown in Figure 15.1:

```
NSInteger choice = NSRunAlertPanel(@"Title", @"Message",
                          @"Default", @"Alternate", @"Other");
```

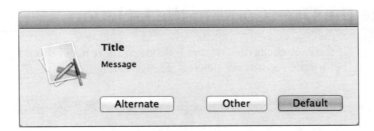

**Figure 15.1**  Example Alert Panel

Note that the icon on the panel will be the icon for the responsible application. The second and third buttons are optional. To prevent a button from appearing, replace its label with `nil`.

The **NSRunAlertPanel()** function returns an `int` that indicates which button the user clicked. There are global variables for these constants: NSAlert DefaultReturn, NSAlertAlternateReturn, and NSAlertOtherReturn.

Note that **NSRunAlertPanel()** takes a variable number of arguments. The second string may include printf-like tokens. Values supplied after the otherButton label will be substituted in. Thus, the following code would result in the Alert panel shown in Figure 15.2:

```
NSInteger choice = NSRunAlertPanel(@"Title", @"Message can have %@",
                                   @"Default", @"Alternate", nil,
                                   @"Format Specifiers");
```

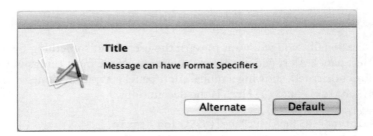

**Figure 15.2**   Another Example Alert Panel

Alert panels run *modally*; that is, other windows in the application don't receive events until the Alert panel has been dismissed.

Alerts can also be run as a sheet.

# Make the User Confirm the Deletion

If the user clicks the Remove button, an Alert panel should appear as a sheet before the records are deleted (Figure 15.3).

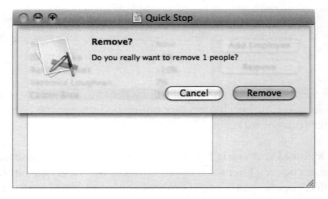

**Figure 15.3**   Completed Application

To enable this behavior, open RMDocument.xib, select the table view, and open the Attributes Inspector. Allow the user to make multiple selections (Figure 15.4).

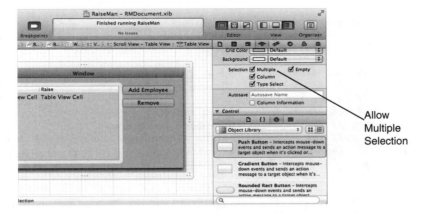

**Figure 15.4**   Inspect Table View

You now want the Remove button to send to **RMDocument** a message which will ask the user to confirm the deletion. If the user confirms this choice, **RMDocument** will send the **removeEmployee:** message to the array controller to remove the selected **Person** objects.

In Xcode, open the RMDocument.h file and add the method that will be triggered by the Remove button:

```
- (IBAction)removeEmployee:(id)sender;
```

In RMDocument.m, implement the removeEmployee: method that will start the Alert panel as a sheet:

```
- (IBAction)removeEmployee:(id)sender
{
    NSArray *selectedPeople = [employeeController selectedObjects];
    NSAlert *alert = [NSAlert alertWithMessageText:
                        @"Do you really want to remove these people?"
                defaultButton:@"Remove"
            alternateButton:@"Cancel"
                otherButton:nil
informativeTextWithFormat:@"%d people will be removed.",
                        [selectedPeople count]];

    NSLog(@"Starting alert sheet");
    [alert beginSheetModalForWindow:[tableView window]
                    modalDelegate:self
                    didEndSelector:@selector(alertEnded:code:context:)
                        contextInfo:NULL];
}
```

This method will start the sheet. When the user clicks a button, the document object will get sent the message **alertEnded:code:context:**

```
- (void)alertEnded:(NSAlert *)alert
           code:(NSInteger)choice
        context:(void *)v
{
    NSLog(@"Alert sheet ended");
    // If the user chose "Remove", tell the array controller to
    // delete the people
    if (choice == NSAlertDefaultReturn) {
        // The argument to remove: is ignored
        // The array controller will delete the selected objects
        [employeeController remove:nil];
    }
}
```

Open `RMDocument.xib`. Control-drag from the Remove button to the File's Owner icon to make the File's Owner be the new `target`. Set the `action` to **removeEmployee:** (Figure 15.5).

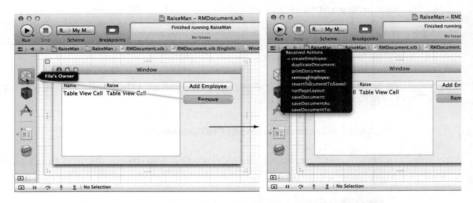

**Figure 15.5**    Change Target and Action of Remove Button

Build and run your application.

# Challenge

Add to the Alert sheet a button that says Keep, but no raise. Instead of deleting the employees, this button will simply set the raises of the selected employees to zero.

# Chapter 16
# LOCALIZATION

If the application you create is useful, you will want to share it with all the people of the world. Unfortunately, we don't all speak the same language. Suppose that you wish to make your RaiseMan application available to French speakers. We would say, "You are going to *localize* RaiseMan for French speakers."

If you are creating an application for the world, you should plan on localizing it for at least the following languages: English, French, Spanish, German, Dutch, Italian, and Japanese. Clearly, you do not want to have to rewrite the entire app for each language. In fact, our goal is to ensure that you don't have to rewrite any Objective-C code for each language. That way, all the nations of the world can use a single executable in peace and harmony.

Instead of creating multiple executables, you will localize resources and create string tables. Inside your project directory, an `en.lproj` directory holds all the resources for English speakers: XIB files, images, and sounds. To localize the app for French speakers, you will add a `fr.lproj` directory. The XIBs, images, and sounds in this directory will be appropriate for French speakers. At runtime, the app will automatically use the version of the resource appropriate to the user's language preference.

What about the places in your application where you use the language programmatically? For example, in `RMDocument.m`, you have the following line of code:

```
NSAlert *alert = [NSAlert alertWithMessageText:
                @"Do you really want to remove these people?"
        defaultButton:@"Remove"
      alternateButton:@"Cancel"
          otherButton:nil
 informativeTextWithFormat:@"%d people will be removed.",
                      [selectedPeople count]];
```

*That* Alert sheet is not going to bring about world peace. For each language, you will have a table of strings. You will ask **NSBundle** to look up the string, and NSBundle will automatically use the version appropriate to the user's language preference (Figure 16.1).

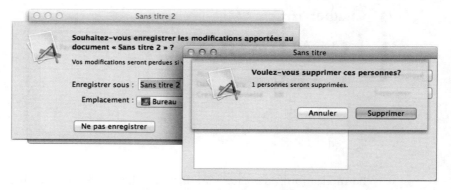

**Figure 16.1**   Completed Application

# Localizing a NIB File

In Xcode, open RMDocument.xib and bring up the File Inspector. Click the + button under the Localization section (Figure 16.2).

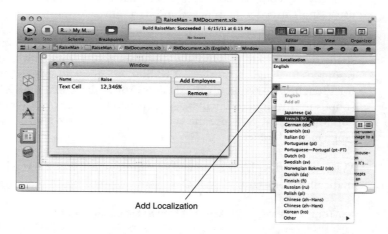

**Figure 16.2**   Create a French Version of RMDocument.xib

You will be prompted for a locale. Choose French.

If you look in Finder, you will see that a copy of en.1proj/RMDocument.xib has been created in fr.1proj. You will francophize this copy. In the Xcode Project Navigator, you will have two versions of RMDocument.xib: English and French, as shown in Figure 16.3. Click on the French version to open it in the editor.

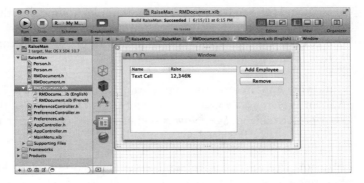

**Figure 16.3**  Two Versions of MainMenu.xib

Make your window look like Figure 16.4.

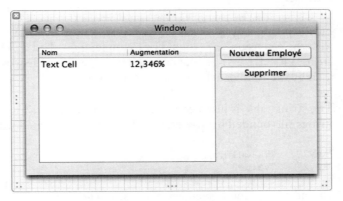

**Figure 16.4**  Completed Interface

To type in characters with accents, you will need to use the Option key. For example, to type é, type the e, while holding down the Option key, and then type e again. In Mac OS X Lion you can also hold down a key for a second to see a popup with its diacritical marks (In the International page of System Preferences, you can add the Keyboard Viewer to your input menu. If you are using a lot of unusual characters, the Keyboard Viewer can help you learn which key combinations create which characters.)

At this point, you have created a localized resource. Note that if you make a lot of changes to your program, you may need to update both XIB files (the French version and the English version). For example, finding that the buttons were too narrow for the French translation, Aaron resized the window accordingly. For this reason, it is a good idea to wait until the application is completed and tested before localizing it.

Build your app. Before running it, bring up the Language & Text page of the System Preferences application. Drag Français to the top of the list to set it as your preferred language. Now run your application. Note that the French version of the NIB is used automatically.

Also note that the document architecture takes care of some localization for you. For example, if you try to close an unsaved document, you will be asked in French whether you want to save the changes.

# String Tables

For each language, you can create several string tables. A string table is a file with the extension .strings. For example, if you had a Find panel, you might create a Find.strings file for each language. This file would have the phrases used by the Find panel, such as "None found."

The string table is just a collection of key-value pairs. The key and the value are strings surrounded by quotes, and the pair is terminated with a semicolon:

```
"Key1" = "Value1";
"Key2" = "Value2";
```

To find a value for a given key, you use **NSBundle**:

```
NSBundle *main;
NSString *aString;

main = [NSBundle mainBundle];
aString = [main localizedStringForKey:@"Key1"
                                value:@"DefaultValue1"
                                table:@"Find"];
```

This would search for the value for "Key1" in the Find.strings file. If it is not found in the user's preferred language, the second-favorite language is searched, and so on. If the key is not found in any of the user's languages, "DefaultValue1" is returned. If you do not supply the name of the table, Localizable is used. Most simple applications just have one string table for each language: Localizable.strings.

# Creating String Tables

To create a `Localizable.strings` file for English speakers, choose the New -> New File... menu item in Xcode. In the Mac OS X Resource category, create a new Strings file, and name it `Localizable.strings`. Save it in the `en.lproj` directory (Figure 16.5).

**Figure 16.5**    Create an English String Table

Edit the new file to have the following text:

```
"REMOVE_MSG" = "Do you really want to remove these people?";
"REMOVE_INF" = "%d people will be removed.";
"REMOVE" = "Remove";
"CANCEL" = "Cancel";
```

Save it. (Don't forget the semicolons!)

Now create a localized version of that file for French. Select the English version of the `Localizable.strings` file in Xcode (it is the only version so far), bring up the File Inspector, and create a localized variant (Figure 16.6).

Edit the file to look like this:

```
"REMOVE_MSG" = "Voulez-vous supprimer ces personnes?";
"REMOVE_INF" = "%d personnes seront supprimées.";
"REMOVE" = "Supprimer";
"CANCEL" = "Annuler";
```

(To create the e with the accent aigu, type e while holding down the Option key, and then type e.)

**Figure 16.6**   Create a French String Table

When saving a file with unusual characters, you should use the Unicode (UTF-8) file encoding. In the File Inspector for fr.lproj/Localizable.strings, ensure that the Text Encoding is set to UTF-8. (If it is not and you are presented with a panel asking whether you wish to convert the file to UTF-8, click the + button labeled Convert.)

Save the file.

## Using the String Table

In an app with just one string table, you would write code like this a lot:

```
NSString *deleteString;
deleteString = [[NSBundle mainBundle]
    localizedStringForKey:@"REMOVE"
                    value:@"Do you want to remove these people?"
                    table:nil];
```

Fortunately, a macro is defined in NSBundle.h for this purpose:

```
#define NSLocalizedString(key, comment)
        [[NSBundle mainBundle] localizedStringForKey:(key)
                                               value:@""
                                               table:nil]
```

(Note that this macro completely ignores the comment. It is, however, used by a tool called `genstrings`, which scans through your code for calls to the macro `NSLocalizedString` and creates a skeleton string table. This string table includes the comment.)

In `RMDocument.m`, find the place where you run the Alert panel. Replace that line with this one:

```
NSAlert *alert = [NSAlert
    alertWithMessageText:NSLocalizedString(@"REMOVE_MSG", @"Remove")
           defaultButton:NSLocalizedString(@"REMOVE", @"Remove")
         alternateButton:NSLocalizedString(@"CANCEL", @"Cancel")
             otherButton:nil
    informativeTextWithFormat:NSLocalizedString(@"REMOVE_INF",
                        @"%d people will be removed."),
                    [selectedPeople count]];
```

Build the app. Change your preferred language back to French in System Preferences, and run the app again. When you delete a row from the table, you should get an Alert panel in French.

# For the More Curious: ibtool

Clearly, as you develop and localize many applications, you will develop a set of common translations. It would be handy to have an automated way to get the translated strings into a XIB file. This is one of several uses for `ibtool`.

The `ibtool` command, which is run from the terminal, can list the classes or objects in a XIB and can also dump the localizable strings into a `plist`. Here is how you would dump the localizable strings from the `en.lproj/RMDocument.xib` file into a file named `Doc.strings`:

```
> cd RaiseMan/en.lproj
> ibtool --generate-stringsfile Doc.strings RMDocument.xib
```

The resulting `Doc.strings` file would have a bunch of entries something like this:

```
/* Class="NSTableColumn";headerCell.title="Name";ObjectID="100026"; */
"100026.headerCell.title" = "Name";
```

To create a Spanish dictionary for this XIB file, you could edit the file to have Spanish entries:

```
/* Class="NSTableColumn";headerCell.title="Name";ObjectID="100026"; */
"100026.headerCell.title" = "Nombre";
```

To substitute the strings in a XIB file with their Spanish equivalents from this dictionary, you could create a new NIB file like this:

```
> mkdir ../es.lproj
> ibtool --strings-file Doc.strings
        --write ../es.lproj/RMDocument.xib RMDocument.xib
```

To learn more about ibtool, use Unix's man command:

```
> man ibtool
```

# For the More Curious: Explicit Ordering of Tokens in Format Strings

As text is moved from language to language, both the words and the order of the words change. For example, the words in one language may be laid out like this: "Ted wants a scooter." In another, the order might be "A scooter is what Ted wants." Suppose that you try to localize the format string to be used like this:

```
NSString * theFormat = NSLocalizedString(@"WANTS", @"%@ wants a %@");
x = [NSString stringWithFormat:theFormat, @"Ted", @"Scooter"];
```

The following will work fine for the first language:

```
"WANTS" = "%@ wants a %@";
```

For the second language, you would need to explicitly indicate the index of the token you want to insert. This is done with a number and the dollar sign:

```
"WANTS =  "A %2$@ is what %1$@ wants".
```

# Chapter 17

# CUSTOM VIEWS

All visible objects in an application are either windows or views. In this chapter, you will create a subclass of **NSView**. From time to time, you may need to create a custom view to do custom drawing or event handling. Even if you do not plan to do custom drawing or event handling, you will learn a lot about how Cocoa works by learning how to create a new view class.

Windows are instances of the class **NSWindow**. Each window has a collection of views, each of which is responsible for a rectangle of the window. The view draws inside that rectangle and handles mouse events that occur there. A view may also handle keyboard events. You have worked with several subclasses of **NSView** already: **NSButton**, **NSTextField**, **NSTableView**, and **NSColorWell** are all views. (Note that a window is not a subclass of **NSView**.)

## The View Hierarchy

Views are arranged in a hierarchy (Figure 17.1). The window has a content view that completely fills its interior. The content view usually has several subviews. Each subview may have subviews of its own. Every view knows its superview, its subviews, and the window it lives on.

Here are the relevant methods from **NSView**:

```
- (NSView *)superview;
- (NSArray *)subviews;
- (NSWindow *)window;
```

Any view can have subviews, but most don't. The following five views commonly have subviews:

1. The content view of a window.

2. **NSBox**. The contents of a box are its subviews.

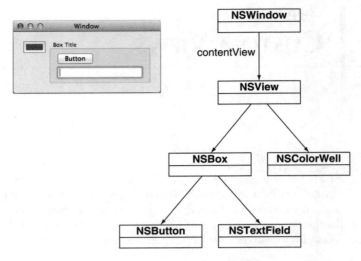

**Figure 17.1** Views Hierarchy

3. **NSScrollView.** A view that appears in a scroll view is a subview of the scroll view. The scroll bars are also subviews of the scroll view.

4. **NSSplitView.** Each view in a split view is a subview (Figure 17.2).

**Figure 17.2** A Scroll View in a Split View

5. **NSTabView.** As the user chooses different tabs, different subviews are swapped in and out (Figure 17.3).

**Figure 17.3**    A Tab View

# Get a View to Draw Itself

In this section, you will create a very simple view that will appear and paint itself green. It will look like Figure 17.4, except greener.

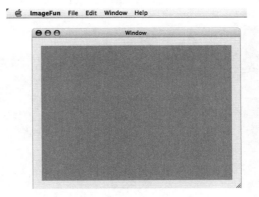

**Figure 17.4**    Completed Application

Create a new project of type Cocoa Application. Name it DrawingFun, and set the Class Prefix to DrawingFun. Turn off Create Document-Based Application, Use Core Data, and Include Unit Tests.

Using the File->New->New File... menu item, create a new Objective-C class that is an NSView subclass, and name it `StretchView`.

## Create an Instance of a View Subclass

Open `MainMenu.xib` and click the window in the editor dock to show it. Create an instance of your class by dragging out a Custom View from the Library (under Cocoa -> Layout Views) and dropping it onto the window (Figure 17.5).

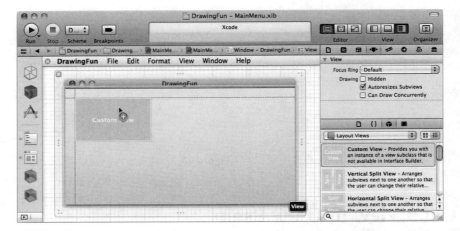

**Figure 17.5**    Drop a View onto the Window

Resize the view to fill most of the window. Open the Identity Inspector and set the class of the view to be **StretchView** (Figure 17.6).

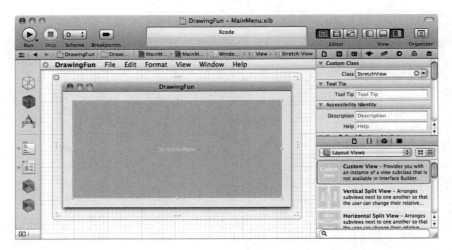

**Figure 17.6**    Set the Class of the View to StretchView

## Size Inspector

Your **StretchView** object is a subview of the window's content view. This point raises an interesting question: What happens to the view when the superview resizes? The Size Inspector allows you to specify that behavior. Open the Size Inspector, and make all the lines inside the Autosizing view red, as shown in Figure 17.7. Now the view will grow and shrink as necessary to keep the distance from its edges to the edges of its superview constant.

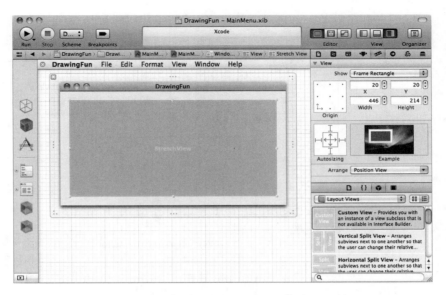

**Figure 17.7**  Make the View Resize with the Window

If you wanted the view to stay the same height, you could let the distance between the bottom of the view and the bottom of the superview grow and shrink. You could also let the distance between the right edge of the view and the right edge of the window grow and shrink. In this exercise, you do not want this behavior. But in a parallel universe where you did want the view to stick to the upper-left corner of the window, the inspector would look like Figure 17.8.

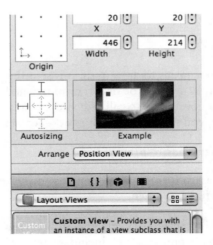

**Figure 17.8**  Don't Do This—This View Will Not Resize with the Window

Figure 17.9 is a complete diagram of what the red lines in the Size Inspector mean.

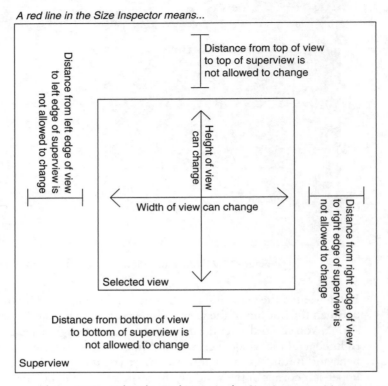

**Figure 17.9**    What the Red Lines in the Size Inspector Mean

## drawRect

When a view needs to draw itself, it is sent the message **drawRect:** with the rectangle that needs to be drawn or redrawn. The method is called automatically—you never need to call it directly. Instead, if you know that a view needs redrawing, you send the view the **setNeedsDisplay:** message:

```
[myView setNeedsDisplay:YES];
```

This message informs myView that it is "dirty." After the event has been handled, the view will be redrawn.

Before calling **drawRect:**, the system *locks focus* on the view. Each view has its own graphics context, which includes the view's coordinate system, its current color, its current font, and the clipping rectangle. When the focus is locked on a view, the view's graphics context is active. When the focus is unlocked, the graphics context is no longer active. Whenever you issue drawing commands, they will be executed in the current graphics context.

You can use **NSBezierPath** to draw lines, circles, curves, and rectangles. You can use **NSImage** to create composite images on the view. In this example, you will fill the entire view with a green rectangle.

Open StretchView.m and add the following code to the **drawRect:** method:

```
- (void)drawRect:(NSRect)dirtyRect
{
    NSRect bounds = [self bounds];
    [[NSColor greenColor] set];
    [NSBezierPath fillRect:bounds];
}
```

As shown in Figure 17.10, NSRect is a struct with two members: origin, which is an NSPoint, and size, which is an NSSize.

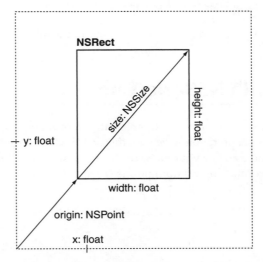

**Figure 17.10**   NSRect, NSSize, and NSPoint

NSSize is a struct with two members: width and height (both floats).

NSPoint is a struct with two members: x and y (both floats).

For performance reasons, structs are used in a few places instead of Objective-C classes. For completeness, here is the list of all the Cocoa structs that you are likely to use: NSSize, NSPoint, NSRect, NSRange, NSDecimal, and

NSAffineTransformStruct. NSRange is used to define subranges. NSDecimal describes numbers with very specific precision and rounding behavior. NSAffine-TransformStruct describes linear transformations of graphics.

Note that your view knows its dimensions as an NSRect called bounds. In this method, you fetched the bounds rectangle, set the current color to green, and filled the entire bounds rectangle with the current color.

The NSRect that is passed as an argument to the view is the region that is "dirty" and needs redrawing. It may be less than the entire view. If you are doing very time-consuming drawing, redrawing only the dirty rectangle may speed up your application considerably.

Note that **setNeedsDisplay:** will trigger the entire visible region of the view to be redrawn. If you wanted to be more precise about which part of the view needs redrawing, you would use **setNeedsDisplayInRect:** instead:

```
NSRect dirtyRect;
dirtyRect = NSMakeRect(0, 0, 50, 50);
[myView setNeedsDisplayInRect:dirtyRect];
```

Build and run your app. Try resizing the window.

# Drawing with NSBezierPath

If you want to draw lines, ovals, curves, or polygons, you can use **NSBezierPath**. In this chapter, you have already used the **NSBezierPath**'s **fillRect:** class method to color your view. In this section, you will use **NSBezierPath** to draw lines connecting random points (Figure 17.11).

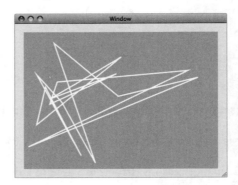

**Figure 17.11**    Completed Application

The first thing you will need is an instance variable to hold the instance of
**NSBezierPath**. You will also create an instance method that returns a random
point in the view. Open StretchView.h and make it look like this:

```
#import <Cocoa/Cocoa.h>

@interface StretchView : NSView {
    NSBezierPath *path;
}
- (NSPoint)randomPoint;

@end
```

In StretchView.m, you will override **initWithFrame:**. As the designated
initializer for **NSView**, **initWithFrame:** will be called automatically when an
instance of your view is created. In your version of **initWithFrame:**, you will
create the path object and fill it with lines to random points. Make
StretchView.m look like this:

```
#import "StretchView.h"

@implementation StretchView

- (id)initWithFrame:(NSRect)frame
{
    self = [super initWithFrame:frame];
    if (self) {
        // Seed the random number generator
        srandom((unsigned)time(NULL));

        // Create a path object
        path = [NSBezierPath bezierPath];
        [path setLineWidth:3.0];
        NSPoint p = [self randomPoint];
        [path moveToPoint:p];
        int i;
        for (i = 0; i < 15; i++) {
            p = [self randomPoint];
            [path lineToPoint:p];
        }
        [path closePath];
    }
    return self;
}

// randomPoint returns a random point inside the view
- (NSPoint)randomPoint
{
    NSPoint result;
    NSRect r = [self bounds];
    result.x = r.origin.x + random() % (int)r.size.width;
    result.y = r.origin.y + random() % (int)r.size.height;
    return result;
}
```

```
- (void)drawRect:(NSRect)rect
{
    NSRect bounds = [self bounds];

    // Fill the view with green
    [[NSColor greenColor] set];
    [NSBezierPath fillRect: bounds];

    // Draw the path in white
    [[NSColor whiteColor] set];
    [path stroke];
}

@end
```

Build and run your app. Pretty, eh?

OK, now try replacing [path stroke] with [path fill]. Build and run it.

# NSScrollView

In the art world, a larger work is typically more expensive than a smaller one of equal quality. Your beautiful view is lovely, but it would be more valuable if it were larger. How can it be larger, yet still fit inside that tiny window? You are going to put it in a scroll view (Figure 17.12).

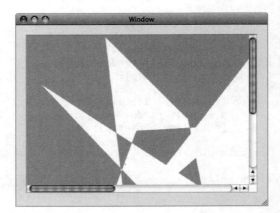

**Figure 17.12**   Completed Application

A scroll view has three parts: the document view, the content view, and the scroll bars. In this example, your view will become the document and will be displayed in the content view, which is an instance of **NSClipView**.

It looks tricky, but this change is very simple to make. In fact, it requires no code at all. Open `MainMenu.xib` in Interface Builder. Select the view, and choose Embed -> Scroll View from the Editor menu (Figure 17.13).

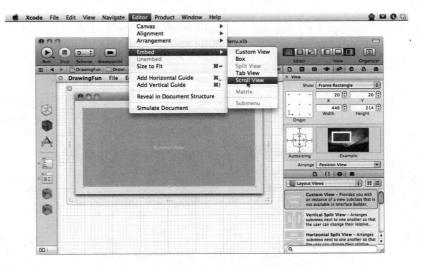

**Figure 17.13**     Embed StretchView in a Scroll View

As the window resizes, you want the scroll view to resize, but you do not want your document to resize. Open the Size Inspector, select the scroll view, and set the Size Inspector so that it resizes with the window (Figure 17.14).

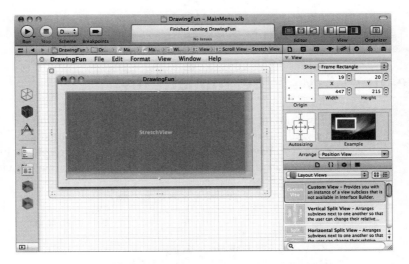

**Figure 17.14**     Make Scroll View Resize with Window

Note the width and height of the view.

To select the document view, double-click inside the scroll view. You should see the title in the rightmost part of the jump bar change to Stretch View. Make the view about twice as wide and twice as tall as the scroll view. Set the Size Inspector so that the view will stick to the lower-left corner of its superview and not resize (Figure 17.15). Build the application and run it.

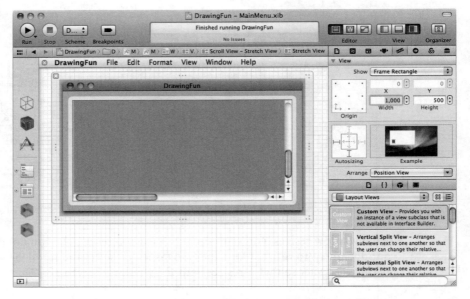

**Figure 17.15**   Make StretchView Larger and Nonresizing

# Creating Views Programmatically

You will instantiate most of your views in the Interface Builder editor. Every once in a while, you will need to create views programmatically. For example, assume that you have a pointer to a window and want to put a button on it. This code would create a button and put it on the window's content view:

```
NSView *superview = [window contentView];
NSRect frame = NSMakeRect(10, 10, 200, 100);
NSButton *button = [[NSButton alloc] initWithFrame:frame];
[button setTitle:@"Click me!"];
[superview addSubview:button];
```

# For the More Curious: Cells

**NSControl** inherits from **NSView**. **NSView** (with its graphics context) is a relatively large and expensive object to create. When the **NSButton** class was created, the first thing someone did was to create a calculator with ten rows and ten columns of buttons. The performance was less than it could have been, because of the 100 tiny views. Later, someone had the clever idea of moving the brains of the button into another object (not a view) and creating one big view (called an **NSMatrix**) that would act as the view for all 100 button brains. The class for the button brains was called **NSButtonCell** (Figure 17.16).

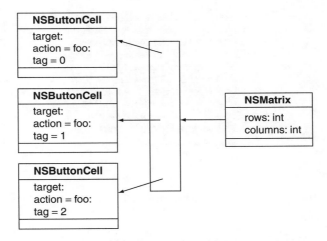

**Figure 17.16**  NSMatrix

In the end, **NSButton** became just a view that had an **NSButtonCell**. The button cell does everything, and **NSButton** simply claims a space in the window (Figure 17.17).

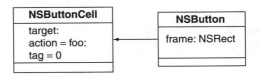

**Figure 17.17**  NSButton and NSButtonCell

Similarly, **NSSlider** is a view with an **NSSliderCell**, and **NSTextField** is a view with an **NSTextFieldCell**. By contrast, **NSColorWell** has no cell.

To create an instance of **NSMatrix** in the Interface Builder editor, drop a control with a cell onto the window, choose Editor -> Embed In -> Matrix, and then Option-drag the size handles until the matrix has the correct number of rows and columns (Figure 17.18).

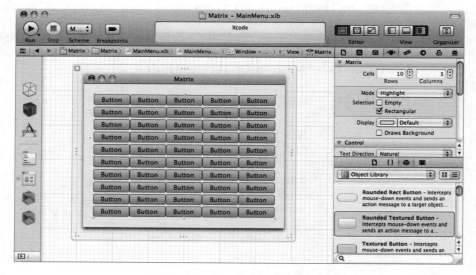

**Figure 17.18**    A Matrix of Buttons

An **NSMatrix** has a target and an action. A cell may also have a target and an action. If the cell is activated, the cell's target and action are used. If the target and action of the selected cell are not set, the matrix's target and action will be used.

When dealing with matrices, you will often ask which cell was activated. Cells can also be given a tag:

```
- (IBAction)myAction:(id)sender {
    id theCell = [sender selectedCell];
    int theTag = [theCell tag];
    ...
}
```

The cell's tag can be set in Interface Builder.

Cells are used in several other types of objects. The data in a cell-based **NSTableView**, for example, is drawn by cells.

# For the More Curious: isFlipped

Both PDF and PostScript use the standard Cartesian coordinate system, whereby *y* increases as you move up the page. Quartz follows this model by default. The origin is usually at the lower-left corner of the view.

For some types of drawing, the math becomes easier if the upper-left corner is the origin and *y* increases as you move down the page. We say that such a view is *flipped*.

To flip a view, you override **isFlipped** in your view class to return YES:

```
- (BOOL)isFlipped
{
    return YES;
}
```

While we are discussing the coordinate system, note that *x*- and *y*-coordinates are measured in *points*. A point is typically defined as "72.0 points = 1 inch." In reality, by default "1.0 point = 1 pixel" on your screen. You can, however, change the size of a point by changing the coordinate system:

```
// Make everything in the view twice as large
NSSize newScale;
newScale.width = 2.0;
newScale.height = 2.0;
[myView scaleUnitSquareToSize:newScale];
[myView setNeedsDisplay:YES];
```

# Challenge

**NSBezierPath** can also draw Bezier curves. Replace the straight lines with randomly curved ones. (*Hint:* Look in the documentation for **NSBezierPath**.)

## Chapter 18

# IMAGES AND MOUSE EVENTS

In the previous chapter, you drew lines connecting random points. A more interesting project would have been to write a drawing application. To write this sort of application, you will need to be able to get and handle mouse events.

## NSResponder

**NSView** inherits from **NSResponder**. All the event-handling methods are declared in **NSResponder**. We will discuss keyboard events in the next chapter. For now, we are interested just in mouse events. **NSResponder** declares these methods:

```
- (void)mouseDown:(NSEvent *)theEvent;
- (void)rightMouseDown:(NSEvent *)theEvent;
- (void)otherMouseDown:(NSEvent *)theEvent;

- (void)mouseUp:(NSEvent *)theEvent;
- (void)rightMouseUp:(NSEvent *)theEvent;
- (void)otherMouseUp:(NSEvent *)theEvent;

- (void)mouseDragged:(NSEvent *)theEvent;
- (void)scrollWheel:(NSEvent *)theEvent;
- (void)rightMouseDragged:(NSEvent *)theEvent;
- (void)otherMouseDragged:(NSEvent *)theEvent;
```

Notice that the argument is always an **NSEvent** object.

## NSEvent

An event object has all the information about what the user did to trigger the event. When you are dealing with mouse events, you might be interested in the following methods:

```
- (NSPoint)locationInWindow
```

Returns the location of the mouse event.

```
- (NSUInteger)modifierFlags
```

Tells you which modifier keys the user is holding down on the keyboard. This enables the programmer to tell a Control-click from a Shift-click, for example. The code would look like this:

```
- (void)mouseDown:(NSEvent *)e
{
    NSUInteger flags;
    flags = [e modifierFlags];
    if (flags & NSControlKeyMask) {
        ...handle control click...
    }
    if (flags & NSShiftKeyMask) {
        ...handle shift click...
    }
}
```

Here are the constants that you commonly AND (&) against the modifier flags:

```
NSShiftKeyMask

NSControlKeyMask

NSAlternateKeyMask

NSCommandKeyMask
```

```
- (NSTimeInterval)timestamp
```

Gives the time interval in seconds between the time the machine booted and the time of the event. NSTimeInterval is a `double`.

```
- (NSWindow *)window
```

Returns the window associated with the event.

```
- (NSInteger)clickCount
```

Indicates whether the click was single, double, or triple.

```
- (float)pressure
```

Returns the pressure if the user is using an input device that gives pressure (a tablet, for example). It is between 0 and 1.

```
- (float)deltaX;
- (float)deltaY;
- (float)deltaZ;
```

Give the change in the position of the mouse or scroll wheel.

# Getting Mouse Events

To get mouse events, you need to override the mouse event methods in
`StretchView.m`:

```
#pragma mark Events

- (void)mouseDown:(NSEvent *)event
{
    NSLog(@"mouseDown: %ld", [event clickCount]);
}

- (void)mouseDragged:(NSEvent *)event
{
    NSPoint p = [event locationInWindow];
    NSLog(@"mouseDragged:%@", NSStringFromPoint(p));
}

- (void)mouseUp:(NSEvent *)event
{
    NSLog(@"mouseUp:");
}
```

Build and run your application. Try double-clicking, and check the click count.
Note that the first click is sent and then the second click. The first click has a
click count of 1; the second click has a click count of 2.

Note the use of `#pragma mark`. The jump bar at the top of any Xcode editing
window enables you to jump to any of the declarations and definitions in the file;
`#pragma mark` puts a label into that pop-up. Stylish programmers (like you, dear
reader) use it to group their methods.

# Using NSOpenPanel

It would be fun to composite an image onto the view, but first you need to create
a controller object that will read the image data from a file. This is a good
opportunity to learn how to use **NSOpenPanel**. Note that the RaiseMan
application used **NSOpenPanel**, but it was done automatically by the **NSDocument**
class. Here you will use **NSOpenPanel** explicitly. Figure 18.1 shows what your
application will look like once the user has chosen an image. The slider at the
bottom of the window will control how opaque the image is.

Figure 18.2 shows the object diagram.

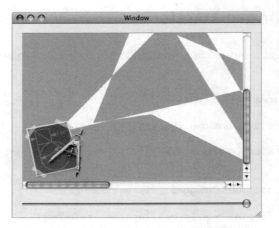

**Figure 18.1**  Completed Application

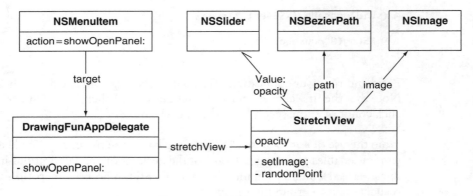

**Figure 18.2**  Object Diagram

# Change the XIB File

Open the DrawingFun project from Chapter 17. In DrawingFunAppDelegate.h, add an outlet for the **StretchView** and an action that will start the Open panel:

```
#import <Cocoa/Cocoa.h>
@class StretchView;

@interface DrawingFunAppDelegate : NSObject <NSApplicationDelegate> {
    IBOutlet StretchView *stretchView;
}
@property (strong) IBOutlet NSWindow *window;
- (IBAction)showOpenPanel:(id)sender;
@end
```

Open `MainMenu.xib` and bring up our drawing window. Drop a slider onto the window. In the Inspector, set its range from 0 to 1. Also, check the box labeled Continuous. This slider will control how opaque the image is (Figure 18.3).

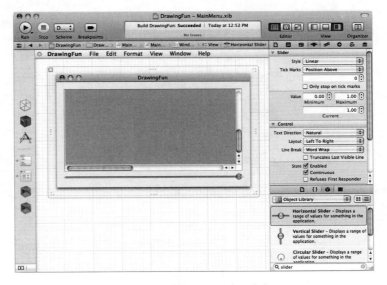

**Figure 18.3**    Inspect the Slider

Switch to the Size Inspector and configure the slider to stretch horizontally and maintain the left, right, and bottom margins (Figure 18.4). This will make the slider resize appropriately with the window.

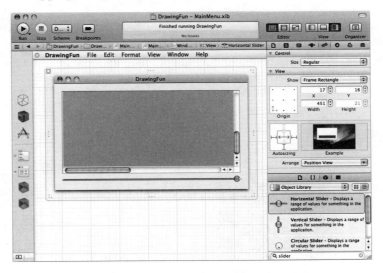

**Figure 18.4**    Configure the Slider's Autoresizing

Bind the value of the slider to the app delegate's `stretchView.opacity` key path.

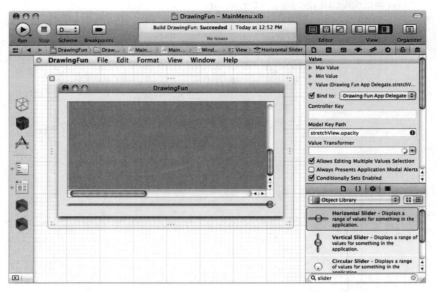

**Figure 18.5** Bind the Slider's Value

Control-click on the **DrawingFunAppDelegate**. Connect the `stretchView` outlet to the **StretchView** on the window (Figure 18.6).

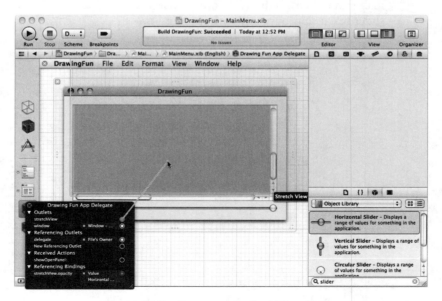

**Figure 18.6** Connect the stretchView Outlet

Look at the main menu in your XIB. Open the File menu and delete all menu items except Open. Control-drag to connect the menu item to the **DrawingFunAppDelegate**'s **showOpenPanel:** action (Figure 18.7). Save the file.

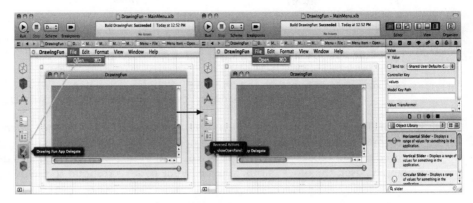

**Figure 18.7**    Connect the Menu Item

# Edit the Code

Edit DrawingFunAppDelegate.m to read as follows. Note that there's some new syntax, called a block, in this method. We'll discuss blocks in detail in Chapter 29. Note that you may see a warning that **StretchView** may not respond to **setImage:**; this is fine for now. We will fix it in the next section.

```
#import "DrawingFunAppDelegate.h"
#import "StretchView.h"

@implementation DrawingFunAppDelegate

@synthesize window;

- (IBAction)showOpenPanel:(id)sender
{
    __block NSOpenPanel *panel = [NSOpenPanel openPanel];
    [panel setAllowedFileTypes:[NSImage imageFileTypes]];

    [panel beginSheetModalForWindow:[stretchView window]
              completionHandler:^ (NSInteger result) {

        if (result == NSOKButton) {
            NSImage *image = [[NSImage alloc]
                                initWithContentsOfURL:[panel URL]];
```

```
                    [stretchView setImage:image];
            }
            panel = nil; // prevent strong ref cycle
    }];
}

@end
```

The line where you start the sheet is a very handy method:

```
- (void)beginSheetModalForWindow:(NSWindow *)window
              completionHandler:(void (^)(NSInteger result))handler
```

This method brings up an Open panel as a sheet attached to the window. The second parameter, handler, is the block. The block syntax takes some getting used to, but blocks are a very powerful tool. When the Open panel is dismissed by the user, the block is run, allowing your code to respond to the user's actions.

# Composite an Image onto Your View

You will also need to change **StretchView** so that it uses the opacity and image. First, declare variables and methods in your StretchView.h file:

```
#import <Cocoa/Cocoa.h>

@interface StretchView : NSView
{
    NSBezierPath *path;
    NSImage *image;
    float opacity;
}
@property (assign) float opacity;
@property (strong) NSImage *image;
- (NSPoint)randomPoint;

@end
```

Now implement these methods in your StretchView.m file:

```
#pragma mark Accessors

- (NSImage *)image
{
    return image;
}
- (void)setImage:(NSImage *)newImage
{
    image = newImage;
    [self setNeedsDisplay:YES];
}
```

```
- (float)opacity
{
    return opacity;
}

- (void)setOpacity:(float)x
{
    opacity = x;
    [self setNeedsDisplay:YES];
}
```

At the end of each of the methods, you inform the view that it needs to redraw itself. Near the end of the **initWithFrame:** method, set opacity to be 1.0:

```
        [path closePath];
        opacity = 1.0;
    }
    return self;
}
```

Also in StretchView.m, you need to add compositing of the image to the **drawRect:** method:

```
- (void)drawRect:(NSRect)rect
{
    NSRect bounds = [self bounds];
    [[NSColor greenColor] set];
    [NSBezierPath fillRect:bounds];
    [[NSColor whiteColor] set];
    [path fill];
    if (image) {
        NSRect imageRect;
        imageRect.origin = NSZeroPoint;
        imageRect.size = [image size];
        NSRect drawingRect = imageRect;
        [image drawInRect:drawingRect
                 fromRect:imageRect
                operation:NSCompositeSourceOver
                 fraction:opacity];
    }
}
```

Note that the **drawInRect:fromRect:operation:fraction:** method composites the image onto the view. The fraction determines the image's opacity.

Build and run your application. You will find a few images in /Developer/ Examples/Sketch . When you open an image, it will appear in the lower-left corner of your **StretchView** object.

# The View's Coordinate System

The final bit of fun comes from being able to choose the location and dimensions of the image, based on the user's dragging. The mouse down will indicate one corner of the rectangle where the image will appear, and the mouse up will indicate the opposite corner. The final application will look something like Figure 18.8.

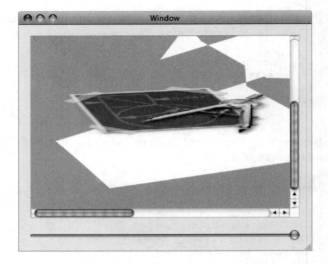

**Figure 18.8**   Completed Application

Each view has its own coordinate system. By default, (0, 0) is in the lower-left corner. This is consistent with PDF and PostScript. You can change the coordinate system of the view if you wish. You can move the origin, change the scale, or rotate the coordinates. The window also has a coordinate system.

If you have two views, a and b, and you need to translate an NSPoint pb from b's coordinate system to a's coordinate system, it would look like this:

```
NSPoint pa = [a convertPoint:pb fromView:b];
```

If b is nil, the point is converted from the window's coordinate system.

Mouse events have their locations in the window's coordinate system, so you will nearly always have to convert the point to the local coordinate system. You are going to create variables to hold onto the corners of the rectangle where the image will be drawn.

Add these instance variables to StretchView.h:

```
NSPoint downPoint;
NSPoint currentPoint;
```

The location of the **mouseDown:** will be downPoint and currentPoint will be updated by **mouseDragged:** and **mouseUp:**.

Edit the mouse-event-handling methods in StretchView.m to update downPoint and currentPoint:

```
- (void)mouseDown:(NSEvent *)event
{
    NSPoint p = [event locationInWindow];
    downPoint = [self convertPoint:p fromView:nil];
    currentPoint = downPoint;
    [self setNeedsDisplay:YES];
}

- (void)mouseDragged:(NSEvent *)event
{
    NSPoint p = [event locationInWindow];
    currentPoint = [self convertPoint:p fromView:nil];
    [self setNeedsDisplay:YES];
}

- (void)mouseUp:(NSEvent *)event
{
    NSPoint p = [event locationInWindow];
    currentPoint = [self convertPoint:p fromView:nil];
    [self setNeedsDisplay:YES];
}
```

Add a method to calculate the rectangle based on the two points:

```
- (NSRect)currentRect
{
    float minX = MIN(downPoint.x, currentPoint.x);
    float maxX = MAX(downPoint.x, currentPoint.x);
    float minY = MIN(downPoint.y, currentPoint.y);
    float maxY = MAX(downPoint.y, currentPoint.y);

    return NSMakeRect(minX, minY, maxX-minX, maxY-minY);
}
```

(For some reason, many people mistype that last method. Look at yours once more before going on. If you get it wrong, the results are disappointing.)

Declare the **currentRect** method in StretchView.h.

So that the user will see something even if he or she has not dragged, initialize downPoint and currentPoint in the **setImage:** method:

```
- (void)setImage:(NSImage *)newImage
{
    image = newImage;
    NSSize imageSize = [newImage size];
    downPoint = NSZeroPoint;
    currentPoint.x = downPoint.x + imageSize.width;
    currentPoint.y = downPoint.y + imageSize.height;
    [self setNeedsDisplay:YES];
}
```

In the **drawRect:** method, composite the image inside the rectangle:

```
- (void)drawRect:(NSRect)rect
{
    NSRect bounds = [self bounds];
    [[NSColor greenColor] set];
    [NSBezierPath fillRect:bounds];
    [[NSColor whiteColor] set];
    [path stroke];
    if (image) {
        NSRect imageRect;
        imageRect.origin = NSZeroPoint;
        imageRect.size = [image size];
        NSRect drawingRect = [self currentRect];
        [image drawInRect:drawingRect
                 fromRect:imageRect
                operation:NSCompositeSourceOver
                 fraction:opacity];
    }
}
```

Build and run your application. Note that the view doesn't scroll when you drag past the edge. It would be nice if the scroll view would move to allow users to see where they have dragged to, a technique known as *autoscrolling*. In the next section, you will add autoscrolling to your application.

# Autoscrolling

To add autoscrolling to your application, you will send the message **autoscroll:** to the clip view when the user drags. You will include the event as an argument. Open StretchView.m and add the following line to the **mouseDragged:** method:

```
- (void)mouseDragged:(NSEvent *)event
{
    NSPoint p = [event locationInWindow];
    currentPoint = [self convertPoint:p fromView:nil];
    [self autoscroll:event];
    [self setNeedsDisplay:YES];
}
```

Build and run your application.

Note that autoscrolling happens only as you drag. For smoother autoscrolling, most developers will create a timer that sends the view the **autoscroll:** method periodically while the user is dragging. Timers are discussed in Chapter 24.

# For the More Curious: NSImage

In most cases, it suffices to read in an image, resize it, and composite it onto a view, as you did in this exercise.

An **NSImage** object has an array of representations. For example, your image might be a drawing of a cow. That drawing can be in PDF, a color bitmap, and a black-and-white bitmap. Each of these versions is an instance of a subclass of **NSImageRep**. You can add representations to and remove representations from your image. When you sit down to rewrite Adobe Photoshop, you will be manipulating the image representations.

Here is a list of the subclasses of **NSImageRep**:

- **NSBitmapImageRep**

- **NSEPSImageRep**

- **NSCachedImageRep**

- **NSCustomImageRep**

- **NSPDFImageRep**

Although **NSImageRep** has only five subclasses, it is important to note that **NSImage** knows how to read dozens of image formats, including all the common formats: PNG, JPEG, PDF, GIF, BMP, TIFF and so on.

# Challenge

Create a new document-based application that allows the user to draw ovals in arbitrary locations and sizes. **NSBezierPath** has the following method:

```
+ (NSBezierPath *)bezierPathWithOvalInRect:(NSRect)rect;
```

If you are feeling ambitious, add the ability to save and read files.

If you are feeling extra ambitious, add undo capabilities.

## Chapter 19
# KEYBOARD EVENTS

When the user types, where are the corresponding events sent? First, the window manager gets the event and forwards it to the active application. The active application forwards the keyboard events to the key window. The key window forwards the event to the "active" view. Which view, then, is the active one? Each window has an outlet called firstResponder that points to one view of that window. That view is the "active" one for that window. For example, when you click on a text field, it becomes the firstResponder of that window (Figure 19.1).

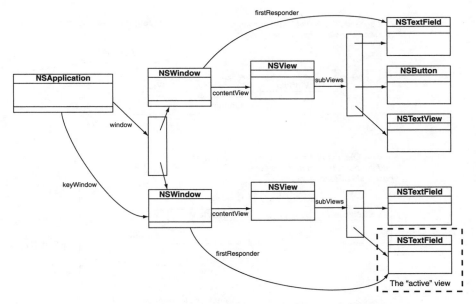

**Figure 19.1**    The First Responder of the Key Window Is "Active"

When the user tries to change the firstResponder to another view (by tabbing or clicking the other view), the views go through a certain ritual before the firstResponder outlet is changed. First, the view that may become the firstResponder is asked whether it accepts first-responder status. A return of NO means that the view is not interested in keyboard events. For example, you can't type into a slider, so it refuses to accept first-responder status. If the view does accept first-responder status, the view that is currently the first responder is asked whether it resigns its role as the first responder. If the editing is not done, the view can refuse to give up first-responder status. For example, if the user had not typed in his or her entire phone number, the text field could refuse to resign this status. Finally, the view is told that it is becoming the first responder. Often, this triggers a change in its appearance (Figure 19.2).

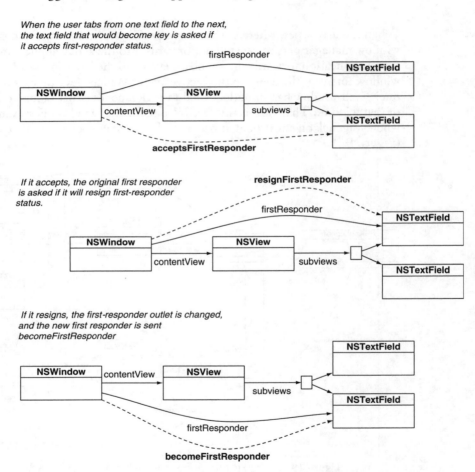

**Figure 19.2**   Becoming the First Responder

Note that each window has its own first responder. Several windows may be open, but only the first responder of the key window gets the keyboard events.

# NSResponder

We are interested in the following methods that are inherited from
**NSResponder**:

- (BOOL)acceptsFirstResponder

Overridden by a subclass to return YES if it handles keyboard events.

- (BOOL)resignFirstResponder

Asks whether the receiver is willing to give up first-responder status.

- (BOOL)becomeFirstResponder

Notifies the receiver that it has become first responder in its **NSWindow**.

- (void)keyDown:(NSEvent *)theEvent

Informs the receiver that the user has pressed a key.

- (void)keyUp:(NSEvent *)theEvent

Informs the receiver that the user has released a key.

- (void)flagsChanged:(NSEvent *)theEvent

Informs the receiver that the user has pressed or released a modifier key
(Shift, Control, or so on).

# NSEvent

We discussed **NSEvent** in terms of mouse events in the previous chapter. Here
are some of the methods commonly used when getting information about a
keyboard event:

- (NSString *)characters

Returns the characters created by the event.

- (BOOL)isARepeat

Returns YES if the key event is a repeat caused by the users holding the key
down; returns NO if the key event is new.

```
- (unsigned short)keyCode
```

Returns the code for the keyboard key that caused the event.

```
- (NSUInteger)modifierFlags
```

Returns an integer bit field indicating the modifier keys in effect for the receiver. For information about what the bits of the integer mean, refer to the discussion in Chapter 18.

# Create a New Project with a Custom View

Create a new project of type Cocoa Application. Name it TypingTutor and set the Class Prefix to TypingTutor.

In Xcode, create an Objective-C class that is a subclass of NSView subclass, and name it **BigLetterView**.

## Lay Out the Interface

Open MainMenu.xib and click on the TypingTutor window in the dock to open it. Create an instance of your class by dragging out a Custom View (under Cocoa -> Layout Views) and dropping it onto the window (Figure 19.3).

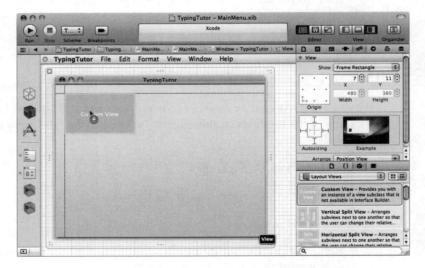

**Figure 19.3**    Drop a View onto the Window

In the Identity Inspector, set the class of the view to be **BigLetterView** (Figure 19.4).

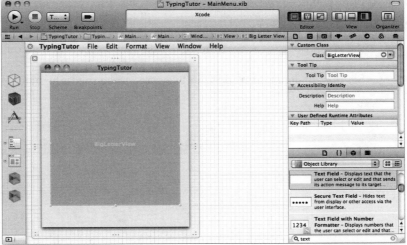

**Figure 19.4**    Set the Class of the View to BigLetterView

Drop two text fields (under Cocoa -> Controls) onto the window (Figure 19.5).

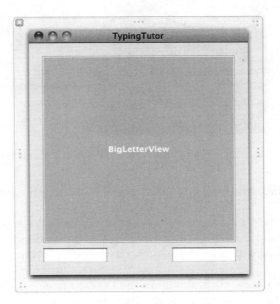

**Figure 19.5**    Completed Interface

## Make Connections

Now you need to create the loop of key views for your window. That is, you are setting the order in which the views will be selected as the user tabs from one element to the next. The order will be the text field on the left, the text field on the right, the **BigLetterView**, and then back to the text field on the left.

Set the left-hand text field's nextKeyView to be the right-hand text field (Figure 19.6).

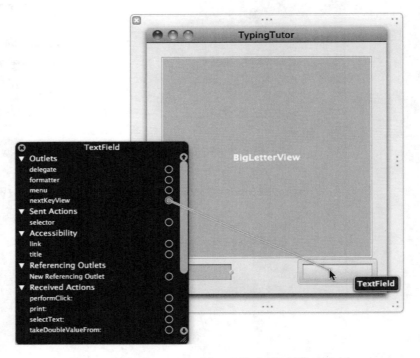

**Figure 19.6**    Set nextKeyView of Left-Hand Text Field

Set the right-hand text field's nextKeyView to be the **BigLetterView** (Figure 19.7).

Finally, set the nextKeyView of the **BigLetterView** to be the left-hand text field (Figure 19.8). This will enable the user to tab between the three views. Shift-tabbing will move the selection in the opposite direction.

Which view, then, should be the firstResponder when the window first appears? To make the **BigLetterView** the initialFirstResponder of the window, Control-click on the title bar of the window in the editor to see

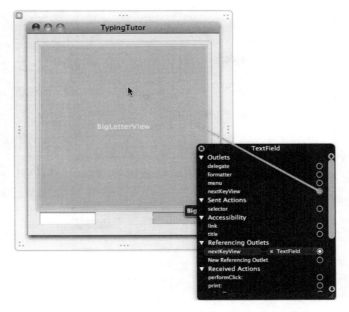

**Figure 19.7**    Set nextKeyView of Right-Hand Text Field

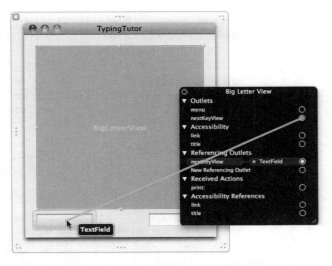

**Figure 19.8**    Set nextKeyView of the BigLetterView

the Connection panel, then drag from the `initialFirstResponder` outlet to the **BigLetterView** (Figure 19.9). You can also use the icon of the window on the dock to set the outlet.

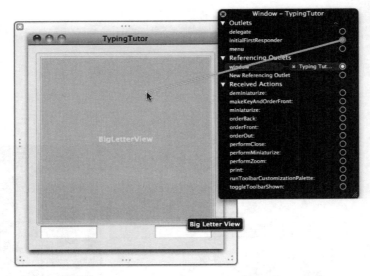

**Figure 19.9** Set the initialFirstResponder of the Window

# Write the Code

In this section, you will make your **BigLetterView** respond to key events and accept first-responder status. The characters typed by the user will appear in the console. The completed application will look like Figure 19.10.

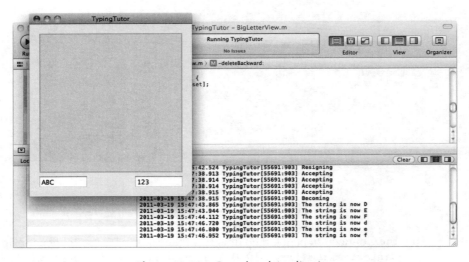

**Figure 19.10** Completed Application

## In BigLetterView.h

Your **BigLetterView** will have two instance variables and accessor methods for those variables. The bgColor variable will identify the background color of the view and will be an **NSColor** object. The string variable will hold onto the letter that the user most recently typed and will be an **NSString** object.

```
#import <Cocoa/Cocoa.h>

@interface BigLetterView : NSView {
    NSColor *bgColor;
    NSString *string;
}
@property (strong) NSColor *bgColor;
@property (copy) NSString *string;
@end
```

## In BigLetterView.m

The designated initializer for a view is **initWithFrame:**. In this method, you will call the superclass's **initWithFrame:** method and initialize bgColor and string to default values. Add the following methods to BigLetterView.m:

```
- (id)initWithFrame:(NSRect)frame
{
    self = [super initWithFrame:frame];
    if (self)
    {
        NSLog(@"initializing view");
        bgColor = [NSColor yellowColor];
        string = @" ";
    }
    return self;
}
```

Create accessor methods for bgColor and string:

```
#pragma mark Accessors

- (void)setBgColor:(NSColor *)c
{
    bgColor = c;
    [self setNeedsDisplay:YES];
}

- (NSColor *)bgColor
{
    return bgColor;
}
```

```
- (void)setString:(NSString *)c
{
    string = c;
    NSLog(@"The string is now %@", string);
}

- (NSString *)string
{
    return string;
}
```

Add the following code to the **drawRect:** method to fill the view with bgColor. If it is the window's *firstResponder*, the view will stroke a blue rectangle around its bounds to show the user that it will be the view receiving keyboard events:

```
- (void)drawRect:(NSRect)rect
{
    NSRect bounds = [self bounds];
    [bgColor set];
    [NSBezierPath fillRect:bounds];

    // Am I the window's first responder?
    if ([[self window] firstResponder] == self) {
        [[NSColor keyboardFocusIndicatorColor] set];
        [NSBezierPath setDefaultLineWidth:4.0];
        [NSBezierPath strokeRect:bounds];
    }
}
```

The system can optimize your drawing a bit if it knows that the view is completely opaque. Override **NSView**'s **isOpaque** method:

```
- (BOOL)isOpaque
{
    return YES;
}
```

The methods to become firstResponder are as follows:

```
- (BOOL)acceptsFirstResponder
{
    NSLog(@"Accepting");
    return YES;
}

- (BOOL)resignFirstResponder
{
    NSLog(@"Resigning");
    [self setNeedsDisplay:YES];
    return YES;
}
```

```
- (BOOL)becomeFirstResponder
{
    NSLog(@"Becoming");
    [self setNeedsDisplay:YES];
    return YES;
}
```

Once the view becomes the first responder, it will handle key events. For most **keyDowns**, the view will simply change `string` to be whatever the user typed. If, however, the user presses Tab or Shift-Tab, the view will ask the window to change the first responder.

**NSResponder** (from which **NSView** inherits) has a method called **interpret-KeyEvents:**. For most key events, it just tells the view to insert the text. For events that might do something else (such as Tab or Shift-Tab), it calls methods on itself.

In **keyDown:**, you simply call **interpretKeyEvents:**

```
- (void)keyDown:(NSEvent *)event
{
    [self interpretKeyEvents:[NSArray arrayWithObject:event]];
}
```

Then you need to override the methods that **interpretKeyEvents:** will call:

```
- (void)insertText:(NSString *)input
{
    // Set string to be what the user typed
    [self setString:input];
}

- (void)insertTab:(id)sender
{
    [[self window] selectKeyViewFollowingView:self];
}

// Be careful with capitalization here, "backtab" is considered
// one word.
- (void)insertBacktab:(id)sender
{
    [[self window] selectKeyViewPrecedingView:self];
}


- (void)deleteBackward:(id)sender
{
    [self setString:@" "];
}

@end
```

Build and run your program. You should see that your view becomes the first responder. While it is first responder, it should take keyboard events and log them to the terminal. Also, note that you can Tab and Shift-Tab between the views (Figure 19.11).

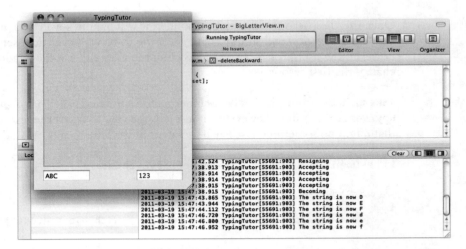

**Figure 19.11**   Completed Application

(Yes, **acceptsFirstResponder** gets called more times than you might expect (each time the view is selected)).

# For the More Curious: Rollovers

Three mouse events were not discussed in Chapter 18: **mouseMoved:**, **mouseEntered:**, and **mouseExited:**.

- (void)mouseMoved:(NSEvent *)event

To receive **mouseMoved:**, the view's window needs to accept "mouse-moved" events. If it does, the **mouseMoved:** message is sent to the window's first responder. To set the window to get mouse-moved events, you send it the message **setAcceptsMouseMovedEvents:**

[[self window] setAcceptsMouseMovedEvents:YES];

At this point, the view will be sent the message every time the mouse moves. This is a lot of events. When people ask us about mouse-moved events, we ask them why they want it. They usually say, "Uh, rollovers."

Rollovers are very popular in Web browsers. As you roll over a region, its appearance changes to make it clear that if you clicked now, that region would accept the click. Hyperlinks in Safari, for example, become highlighted when you roll over them.

To do rollovers, you don't typically use **mouseMoved:**. Instead, you set up a tracking area and override **mouseEntered:** and **mouseExited:**.

When a view is put on a window, **viewDidMoveToWindow** gets called. This is a pretty good place to create tracking areas. By passing the NSTrackingInVisibleRect, the tracking area will automatically match the visible rect of the owner.

```
- (void)viewDidMoveToWindow
{
    int options = NSTrackingMouseEnteredAndExited |
                  NSTrackingActiveAlways |
                  NSTrackingInVisibleRect;
    NSTrackingArea *ta;
    ta = [[NSTrackingArea alloc] initWithRect:NSZeroRect
                                      options:options
                                        owner:self
                                     userInfo:nil];
    [self addTrackingArea:ta];
}
```

Then, you change the appearance when **mouseEntered:** and **mouseExited:** are called. Assuming that you have a variable called isHighlighted of type BOOL, here is the code:

```
- (void)mouseEntered:(NSEvent *)theEvent
{
    isHighlighted = YES;
    [self setNeedsDisplay:YES];
}

- (void)mouseExited:(NSEvent *)theEvent
{
    isHighlighted = NO;
    [self setNeedsDisplay:YES];
}
```

You would then check isHighlighted in your **drawRect:** method and draw the view appropriately.

# The Fuzzy Blue Box

Your **BigLetterView** gets a blue box around its edge when it is firstResponder. Note, however, that the box isn't nice and fuzzy like the box around text fields. You want the fuzzy blue box? It takes a little work.

See where you draw the blue box in **drawRect:** in BigLetterView.m? Change it to look like this:

```
if ((([[self window] firstResponder] == self) &&
        [NSGraphicsContext currentContextDrawingToScreen]) {
    [NSGraphicsContext saveGraphicsState];
    NSSetFocusRingStyle(NSFocusRingOnly);
    [NSBezierPath fillRect:bounds];
    [NSGraphicsContext restoreGraphicsState];
}
```

Now, when you lose first-responder status, you need to redraw the view *and the area occupied by the fuzzy blue glow around it*:

```
- (BOOL)resignFirstResponder
{
    NSLog(@"Resigning");
    [self setKeyboardFocusRingNeedsDisplayInRect:[self bounds]];
    return YES;
}
```

Build and run your application.

## Chapter 20
# DRAWING TEXT WITH ATTRIBUTES

The next step is to get the string to appear in our view. At the end of this chapter, your application will look like Figure 20.1. The character being displayed will change as you type.

**Figure 20.1** Completed Application

## NSFont

Overall, the class **NSFont** has only two types of methods:

1. Class methods for getting the font you want

2. Methods for getting metrics on the font, such as letter height

The following are commonly used methods in **NSFont:**

```
+ (NSFont *)userFontOfSize:(float)fontSize

+ (NSFont *)userFixedPitchFontOfSize:(float)fontSize

+ (NSFont *)messageFontOfSize:(float)fontSize

+ (NSFont *)toolTipsFontOfSize:(float)fontSize

+ (NSFont *)titleBarFontOfSize:(float)fontSize
```

Return a font object for the user's default font for the corresponding string types. If you send a fontSize of 0.0, these methods will use the default font size.

User fonts are intended to be used in areas representing user input: a text field, for example. The other methods are useful when implementing custom user interface controls.

```
+ (NSFont *)fontWithName:(NSString *)fontName size:(float)fontSize
```

Returns a font object; fontName is a family-face name, such as "HelveticaBoldOblique" or "Times-Roman." Again, a fontSize of 0.0 uses the default font size.

Unless your application calls for using a specific font, we recommend using the prior set of methods in place of this one, in order to maintain consistency.

# NSAttributedString

Sometimes, you want to display a string that has certain attributes for a range of characters. As an example, suppose that you want to display the string "Big Nerd Ranch" and want the letters 0 through 2 to be underlined, the letters 0 through 7 to be green, and the letters 9 through 13 to be subscripts.

When dealing with a range of numbers, Cocoa uses the struct NSRange. NSRange has two members: location and length are both integers. The location is the index of the first item, and the length is the number of items in the range. You can use the function **NSMakeRange()** to create an NSRange.

To create strings with attributes that remain in effect over a range of characters, Cocoa has **NSAttributedString** and **NSMutableAttributedString**. Here is how you could create the **NSAttributedString** just described:

```
NSMutableAttributedString *s;
s = [[NSMutableAttributedString alloc]
        initWithString:@"Big Nerd Ranch"];
```

```
[s addAttribute:NSFontAttributeName
        value:[NSFont userFontOfSize:22]
        range:NSMakeRange(0, 14)];

[s addAttribute:NSUnderlineStyleAttributeName
        value:[NSNumber numberWithInt:1]
        range:NSMakeRange(0,3)];

[s addAttribute:NSForegroundColorAttributeName
        value:[NSColor greenColor]
        range:NSMakeRange(0, 8)];

[s addAttribute:NSSuperscriptAttributeName
        value:[NSNumber numberWithInt:-1]
        range:NSMakeRange(9,5)];
```

Once you have an attributed string, you can do lots of stuff with it.

```
[s drawInRect:[self bounds]];

// Put it in a text field
[textField setAttributedStringValue:s];

// Put it on a button
[button setAttributedTitle:s];
```

Figure 20.2 shows the result of this code's execution.

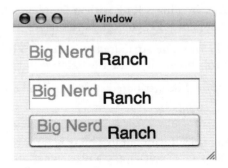

**Figure 20.2**   Using the Attributed String

Here are the names of the global variables for the most commonly used attributes, the type of object they correspond to, and their default values:

| Global Variable Name | Corresponds to | Default Value |
| --- | --- | --- |
| NSFontAttributeName | A font object | 12-point Helvetica |
| NSForegroundColorAttributeName | A color | Black |

| | | |
|---|---|---|
| `NSParagraphStyleAttributeName` | An `NSParagraph-Style` object | Standard paragraph style |
| `NSUnderlineColorAttributeName` | A color | The same as the foreground |
| `NSUnderlineStyleAttributeName` | A number | 0 (which means no underline) |
| `NSSuperscriptAttributeName` | A number | 0 (which means no superscripting or subscripting) |
| `NSShadowAttributeName` | An **NSShadow** object | `Nib` (no shadow) |

A list of all the attribute names can be found in `NSAttributedString.h`.

The easiest way to create attributed strings is from a file. **NSAttributedString** can read and write the following file formats:

- *A string*: Typically from a plain text file.
- *RTF*: Rich Text Format is a standard for text with multiple fonts and colors. In this case, you will read and set the contents of the attributed string with an instance of **NSData**.
- *RTFD*: This is RTF with attachments. Besides the multiple fonts and colors of RTF, you can have images.
- *HTML*: The attributed string can do basic HTML layout, but you probably want to use the **WebView** for best quality.
- *Word*: The attributed string can read and write simple `.doc` files.
- *OpenOffice*

When you read a document in, you may want to know some things about it, such as the paper size. If you supply a place where the method can put a pointer to a dictionary, the dictionary will have all the extra information that it could get from the data. For example:

```
NSDictionary *myDict;
NSData *data = [NSData dataWithContentsOfFile:@"myfile.rtf"];
NSAttributedString *aString;
aString = [[NSAttributedString alloc] initWithRTF:data
                            documentAttributes:&myDict];
```

If you don't care about the document attributes, just supply NULL.

# Drawing Strings and Attributed Strings

Both **NSString** and **NSAttributedString** have methods that cause them to be drawn onto a view. **NSAttributedString** has the following methods:

```
- (void)drawAtPoint:(NSPoint)aPoint
```

Draws the receiver. aPoint is the lower-left corner of the string.

```
- (void)drawInRect:(NSRect)rect
```

Draws the receiver; all drawing occurs inside rect. If rect is too small for the string to fit, the drawing is clipped to fit inside rect.

```
- (NSSize)size
```

Returns the size that the receiver would be if drawn.

**NSString** has analogous methods. With **NSString**, you need to supply a dictionary of attributes to be applied for the entire string.

```
- (void)drawAtPoint:(NSPoint)aPoint
    withAttributes:(NSDictionary *)attribs
```

Draws the receiver with the attributes in attribs.

```
- (void)drawInRect:(NSRect)aRect
    withAttributes:(NSDictionary *)attribs
```

Draws the receiver with the attributes in attribs.

```
- (NSSize)sizeWithAttributes:(NSDictionary *)attribs
```

Returns the size that the receiver would be if drawn with the atttibutes in attribs.

# Making Letters Appear

Open BigLetterView.h. Add an instance variable to hold the attributes dictionary and declare **prepareAttributes**.

```
#import <Cocoa/Cocoa.h>

@interface BigLetterView : NSView {
    NSColor *bgColor;
    NSString *string;
    NSMutableDictionary *attributes;
}
- (void)prepareAttributes;
```

Open `BigLetterView.m`. Create a method that creates the `attributes` dictionary with a font and a foreground color:

```
- (void)prepareAttributes
{
    attributes = [NSMutableDictionary dictionary];

    [attributes setObject:[NSFont userFontOfSize:75]
                   forKey:NSFontAttributeName];

    [attributes setObject:[NSColor redColor]
                   forKey:NSForegroundColorAttributeName];
}
```

In the **initWithFrame:** method, call the new method:

```
- (id)initWithFrame:(NSRect)rect
{
    self = [super initWithFrame:rect];
    if (self) {
        NSLog(@"initializing view");
        [self prepareAttributes];
        bgColor = [NSColor yellowColor];
        string = @" ";
    }
    return self;
}
```

In the **setString:** method, tell the view that it needs to redisplay itself:

```
- (void)setString:(NSString *)c
{
    string = c;
    NSLog(@"The string: %@", string);
    [self setNeedsDisplay:YES];
}
```

Create a method that will display the string in the middle of a rectangle:

```
- (void)drawStringCenteredIn:(NSRect)r
{
    NSSize strSize = [string sizeWithAttributes:attributes];
    NSPoint strOrigin;
    strOrigin.x = r.origin.x + (r.size.width - strSize.width)/2;
    strOrigin.y = r.origin.y + (r.size.height - strSize.height)/2;
    [string drawAtPoint:strOrigin withAttributes:attributes];
}
```

Call that method from inside your **drawRect:** method:

```
- (void)drawRect:(NSRect)rect
{
    NSRect bounds = [self bounds];
    [bgColor set];
    [NSBezierPath fillRect:bounds];

    [self drawStringCenteredIn:bounds];

    if ((([[self window] firstResponder] == self) && ...
```

Build and run the application. Note that keyboard events go to your view unless they trigger a menu item. Try pressing Command-W. It should close the window (even if your view is the first responder for the key window).

# Getting Your View to Generate PDF Data

All the drawing commands can be converted into PDF by the AppKit framework. The PDF data can be sent to a printer or to a file. Note that the PDF will always look as good as possible on any device, because it is resolution independent.

You have already created a view that knows how to generate PDF data to describe how it is supposed to look. Getting the PDF data into a file is really quite easy. **NSView** has the following method:

```
- (NSData *)dataWithPDFInsideRect:(NSRect)aRect
```

This method creates a data object and then calls **drawRect:**. The drawing commands that would usually go to the screen instead go into the data object. Once you have this data object, you simply save it to a file.

Open `BigLetterView.m` and add a method that will create a Save panel as a sheet. We'll use a block again, as we did with `NSOpenPanel` in Chapter 18, to respond to the user's actions.

```
- (IBAction)savePDF:(id)sender
{
    __block NSSavePanel *panel = [NSSavePanel savePanel];
    [panel setAllowedFileTypes:[NSArray arrayWithObject:@"pdf"]];

    [panel beginSheetModalForWindow:[self window]
               completionHandler:^ (NSInteger result) {
```

```
    if (result == NSOKButton)
    {
        NSRect r = [self bounds];
        NSData *data = [self dataWithPDFInsideRect:r];
        NSError *error;
        BOOL successful = [data writeToURL:[panel URL]
                                  options:0
                                    error:&error];

        if (!successful) {
            NSAlert *a = [NSAlert alertWithError:error];
            [a runModal];
        }
    }
    panel = nil; // avoid strong ref cycle
}];
}
```

Also, declare the action method in the `BigLetterView.h` file:

`- (IBAction)savePDF:(id)sender;`

Open `MainMenu.xib`. Select the Save As... item under the File menu. If there is no a Save As item, drag a new Menu Item from the Library onto the *File* menu. Relabel it Save As PDF.... (You may delete all the other menu items from the menu, if you wish.) Make the Save As PDF... menu item trigger the **BigLetter-View**'s **savePDF:** method (Figure 20.3).

Save and build the application. You should be able to generate a PDF file and view it in Preview (Figure 20.4).

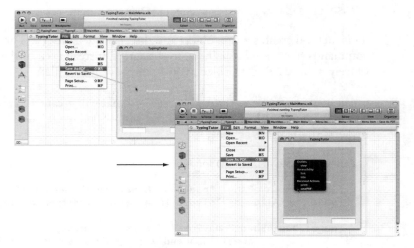

**Figure 20.3**    Connect Menu Item

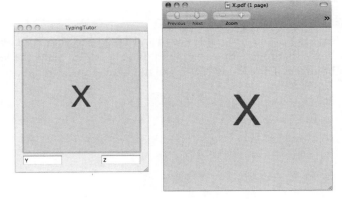

**Figure 20.4**   Completed Application

You will notice that multikeystroke characters (such as é) are not handled by your **BigLetterView**. To make this possible, you would need to add several methods that the **NSInputManager** uses. This topic is beyond the scope of this book (we just wanted to show you how to get keyboard events), but you can learn about it in Apple's discussion of **NSInputManager** in the documentation.

# For the More Curious: NSFontManager

Sometimes, you will have a font that is good but would be perfect if it were bold or italicized or condensed. **NSFontManager** can be used to make this sort of conversion. You can also use a font manager to change the size of the font.

For example, imagine that you have a font and would like a similar font but bold. Here is the code:

```
fontManager = [NSFontManager sharedFontManager];
boldFont = [fontManager convertFont:aFont toHaveTrait:NSBoldFontMask];
```

# Challenge 1

Give the letter a shadow. The **NSShadow** class has the following methods:

- (id)init;
- (void)setShadowOffset:(NSSize)offset;
- (void)setShadowBlurRadius:(float)val;
- (void)setShadowColor:(NSColor *)color;

# Challenge 2

Add the Boolean variables `bold` and `italic` to your **BigLetterView**. Add check boxes that toggle these variables. If `bold` is YES, make the letter appear in boldface; if `italic` is YES, make the letter appear in italics.

# Chapter 21

# PASTEBOARDS AND NIL-TARGETED ACTIONS

A process called the pasteboard server (`/usr/bin/pboard`) runs on your Mac. Applications use the **NSPasteboard** class to write data into that process and to read data from that process. The pasteboard server makes possible such operations as copying, cutting, and pasting between applications.

An application can copy the same data onto the pasteboard in several formats. For example, an image can be copied onto the pasteboard as a PDF document and as a PNG image. Then the application that reads the data can choose the format that it likes most. The pasteboard uses UTIs to identify the various types used on the pasteboard.

Prior to Mac OS X 10.6, the pasteboard APIs allowed for only one item on the pasteboard at any one time (although that item could have an arbitrary number of representations, or types). In 10.6, Apple updated the pasteboard APIs to allow for multiple items on a pasteboard: for example, multiple URLs copied from Finder. Each item can have multiple types associated with it, such as string and URL representations.

When putting data on the pasteboard, your application typically clears the pasteboard and then writes one or more objects directly to the pasteboard. Each of those objects forms an individual item on the pasteboard. The objects must conform to a pasteboard-writing protocol, which supplies the data. In this case the data for those items is immediately copied to the pasteboard.

The receiving application will then ask the pasteboard for an array of objects. It supplies an array of classes along with this request, which enables the pasteboard to provide the richest representations available for each item. In this scenario, the classes must conform to the pasteboard-reading protocol.

Data can also be passed via the pasteboard lazily. To do so, a class declares the data it will provide and then promises to provide that data when asked to do so by means of a delegate method in the future. We will talk about lazy copying at the end of the chapter.

Apple also provides APIs to work with the pasteboard on a per type basis, which may be useful if your application requires very fine control of the pasteboard. These APIs match the pre-10.6 APIs very closely.

Multiple pasteboards are available. There is a pasteboard called the general pasteboard, for copy-and-paste operations and another for drag-and-drop tasks. One pasteboard stores the last string that the user searched for, another copies rulers, and another copies fonts.

In this chapter, you will add cut, copy, and paste capabilities to your **BigLetterView**. First, you will implement the methods that will read from and write to the pasteboard. Then we will discuss how those methods get called.

# NSPasteboard

As mentioned earlier, the **NSPasteboard** class acts as an interface to the pasteboard server. Following are some of the commonly used methods of **NSPasteboard**:

> `+ (NSPasteboard *)generalPasteboard`

Returns the general **NSPasteboard**. You will use this pasteboard to copy, cut, and paste.

> `+ (NSPasteboard *)pasteboardWithName:(NSString *)name`

Returns the pasteboard identified by name. Here are the global variables that contain the names of the standard pasteboards:

> NSGeneralPboard
>
> NSFontPboard
>
> NSRulerPboard
>
> NSFindPboard
>
> NSDragPboard

> `- (NSInteger)clearContents`

Clears the contents of the pasteboard before writing objects to it. Returns the current change count of this pasteboard, which is not needed in most applications.

```
- (BOOL)writeObjects:(NSArray *)objects
```

Writes to the pasteboard objects that conform to the **NSPasteboardWrit-ing** protocol. Conforming classes include **NSString**, **NSAttributed-String**, **NSURL**, and **NSImage**. Each object represents an individual pasteboard item. If multiple types are to be written for each item, the object must write those types through the pasteboard-writing protocol.

For example, if an array of **NSURL** objects is written to the pasteboard, a pasteboard item will be created for each **NSURL**. Each of those pasteboard items will have two types associated with it: `public.url` and `public.utf8-plain-text`.

```
- (NSArray *)readObjectsForClasses:(NSArray *)classes
                   options:(NSDictionary *)options
```

Reads objects from the pasteboard. One object will be returned per pasteboard item. An array of classes must be passed that describe the order in which the types are desired, usually with the richest representation first. The classes must conform to the **NSPasteboardReading** protocol.

Following on the previous example, if the `classes` array contains only [NSURL class], an array of **NSURL** instances will be returned. If it contains only [NSString class], **NSString** instances will be returned.

Note that UTIs are not used directly in any of the preceding methods. Instead, they are class focused.

**NSPasteboardItem**, which itself conforms to **NSPasteboardReading** and **NSPasteboardWriting**, allows you to work much more closely with the pasteboard contents using UTIs. Here are some of the more commonly used methods on **NSPasteboardItem**:

```
- (BOOL)setDataProvider:(id<NSPasteboardItemDataProvider)provider
              forTypes:(NSArray *)types
```

Used for providing pasteboard data lazily, declares that `provider` will provide the given `types` when requested. Here are a few of the global variables for the standard types. Each of these evaluates to a UTI.

```
NSPasteboardTypeColor

NSPasteboardTypeFont

NSPasteboardTypePDF

NSPasteboardTypeRuler

NSPasteboardTypeRTF

NSPasteboardTypeRTFD
```

```
NSPasteboardTypeHTML

NSPasteboardTypeString

NSPasteboardTypeTabularText

NSPasteboardTypeTIFF

kUTTypeURL
```

You can also create your own UTIs for use with the pasteboard.

```
- (BOOL)setData:(NSData *)aData forType:(NSString *)dataType
- (BOOL)setString:(NSString *)s forType:(NSString *)dataType
- (BOOL)setPropertyList:(id)plist forType:(NSString *)dataType
```

Write data to the pasteboard.

```
- (NSArray *)types
```

Returns an array containing the types of data that are available to be read from the pasteboard.

```
- (NSString *)availableTypeFromArray:(NSArray *)types
```

Returns the first type found in types that is available for reading from the pasteboard; types should be a list of all types that you would be able to read.

```
- (NSData *)dataForType:(NSString *)dataType
```

```
- (NSString *)stringForType:(NSString *)dataType
```

```
- (id)propertyListForType:(nSString *)dataType
```

Read data from the pasteboard.

# Add Cut, Copy, and Paste to BigLetterView

You will create methods named cut:, copy:, and paste: in the BigLetterView class. To make these methods easier to write, you will first create methods for putting data onto and reading data off a pasteboard. Add these methods to Big-LetterView.m:

```
- (void)writeToPasteboard:(NSPasteboard *)pb
{
    // Copy data to the pasteboard
    [pb clearContents];
    [pb writeObjects:[NSArray arrayWithObject:string]];
}
```

```
- (BOOL)readFromPasteboard:(NSPasteboard *)pb
{
    NSArray *classes = [NSArray arrayWithObject:[NSString class]];
    NSArray *objects = [pb readObjectsForClasses:classes
                                          options:nil];
    if ([objects count] > 0)
    {
        // Read the string from the pasteboard
        NSString *value = [objects objectAtIndex:0];

        // Our view can handle only one letter
        if ([value length] == 1) {
            [self setString:value];
            return YES;
        }
    }
    return NO;
}
```

Note how we have implemented the write and read methods. When writing to
the pasteboard, we clear its contents and then write objects to it. When reading
from the pasteboard, we supply an array of the classes we are interested in and
then request the matching objects from the pasteboard. By implementing the
**NSPasteboardWriting** and **NSPasteboardReading** protocols, the **NSString**
class has made this task very simple.

Declare the **cut:**, **copy:**, and **paste:** methods in BigLetterView.h:

```
- (IBAction)cut:(id)sender;
- (IBAction)copy:(id)sender;
- (IBAction)paste:(id)sender;
```

Implement these methods in BigLetterView.m:

```
- (IBAction)cut:(id)sender
{
    [self copy:sender];
    [self setString:@""];
}


- (IBAction)copy:(id)sender
{
    NSPasteboard *pb = [NSPasteboard generalPasteboard];
    [self writeToPasteboard:pb];
}
```

```
- (IBAction)paste:(id)sender
{
    NSPasteboard *pb = [NSPasteboard generalPasteboard];
    if(![self readFromPasteboard:pb]) {
        NSBeep();
    }
}
```

Build and run the application. Note that the Cut, Copy, and Paste menu items now work when the **BigLetterView** is selected. The keyboard equivalents also work. You can copy only strings that have one character into the **BigLetterView**.

# Nil-Targeted Actions

How is the right view sent the **cut:**, **copy:**, or **paste:** message? After all, there are many, many views. If you select a text field, it should get the message. When you select another view and then choose the Copy or Paste menu item, the message should go to the newly selected view.

To solve this problem, the clever engineers at NeXT came up with *nil-targeted actions*. If you set the `target` of a control to `nil`, the application will try to send the `action` message to several objects until one of them responds. The application first tries to send the message to the first responder of the key window. This is exactly the behavior that you want for Cut and Paste. You can have several windows, each of which can have several views. The active view on the active window gets sent the cut-and-paste messages.

The beauty of targeted actions doesn't end there. **NSView**, **NSApplication**, and **NSWindow** all inherit from **NSResponder**, which has an instance variable called `nextResponder`. If an object doesn't respond to a nil-targeted action, its `nextResponder` gets a chance. The `nextResponder` for a view is usually its superview. The `nextResponder` of the content view of the window is the window. Thus, the responders are linked together in what we call the *responder chain*.

Note that `nextResponder` has nothing to do with `nextKeyView`.

For example, one menu item closes the key window. It has a `target` of `nil`. The action is **performClose:**. None of the standard objects respond to **performClose:** except **NSWindow**. Thus, the selected text field, for example, refuses to respond to **performClose:**. Then the superview of the text field refuses, and on up the view hierarchy. Ultimately, the window (the key window) accepts the **performClose:** method. So, to the user, the "active" window is closed.

As was mentioned in Chapter 12, a panel can become the key window but not the main window. If the key window and the main window are different, both windows get a chance to respond to the nil-targeted action.

Your question at this point should be: In what order will the objects be tested before a nil-targeted action is discarded?

1. The `firstResponder` of the `keyWindow` and its responder chain. The responder chain would typically include the superviews and, finally, the key window.

2. The `delegate` of the key window.

3. If it is a document-based application, the **NSWindowController** and then **NSDocument** object for the key window.

4. If the main window is different from the key window, it then goes through the same ritual with the main window: the `firstResponder` of the main window and its responder chain (including the main window itself), the main window's `delegate`, and the **NSWindowController** and then **NSDocument** object for the main window.

5. The instance of **NSApplication**.

6. The `delegate` of the **NSApplication**.

7. The **NSDocumentController**.

This series of objects represents the responder chain introduced above. Figure 21.1 presents an example. The numbers indicate the order in which the objects would be asked whether they respond to the nil-targeted action.

Note that in document-based applications (such as RaiseMan), the **NSDocument** object gets a chance to respond to the nil-targeted action. The object receives the messages from the following menu items: Save, Save As..., Revert To Saved, Print..., and Page Layout....

## Looking at the XIB File

To continue with our example, open `MainMenu.xib`. Note that the cut, copy, and paste items are connected to the icon labeled First Responder. The First Responder icon represents `nil`. It gives you something to drag to when you want an object to have a `nil` target (Figure 21.2).

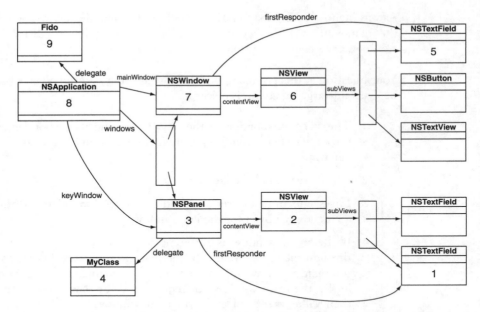

**Figure 21.1**    An Example of the Order in Which Responders Get a Chance to Respond

**Figure 21.2**    Check Menu Item

# For the More Curious: Which Object Sends the Action Message?

The `target` on the cut, copy, and paste menu items is `nil`. We know that sending a message to `nil` will not do anything. All target-action messages are handled by **NSApplication**. It has the following method:

```
- (BOOL)sendAction:(SEL)anAction to:(id)aTarget from:(id)sender
```

When the target is `nil`, **NSApplication** knows to try to send messages to the objects in the responder chain.

# For the More Curious: UTIs and the Pasteboard

In Chapter 10, we discussed how UTIs are used by Mac OS X to identify file types. The pasteboard also uses UTIs for this purpose. Although we did not use UTIs directly in this exercise, **NSString** uses NSPasteboardTypeString as its type when it reads and writes itself from the pasteboard. If you were to log the value of NSPasteboardTypeString, you would find that its value is `public.utf8-plain-text`.

The hierarchical nature of UTIs enables an application to be broad (`public.image`) or specific (`public.png`) when requesting objects from the pasteboard. The system will work out whether a type is permissable, based on what types it conforms to.

## Custom UTIs

At some point, you will want to use the pasteboard for custom, application-specific data. In such cases, you can simply use your own UTI. Custom UTIs should take the form of a reverse DNS name, such as `com.bignerdranch.raiseman.person`. You would then want to implement **NSPasteboardWriting** and **NSPasteboardReading** on your custom object or use **NSPasteboardItem** as an abstraction layer.

Note that custom UTIs do not need to be exported (using `Info.plist`) unless they are to be used by other applications. If they are exported, they must conform to `public.data`.

# For the More Curious: Lazy Copying

An application can implement copying to a pasteboard in a lazy manner. For example, imagine a graphics application that copies large images to the pasteboard in several formats: PNG, TIFF, PDF, and so on. You can imagine that copying all these formats onto the pasteboard would be hard on the application and the pasteboard server. Instead, such an application might do a lazy copy. That is, the application will declare all the types that it could put on the pasteboard but will put off copying the data until another application asks for it.

Essentially, the application puts an "IOU" (instead of the data) on the pasteboard and gives an object that will provide the data when they are needed. When another application actually asks for the data, the pasteboard server calls back for the data.

You will use an **NSPasteboardItem** to create this IOU object:

```
NSPasteboard *pboard = [NSPasteboard generalPasteboard];
[pboard clearContents];
NSPasteboardItem *item = [[NSPasteboardItem alloc] init];
[item setDataProvider:self forTypes:...];
[pboard writeObjects:[NSArray arrayWithObject:item]];
```

Then implement **pasteboard:item:provideDataForType:**:

```
- (void)pasteboard:(NSPasteboard *)pasteboard
              item:(NSPasteboardItem *)item
provideDataForType:(NSString *)type
{
    [item setData:... forType:type];
}
```

When another application needs the data, this method will be called. At that point, the application must copy the data it promised to the supplied pasteboard item.

As you can imagine, a problem would arise if the pasteboard server asked for the data after the application had terminated. When the application is terminating, if it has an "IOU" currently on the pasteboard, it will be asked to supply all the data promised before terminating. Thus, it is not uncommon for an "IOU" data provider to be sent **pasteboard:item:provideDataForType:** several times while the application is in the process of terminating.

The trickiest part of a lazy copy is that when the user copies data to the pasteboard and later pastes it into another application, he or she doesn't want the most recent state of the data. Rather, the user wants it *the way it was when he or she copied it*. When implementing a lazy copy, most developers will take some sort of a snapshot of the information when declaring the types. When providing the data, the developer will copy the snapshot, instead of the current state, onto the pasteboard.

Of course, when the user does a copy somewhere else, your object will no longer be responsible for keeping the snapshot.

```
- (void)pasteboardFinishedWithDataProvider:(NSPasteboard *)sender;
```

If you implement this method, it will be called when you are no longer responsible for keeping the snapshot.

# Challenge 1

You are putting the string onto the pasteboard. Create the PDF for the view and put that on the pasteboard, too. Now you will be able to copy the image of the letter into graphics programs. Test it using Preview's New from Clipboard menu item. (Don't break the string copy and paste: Put both the string and the PDF onto the pasteboard.) <u>Hint:</u> You will need to create an **NSPasteboardItem**.

# Challenge 2

In the **RaiseMan** project, add a menu item that triggers the **removeEmployee:** method in **RMDocument**.

# Chapter 22
# CATEGORIES

Although the engineers at Apple are very wise, one day you will think, "Golly, if only they had put that method on that class, my life would be so much easier." When this happens, you will want to create a *category*. A category is simply a collection of methods that you would like added to an existing class. The category concept is very useful, and it is surprising that so few object-oriented languages include this powerful idea.

Creating categories is easier than talking about them. In the previous chapter, you added pasting capabilities to your **BigLetterView**. Note, however, that if the string on the pasteboard has more than one letter, the paste attempt will fail because **BigLetterView** is capable of displaying only one letter at a time. Let's extend the example to take just the first letter of the string instead of failing.

## Add a Method to NSString

It would be nice if every **NSString** object had a method that returned its first letter. It does not, so you will use a category to add it.

Open the TypingTutor project and create a new file of type Objective-C category. In the Category field enter FirstLetter, and for Category on enter NSString. Two files will be created: NSString+FirstLetter.m and NSString+FirstLetter.h. Edit NSString+FirstLetter.h to look like this:

```
#import <Foundation/Foundation.h>

@interface NSString (FirstLetter)

- (NSString *)bnr_firstLetter;

@end
```

You appear to be declaring the class **NSString**, but you are not giving it any instance variables or a superclass. Instead, you are naming the category **FirstLetter** and declaring a method. A category cannot add instance variables to the class, only methods.

Now implement the method **bnr_firstLetter** in the file NSString+ FirstLetter.m. Make the file look like this:

```
#import "NSString+FirstLetter.h"

@implementation NSString (FirstLetter)

- (NSString *)bnr_firstLetter
{
    if ([self length] < 2) {
        return self;
    }
    NSRange r;
    r.location = 0;
    r.length = 1;
    return [self substringWithRange:r];
}
@end
```

Now you can use this method as if it were part of **NSString**. In Big LetterView.m, change **readFromPasteboard:** to look like this:

```
- (BOOL)readFromPasteboard:(NSPasteboard *)pb
{
    NSArray *classes = [NSArray arrayWithObject: NSString class]];
    NSArray *objects = [pb readObjectsForClasses:classes
                options:nil];
    if ([objects count] > 0)
{

        // Read the string from the pasteboard
        NSString *value = [objects objectAtIndex:0];

        [self setString:[value bnr_firstLetter]];
        return YES;
    }
    return NO;
}
```

At the beginning of BigLetterView.m, import the header:

```
#import "NSString+FirstLetter.h"
```

Build and run your application. You will be able to copy strings with more than one letter into **BigLetterView**. Only the first letter of the string will be copied.

In this example, you added only one method, but note that you can add as many methods to the class as you wish. Also, you used only the methods of the class here, but you can also access the class's instance variables directly.

Notice that I added a prefix "bnr_" to the method name in my category. I would like to just name the method **firstLetter**. But, what if Apple adds a **firstLetter** method to **NSString** in Mac OS X 10.9? There would be a conflict. For safety, I added the prefix. Also, note the file naming convention: ClassName+CategoryName.h. Stylish Objective-C developers name their category files in this fashion to clearly indicate the class and category names. The purpose of NSString+FirstLetter.h is much more apparent than FirstLetter.h.

Cocoa itself has many categories. For example, **NSAttributedString** is part of the Foundation framework. However, **NSAttributedString**'s **drawInRect:** method is part of a category from the AppKit framework. As a result, the documention for the methods on **NSAttributedString** are distributed between the two frameworks. There are also separate header files for **NSAttributedString** and its categories, which tends to cause some confusion.

# For the More Curious: Declaring Private Methods

Often, you will have in your .m file methods defined that you do not want to advertise by declaring them in your .h file. These are known as *private methods*.

If you call a private method before you declare or define it, you will get a warning from the compiler. One common technique to prevent these warnings is to declare the private methods in a category at the beginning of the .m file:

```
#import  "Megatron.h"

// Declare the private methods
@interface Megatron ()
- (void)blowTheLidOff;
- (void)putTheLidBackOn;
@end

@implementation Megatron

...actually implement all the private and public methods...

@end
```

# Chapter 23
# DRAG-AND-DROP

Drag-and-drop is little more than a flashy copy-and-paste operation. When the drag starts, some data is copied onto the dragging pasteboard. When the drop occurs, the data is read off the dragging pasteboard. The only thing that makes this technique trickier than copy-and-paste is that users need feedback: an image that appears as they drag, a view that becomes highlighted when they drag into it, and maybe a big gulping sound when they drop the image.

Several things can happen when data is dragged from one application to another: nothing may happen, a copy of the data may be created, or a link to the existing data may be created. Constants represent these operations:

    NSDragOperationNone

    NSDragOperationCopy

    NSDragOperationLink

There are several other operations that you see less frequently:

    NSDragOperationGeneric

    NSDragOperationPrivate

    NSDragOperationMove

    NSDragOperationDelete

    NSDragOperationEvery

Both the source and the destination must agree on the operation that will occur when the user drops the image.

When you add drag-and-drop to a view, there are two distinct parts of the change:

1. Make it a drag source.

2. Make it a drag destination.

Let's take these steps separately. First, you will make your view a drag source. When that is working, you will make it a drag destination.

# Make BigLetterView a Drag Source

When you finish this section, you will be able to drag a letter off the **BigLetterView** and drop it into any text editor. It will look like Figure 23.1.

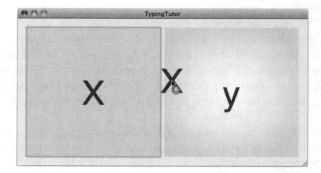

**Figure 23.1**  Completed Application

To be a drag source, your view must implement **draggingSourceOperationMask-ForLocal:**. This method declares what operations the view is willing to participate in as a source. Add the following method to BigLetterView.m:

```
- (NSDragOperation)draggingSourceOperationMaskForLocal:(BOOL)isLocal
{
    return NSDragOperationCopy;
}
```

This method is automatically called twice: once with isLocal as YES, which determines what operations it is willing to participate in for destinations within your application; and a second time, with isLocal as NO, which determines what operations it is willing to participate in for destinations in other applications.

## Starting a Drag

To start a drag operation, you will use a method on **NSView**:

```
- (void)dragImage:(NSImage *)anImage
               at:(NSPoint)imageLoc
           offset:(NSSize)mouseOffset
```

```
    event:(NSEvent *)theEvent
pasteboard:(NSPasteboard *)pboard
    source:(id)sourceObject
 slideBack:(BOOL)slideBack
```

You will supply the method with the image to be dragged and the point at which you want the drag to begin. The event supplied should be the mouseDown event. The offset is completely ignored. The pasteboard is usually the standard drag pasteboard. If the drop does not occur, you can choose whether the icon should slide back to the place from which it came.

Add an instance variable to BigLetterView.h to hold the mouseDown event:

**NSEvent *mouseDownEvent;**

In BigLetterView.m, define **mouseDown:** and put the event into that instance variable:

```
- (void)mouseDown:(NSEvent *)event
{
    mouseDownEvent = event;
}
```

You will also need to create an image to drag. You can draw on an image just as you can on a view. To make the drawing appear on the image instead of on the screen, you must first lock focus on the image. When the drawing is complete, you must unlock the focus.

Here is the whole method to add to BigLetterView.m:

```
- (void)mouseDragged:(NSEvent *)event
{
    NSPoint down = [mouseDownEvent locationInWindow];
    NSPoint drag = [event locationInWindow];
    float distance = hypot(down.x - drag.x, down.y - drag.y);
    if (distance < 3) {
        return;
    }

    // Is the string of zero length?
    if ([string length] == 0) {
        return;
    }

    // Get the size of the string
    NSSize s = [string sizeWithAttributes:attributes];

    // Create the image that will be dragged
    NSImage *anImage = [[NSImage alloc] initWithSize:s];
```

```
// Create a rect in which you will draw the letter
// in the image
NSRect imageBounds;
imageBounds.origin = NSZeroPoint;
imageBounds.size = s;

// Draw the letter on the image
[anImage lockFocus];
[self drawStringCenteredIn:imageBounds];
[anImage unlockFocus];

// Get the location of the mouseDown event
NSPoint p = [self convertPoint:down fromView:nil];

// Drag from the center of the image
p.x = p.x - s.width/2;
p.y = p.y - s.height/2;

// Get the pasteboard
NSPasteboard *pb = [NSPasteboard pasteboardWithName:NSDragPboard];

// Put the string on the pasteboard
[self writeToPasteboard:pb];

// Start the drag
[self dragImage:anImage
             at:p
         offset:NSZeroSize
          event:mouseDownEvent
     pasteboard:pb
         source:self
      slideBack:YES];
}
```

That's it. Build and run the application. You should be able to drag a letter off the view and into any text editor. (Try dragging it into Xcode.)

## After the Drop

When a drop occurs, the drag source will be notified if you implement the following method:

```
- (void)draggedImage:(NSImage *)image
             endedAt:(NSPoint)screenPoint
           operation:(NSDragOperation)operation;
```

For example, to make it possible to clear the **BigLetterView** by dragging the letter to the trashcan in the dock, advertise your willingness in **draggingSource-OperationMaskForLocal:**

```
- (NSDragOperation)draggingSourceOperationMaskForLocal:(BOOL)isLocal
{
    return NSDragOperationCopy | NSDragOperationDelete;
}
```

Then implement **draggedImage:endedAt:operation:**

```
- (void)draggedImage:(NSImage *)image
            endedAt:(NSPoint)screenPoint
          operation:(NSDragOperation)operation
{
    if (operation == NSDragOperationDelete) {
        [self setString:@""];
    }
}
```

Build and run the application. Drag a letter into the trashcan. It should disappear
from the view.

# Make BigLetterView a Drag Destination

There are several parts to being a drag destination. First, you need to declare
your view a destination for the dragging of certain types. **NSView** has a method
for this purpose:

```
- (void)registerForDraggedTypes:(NSArray *)pboardTypes
```

You typically call this method in your **initWithFrame:** method.

Then you need to implement six methods. (Yes, six!) All six methods have the
same argument: an object that conforms to the **NSDraggingInfo** protocol. That
object has the dragging pasteboard. The six methods are invoked as follows:

1. As the image is dragged into the destination, the destination is sent a
   **draggingEntered:** message. Often, the destination view updates its
   appearance. For example, it might highlight itself.

2. While the image remains within the destination, a series of
   **draggingUpdated:** messages are sent. Implementing **draggingUp-
   dated:** is optional.

3. If the image is dragged outside the destination, **draggingExited:** is sent.

4. If the image is released on the destination, either it slides back to its
   source (and breaks the sequence) or a **prepareForDragOperation:**
   message is sent to the destination, depending on the value returned by

the most recent invocation of **draggingEntered:** (or **draggingUp-dated:** if the view implemented it).

5. If the **prepareForDragOperation:** message returns YES, then a **performDragOperation:** message is sent. This is typically where the application reads data off the pasteboard.

6. Finally, if **performDragOperation:** returned YES, **concludeDragOperation:** is sent. The appearance may change. This is where you might generate the big gulping sound that implies a successful drop.

## registerForDraggedTypes:

Add a call to **registerForDraggedTypes:** to the **initWithFrame:** method in BigLetterView.m:

```
- (id)initWithFrame:(NSRect)rect
{
    self = [super initWithFrame:rect];
    if (self) {
        NSLog(@"initializing view");
        [self prepareAttributes];
        bgColor = [NSColor yellowColor];
        string = @"";
        [self registerForDraggedTypes:
                [NSArray arrayWithObject:NSPasteboardTypeString]];
    }
    return self;
}
```

## Add Highlighting

To signal the user that the drop is acceptable, your view will highlight itself. Add a highlighted instance variable to BigLetterView.h:

```
@interface BigLetterView : NSView
{
    NSColor *bgColor;
    NSString *string;
    NSMutableDictionary *attributes;
    NSEvent *mouseDownEvent;
    BOOL highlighted;
}
```

Now you are going to add highlighting to **drawRect:**. The class **NSGradient** makes it easy to draw with gradients. In this case, you are going to draw a radial gradient: white in the center and fading into the bgColor.

```
- (void)drawRect:(NSRect)rect
{
 NSRect bounds = [self bounds];
 // Draw gradient background if highlighted
 if (highlighted) {
   NSGradient *gr;
   gr = [[NSGradient alloc] initWithStartingColor:[NSColor whiteColor]
                                      endingColor:bgColor];
   [gr drawInRect:bounds relativeCenterPosition:NSZeroPoint];
 } else {
   [bgColor set];
   [NSBezierPath fillRect:bounds];
 }
 [self drawStringCenteredIn:bounds];
```

## Implement the Dragging Destination Methods

So far, we have seen two ways to declare a pointer to an object. If the pointer can refer to any type of object, we would declare it like this:

```
id foo;
```

If the pointer should refer to an instance of a particular class, we can declare it like this:

```
MyClass *foo;
```

A third possibility also exists. If we have a pointer that should refer to an object that conforms to a particular protocol, we can declare it like this:

```
id <MyProtocol> foo;
```

**NSDraggingInfo** is a protocol, not a class. All the dragging destination methods expect an object that conforms to the **NSDraggingInfo** protocol.

Add the following methods to BigLetterView.m:

```
#pragma mark Dragging Destination

- (NSDragOperation)draggingEntered:(id <NSDraggingInfo>)sender
{
    NSLog(@"draggingEntered:");
    if ([sender draggingSource] == self) {
        return NSDragOperationNone;
    }

    highlighted = YES;
    [self setNeedsDisplay:YES];
    return NSDragOperationCopy;
}
```

```
- (void)draggingExited:(id <NSDraggingInfo>)sender
{
    NSLog(@"draggingExited:");
    highlighted = NO;
    [self setNeedsDisplay:YES];
}

- (BOOL)prepareForDragOperation:(id <NSDraggingInfo>)sender
{
    return YES;
}

- (BOOL)performDragOperation:(id <NSDraggingInfo>)sender
{
    NSPasteboard *pb = [sender draggingPasteboard];
    if(![self readFromPasteboard:pb]) {
        NSLog(@"Error: Could not read from dragging pasteboard");
        return NO;
    }
    return YES;
}

- (void)concludeDragOperation:(id <NSDraggingInfo>)sender
{
    NSLog(@"concludeDragOperation:");
    highlighted = NO;
    [self setNeedsDisplay:YES];
}
```

## Add a Second BigLetterView

Open `MainMenu.xib` and add another **BigLetterView** to the window. Delete the text fields. Make sure to set the `nextKeyView` for each **BigLetterView** so that you can tab between them (Figure 23.2).

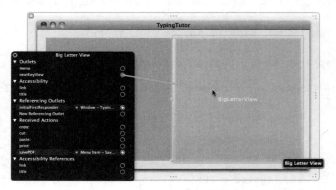

**Figure 23.2**   Set nextKeyView for Each BigLetterView

Build and run the application. Note that you can drag characters between the views and from other applications.

# For the More Curious: Operation Mask

For some apps, the negotiations of what operation will occur when the user drops can be quite complicated. After all, the source advertises its willingness to participate in some kinds of operations through **draggingSourceOperation-MaskForLocal:**. The user may also indicate preferences by holding down the Control, Option, or Command key. It is the job of the destination to determine what happens.

The dragging info object will do most of the work for you. It will get the source's advertised operation mask and filter it, depending on what modifier keys the user holds down. To see this, implement **draggingUpdated:** and log out the dragging info's operation mask:

```
- (NSDragOperation)draggingUpdated:(id <NSDraggingInfo>)sender
{
    NSDragOperation op = [sender draggingSourceOperationMask];
    NSLog(@"operation mask = %ld", op);
    if ([sender draggingSource] == self) {
        return NSDragOperationNone;
    }
    return NSDragOperationCopy;
}
```

Now build and run the application. Try dragging text from different sources and holding down different modifier keys. Note what happens to the mask and the cursor.

## Chapter 24

# NSTimer

An instance of **NSButton** has a target and a selector (the action). When the button is clicked, the action message is sent to the target. Timers work in a similar way. A timer is an object that has a target, a selector, and a delay, which is given in seconds (Figure 24.1). After the delay, the selector message is sent to the target. The timer sends itself as an argument to the message. The timer can also be set to send the message repeatedly.

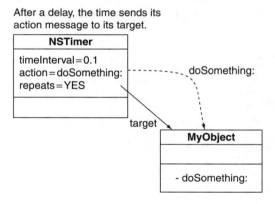

**Figure 24.1**   NSTimer

To play with timers a bit, you will create a typing tutor application. The application will have two **BigLetterView** objects. One will display what the user should type, and the other will display what the user has typed (Figure 24.2). An **NSProgressIndicator** will display how much time is left. After 2 seconds, the application will beep to indicate that the user took too long. Then the user is given 2 more seconds.

You will create a **TutorController** class. When the user clicks the Go button, an instance of **NSTimer** will be created. The timer will send a message every 0.1 second. The method triggered will check whether the two views match. If so, the user is given a new letter to type. Otherwise, the progress indicator is updated

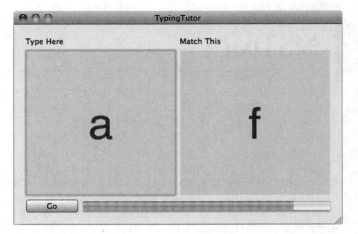

**Figure 24.2**  Completed Application

to reflect the elapsed time. If the user clicks the Stop button, the timer is invalidated. Figure 24.3 shows the object diagram.

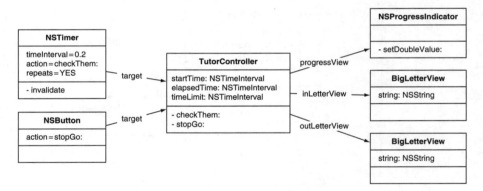

**Figure 24.3**  Object Diagram

Go back to your TypingTutor project in Xcode. Create a new Objective-C class called **TutorController**. In TutorController.h, give it two outlets and an action. You will also need a timer, an array for the letters, the index of the last letter displayed, and three time intervals that will help track how long the current letter has been visible:

```
#import <Cocoa/Cocoa.h>
@class BigLetterView;

@interface TutorController : NSObject {
```

```
    // Outlets
    IBOutlet BigLetterView *inLetterView;
    IBOutlet BigLetterView *outLetterView;

    // Data
    NSArray *letters;
    int lastIndex;

    // Time
    NSTimeInterval startTime;
    NSTimeInterval elapsedTime;
    NSTimeInterval timeLimit;
    NSTimer *timer;
}
- (IBAction)stopGo:(id)sender;
- (void)updateElapsedTime;
- (void)resetElapsedTime;
- (void)showAnotherLetter;
@end
```

# Lay Out the Interface

Open MainMenu.xib. Create an instance of **TutorController** by dragging an Object into the editor (from under Cocoa -> Objects & Controllers). Set the class to be **TutorController** (Figure 24.4).

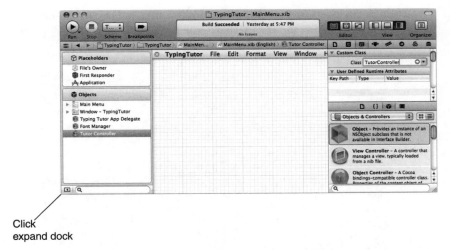

Click
expand dock

**Figure 24.4**    Create an Instance of TutorController

Add two labels (from Cocoa -> Controls) and place them above each of the
BigLetterView instances. Set the left label to read Type Here and the right label
to Match This.

Drop an **NSProgressIndicator** onto the window. Use the Inspector to make it
not indeterminate. Set its range to be 0 to 100 (Figure 24.5).

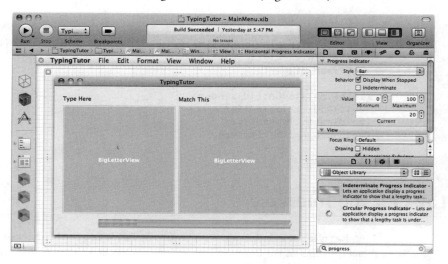

**Figure 24.5**   Inspect the Progress Indicator

Put a Rounded Textured Button onto the window. Using the Attributes Inspector,
set its title to Go and its alternate title to Stop. Set its type to Toggle and its state
to Off (Figure 24.6).

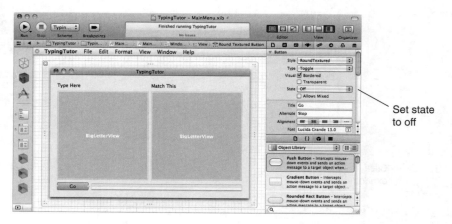

**Figure 24.6**   Inspect the Button

# Make Connections

Control-drag from the button to the **TutorController** object. Set the action to be **stopGo:** (Figure 24.7).

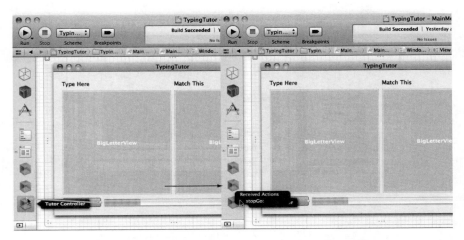

**Figure 24.7**   Connect the Button to the TutorController

Open the Bindings Inspector of the Progress Indicator (Figure 24.8). Bind Value to **TutorController**'s model key elapsedTime. Bind Max Value, also on the Progress Indicator, to the tutor controller's timeLimit.

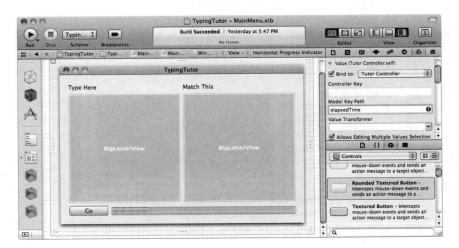

**Figure 24.8**   NSProgressIndicator Bindings

Control-click on the **TutorController** to display the Connection panel. Drag from inLetterView to the **BigLetterView** on the left. Drag from outLetterView to the **BigLetterView** on the right (Figure 24.9).

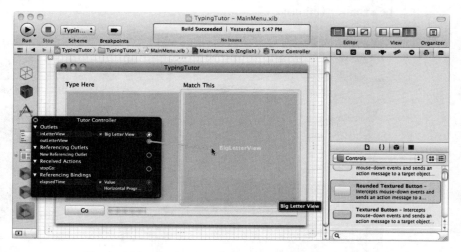

**Figure 24.9**   Connecting the outLetterView Outlet

# Add Code to TutorController

Implement the following methods in `TutorController.m`:

```
#import "TutorController.h"
#import "BigLetterView.h"

@implementation TutorController

- (id)init
{
    self = [super init];
    if (self) {
        // Create an array of letters
        letters = [NSArray arrayWithObjects:@"a", @"s",
                    @"d",@"f", @"j", @"k", @"l", @";",nil];

        // Seed the random number generator
        srandom((unsigned)time(NULL));
        timeLimit = 5.0;
    }
    return self;
}
```

```objc
- (void)awakeFromNib
{
    [self showAnotherLetter];
}

- (void)resetElapsedTime
{
    startTime = [NSDate timeIntervalSinceReferenceDate];
    [self updateElapsedTime];
}

- (void)updateElapsedTime
{
    [self willChangeValueForKey:@"elapsedTime"];
    elapsedTime = [NSDate timeIntervalSinceReferenceDate] - startTime;
    [self didChangeValueForKey:@"elapsedTime"];
}

- (void)showAnotherLetter
{
    //Choose random numbers until you get a different
    // number than last time
    int x = lastIndex;
    while (x == lastIndex){
        x = (int)(random() % [letters count]);
    }
    lastIndex = x;
    [outLetterView setString:[letters objectAtIndex:x]];

    // Start the count again
    [self resetElapsedTime];
}

- (IBAction)stopGo:(id)sender
{
    [self resetElapsedTime];

    if (timer == nil) {
        NSLog(@"Starting");

        // Create a timer
        timer = [NSTimer scheduledTimerWithTimeInterval:0.1
                                    target:self
                                    selector:@selector(checkThem:)
                                    userInfo:nil
                                     repeats:YES];
    } else {
        NSLog(@"Stopping");

        // Invalidate the timer
        [timer invalidate];
        timer = nil;
    }
}
```

```
- (void)checkThem:(NSTimer *)aTimer
{
    if ([[inLetterView string] isEqual:[outLetterView string]]) {
        [self showAnotherLetter];
    }
    [self updateElapsedTime];
    if (elapsedTime >= timeLimit) {
        NSBeep();
        [self resetElapsedTime];
    }
}

@end
```

Build and run your application.

Note, once again, that we have separated our classes into views (**BigLetterView**) and controllers (**TutorController**). If we were creating a full-featured application, we would probably also create model classes, such as **Lesson** and **Student**.

# For the More Curious: NSRunLoop

**NSRunLoop** is an object that waits. It waits for events to arrive and then forwards them to **NSApplication**. It waits for timer events to arrive and then forwards them to **NSTimer**. You can even attach a network socket to the run loop, and it will wait for data to arrive on that socket.

# Challenge

Change your DrawingFun application so that autoscrolling is timer driven. Delete your **mouseDragged:** method from **StretchView**. In **mouseDown:**, create a repeating timer that invokes a method in the view every tenth of a second. In the invoked method, autoscroll using the current event. To get the current event, use **NSApplication**'s **currentEvent** method:

```
NSEvent *e = [NSApp currentEvent];
```

(Remember that NSApp is a global variable that points to the instance of **NSApplication**.) Invalidate the timer in **mouseUp:**. Note that the autoscrolling becomes much smoother and more predictable.

# Chapter 25
# SHEETS

A sheet is simply an **NSWindow** instance that is attached to another window. The sheet comes down over the window, and the window stops getting events until the sheet is dismissed. Typically, you will compose a sheet as an off-screen window in your XIB file.

**NSApplication** has several methods that make sheets possible:

```
// Start a sheet
- (void)beginSheet:(NSWindow *)sheet
    modalForWindow:(NSWindow *)docWindow
     modalDelegate:(id)modalDelegate
    didEndSelector:(SEL)didEndSelector
       contextInfo:(void *)contextInfo;

// End the sheet
- (void)endSheet:(NSWindow *)sheet returnCode:(NSInteger)returnCode;
```

Besides the sheet window and the window to which it is attached, you supply a modal delegate, a selector, and a `contextInfo` pointer when you start the sheet. The `modalDelegate` will be sent the `didEndSelector`, and the sheet, its return code, and the `contextInfo` will be sent as arguments. Thus, the method triggered by the `didEndSelector` should have a signature like this:

```
- (void)rex:(NSWindow *)sheet
       fido:(NSInteger)returnCode
      rover:(void *)contextInfo;
```

The dog names are used here to indicate that you could name the method anything you wish. Most programmers name the method something more meaningful, such as **sheetDidEnd:returnCode:contextInfo:**.

# Adding a Sheet

You are going to add a sheet that will allow the user to adjust the speed of TypingTutor. You will bring up the sheet when the user selects the Adjust speed... menu item. You will end the sheet when the user clicks the OK button. The final application will look like Figure 25.1.

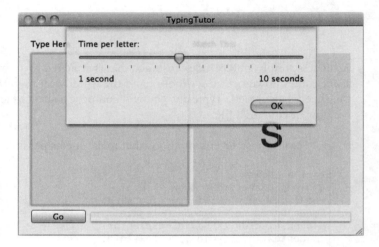

**Figure 25.1**    Completed Application

Your **TutorController** will control the slider and the window, so you will need to add outlets for them. Also, your **TutorController** will be sent a message when the user selects the Adjust speed... menu item or clicks the OK button, so you will need to add two action methods to the **TutorController**.

Figure 25.2 presents the object diagram.

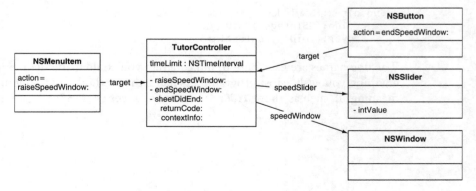

**Figure 25.2**    Object Diagram

## Add Outlets and Actions

Edit TutorController.h as follows:

```
#import <Cocoa/Cocoa.h>
@class BigLetterView;

@interface TutorController : NSObject
{
    // Outlets
    IBOutlet BigLetterView *inLetterView;
    IBOutlet BigLetterView *outLetterView;
    IBOutlet NSWindow *speedSheet;

    // Data
    NSArray *letters;
    int lastIndex;

    // Time
    NSTimeInterval startTime;
    NSTimeInterval timeLimit;
    NSTimeInterval elapsedTime;
    NSTimer *timer;
}
- (IBAction)stopGo:(id)sender;
- (IBAction)showSpeedSheet:(id)sender;
- (IBAction)endSpeedSheet:(id)sender;

- (void)updateElapsedTime;
- (void)resetElapsedTime;
- (void)showAnotherLetter;

@end
```

Save the file.

## Lay Out the Interface

Open MainMenu.xib. Add a menu item to the main menu for your application by dragging it out of the Library (under Cocoa -> Windows & Menus) (Figure 25.3).

Change the title of the menu item to Adjust Speed.... Control-drag from the menu item to the **TutorController**. Set the action to be **showSpeedSheet:** (Figure 25.4).

Create a new window by dragging one out of the Library (under Cocoa -> Windows & Menus) (Figure 25.5). Disable resizing for the window. Uncheck Visible at launch.

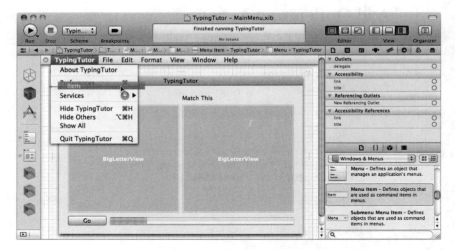

**Figure 25.3**   Add a Menu Item

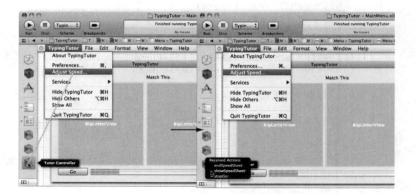

**Figure 25.4**   Connect the Menu Item

Put a slider on the new window. To label the left end of the slider as "1 second" and the right end as "10 seconds," drop two labels onto the window. Add a third label above the slider to read Time per letter:. Add a button and change its title to OK. Inspect the slider and set its range to be 1 to 10 (Figure 25.6).

Bind the Value of the slider to the **TutorController**'s timeLimit as shown in Figure 25.7.

When the user clicks the OK button, it should send to the **TutorController** a message that will end the sheet. Control-drag from the button to the **TutorController** and choose **endSpeedSheet:** as the action (Figure 25.8).

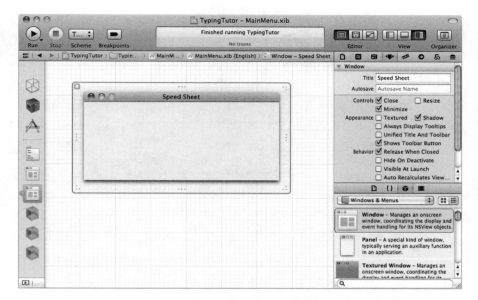

**Figure 25.5**  Inspect New Window

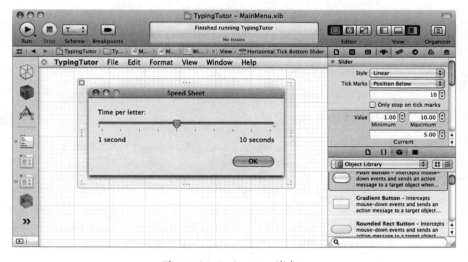

**Figure 25.6**  Inspect Slider

To raise the window as a sheet, your **TutorController** must have a pointer to it. Control-click on the **TutorController** to get the Connection panel. Connect the speedSheet outlet to the window (Figure 25.9).

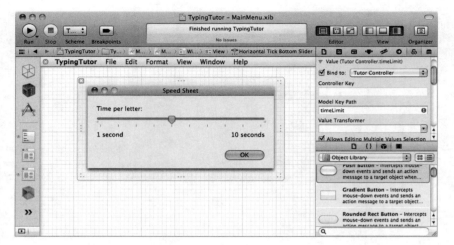

**Figure 25.7**    Bind the Slider's Value to timeLimit

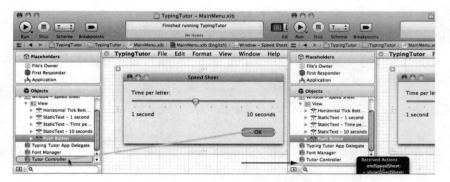

**Figure 25.8**    Set the Target of the Button

# Add Code

When the user chooses the Adjust Speed… menu item, the sheet will run. Add the following method to `TutorController.m`:

```
- (IBAction)showSpeedSheet:(id)sender
{
    [NSApp beginSheet:speedSheet
        modalForWindow:[inLetterView window]
         modalDelegate:nil
        didEndSelector:NULL
           contextInfo:NULL];
}
```

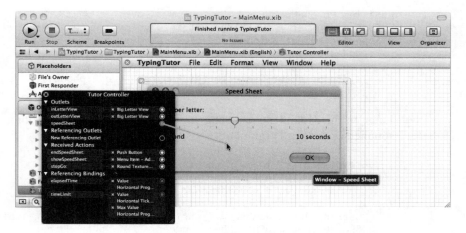

**Figure 25.9**   Connect speedSheet Outlet

Note that you are attaching the sheet to the window that the `inLetterView` is on. Also, when the sheet is dismissed, you are choosing not to get any sort of callback.

The sheet will end when the user clicks the **OK** button. Add the following method to `TutorController.m`:

```
- (IBAction)endSpeedSheet:(id)sender
{
  // Return to normal event handling
  [NSApp endSheet:speedSheet];

  // Hide the sheet
  [speedSheet orderOut:sender];

}
```

Build and run your application. Bring up the sheet, adjust the speed, and dismiss the sheet.

# For the More Curious: contextInfo

The `contextInfo` parameter is a pointer to some data. You can supply this parameter when you start the sheet, and the delegate will get the pointer when you end the sheet. For example, here the developer has started a sheet and inserted a phone number for the context info:

```
NSString *phoneNumber = ...;
void *voidNumber = (__bridge_retained void *)phoneNumber;
[NSApp beginSheet:aWindow
    modalForWindow:someOtherWindow
     modalDelegate:self
    didEndSelector:@selector(didEnd:returnCode:phone:)
       contextInfo:voidPhone];
```

Later, in the **didEnd:returnCode:phone:** method, the phone number will be
supplied as the third argument:

```
- (void)didEnd:(NSWindow *)sheet
    returnCode:(NSInteger)returnCode
         phone:(void *)voidPhone
{
    NSString *phoneNumber = (__bridge_transfer NSString *)voidPhone;
    NSLog(@"sheetDidEnd: Phone number = %@", phoneNumber);
}
```

Note also that the context info and the NSNotification's user info dictionary
serve similar purposes.

You probably noticed that we had to do some rather unsightly casting to turn the
NSString * type into a void *. The reason it that ARC requires hints from the
developer so that it knows how to account for the object reference. In this case,
__bridge_retained instructs ARC that it should retain phoneNumber, leaving it
at +1 as **beginSheet:modalForWindow:modalDelegate:didEndSelector:
contextInfo:** is called. In **didEnd:returnCode:phone:**, ownership of the
phoneNumber reference is being transferred to the local phoneNumber variable by
using the __bridge_transfer cast. The object is then released once the local
variable phoneNumber goes out of scope.

Before ARC, it was not uncommon when using manual reference counting to see
an object pointer cast to void *; the developer was responsible for ensuring that
the object was retained and released appropriately. Expect to see APIs like this
one revised in the future.

# For the More Curious: Modal Windows

When a sheet is active, the user is prevented from sending events to the window
to which it is attached. When an Alert panel is run, it is a modal window—that is,
the user is prevented from sending events to any other window.

To make a window modal, use the following method of NSApp:

- (NSInteger)runModalForWindow:(NSWindow *)aWindow

This method will block, and only events destined for aWindow will be processed; clicking on the menu and other windows will do nothing. When you are ready to make the aWindow nonmodal, send this message to the **NSApplication** object:

- (void)stopModalWithCode:(NSInteger)returnCode

At that point, **runModalForWindow:** will end and return returnCode.

## Chapter 26
# CREATING NSFORMATTERS

A formatter takes a string and makes another object, typically so that the user can type something that is more than just a string. For example, the **NSDateFormatter**, when passed the string August 17, 1967, converts it into an **NSDate** object that represents the seventeenth day of August in the year 1967 (Figure 26.1).

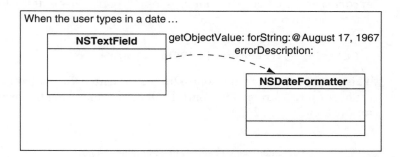

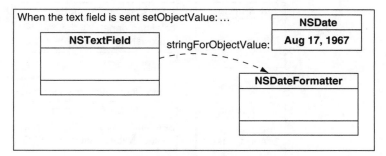

**Figure 26.1** NSDateFormatter

Also, a formatter can take an object and create a string for the user to see. For example, imagine a text field that has an **NSDateFormatter**. When the text field is sent **setObjectValue:** with an **NSDate** object, the date formatter will create a string that represents that date. The user will then see that string.

All formatters are subclasses of the **NSFormatter** class. Two of these subclasses come with Cocoa: **NSDateFormatter** and **NSNumberFormatter**. You used **NSDateFormatter** in Chapter 3 to format the lottery date and **NSNumber-Formatter** in Chapter 8 to format the expected raise as a percentage.

The most basic formatter will implement two methods:

```
- (BOOL)getObjectValue:(id *)anObject
            forString:(NSString *)aString
    errorDescription:(NSString **)errorPtr
```

This message is sent by the control (such as a text field) to the formatter when it has to convert aString into an object; aString is the string that the user typed in. The formatter can return YES and set anObject to point to the new object. A return of NO indicates that the string could not be converted, and the errorPtr is set to indicate what went wrong. Note that errorPtr is a pointer to a pointer, as is anObject. That is, it is a location where you can put a pointer to the string.

```
- (NSString *)stringForObjectValue:(id)anObject
```

This message is sent by the control to the formatter when it has to convert anObject into a string. The control will display the string that is returned for the user (Figure 26.2).

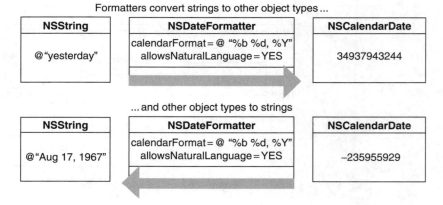

**Figure 26.2**   NSFormatter

Often the object that is created from the string is also a string. For example, you might have a **TelephoneNumberFormatter** that properly inserts the parentheses and dashes into a telephone number.

# A Basic Formatter

In this chapter, you will write your own formatter class. You will create a formatter that allows the user to type in the name of a color, and the formatter will in turn create the appropriate **NSColor** object. Then you will set the background of the **BigLetterView** with that color object. Figure 26.3 shows what the application will look like when you are done.

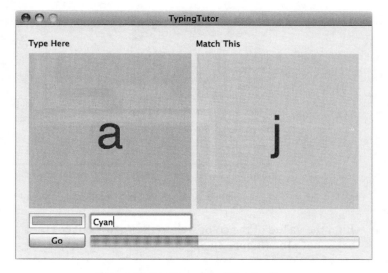

**Figure 26.3**  Completed Application

## Create ColorFormatter.h

Open the **TypingTutor** project in Xcode and create a new Objective-C class that is a subclass of **NSFormatter**. Name it **ColorFormatter**.

In ColorFormatter.h, add an instance variable:

```
#import <Foundation/Foundation.h>

@interface ColorFormatter : NSFormatter {
    NSColorList *colorList;
}
@end
```

Save the file.

## Edit the XIB File

Open `MainMenu.xib`. Drop a color well and a text field onto the window
(Figure 26.4).

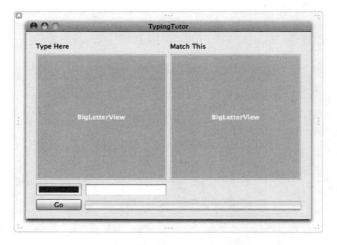

**Figure 26.4**    Add Color Well and Text Field

Bind the `value` of the color well to the **TutorController**'s `inLetter-`
`View.bgColor` (Figure 26.5).

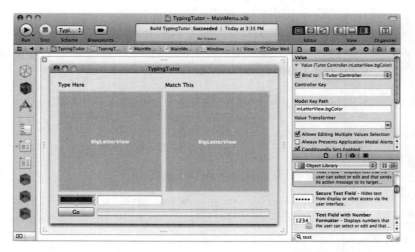

**Figure 26.5**    Bind Value of Color Well to bgColor of inLetterView

Bind the value of the text field to the same key path (Figure 26.6).

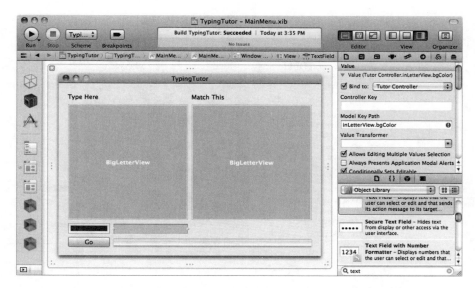

**Figure 26.6**    Bind Value of Text Field to bgColor of inLetterView

Drop an **NSObject** in the editor. Set its class to be **ColorFormatter** (Figure 26.7).

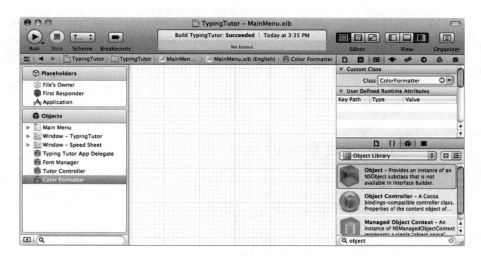

**Figure 26.7**    Create an Instance of ColorFormatter

Control-click on the text field to bring up its Connection panel. Set the formatter outlet to point to the **ColorFormatter** object (Figure 26.8).

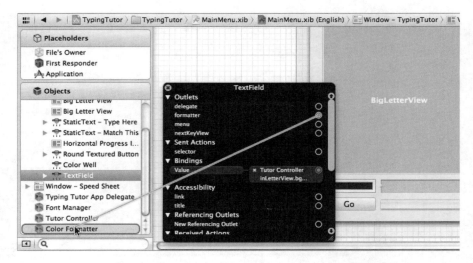

**Figure 26.8**  Set the Text Field's Formatter Outlet

## NSColorList

For this exercise, you will use an **NSColorList**, a dictionary of color objects that maps a name to an instance of **NSColor** objects. Several color lists come standard with Mac OS X. In particular, the color list named "Apple" includes many of the standard colors, such as "Purple" and "Yellow."

**NSColorList** is not a particularly useful class, but it makes this exercise very elegant. We will not spend much time discussing it.

## Searching Strings for Substrings

When you have a string dakakookookakoo and are searching through it for a shorter string, such as ka, the result will be an NSRange. The location is the first letter of the matching substring in the longer string. The length is the length of the substring.

Of course, there are a couple of options that you might want to set. For example, you might want to do a case-insensitive search. Or you might want to do a backward search (from the end of the string instead of the beginning). To search backward for the string KA in abbakachakaza in a case-insensitive manner, you would use the following code:

```
NSRange aRange;
NSString *big = @"abbakachakazazzz";
```

```
NSString *small = @"KA";
aRange = [big rangeOfString:small
                options:(NSCaseInsensitiveSearch | NSBackwardsSearch)];
```

After this code executes, aRange.location would be 9, and aRange.length would be 2.

If the substring is not found, the length will be 0.

## Implement the Basic Formatter Methods

Edit ColorFormatter.m to look like this:

```
#import "ColorFormatter.h"

@interface ColorFormatter ()
- (NSString *)firstColorKeyForPartialString:(NSString *)string;
@end

@implementation ColorFormatter

- (id)init
{
    self = [super init];
    if (self) {
        colorList = [NSColorList colorListNamed:@"Apple"];
    }
    return self;
}

- (NSString *)firstColorKeyForPartialString:(NSString *)string
{
    // Is the key zero-length?
    if ([string length] == 0) {
        return nil;
    }

    // Loop through the color list
    for (NSString *key in [colorList allKeys]) {
        NSRange whereFound = [key rangeOfString:string
                                    options:NSCaseInsensitiveSearch];
        // Does the string match the beginning of the color name?
        if ((whereFound.location == 0) && (whereFound.length > 0)) {
            return key;
        }
    }
    // If no match is found, return nil
    return nil;
}
```

```objc
- (NSString *)stringForObjectValue:(id)obj
{
    // Not a color?
    if (![obj isKindOfClass:[NSColor class]]) {
        return nil;
    }

    // Convert to an RGB Color Space
    NSColor *color;
    color = [obj colorUsingColorSpaceName:NSCalibratedRGBColorSpace];

    // Get components as floats between 0 and 1
    CGFloat red, green, blue;
    [color getRed:&red
            green:&green
             blue:&blue
            alpha:NULL];

    // Initialize the distance to something large
    float minDistance = 3.0;
    NSString *closestKey = nil;

    // Find the closest color
    for (NSString *key in [colorList allKeys]) {
        NSColor *c = [colorList colorWithKey:key];
        CGFloat r, g, b;
        [c getRed:&r
            green:&g
             blue:&b
            alpha:NULL];

        // How far apart are 'color' and 'c'?
        float dist;
        dist = pow(red - r, 2) + pow(green -g, 2) + pow(blue - b, 2);

        // Is this the closest yet?
        if (dist < minDistance) {
            minDistance = dist;
            closestKey = key;
        }
    }
    // Return the name of the closest color
    return closestKey;
}

- (BOOL)getObjectValue:(id *)obj
             forString:(NSString *)string
     errorDescription:(NSString **)errorString
{
    // Look up the color for 'string'
    NSString *matchingKey = [self firstColorKeyForPartialString:string];
```

```
    if (matchingKey) {
      *obj = [colorList colorWithKey:matchingKey];
      return YES;
    } else {
      // Occasionally, 'errorString' is NULL
      if (errorString != NULL) {
        *errorString = [NSString stringWithFormat:
                                   @" is not a color", string];
      }
      return NO;
    }
  }
}
@end
```

Build and run your application. You should be able to type in color names and see the background of the **BigLetterView** change accordingly. Also, if you use the color well, you should see the name of the color change in the text field. Try typing in a string that is not a color.

# The Delegate of the NSControl Class

Note that the bindings mechanism makes a nice Alert sheet when the formatting fails. The text field's delegate can also be informed of the failed formatting. If the formatter decides that the string is invalid, the delegate is sent the following error message:

```
- (BOOL)control:(NSControl *)control
      didFailToFormatString:(NSString *)string
          errorDescription:(NSString *)error
```

The delegate can override the opinion of the formatter. If it returns YES, the control displays the string as is. If it returns NO, the delegate agrees with the formatter: The string is invalid.

Implement the following method in TutorController.m:

```
- (BOOL)control:(NSControl *)control
    didFailToFormatString:(NSString *)string
        errorDescription:(NSString *)error
{
    NSLog(@"TutorController told that formatting of %@ failed: %@",
             string, error);
    return NO;
}
```

Now open MainMenu.xib and make the **TutorController** the delegate of the text field (Figure 26.9).

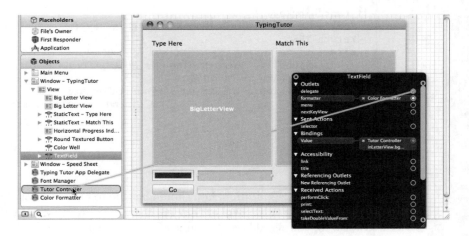

**Figure 26.9**   Connect the Text Field's delegate Outlet

Build and run your application. When validation fails, you will see a message on the console indicating what the string was and why it failed.

# Checking Partial Strings

You might want to create a formatter that prevents the user from typing letters that are not part of a color name. To make the formatter check the string after every keystroke, implement the following method:

```
- (BOOL)isPartialStringValid:(NSString *)partial
         newEditingString:(NSString **)newString
         errorDescription:(NSString **)errorString
```

Here partial is the string, including the last keystroke. If your formatter returns NO, it indicates that the partial string is not acceptable. Also, if your formatter returns NO, it can supply the newString and an errorString. The newString will appear in the control. The errorString should give the user an idea of what she or he did wrong. If your formatter returns YES, the newString and the errorString are ignored.

Add the following method to ColorFormatter.m:

```
- (BOOL)isPartialStringValid:(NSString *)partial
         newEditingString:(NSString **)newString
         errorDescription:(NSString **)error
{
    // Zero-length strings are OK
    if ([partial length] == 0){
```

```
        return YES;
    }
    NSString *match = [self firstColorKeyForPartialString:partial];
    if (match) {
        return YES;
    } else {
        if (error) {
            *error = @"No such color";
        }
        return NO;
    }
}
```

Build and run your application. You will not be able to type in anything except the color names.

Notice something annoying about this app: You can't see what color would be chosen until you tab out of the field. What you would like is a formatter that does autocompletion. To enable autocompletion, you need to control the range of the selection as well. Comment out the **isPartialStringValid:newEditingString:errorDescription:** method and replace it with this method:

```
- (BOOL)isPartialStringValid:(NSString **)partial
        proposedSelectedRange:(NSRange *)selPtr
              originalString:(NSString *)origString
        originalSelectedRange:(NSRange)origSel
            errorDescription:(NSString **)error
{
    // Zero-length strings are fine
    if ([*partial length] == 0) {
        return YES;
    }
    NSString *match = [self firstColorKeyForPartialString:*partial];

    // No color match?
    if (!match) {
        return NO;
    }

    // If this would not move the beginning of the selection, it
    // is a delete
    if (origSel.location == selPtr->location) {
        return YES;
    }

    // If the partial string is shorter than the
    // match, provide the match and set the selection
    if ([match length] != [*partial length]) {
        selPtr->location = [*partial length];
        selPtr->length = [match length] - selPtr->location;
        *partial = match;
```

```
            return NO;
        }
        return YES;
    }
```

Build and run your application. Your formatter will now autocomplete color names as you type them.

# Formatters That Return Attributed Strings

Sometimes, it is nice for the formatter to define not only the string that is to be displayed but also the attributes of that string. For example, a number formatter might print the number in red if it is negative. For this purpose, you will use **NSAttributedString**.

Your formatter can implement the following method:

```
- (NSAttributedString *)attributedStringForObjectValue:(id)anObj
                        withDefaultAttributes:(NSDictionary *)aDict
```

If the method exists, it will be called instead of **stringForObjectValue:**. The dictionary that you are passed contains the default attributes for the view where the data will be displayed. It is a good idea to merge the dictionary with your added attributes. For example, use the font from the text field where the data will be displayed, but make the foreground color red to show that the profits are negative.

Implement the following method to display the name of the color in that color:

```
- (NSAttributedString *)attributedStringForObjectValue:(id)anObj
                        withDefaultAttributes:(NSDictionary *)attributes
{
    NSString *match = [self stringForObjectValue:anObj];
    if (!match) {
        return nil;
    }
    NSMutableDictionary *attDict = [attributes mutableCopy];
    [attDict setObject:anObj
                forKey:NSForegroundColorAttributeName];
    NSAttributedString *atString
            = [[NSAttributedString alloc] initWithString:match
                                            attributes:attDict];
    return atString;
}
```

Build and run the application. Note that the text field will not change colors until it gives up first-responder status.

# For the More Curious: NSValueTransformer

Bindings read values from objects. Sometimes, a value will need some massaging before it can be used. To fulfill this purpose, Apple created **NSValueTransformer**. There is, for example, a negating value transformer that transforms YES into NO, and NO into YES.

You can create your own **NSValueTransformer** subclasses and attach them to bindings in your application. Unlike formatters, value transformers are used only by bindings.

## Chapter 27

# PRINTING

Code to handle printing is always relatively hard to write. Many factors are at play: pagination, margins, and page orientation (landscape versus portrait). This chapter is designed to get you started on your journey toward the perfect printout.

Compared to most operating systems, Mac OS X makes writing print routines considerably easier. After all, your views already know how to generate PDF, and Mac OS X knows how to print PDF. If you have a document-based application and a view that knows how to draw itself, you simply implement **printOperationWithSettings:error:**. In this method, you create an **NSPrintOperation** object, using a view, and return it. The code, in your **NSDocument** subclass, would look like this:

```
- (NSPrintOperation *)printOperationWithSettings:(NSDictionary *)ps
                                           error:(NSError **)e;
{
    NSPrintInfo *printInfo = [self printInfo];
    NSPrintOperation *printOp
            = [NSPrintOperation printOperationWithView:aView
                                             printInfo:printInfo];
    return printOp;
}
```

# Dealing with Pagination

What about multiple pages? A view, after all, has only a single page. How will you get a view to print multiple-page documents? Off-screen, you will make a huge view that can display all the pages of the document simultaneously (Figure 27.1). The print system will ask the view how many pages it is displaying and will ask the view where each page can be found in the view.

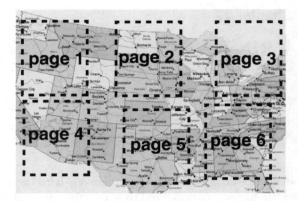

**Figure 27.1**    Each Page Is a Rectangle on the View

Your view, then, must override two methods:

```
// How many pages?
- (BOOL)knowsPageRange:(NSRange *)rptr;

// Where is each page?
- (NSRect)rectForPage:(NSInteger)pageNum;
```

Instead of creating a huge view and returning a different rectangle for each page, you can note what page is being printed and always return the same rectangle in `rectForPage:`. This is the technique you will be using in the exercise.

As an example, you will add printing to the RaiseMan application. You will print the name and expected raise for as many people as will fit on the paper size that the user selected from the Print panel (Figure 27.2).

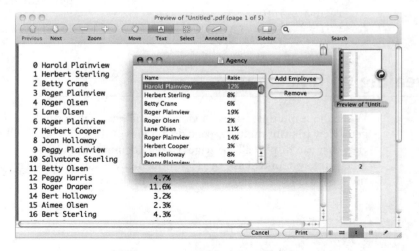

**Figure 27.2**    Completed Application

To do so, you will create a view that does the printing. Instead of making the view big enough to display all the people simultaneously, we will simply note which page the system is printing and draw only the names on that page in **drawRect:**.

Create a class called **PeopleView** that is a subclass of **NSView**. Make PeopleView.h look like this:

```
#import <Cocoa/Cocoa.h>

@interface PeopleView : NSView {
    NSArray *people;
    NSMutableDictionary *attributes;
    float lineHeight;
    NSRect pageRect;
    NSInteger linesPerPage;
    NSInteger currentPage;
}
- (id)initWithPeople:(NSArray *)array;
@end
```

In PeopleView.m, you will implement the **initWithPeople:** method. This initializer will call **NSView**'s **initWithFrame:** method.

```
#import "PeopleView.h"
#import "Person.h"

@implementation PeopleView

- (id)initWithPeople:(NSArray *)persons
{
    // Call the superclass's designated initializer with some
    // dummy frame
    self = [super initWithFrame:NSMakeRect(0, 0, 700, 700)];
    if (self) {
        people = [persons copy];
        // The attributes of the text to be printed
        attributes = [[NSMutableDictionary alloc] init];
        NSFont *font = [NSFont fontWithName:@"Monaco" size:12.0];
        lineHeight = [font capHeight] * 1.7;
        [attributes setObject:font
                       forKey:NSFontAttributeName];
    }
    return self;
}

#pragma mark Pagination
```

```
- (BOOL)knowsPageRange:(NSRange *)range
{
    NSPrintOperation *po = [NSPrintOperation currentOperation];
    NSPrintInfo *printInfo = [po printInfo];

    // Where can I draw?
    pageRect = [printInfo imageablePageBounds];
    NSRect newFrame;
    newFrame.origin = NSZeroPoint;
    newFrame.size = [printInfo paperSize];
    [self setFrame:newFrame];

    // How many lines per page?
    linesPerPage = pageRect.size.height / lineHeight;

    // Pages are 1-based
    range->location = 1;

    // How many pages will it take?
    range->length = [people count] / linesPerPage;
    if ([people count] % linesPerPage) {
        range->length = range->length + 1;
    }
    return YES;
}

- (NSRect)rectForPage:(NSInteger)i
{
    // Note the current page
    currentPage = i - 1;

    // Return the same page rect everytime
    return pageRect;
}

#pragma mark Drawing

// The origin of the view is at the upper-left corner
- (BOOL)isFlipped
{
    return YES;
}

- (void)drawRect:(NSRect)r
{
    NSRect nameRect;
    NSRect raiseRect;
    raiseRect.size.height = nameRect.size.height = lineHeight;
    nameRect.origin.x = pageRect.origin.x;
    nameRect.size.width = 200.0;
    raiseRect.origin.x = NSMaxX(nameRect);
    raiseRect.size.width = 100.0;
```

```
NSInteger i;
for (i=0; i<linesPerPage; i++) {
    NSInteger index = (currentPage * linesPerPage) + i;
    if (index >= [people count]) {
        break;
    }
    Person *p = [people objectAtIndex:index];

    // Draw index and name
    nameRect.origin.y = pageRect.origin.y + (i * lineHeight);
    NSString *nameString = [NSString stringWithFormat:@"%2d %@",
                                          index, [p personName]];
    [nameString drawInRect:nameRect withAttributes:attributes];

    raiseRect.origin.y = nameRect.origin.y;
    NSString *raiseString=[NSString stringWithFormat:@"%4.1f%%",
                                              [p expectedRaise]];
    [raiseString drawInRect:raiseRect withAttributes:attributes];
}
}

@end
```

The code in RMDocument.m is pretty simple. First, import PeopleView.h at the top:

```
#import PeopleView.h
```

Then implement **printOperationWithSettings:error:**:

```
- (NSPrintOperation *)printOperationWithSettings:(NSDictionary *)ps
                                       error:(NSError **)e;
{
    PeopleView *view = [[PeopleView alloc] initWithPeople:employees];
    NSPrintInfo *printInfo = [self printInfo];
    NSPrintOperation *printOp
            = [NSPrintOperation printOperationWithView:view
                                          printInfo:printInfo];
    return printOp;
}
```

In the MainMenu.xib file, note that the Print... menu item is nil-targeted and that its action is **printDocument:**, which will trigger **printOperationWithSettings:error:**.

Build and run the application. Note that a setup of multiple pages per sheet (4-up, for example) works. Notice that you can change the paper size and more or fewer people subsequently appear on each page.

# For the More Curious: Are You Drawing to the Screen?

In an application, you will often want to draw things differently on screen than on the printer. For example, in a drawing program, the on-screen view might show a grid on-screen but not when printed on paper.

In your **drawRect:** method, you can ask the current graphics context if it is currently drawing to the screen:

```
if ([[NSGraphicsContext currentContext] isDrawingToScreen]) {
    ...draw grid...
}
```

# Challenge

Add page numbers to the printout.

## Chapter 28
# WEB SERVICES

Web services are getting a lot of hype. In the end, however, a Web service is just an HTTP request and response where each may be carrying XML data (Figure 28.1). So using a Web service from Cocoa is simply a matter of being able to send HTTP requests and receive responses and it also may require generating and parsing XML or JSON.

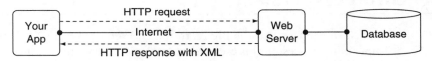

**Figure 28.1**   Your Average Web Service in Action

HTTP requests and responses are handled by **NSURL, NSURLRequest**, and **NSURLConnection** (Figure 28.2).

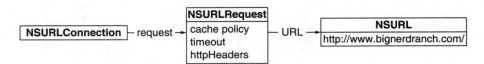

**Figure 28.2**   Classes for Making HTTP Requests

Generating and parsing XML is typically done in one of two ways. The high-level method is to use **NSXMLDocument** and **NSXMLNode**. If you have an **NSData** containing the following XML, **NSXMLDocument** will parse it into a handy tree (Figure 28.3):

```
<?xml version="1.0" encoding="UTF-8"?>
<person>
<first>Larry</first>
<last>Furg</last>
</person>
```

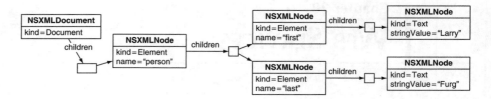

**Figure 28.3**    Parsed XML Document

Low-level XML parsing is done with **NSXMLParser**. As it parses **NSData** containing XML, NSXMLParser makes calls to its delegate as it encounters XML elements and other structures. Low-level XML parsing is most appropriate when working with a large XML document or when memory resources are limited, such as on iOS devices.

# RanchForecast Project

It just so happens that the Big Nerd Ranch Web site has an XML feed of upcoming classes. In this exercise, you are going to write an application that uses this Web service to show the upcoming classes at Big Nerd Ranch in a table view. The app will look like Figure 28.4.

| Date | Class | Location |
| --- | --- | --- |
| Apr 2, 2011 | Beginning Cocoa | Atlanta, Georgia |
| Apr 8, 2011 | iOS Seminar | Marina Room – S... |
| Apr 11, 2011 | Cocoa Commuter Class in ... | Miami, FL |
| Apr 11, 2011 | iOS (iPhone/iPad) | Atlanta, Georgia |
| Apr 18, 2011 | Android | Atlanta, Georgia |
| May 7, 2011 | Beginning iOS (iPhone/iPad) | Atlanta, Georgia |
| Jun 6, 2011 | Django | Atlanta, Georgia |
| Jun 18, 2011 | Beginning Ruby on Rails | Atlanta, Georgia |
| Jul 18, 2011 | OpenGL | Atlanta, Georgia |
| Aug 29, 2011 | Advanced Mac OS X | Atlanta, Georgia |
| Apr 18, 2011 | iOS (iPhone/iPad) | Frankfurt, Germany |
| May 16, 2011 | Android | Frankfurt, Germany |
| Jul 25, 2011 | Cocoa II | Frankfurt, Germany |
| Sep 5, 2011 | Cocoa I | Frankfurt, Germany |
| Oct 17, 2011 | Python Mastery | Frankfurt, Germany |

**Figure 28.4**    Completed Application

Create a new project of type Cocoa Application. Disable Create Document-Based Application, Uses Core Data, and Create Unit Tests. Name the project RanchForecast. Set the Class Prefix to RanchForecast also.

We'll build this application from the model upward. Create a new Objective-C class called **ScheduledClass** that subclasses **NSObject**. Add four properties: name, location, href, and begin in ScheduledClass.h:

```
#import <Foundation/Foundation.h>

@interface ScheduledClass : NSObject {
    NSString *name;
    NSString *location;
    NSString *href;
    NSDate *begin;
}
@property (nonatomic, copy) NSString *name;
@property (nonatomic, copy) NSString *location;
@property (nonatomic, copy) NSString *href;
@property (nonatomic, strong) NSDate *begin;
@end
```

Then synthesize the properties in ScheduledClass.m:

```
#import "ScheduledClass.h"

@implementation ScheduledClass

@synthesize name, location, href, begin;

@end
```

With a simple model, it can often be tempting to use an **NSDictionary**. Frequently, however, taking the time to create a class will make life easier in the long run, especially when a project grows beyond its initial scope.

## NSURLConnection

Now that we have the model defined, we will turn our attention to fetching the data from the Web service. In Cocoa, this is typically done using the **NSURLConnection** class. In order to create a connection, we must first create an **NSURLRequest**, which describes the request to the connection object. **NSURLRequest** is sufficient for simple requests. Requests requiring more conrol, such as specific request headers, should use **NSMutableURLRequest**.

**NSURLConnection** can be used synchronously and asynchronously. In a synchronous connection, the current thread blocks while the request is completed, making it unsuitable for use in the main thread, as this will make the user interface unresponsive while the request is completed.

Asynchronous connections are scheduled in the run loop, and a delegate is specified to respond to various events in the connection's lifetime. In this chapter, we will use an synchronous connection for simplicity.

Create a new subclass of **NSObject** called **ScheduleFetcher**. This class will encapsulate the hard work of communicating with the Web service and parsing the result into the model object. By abstracting away this functionality, we keep our user interface controller classes simple and uncluttered, and we can easily use this class in other projects. Define the interface in ScheduleFetcher.h:

```
#import <Foundation/Foundation.h>

@interface ScheduleFetcher : NSObject <NSXMLParserDelegate> {
    NSMutableArray *classes;
    NSMutableString *currentString;
    NSMutableDictionary *currentFields;
    NSDateFormatter *dateFormatter;
}

// Returns an NSArray of ScheduledClass objects if successful.
// Returns nil on failure.
- (NSArray *)fetchClassesWithError:(NSError **)outError;
@end
```

Define **init** and **fetchClassesWithError:** in ScheduleFetcher.m:

```
#import "ScheduleFetcher.h"
#import "ScheduledClass.h"

@implementation ScheduleFetcher

- (id)init
{
    self = [super init];
    if (self) {
        classes = [[NSMutableArray alloc] init];
        dateFormatter = [[NSDateFormatter alloc] init];
        [dateFormatter setDateFormat:@"yyyy-MM-dd HH:mm:ss zzzz"];
    }
    return self;
}

- (NSArray *)fetchClassesWithError:(NSError **)outError
{
    NSURL *xmlURL = [NSURL URLWithString:
                        @"http://bignerdranch.com/xml/schedule"];

    NSURLRequest *req = [NSURLRequest requestWithURL:xmlURL
                            cachePolicy:NSURLRequestReturnCacheDataElseLoad
                        timeoutInterval:30];
```

```
    NSURLResponse *resp = nil;

    NSData *data = [NSURLConnection sendSynchronousRequest:req
                                        returningResponse:&resp
                                                    error:outError];
    if (!data)
        return nil;

    NSLog(@"Received %ld bytes.", [data length]);

    return nil;
}
```

`@end`

We will use the **NSDateFormatter** later in the parsing process. Before we get into XML parsing, however, let's test our **fetchClassesWithError:** method. In RanchForecastAppDelegate.m:

```
#import "RanchForecastAppDelegate.h"
#import "ScheduleFetcher.h"

@implementation RanchForecastAppDelegate

@synthesize window;

- (void)applicationDidFinishLaunching:(NSNotification *)aNotification
{
    ScheduleFetcher *fetcher = [[ScheduleFetcher alloc] init];
    NSError *error = nil;
    [fetcher fetchClassesWithError:&error];
}
```

Build and run your application. You should see a log message indicating that data was received. Resolve any problems before continuing. It may help to log the error, if an error is being set.

# Add XML Parsing to ScheduleFetcher

Now we need to parse the XML data from the Web service. We will do this by using an instance of **NSXMLParser**. Modify **fetchClassesWithError:** to instantiate and run the parser:

```
- (NSArray *)fetchClassesWithError:(NSError **)outError
{
    BOOL success;
    NSURL *xmlURL = [NSURL URLWithString:
                    @"http://bignerdranch.com/xml/schedule"];
```

```
NSURLRequest *req = [NSURLRequest requestWithURL:xmlURL
                cachePolicy:NSURLRequestReturnCacheDataElseLoad
            timeoutInterval:30];

NSURLResponse *resp = nil;

NSData *data = [NSURLConnection sendSynchronousRequest:req
                                     returningResponse:&resp
                                                 error:outError];
if (!data)
    return nil;

[classes removeAllObjects];

NSXMLParser *parser;
parser = [[NSXMLParser alloc] initWithData:data];
[parser setDelegate:self];

success = [parser parse];
if (!success)
{
    *outError = [parser parserError];
    return nil;
}

NSArray *output = [classes copy];
return output;
}
```

Note that the parser's delegate is set to self. As all the **NSXMLParserDelegate** protocol methods are optional, we need to add only the ones we are interested in. Add them now to ScheduleFetcher.m:

```
#pragma mark -
#pragma mark NSXMLParserDelegate Methods

- (void)parser:(NSXMLParser *)parser
  didStartElement:(NSString *)elementName
    namespaceURI:(NSString *)namespaceURI
    qualifiedName:(NSString *)qName
      attributes:(NSDictionary *)attributeDict
{
    if ([elementName isEqual:@"class"])
    {
        currentFields = [[NSMutableDictionary alloc] init];
    }
    else if ([elementName isEqual:@"offering"])
    {
        [currentFields setObject:[attributeDict objectForKey:@"href"]
                    forKey:@"href"];
    }
}
```

```objc
- (void)parser:(NSXMLParser *)parser
 didEndElement:(NSString *)elementName
  namespaceURI:(NSString *)namespaceURI
 qualifiedName:(NSString *)qName
{
    if ([elementName isEqual:@"class"])
    {
        ScheduledClass *currentClass = [[ScheduledClass alloc] init];

        [currentClass setName:[currentFields
                                    objectForKey:@"offering"]];
        [currentClass setLocation:[currentFields
                                    objectForKey:@"location"]];
        [currentClass setHref:[currentFields
                                    objectForKey:@"href"]];

        NSString *beginString = [currentFields objectForKey:@"begin"];
        NSDate *beginDate = [dateFormatter
                                    dateFromString:beginString];
        [currentClass setBegin:beginDate];

        [classes addObject:currentClass];
        currentClass = nil;

        currentFields = nil;
    }
    else if (currentFields && currentString)
    {
        NSString *trimmed;
        trimmed = [currentString stringByTrimmingCharactersInSet:
                        [NSCharacterSet whitespaceAndNewlineCharacterSet]];
        [currentFields setObject:trimmed forKey:elementName];
    }
    currentString = nil;
}

- (void)parser:(NSXMLParser *)parser
  foundCharacters:(NSString *)string
{
    if (!currentString) {
        currentString = [[NSMutableString alloc] init];
    }
    [currentString appendString:string];
}
```

As mentioned at the start of the chapter, when **NSXMLParser**'s **parse** method is called, it scans through the data provided, calling its delegate for each change in the structure of the XML data that it encounters. As is this case in this exercise, you will frequently be interested only in the start and end of elements, as well as the character data that occurs in between them.

The delegate is responsible for managing any state information during the parsing process. **ScheduleFetcher** uses its currentString, currentFields, and `classes` instance variables for this purpose. The string data that `currentString` accumulates for the current element is then stored in `currentFields` once the element ends. Once each `class` element ends, a **ScheduledClass** instance is created and populated with the values from `currentFields`, and the process starts over again for the next class.

Once the parsing is completed, a copy is made of the `classes` array (to make it immutable), and the result is returned.

Run the application again and use the debugger to inspect the `classes` array before it is returned to see that the XML is being parsed.

## Lay Out the Interface

In `RanchForecastAppDelegate.h`, declare a table view outlet and an array of classes:

```
#import <Cocoa/Cocoa.h>

@interface RanchForecastAppDelegate : NSObject <NSApplicationDelegate>
{
    IBOutlet NSTableView *tableView;
    NSArray *classes;
}
@property (strong) IBOutlet NSWindow *window;
@end
```

Open `MainMenu.xib`. Drop a table view onto the window. Ensure that the table view's Content Mode is set to Cell Based. Set the table view to have three columns: Date, Class, and Location. Drag a date formatter onto the Date column cell and set its Date Style to Medium (Figure 28.5).

Control-click on the **RanchForecastAppDelegate** to bring up the Connection panel and connect the `tableView` outlet.

Control-click on the table view to bring up its Connection panel. Make **RanchForecastAppDelegate** the data source for the table view. (Don't see the `dataSource` outlet? Did you select the scroll view instead of the table view?)

In Chapter 7, we talked about how powerful key-value coding can be. Let's use that now to make things easy on the coding end and set the identitier of each table column to be the name of the **ScheduledClass** property we want to display in that column. Use the Identity Inspector for each column of the table view to set the identifiers to `begin`, `name`, and `location` for the Date, Class, and Location

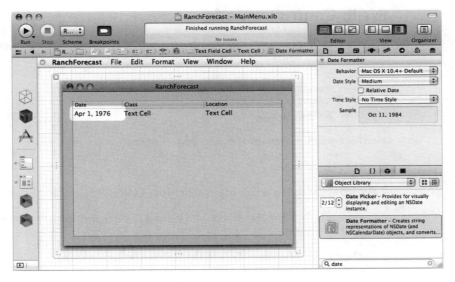

**Figure 28.5**  Lay Out the Interface

columns, respectively (Figure 28.6). If you are using a version of Xcode prior to 4.2, the identifer field will be shown in the Attributes Inspector. Use the Attributes Inspector to make each column not Editable.

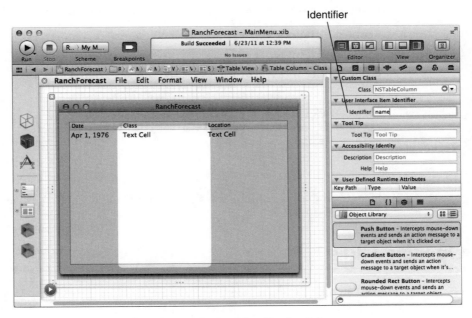

**Figure 28.6**  Setting Identifier for Columns

## Write Controller Code

Update RanchForecastAppDelegate.m to display the fetched classes in the table view:

```
#import "RanchForecastAppDelegate.h"
#import "ScheduleFetcher.h"
#import "ScheduledClass.h"

@implementation RanchForecastAppDelegate

@synthesize window;

- (void)applicationDidFinishLaunching:(NSNotification *)aNotification
{
    ScheduleFetcher *fetcher = [[ScheduleFetcher alloc] init];
    NSError *error;

    classes = [fetcher fetchClassesWithError:&error];
    [tableView reloadData];
}
```

Now add the **NSTableViewDataSource** methods:

```
#pragma mark -
#pragma mark NSTableViewDataSource

- (NSInteger)numberOfRowsInTableView:(NSTableView *)theTableView
{
    return [classes count];
}
- (id)tableView:(NSTableView *)theTableView
  objectValueForTableColumn:(NSTableColumn *)tableColumn
                        row:(NSInteger)row
{
    ScheduledClass *c = [classes objectAtIndex:row];
    return [c valueForKey:[tableColumn identifier]];
}

@end
```

Build and run the application. You should see a list of upcoming classes.

# Opening URLs

The last step is to make it possible for the user to double-click on a class to open it in his or her browser.

In **applicationDidFinishLaunching:**, set the doubleAction and target of the table view:

```
- (void)applicationDidFinishLaunching:(NSNotification *)aNotification
{
    [tableView setTarget:self];
    [tableView setDoubleAction:@selector(openClass:)];

    ScheduleFetcher *fetcher = [[ScheduleFetcher alloc] init];
    NSError *error;

    classes = [fetcher fetchClassesWithError:&error];
    [tableView reloadData];
}
```

Finally, implement **openClass:**. Here you are using the **NSWorkspace** class. **NSWorkspace** represents the Finder.

```
- (void)openClass:(id)sender
{
    ScheduledClass *c = [classes objectAtIndex:
                                    [tableView clickedRow]];

    NSURL *baseUrl = [NSURL URLWithString:
                        @"http://www.bignerdranch.com/"];
    NSURL *url = [NSURL URLWithString:[c href]
                        relativeToURL:baseUrl];
    [[NSWorkspace sharedWorkspace] openURL:url];
}
```

Build and run the application. Double-clicking on a title should open the page for the selected class in your default browser.

# Challenge: Add a WebView

At the moment, you are using **NSWorkspace** to open the Web page in another application. Perhaps the user would like it if the the web page appeared in a sheet in the existing application (Figure 28.7).

The challenge, then, is to add a new window with a **WebView** to your application. Bring the window onto the screen as a sheet.

You will need to add the WebKit framework to your project.

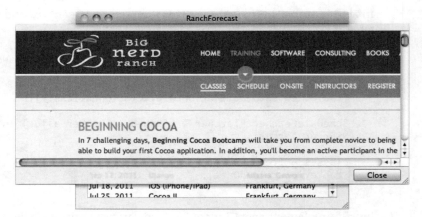

**Figure 28.7**   Use WebView to Display Details

If you have a string representing a URL, you can get a **WebView** to load that URL by sending it the following message:

```
- (void)setMainFrameURL:(NSString *)URLString;
```

That should be all you need. If you want a progress indicator, you will need to make your controller the "frame load delegate" of the **WebView**:

```
[webView setFrameLoadDelegate:self];
```

Then your controller can implement the following methods:

```
- (void)webView:(WebView *)wv
        didStartProvisionalLoadForFrame:(WebFrame *)wf;

- (void)webView:(WebView *)wv
        didFinishLoadForFrame:(WebFrame *)wf;

- (void)webView:(WebView *)wv
        didFailProvisionalLoadWithError:(NSError *)error
                            forFrame:(WebFrame *)wf;
```

## Chapter 29
# BLOCKS

Let's pretend that we're writing a zombie game. Specifically, we're working on the zombie AI code. We want a method on our **Zombie** object to find nearby brains. So we start with this:

```
@implementation Zombie

- (NSArray *)brainsForFlags:(NSInteger)flags
{
    return [[self game] allBrains];
}

@end
```

It's a good start, but it would be a lot more useful it if returned the brains in order of proximity to the zombie, that is, sorted by the distance between the zombie and the brain. The zombie is hungry, after all. **NSArray**'s **sortedArrayUsingSelector:** is usually a great first choice for sorting. It calls the given selector on the objects in the array in order to compare them with their neighbors. For example, **NSString** provides a **compare:** method. Thus, we can use it to sort an array of strings:

```
NSArray *sortedStrings =
        [theStrings sortedArrayUsingSelector:@selector(compare:)];
```

We might entertain adding a **compareByDistanceToZombie:** method to the **Brain** class. But how would it know which zombie it's comparing the distance to? The method **sortedArrayUsingSelector:** doesn't provide any way to pass contextual information to the sorting process.

**NSArray**'s **sortedArrayUsingFunction:context:** seems like a better choice. We can write a C function and tell **sortedArrayUsingFunction:context:** what function to use to compare the brains. Using it would look something like this:

```
NSInteger CmpBrainsByZombieDist(id a, id b, void *context)
{
    Brain *brainA = a;
```

```
        Brain *brainB = b;
        Zombie *zombie = (__bridge Zombie *)context;
        float distA = [zombie distanceToBrain:brainA];
        float distB = [zombie distanceToBrain:brainB];
        if (distA == distB) return NSOrderedSame;
        else if (distA < distB) return NSOrderedAscending;
        else return NSOrderedDescending;
}

- (NSArray *)brainsForFlags:(NSInteger)flags
{
        NSArray *allBrains = [[self game] allBrains];
        return [brains sortedArrayUsingFunction:CmpBrainsByZombieDist
                                        context:(__bridge void *)self];
}
```

The void pointer context argument is used to provide additional data to the comparison function; we use this to pass the pointer to the **Zombie** instance (`self`). Note that the `__bridge` casting is necessary to convert an object reference into a type out of ARC's control.

We've got a workable solution now. After some playtesting, however, we decide that we want our zombies to have a more varied palette. If `frenzy` mode is on, the zombies should seek out the brain with the highest IQ, no matter where it is in the game world. Now we need to supply multiple parameters to **CmpBrains-ByZombieDist**, but it all needs to be passed in through a single void pointer argument.

Perhaps you are starting to see that this approach has a number of downsides. Maintaining C functions for custom sorting forces our input parameters to be awkwardly funneled through a void pointer. An **NSDictionary** or custom C struct will get the job done, but they add complexity. Additionally, the C function must be separate from the code that calls it, making it more challenging to efficiently maintain the code.

There is, however, an elegant solution to this problem: blocks. You can think of blocks as functions that can be passed around just like an object. Consider the following solution. The caret (^) in the following code is the start of the block:

```
- (NSArray *)brainsForFlags:(NSInteger)flags
{
        NSArray *allBrains = [[self game] allBrains];
        return [brains sortedArrayUsingComparator:^(id a, id b) {
            Brain *brainA = a;
            Brain *brainB = b;
            float criteriaA, criteriaB;
            if (flags & FrenzyMode)
            {
```

```
            criteriaA = [brainA iq];
            criteriaB = [brainB iq];
        }
        else
        {
            criteriaA = [self distanceToBrain:brainA];
            criteriaB = [self distanceToBrain:brainB];
        }
        if (criteriaA == criteriaB) return NSOrderedSame;
        else if (criteriaA < criteriaB) return NSOrderedAscending;
        else return NSOrderedDescending;
    }];
}
```

We'll get into the particulars of blocks syntax in the next section. Until then, let's look at some of the more interesting parts of this method. The **sortedArrayUsingComparator:** method takes a block as its only parameter. You'll notice that blocks look quite a bit like C functions. They have arguments and a body. Where they differ from C functions is that they do not have to be named (they are anonymous) and can be treated just like an expression. In fact, they are objects.

This particular block takes two arguments (a and b) and refers to variables that are defined outside the block (self and flags). This is one of the more useful aspects of blocks: They capture the value of variables from the scope outside the block. There's generally no need to package up your variables to squeeze into the argument list: You can simply use the variables that are in scope.

Blocks provide an elegant way to address such problems as nontrivial sort criteria, as well as much more sophisticated problems. Next, we'll talk about the particulars of using blocks.

# Block Syntax

Blocks enable the developer to create objects that encapsulate instructions, inline with the rest of their code, which capture the values of variables that are within scope. The resulting object can then be passed about and even copied, just like any other object.

The block syntax can be a little off-putting at first (it is not dissimilar from C function pointer syntax), but the benefits far outweigh the time you will spend getting used to it. Let's define a simple block:

```
int captured = 1; // Local variable 'captured'

int (^offsetter)(int) = ^(int x) { return x + captured; };
```

On the first line, we create a local variable: `captured`. Next, we declare a variable named `offsetter`, which is a block. Whenever we are creating or defining a block, we use the ^ operator. This block returns an integer and takes an integer as its only argument.

On the right side of the equal sign, we define the block (note the ^, again). This part looks a lot like a C function definition. We specify that the integer parameter will be called x, and then we provide the body of the block in braces. An annotated version is shown in Figure 29.1.

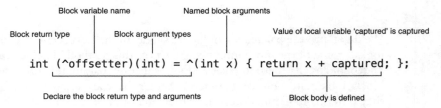

**Figure 29.1**   Anatomy of a Block

Aside from the magic of creating a block of code on the stack like this, two interesting things are happening here: First, our block definition does not specify the return type of the block. The compiler is smart enough to figure it out from the return statement. Second, we refer to the variable `captured` inside the block. A blocks programmer would say that we are capturing the value of `captured` in the block. This is a very powerful feature of blocks.

How do we call a block? As it turns out, it looks quite a bit like a C function call:

```
int answer = offsetter(2);
```

Note that `answer` is now 3 (2 + 1 = 3). What if we change the value of `captured` and call the block again?

```
captured = 64;
answer = offsetter(2);
```

The result is the same; `answer` is still 3 because the *value* of `captured` was captured when we defined the block. We cannot change `captured` from outside the block, and as it happens, we can't change it from inside the block either. To do that, we need the __block type specifier.

By default, captured values are considered `const` within the block. If you need to modify a captured value from inside a block, you can add the __block type specifier:

```
__block BOOL modifiable = YES;
```

However, when a variable is marked with __block, the compiler treats it as what is essentially a global variable. Any block that was created with it in scope can change its value. Because it does come with some performance overhead, __block is not the default. Typically, it is more useful to capture only the value of a variable.

## Memory and Objects within Blocks

When a block is defined, it is created on the stack. When the method or function it was defined in exits, the block is removed from memory along with all the other local stack variables. Sometimes, this is fine; we may wish to use the block only for the lifetime of that particular method call, as in our earlier brain-sorting example. The block is not used after the method returns.

Other times, however, we want the block to live on well after the method returns. Because the block is created on the stack, we must copy it in order to make sure that it is not deallocated with the current stack frame. For this reason, we recommend that you copy blocks when assigning them to instance variables:

```
@property (nonatomic, copy) int (^arithmeticOperationBlock)(int);
```

Just like we can capture scalar values within blocks, we can also capture pointers to objects. When a pointer to an Objective-C object is captured by a block, it is retained (a strong reference is formed). Any objects retained by the block are released when the block goes out of scope or is deallocated:

```
NSMutableArray *array;
array = [NSMutableArray array]; // retain count of 1, autoreleased

void (^simpleBlock)() = ^{
    [array addObject:@"Q"];       // array pointer captured, retained
};

simpleBlock();

return; // simpleBlock is popped from stack, releases array
```

Note that variables with the __block specifier will not be retained by the block. This can be useful in preventing strong reference cycles. Note that this is still the case under ARC; however, ARC still considers a __block pointer a strong reference and thus retains it, unless you mark the variable __weak.

Consider the following code:

```
controller = [[MyController alloc] init];
controller.block = ^{
    [controller doSomething];
};
```

This code creates a strong reference cycle. Do you see it?

**MyController** holds a strong reference to block. The block, however, holds a strong reference to the instance of **MyController**! The simplest approach is to use a temporary weak reference variable, since child objects (the block) should have only weak references to their parents (the controller).

```
controller = [[MyController alloc] init];
__weak MyController *weakController = controller;
controller.block = ^{
    [weakController doSomething];
};
```

This resolves the strong reference cycle.

## Availability of Blocks

Blocks are available beginning with Mac OS X 10.6 and iOS 4.0 and are an extension to the C language. Thus, you don't need to be using Objective-C to take advantage of blocks, but you do need a compiler that understands blocks, as well as runtime support. If you are targeting Mac OS X 10.5 or iOS 2.2, PLBlocks from Plausible Labs provides a solution well worth looking into.

The first high-profile API to make use of blocks was Grand Central Dispatch, a Mac OS X concurrency library. As such, many people think of blocks as being useful only in multithreaded programming. We believe that blocks are extremely handy in a very broad range of programming settings. As you solve problems in your own projects, you may find blocks to be a great fit in some unexpected places.

## RanchForecast: Going Asynchronous

Our RanchForecast application works great in ideal circumstances. That is, with a speedy Internet connection. However, what if our Internet connection is poor? Or what if we were loading a much larger XML document that might take several seconds (or worse) to download?

Our customers will complain, and rightly so, that the application looks as if it has frozen until the request completes and the table updates. The reason is that we are running a synchronous request in the main thread, the very same thread that handles UI events. If we use **NSURLConnection** in the asynchronous style, however, we can avoid blocking the main thread, and the UI will be nice and responsive. Let's update our **ScheduleFetcher** class to do things the Right Way.

Recall that using **NSURLConnection** asynchronously means that we will create the connection and specify a delegate, using **initWithRequest:delegate:**. This call will return immediately, and the delegate will be called to handle various events during the connection's lifetime. **NSURLConnection** works with the run loop to make this possible.

In our application, **ScheduleFetcher** will act as the connection's delegate and implement the three delegate methods needed to handle receiving data and the successful and unsuccessful completion of the request:

```
- (void)connection:(NSURLConnection *)connection
    didReceiveData:(NSData *)data;

- (void)connectionDidFinishLoading:(NSURLConnection *)connection;

- (void)connection:(NSURLConnection *)connection
  didFailWithError:(NSError *)error;
```

## Receiving the Asynchronous Response

If the response loading is taking place asynchronously and **ScheduleFetcher** will not block, how will **RanchForecastAppDelegate** know when the class schedule has been loaded or when an error has occurred?

We can accomplish this in several ways. The most obvious approach would be to add a pointer to **RanchForecastAppDelegate** in the **ScheduleFetcher**. Once the schedule has been fetched, the fetcher would call a method on the app delegate (**updateWithClasses:**, perhaps). The downside of this approach, however, is that we would have just made **ScheduleFetcher** dependent on **RanchForecastAppDelegate**. If we wanted to use **ScheduleFetcher** in another project later on (and we will), we would need to edit its code, which then leaves us with multiple versions of **ScheduleFetcher**.

Another approach is to use the delegate pattern. It works great for **NSURLConnection**; **ScheduleFetcher** could use it as well. We would define a **ScheduleFetcherDelegate** protocol, and **RanchForecastAppDelegate** would conform to the protocol and set itself as the delegate. This approach is very reasonable; it decouples the classes, keeping **ScheduleFetcher** reusable, but it feels somewhat heavy-handed for such a simple Web service response.

Yet another approach is to use our knowledge of blocks to apply the completion block design pattern. In this pattern, our fetch method on **ScheduleFetcher** would take a block as its only parameter. **ScheduleFetcher** then calls the block later when it is ready to deliver the results or report an error. Completion blocks are very compact; no additional methods are needed and they have the advantage of allowing us to keep the response-handling code close to the place where the Web service call is initiated.

Let's modify **ScheduleFetcher** to perform the request asynchronously and report the results using a completion block.

In ScheduleFetcher.h, define the ScheduleFetchResultBlock type. Because the block syntax involves a good bit of punctuation, it is often helpful to typedef block types so that they can be used more gracefully in the future.

```
#import <Foundation/Foundation.h>

typedef void (^ScheduleFetcherResultBlock)(NSArray *classes,
                                           NSError *error);
```

Now add three new instance variables and the replacement for **fetchClass-esWithError:** to **ScheduleFetcher**:

```
@interface ScheduleFetcher : NSObject <NSXMLParserDelegate> {
@private
    NSMutableArray *classes;
    NSMutableString *currentString;
    NSMutableDictionary *currentFields;
    NSDateFormatter *dateFormatter;

    ScheduleFetcherResultBlock resultBlock;
    NSMutableData *responseData;
    NSURLConnection *connection;
}
- (void)fetchClassesWithBlock:(ScheduleFetcherResultBlock)theBlock;

@end
```

Now, in ScheduleFetcher.m, remove **fetchClassesWithError:** and implement **fetchClassesWithBlock::**

```
- (void)fetchClassesWithBlock:(ScheduleFetcherResultBlock)theBlock
{
    // Copy the block to ensure that it is not kept on the stack:
    resultBlock = [theBlock copy];

    NSURL *xmlURL = [NSURL URLWithString:
                    @"http://bignerdranch.com/xml/schedule"];
```

```
NSURLRequest *req = [NSURLRequest requestWithURL:xmlURL
               cachePolicy:NSURLRequestReturnCacheDataElseLoad
           timeoutInterval:30];

    connection = [[NSURLConnection alloc] initWithRequest:req
                                             delegate:self];
    if (connection)
    {
        responseData = [[NSMutableData alloc] init];
    }
}
```

Note that theBlock is copied and the resulting pointer stored in resultBlock. We copy the block because it may still be on the stack of the calling method. If so, the block will be deallocated when that method exits. Because we are starting an asynchronous request and the calling method is guaranteed to return before the request completes, we need to be sure that the block's memory will be valid until we call it with the results. If theBlock were going to be used only within this method and not after we return, copying it would not be necessary.

The resultBlock, connection, and responseData objects are created when the fetch is initiated. It's a good idea to clean them up when the request completes. To reduce repetition, add a new method called **cleanup**:

```
- (void)cleanup
{
    responseData = nil;
    connection = nil;
    resultBlock = nil;
}
```

Still in ScheduleFetcher.m, implement the **NSURLConnection** delegate methods:

```
#pragma mark -
#pragma mark NSURLConnection Delegate

- (void)connection:(NSURLConnection *)theConnection
   didReceiveData:(NSData *)data
{
    [responseData appendData:data];
}

- (void)connectionDidFinishLoading:(NSURLConnection *)theConnection
{
    [classes removeAllObjects];

    NSXMLParser *parser = [[NSXMLParser alloc]
                          initWithData:responseData];
    [parser setDelegate:self];
```

```
        BOOL success = [parser parse];
        if (!success)
        {
            resultBlock(nil, [parser parserError]);
        }
        else
        {
            NSArray *output = [classes copy];
            resultBlock(output, nil);
        }

        [self cleanup];
}

- (void)connection:(NSURLConnection *)theConnection
  didFailWithError:(NSError *)error
{
    resultBlock(nil, error);

    [self cleanup];
}
```

Response data is collected in **connection:didReceiveData:** and then parsed in **connectionDidFinishLoading:**. We then call resultBlock with the results or error condition.

Now it's time to update **RanchForecastAppDelegate** to work with the new interface to **ScheduleFetcher**. In RanchForecastAppDelegate.m, update **applicationDidFinishLaunching:**:

```
- (void)applicationDidFinishLaunching:(NSNotification *)aNotification
{
    [tableView setTarget:self];
    [tableView setDoubleAction:@selector(openClass:)];

    ScheduleFetcher *fetcher = [[ScheduleFetcher alloc] init];

    [fetcher fetchClassesWithBlock:^(NSArray *theClasses,
                                     NSError *error)        {
        if (theClasses)
        {
            classes = theClasses;
            [tableView reloadData];
        }
        else
        {
            NSAlert *alert = [[NSAlert alloc] init];
            [alert setAlertStyle:NSCriticalAlertStyle];
            [alert setMessageText:@"Error loading schedule."];
            [alert setInformativeText:[error localizedDescription]];
            [alert addButtonWithTitle:@"OK"];
```

```
                    [alert beginSheetModalForWindow:self.window
                                   modalDelegate:nil
                                   didEndSelector:nil
                                      contextInfo:nil];
            }
      }];
}
```

Build and run the application. Notice that the application appears more quickly now because the request is performed asynchronously.

# Challenge: Design a Delegate

Earlier in this chapter, we discussed how we might use the delegate design pattern as a means for passing Web service data back to the interested parties. Create a copy of this project and refactor it to use this pattern instead of blocks. Remember that delegate properties should be weak references to prevent a strong reference cycle.

## Chapter 30

# DEVELOPING FOR iOS

Applications for the iPhone and iPad are written using Xcode and the Cocoa Touch Frameworks. Cocoa Touch comprises Foundation, Core Graphics, and UIKit. UIKit is analogous to AppKit, supplying the windows, events, views, buttons, and so on, for iPhone programmers. UIKit is, however, not the same as AppKit. This chapter will get you started developing applications on iOS, with an emphasis on what is not the same.

In particular, you will not have the garbage collector, but you can use ARC on iOS 5 or, if you choose, manual reference counting (retain/release) for memory management. You will use OpenGL ES instead of regular OpenGL. Windows and table-view cells are subclasses of **UIView**.

## Porting RanchForecast to iOS

Most of the stuff that makes RanchForecast work (table views, **NSXMLParser**, **NSURLConnection**) exists on iOS. Porting it all from Cocoa to Cocoa Touch will give you a feel for many of the differences between the two platforms. You will use two common iOS features in your port: a navigation controller and a table view. There will be two view controllers (subclasses of **UIViewController**) (Figure 30.1).

View controllers are just what they sound like: controller classes that are responsible for a **UIView** and its contents. In iOS view controllers are generally used to represent one screen of information. We will discuss the role of view controllers in AppKit in the next chapter.

The navigation controller manages a stack of view controllers, animating them on and off the screen. The navigation bar, at the top, provides users with a sense of their place within the stack, usually with a Back button on the left, a title in the center, and sometimes a button on the right. An iOS app has only one

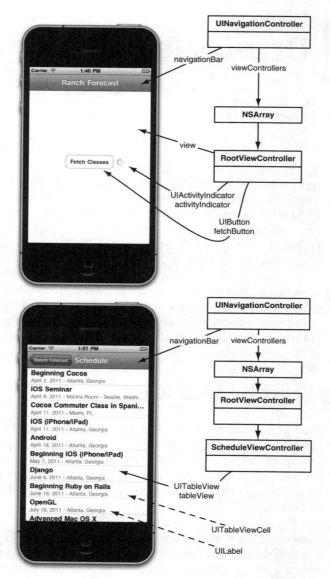

**Figure 30.1**    RootViewController and ScheduleViewController

window. View controllers are used extensively in conjunction with navigation controllers to create the sense of multiple screens.

In Xcode, create a new iOS Application using the Empty Application template (Figure 30.2). Some versions of Xcode refer to this as a Window-Based Application.

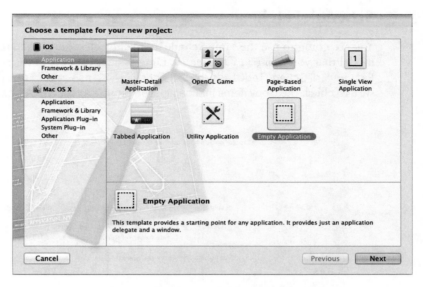

**Figure 30.2**   New iOS Empty Application

Name the project RanchForecastTouch, set the Class Prefix to
RanchForecastTouch, and set Device Family to Universal (Figure 30.3). This
will create more files, but it will be easier in the future to tailor your app for
both iPhone and iPad devices.

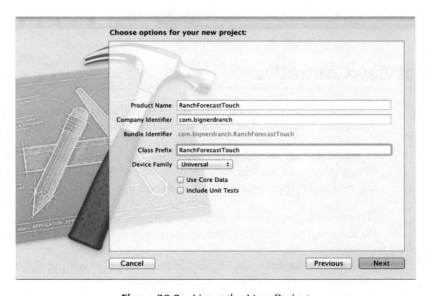

**Figure 30.3**   Name the New Project

## ScheduleFetcher

You are going to use the same **ScheduleFetcher** class and **ScheduledClass** model that you wrote in Chapter 29. Drag ScheduleFetcher.h, Schedule-Fetcher.m, ScheduledClass.h, and ScheduledClass.m into this project. Be sure to check the Copy items into destination group's folder check box (Figure 30.4).

**Figure 30.4**   Copy Files

# RootViewController

Create a new **UIViewController** subclass called **RootViewController**. Check the option box labeled With XIB for user interface  (Figure 30.5).

Open RootViewController.xib. In the Attributes Inspector for the view, under Simulated Metrics, set Top Bar to Navigation Bar (Figure 30.6). This sets the size of the view to be appropriate for a navigation bar.

Drag a button and activity indicator onto the view. Set the button's title to Fetch Classes, and set the activity indicator to Hides When Stopped (Figure 30.7).

Now enable the Assistant Editor. This will simplify creating the outlets and actions that we need. Ensure that the Assistant Editor's jump bar is set to Automatic; this will display RootViewController.h in the editor.

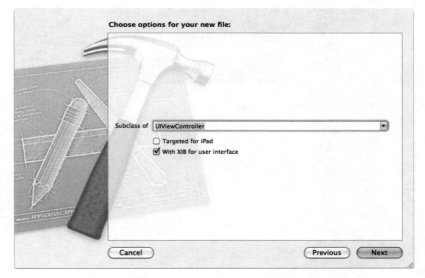

**Figure 30.5**    New UIViewController Subclass

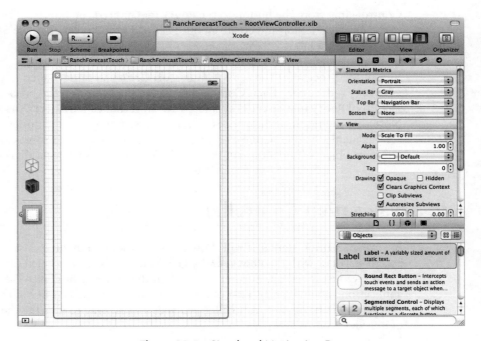

**Figure 30.6**    Simulated Navigation Bar

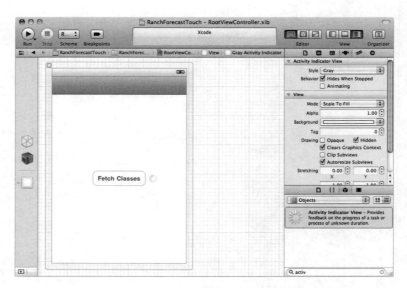

**Figure 30.7**    Set the Activity Indicator to Hides When Stopped

Control-drag from the button to the **RootViewController** interface declaration in the Assistant Editor and create an outlt called fetchButton. See the Storage to Weak (Figure 30.8).

Repeat the process for the activity indicator: Create an outlet called activityIndicator. Then Control-drag from the button to the properties section of **RootViewController** and create an action called **fetchClasses:**. Note that the result of this process is the same as typing out the outlets and actions manually, then Control-dragging between Connection panels and the interface objects. The same can be done in Mac and iOS projects alike.

# Add a Navigation Controller

As our application stands, it will show a blank view on launching. We want the app to start out with the **RootViewController**, which has the Fetch Classes button we just wired up. Furthermore, when the user touches Fetch Classes, the application should display a list of classes. As we mentioned earlier in the chapter, iOS's navigation controller provides an easy way to manage the display of our view controllers.

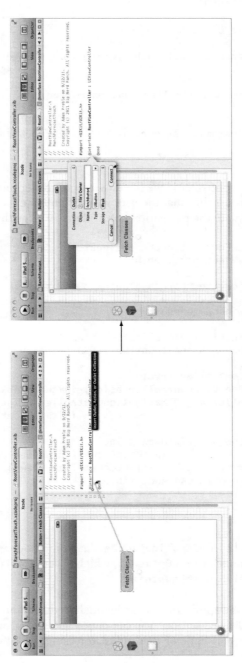

**Figure 30.8** Control-Drag to Create the fetchButton Outlet

Open RanchForecastTouchAppDelegate.h and add an instance variable for the navigation controller:

```
#import <UIKit/UIKit.h>

@interface RanchForecastTouchAppDelegate : NSObject
                                            <UIApplicationDelegate>
{
    UINavigationController *navController;
}

@property (nonatomic, strong) IBOutlet UIWindow *window;

@end
```

The root-view controller is the lowest view controller on the stack and generally the first view controller that the user will see. In RanchForecastTouchAppDelegate.m, instantiate the navigation controller as well as the root-view controller:

```
#import "RanchForecastTouchAppDelegate.h"
#import "RootViewController.h"

@implementation RanchForecastTouchAppDelegate

@synthesize window=_window;

- (BOOL)application:(UIApplication *)application
    didFinishLaunchingWithOptions:(NSDictionary *)launchOptions
{
    RootViewController *rvc;
    rvc = [[RootViewController alloc] initWithNibName:nil bundle:nil];
    navController = [[UINavigationController alloc]
                                    initWithRootViewController:rvc];

    self.window = [[UIWindow alloc]
                        initWithFrame:[[UIScreen mainScreen] bounds]];
    [self.window addSubview:[navController view]];
    [self.window makeKeyAndVisible];

    return YES;
}
```

Note that iOS has a **UIApplicationDelegate** method, **application:didFinishLaunchingWithOptions:**, which is very similar to Cocoa's **applicationDidFinishLaunching:**.

Build and run the application. It will launch in the simulator and you should see the Fetch Classes button. You can choose between launching your application in the iPhone or iPad simulator using the Scheme popup on the Xcode toolbar.

# ScheduleViewController

The second view controller, **ScheduleViewController**, will be used to display the schedule itself once the fetch has completed. Create a new **UIViewController Subclass**, but this time set it to be a subclass of **UITableViewController**. Uncheck With XIB for user interface. Name it **ScheduleViewController**. **UITableViewController** is itself a subclass of **UIViewController**.

Open ScheduleViewController.h and add two instance variables and a property:

```
#import <UIKit/UIKit.h>

@interface ScheduleViewController : UITableViewController {
    NSArray *classes;
    NSDateFormatter *dateFormatter;
}
@property (nonatomic, strong) NSArray *classes;

@end
```

In ScheduleViewController.m, import ScheduledClass.h, synthesize classes and make some additions to **initWithStyle:** and **dealloc**:

```
#import "ScheduleViewController.h"
#import "ScheduledClass.h"

@implementation ScheduleViewController

@synthesize classes;

- (id)initWithStyle:(UITableViewStyle)style
{
    self = [super initWithStyle:style];
    if (self)
    {
        dateFormatter = [[NSDateFormatter alloc] init];
        [dateFormatter setDateStyle:NSDateFormatterLongStyle];
        [[self navigationItem] setTitle:@"Schedule"];
    }
    return self;
}
```

Note that we are setting the title of this view controller's navigation item. Each view controller has a navigation item, which determines what is displayed in the navigation bar when that view controller is topmost. The title is shown in the navigation bar; it is also used to provide the title for the Back button when the topmost view controller is directly above this one. It is also possible to configure within the navigation bar buttons (called bar button items) that are specific to this view controller.

# UITableViewController

Table views, found in nearly every OS application from the iPod to Stocks, provide a highly customizable way of displaying ordered sets of information to the user. After working with table views for a bit, you will quickly see that most of the attractive user interfaces in your favorite apps are simply table views.

**UITableViewController** is a subclass of **UIViewController** specifically designed to manage a **UITableView**. **UITableViewController** automatically creates the table view it manages. It is also the data source and delegate for the table view, so your **UITableViewController** subclass must override the appropriate methods to get data on the table view. Consistent with data source and delegation methods in other Apple frameworks, you do not give the table view data whenever you want. When ready to display data, the table view will ask you for the necessary information.

The Xcode template for a **UITableViewController** subclass includes the necessary **UITableViewDataSource** methods. Fill them in for ScheduleViewController.m:

```
#pragma mark - Table view data source

- (NSInteger)numberOfSectionsInTableView:(UITableView *)tableView
{
    return 1;
}

- (NSInteger)tableView:(UITableView *)tableView
 numberOfRowsInSection:(NSInteger)section
{
    // Return the number of rows in the section.
    return [classes count];
}

- (UITableViewCell *)tableView:(UITableView *)tableView
        cellForRowAtIndexPath:(NSIndexPath *)indexPath
{
    static NSString *CellIdentifier = @"Cell";

    UITableViewCell *cell =
        [tableView dequeueReusableCellWithIdentifier:CellIdentifier];
    if (cell == nil) {
        cell = [[UITableViewCell alloc]
                    initWithStyle:UITableViewCellStyleSubtitle
                    reuseIdentifier:CellIdentifier];
    }
```

```
        ScheduledClass *c = [classes objectAtIndex:[indexPath row]];
        NSString *details =  [NSString stringWithFormat:@"%@ - %@",
                                [dateFormatter stringFromDate:c.begin],
                                c.location];

        [[cell textLabel] setText:[c name]];
        [[cell detailTextLabel] setText:details];
        return cell;
}
```

**UITableView** works very similarly to view-based table views in Cocoa. The table
view asks its data source to provide a **UITableViewCell** for each row. The data
source obtains a view cell (we will talk about that in a moment) and populates its
controls (labels, in this case) with the data values from the model.

Note that the view cell itself is obtained in one of two ways: through a call to
**dequeueReusableCellWithIdentifier:** or by creating one outright.
**UITableView** takes advantage of the fact that most table-view cells will have the
same layout. Thus, when the user scrolls in the table such that a row is no longer
visible, the cell for that row is made available for reuse. In this way, the
**UITableView** keeps memory usage low and minimizes time spent configuring
the view cells. The table view uses identifiers to look up cells of a certain type.
Thus, you can still take advantage of the cell reuse by using unique identifiers for
distinct cell layouts.

# Pushing View Controllers

**ScheduleViewController** is ready to display schedule data in its table. We
need to modify **RootViewController** to obtain the schedule data and then cue
**ScheduleViewController** to display it.

In RootViewController.m, import ScheduleFetcher.h and
ScheduleViewController.h, and set the title of the navigation item:

```
#import "RootViewController.h"
#import "ScheduleFetcher.h"
#import "ScheduleViewController.h"

@implementation RootViewController

- (id)initWithNibName:(NSString *)nibNameOrNil
            bundle:(NSBundle *)nibBundleOrNil
{
    self = [super initWithNibName:nibNameOrNil bundle:nibBundleOrNil];
    if (self) {
```

```
            [[self navigationItem] setTitle:@"Ranch Forecast"];
        }
        return self;
    }
```

Now we are ready to fill in the code for the **fetchClasses:** action. We will use **ScheduleFetcher**, which we copied directly from the Cocoa version of this application, to obtain the results. The block we supply will be called once the results have been received or if an error has occurred. If we receive the schedule, we will create a new instance of **ScheduleViewController** and push it onto the navigation controller's stack, thus presenting it to the user. If an error occurs, we will display an alert.

Fill in the body of **fetchClasses:**:

```
- (IBAction)fetchClasses:(id)sender
{
    [activityIndicator startAnimating];
    [fetchButton setEnabled:NO];

    ScheduleFetcher *fetcher = [[ScheduleFetcher alloc] init];

    [fetcher fetchClassesWithBlock:
                         ^(NSArray *classes, NSError *error) {

        [fetchButton setEnabled:YES];
        [activityIndicator stopAnimating];

        if (classes) {
            ScheduleViewController *svc;
            svc = [[ScheduleViewController alloc]
                            initWithStyle:UITableViewStylePlain];
            [svc setClasses:classes];
            [self.navigationController pushViewController:svc
                                                animated:YES];
        }
        else
        {
            UIAlertView *alert;
            alert = [[UIAlertView alloc]
                        initWithTitle:@"Error Fetching Classes"
                              message:[error localizedDescription]
                             delegate:nil
                    cancelButtonTitle:@"Dismiss"
                    otherButtonTitles:nil];
            [alert show];
        }
    }];
}
```

Build and run the application. Tap on the Fetch Classes button. Once the results are received, you will see the table-view controller being pushed onto the stack and the upcoming class schedule displayed in the table view.

# Challenge

Modify RanchForecastTouch so that when the user taps on a class in the schedule, a Web view for that course is shown. Use the table-view delegate method **tableView:didSelectRowAtIndexPath:** to detect the tap; then push a **UIViewController** containing a **UIWebView**.

## Chapter 31

# VIEW SWAPPING

Often, instead of bringing up a new window, you will simply want to swap out a view and replace it with another. One easy way to do this is to change the content view of a box.

Putting each view in its own XIB results in a more modular design. In Mac OS 10.5, Apple added the class **NSViewController** to Cocoa. We will make a subclass of **NSViewController** for each view that we want to swap in.

This project will, in the next chapter, evolve into a relatively sophisticated Core Data application, so we will want each of our view controllers to have access to an **NSManagedObjectContext**. Figure 31.1 shows where we are going.

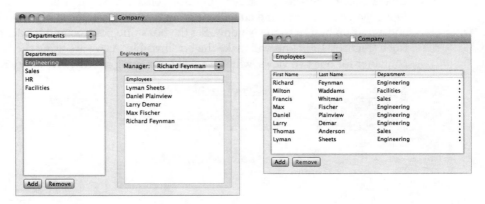

**Figure 31.1** Completed Application

The pop-up button will enable the user to jump back and forth between the two views. In this chapter, you are going to make the jumping back and forth part work. All the really useful parts of this app will be done in the next chapter.

The views (controlled by view controllers) will become the content view of a box. Menu items in the pop-up button will trigger the view swapping. Figure 31.2 is a diagram of the objects involved.

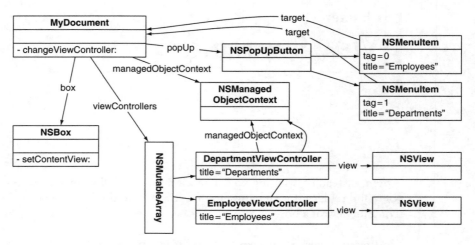

**Figure 31.2**   Object Diagram

# Get Started

In Xcode, create a new Cocoa Application. Name it `Departments`, and enable Create Document-Based Application and Use Core Data. Set the Class Prefix to My. Open `MyDocument.xib` and add a box (from the Library's Cocoa -> Layout Views) and a pop-up button to the window. Set the box's title position and border type to None (Figure 31.3). This will make the box invisible. As we are using the box as a container for our two views, which we will be creating shortly, invisibility is fine.

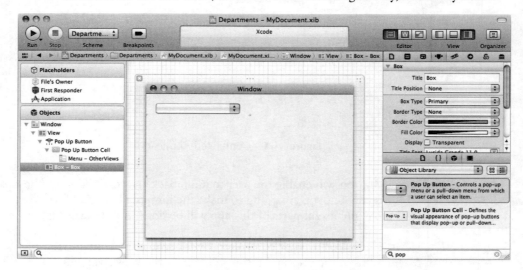

**Figure 31.3**   Set the Box's Title Position and Border Type to None.

Double-click the pop up button to open its menu. Remove all the menu items from the pop up button. You will create those programmatically.

In `MyDocument.h`, add two outlets, an array, and an action:

```
#import <Cocoa/Cocoa.h>

@interface MyDocument : NSPersistentDocument {
    IBOutlet NSBox *box;
    IBOutlet NSPopUpButton *popUp;
    NSMutableArray *viewControllers;
}
- (IBAction)changeViewController:(id)sender;
@end
```

Back in `MyDocument.xib`, control-click on File's Owner to bring up the Connection panel, and set the two outlets.

Now Control-drag from the pop-up button to File's Owner to set its target. The action should be **changeViewController:**.

## Create the ManagedViewController Class

Create a new `Objective-C class` that subclasses **NSViewController**, and name it **ManagingViewController**. We are subclassing **NSViewController** so that each of our view controllers will have an **NSManagedObjectContext**. Use the project navigator to delete the `ManagingViewController.xib` file that Xcode created for us alongside the `.h` and `.m`; we will create XIBs for our **ManagingViewController** subclasses. Edit `ManagingViewController.h`:

```
#import <Cocoa/Cocoa.h>

@interface ManagingViewController : NSViewController {
    NSManagedObjectContext *managedObjectContext;
}
@property (strong) NSManagedObjectContext *managedObjectContext;
@end
```

In `ManagingViewController.m`, remove the initializer created by the Xcode template, synthesize managedObjectContext:

```
#import "ManagingViewController.h"

@implementation ManagingViewController
@synthesize managedObjectContext;

@end
```

## Create ViewControllers and their XIB files

Now you are going to create two separate views that will be swapped into the box you created. Each view has its own controller: a subclass of **ManagingView-Controller**. Thus, you are going to do the same basic steps twice:

1.  Create a subclass of **ManagingViewController** to act as File's Owner.

2.  Create a XIB file for the view.

One view will be for looking at departments in a company. The other view will be for looking at the employees of a company. You will do the Departments view first.

In Xcode, create an Objective-C class that subclasses **ManagingViewController**, and name it **DepartmentViewController**. In DepartmentViewController.h, import ManagingViewController.h.

In Xcode, create a new view XIB (Mac OS X -> User Interface -> View). Name it DepartmentView. Open DepartmentView.xib. Put a few text fields and a couple of butons on the view. (We aren't going to use these controls; we just want you to see something interesting when the view appears in the box.)

In the Identity Inspector, set the class of File's Owner to be **DepartmentView-Controller**. Control-click on File's Owner and drag to the view (labeled Custom View) to set the view outlet. (The view outlet is defined in **NSViewController**.) Save the XIB file.

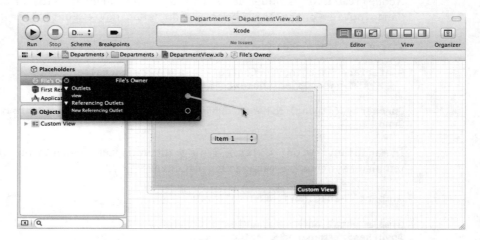

**Figure 31.4**  Introducing the View Controller to Its View

Back in DepartmentViewController.m, give the controller a XIB and a title in its **init** method:

```
- (id)init
{
    self = [super initWithNibName:@"DepartmentView"
                            bundle:nil];
    if (self) {
        [self setTitle:@"Departments"];
    }
    return self;
}
```

OK? Good. Do it again for **EmployeeViewController**:

- Create a class called **EmployeeViewController**, and make it a subclass of **ManagingViewController**.

- Make a XIB file (named EmployeeView.xib) with a view.

- Put a text view (or something else pretty) on the view.

- Set the class of File's Owner to be **EmployeeViewController**.

- Set the view outlet of File's Owner to point to the view.

- Add an **init** method to EmployeeViewController.m:

  ```
  - (id)init
  {
      self = [super initWithNibName:@"EmployeeView"
                              bundle:nil];
      if (self) {
          [self setTitle:@"Employees"];
      }
      return self;
  }
  ```

# Add View Swapping to MyDocument

Now you need to create instances of the controllers in **MyDocument** and add them to the viewControllers array. Add this to MyDocument.m:

```
#import "MyDocument.h"
#import "DepartmentViewController.h"
#import "EmployeeViewController.h"

@implementation MyDocument
```

```
- (id)init
{
    self = [super init];
    if (self) {
        viewControllers = [[NSMutableArray alloc] init];

        ManagingViewController *vc;
        vc = [[DepartmentViewController alloc] init];
        [vc setManagedObjectContext:[self managedObjectContext]];
        [viewControllers addObject:vc];

        vc = [[EmployeeViewController alloc] init];
        [vc setManagedObjectContext:[self managedObjectContext]];
        [viewControllers addObject:vc];
    }
    return self;
}
```

Create the method that swaps the view in:

```
- (void)displayViewController:(ManagingViewController *)vc
{
    // Try to end editing
    NSWindow *w = [box window];
    BOOL ended = [w makeFirstResponder:w];
    if (!ended) {
        NSBeep();
        return;
    }
    // Put the view in the box
    NSView *v = [vc view];
    [box setContentView:v];
}
```

Declare that method in MyDocument.h (also let the complier know about the class **ManagingViewController**):

```
@class ManagingViewController;
...
- (void)displayViewController:(ManagingViewController *)vc;
...
```

A pop-up button is basically a button with a menu. When the NIB file is loaded, you need to load the menu with an item for each controller. Add this code to MyDocument.m:

```
- (void)windowControllerDidLoadNib:(NSWindowController *)wc
{
    [super windowControllerDidLoadNib:wc];
    NSMenu *menu = [popUp menu];
```

```
        NSUInteger i, itemCount;
        itemCount = [viewControllers count];

        for (i = 0; i < itemCount; i++) {
            NSViewController *vc = [viewControllers objectAtIndex:i];
            NSMenuItem *mi = [[NSMenuItem alloc] initWithTitle:[vc title]
                                    action:@selector(changeViewController:)
                          keyEquivalent:@""];
            [mi setTag:i];
            [menu addItem:mi];
        }
        // Initially show the first controller
        [self displayViewController:[viewControllers objectAtIndex:0]];
        [popUp selectItemAtIndex:0];
}
```

Note that the tag of the menu item is set to the index of the controller in the
viewControllers array that the menu item represents. We can use the tag in the
action method that the menu items trigger:

```
- (IBAction)changeViewController:(id)sender
{
    NSUInteger i = [sender tag];
    ManagingViewController *vc = [viewControllers objectAtIndex:i];
    [self displayViewController:vc];
}
```

Build and run the application. The pop-up button should enable you to jump
back and forth between the two views.

# Resizing the Window

What if the two views are radically different sizes? Wouldn't it be nifty if the
window would stretch and shrink to make the box fit the view perfectly? You are
going to add that now.

Open the view XIB files and make the two views different sizes.

In MyDocument.xib, select the box and use the Size Inspector to make it resize
with the window (Figure 31.5).

Select the window. In the Attributes Inspector, prevent the user from resizing the
window (Figure 31.6).

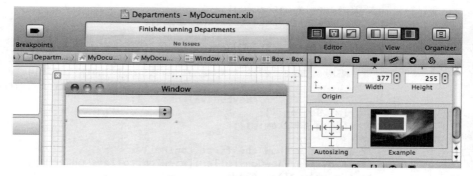

**Figure 31.5**  Size Inspector for Box

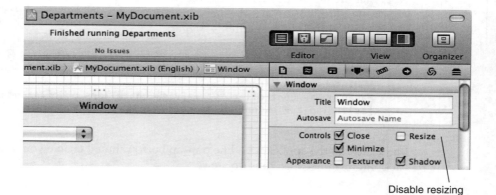

Disable resizing

**Figure 31.6**  Disable Resizing for Window

In MyDocument.m, add the following lines to the **displayViewController:**
method:

```
- (void)displayViewController:(ManagingViewController *)vc
{
    // End editing
    NSWindow *w = [box window];
    BOOL ended = [w makeFirstResponder:w];
    if (!ended) {
        NSBeep();
        return;
    }
    NSView *v = [vc view];

    // Compute the new window frame
    NSSize currentSize = [[box contentView] frame].size;
    NSSize newSize = [v frame].size;
```

```
    float deltaWidth = newSize.width - currentSize.width;
    float deltaHeight = newSize.height - currentSize.height;
    NSRect windowFrame = [w frame];
    windowFrame.size.height += deltaHeight;
    windowFrame.origin.y -= deltaHeight;
    windowFrame.size.width += deltaWidth;

    // Clear the box for resizing
    [box setContentView:nil];
    [w setFrame:windowFrame
        display:YES
        animate:YES];

    [box setContentView:v];
}
```

Build and run the app. When you change views, the window should resize to fit
the new view.

# Chapter 32
# CORE DATA RELATIONSHIPS

It is time to delve a bit deeper into Core Data. In Chapter 11, you dealt with a single entity (**Car**). In most applications, you will have multiple entities and relationships between them. Core Data supports to-one relationships and to-many relationships (ordered or unordered).

In this exercise, there will be two entities: **Employee** and **Department**. An employee will work for one department. A department will have a set of employees; one employee (chosen from its set) will be a manager. Thus, there are three relationships (Figure 32.1).

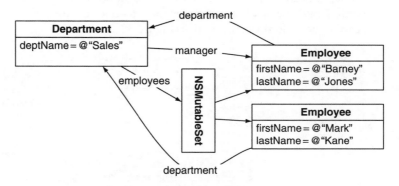

**Figure 32.1**  The Data Model

## Edit the Model

In this section, you are going to be extending the Departments project that you started in the previous chapter. Open MyDocument.xcdatamodel. Add two entities, **Employee** and **Department**.

An **Employee** will have the two attributes firstName and lastName, both strings, as well as a to-one relationship called department with **Department**. Add these properties (Figure 32.2).

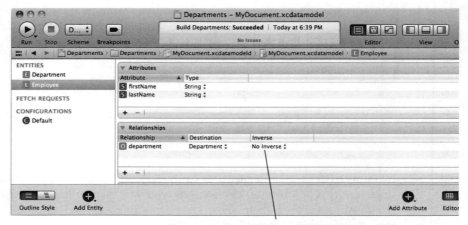

You can't set the inverse until
you have created a relationship
in the Department entity.

**Figure 32.2**   Employee Entity

A **Department** will have an attribute deptName, a string; a to-many relationship called employees with **Employee**; and a to-one relationship called manager with **Employee**. Add these properties (Figure 32.3).

**Figure 32.3**   Department Entity

Note that the department relationship of **Employee** and the employees relationship of **Department** are inverses. Be sure that the inverse is set for both of these relationships (as is shown in the screenshots).

The manager relationship will not have an inverse. You may get a warning about this when you compile: Disregard the warning.

# Create Custom NSManagedObject Classes

You will want to display an employee's full name, so you are going to create a custom class to hold employee data. This class will be a subclass of **NSManaged Object**.

A department can be managed only by an employee who works for that department. When an employee who is the manager leaves the department, you will need to set the manager to nil. This will be handled by the custom **NSManagedObject** subclass for the **Department** entity.

Make sure that your MyDocument.xcdatamodel file is open in the editor, and select one of the entities. In Xcode, select the Editor -> Create NSManagedObject Subclass... menu item. Create classes for **Employee** and **Department**. (Figure 32.4)

**Figure 32.4**    Creating an NSManagedObject Subclass

## Employee

In Employee.h, change firstName and lastName to be copy instead of retain, and declare the read-only property fullName:

```
#import <Foundation/Foundation.h>
#import <CoreData/CoreData.h>
@class Department;
@interface Employee :  NSManagedObject {
```

```
@private
}
@property (nonatomic, copy) NSString *firstName;
@property (nonatomic, copy) NSString *lastName;
@property (nonatomic, retain) Department *department;
@property (nonatomic, readonly) NSString *fullName;
@end
```

In Employee.m, implement the method **fullName:**

```
- (NSString *)fullName
{
    NSString *first = [self firstName];
    NSString *last = [self lastName];
    if (!first)
        return last;

    if (!last)
        return first;

    return [NSString stringWithFormat:@"%@ %@", first, last];
}
```

We are going to bind the column of a table to the fullName key. If firstName or lastName is changed, it is important that observers of fullName get informed that it has also changed. You are going to override a class method to specify what keys cause changes in fullName:

```
+ (NSSet *)keyPathsForValuesAffectingFullName
{
    return [NSSet setWithObjects:@"firstName", @"lastName", nil];
}
```

## Department

In our model, a manager must be a member of a department. As such, if we are asked to remove an employee who is the manager of this department, we want to set the manager to nil. To enforce this, implement these methods in Department.m:

```
#import "Department.h"
#import "Employee.h"

@implementation Department

@dynamic deptName;
@dynamic manager;
@dynamic employees;
```

```
- (void)addEmployeesObject:(Employee *)value
{
    NSLog(@"Dept %@ adding employee %@",
                    [self deptName], [value fullName]);
    NSSet *s = [NSSet setWithObject:value];
    [self willChangeValueForKey:@"employees"
            withSetMutation:NSKeyValueUnionSetMutation
                usingObjects:s];
    [[self primitiveValueForKey:@"employees"] addObject:value];
    [self didChangeValueForKey:@"employees"
            withSetMutation:NSKeyValueUnionSetMutation
                usingObjects:s];
}
- (void)removeEmployeesObject:(Employee *)value
{
    NSLog(@"Dept %@ removing employee %@",
                    [self deptName], [value fullName]);
    Employee *manager = [self manager];
    if (manager == value) {
        [self setManager:nil];
    }
    NSSet *s = [NSSet setWithObject:value];
    [self willChangeValueForKey:@"employees"
            withSetMutation:NSKeyValueMinusSetMutation
                usingObjects:s];
    [[self primitiveValueForKey:@"employees"] removeObject:value];
    [self didChangeValueForKey:@"employees"
            withSetMutation:NSKeyValueMinusSetMutation
                usingObjects:s];
}
@end
```

# Lay Out the Interface

Before you begin editing the XIB files, a warning: There are a lot of bindings to make in this exercise. Be patient. Remember: In this book, you will never bind to a scroll view or a cell. You will, however, bind to table columns. Watch the title of the jump bar to be certain of what you are binding.

In DepartmentView.xib, put two buttons, two table views, and a pop-up button on the view. Place a label that says Manager above the pop-up. Embed the label, the pop-up, and one table view in a box. Create three array controllers and label them Depts, ManagerPopUp, and EmployeeList (Figure 32.5).

Set the target of the two buttons to be the Depts array controller. The Add button's action should be **add:**. The Remove button's action should be **remove:**.

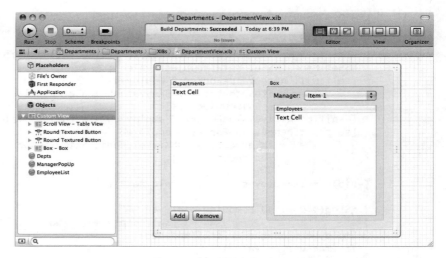

**Figure 32.5**    Basic Layout

The Depts array controller should be in Entity mode and pulling from the **Department** entity. Check the box that says Prepares Content, forcing it to fetch from the object store as soon as the NIB file is loaded (Figure 32.6).

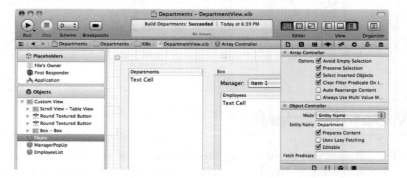

**Figure 32.6**    Depts Array Controller Attributes

Use Table 32.1 to set the bindings. Bindings are set in the Bindings Inspector.

On the last binding, use No selection for the No Selection Placeholder. Use Unnamed Department as the Null Placeholder.

You can build and run your app. You should be able to add and remove departments.

**Table 32.1**   Bindings for DepartmentView.xib (AC = Array Controller)

| Object | Binding | To | Controller Key | Keypath |
|---|---|---|---|---|
| Depts AC | Managed Object Context | File's Owner | | `managedObjectContext` |
| ManagerPopUp AC | Content Set | Depts AC | `selection` | `employees` |
| EmployeeList AC | Content Set | Depts AC | `selection` | `employees` |
| Departments column | Value | Depts AC | `arrangedObjects` | `deptName` |
| Remove button | Enabled | Depts AC | `canRemove` | |
| Employees column | Value | EmployeeList AC | `arrangedObjects` | `fullName` |
| Pop-up | Content | ManagerPopUp AC | `arrangedObjects` | |
| Pop-up | Content values | ManagerPopUp AC | `arrangedObjects` | `fullName` |
| Pop-up | Selected object | Depts AC | `selection` | `manager` |
| Box | Title | Depts AC | `selection` | `deptName` |

## EmployeeView.xib

Open `EmployeeView.xib`, and remove anything on the view. Add a table view
with three columns. Drop a pop-up cell (from the Library's Cocoa->Views &
Cells->Cells) on the third column. Add Add and Remove buttons. Add two array
controllers and label them Employees and DeptPopUp. See Figure 32.7.

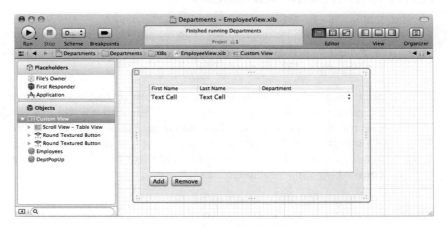

**Figure 32.7**   Basic Layout

The Employees array controller should be in Entity Name mode and pulling from
the **Employee** entity. The DeptPopUp array controller should be in Entity mode
and pulling from the **Department** entity. Both should automatically prepare
content.

Make the Employees array controller the target of the two buttons. The Add button should trigger **add:**. The Remove button should trigger **remove:**.

Set the bindings according to Table 32.2.

**Table 32.2**  Bindings for EmployeeView.xib

| Object | Binding | To | Controller Key | Keypath |
|---|---|---|---|---|
| Employees AC | Managed Object Context | File's Owner | | `managedObjectContext` |
| DeptPopUp AC | Managed Object Context | File's Owner | | `managedObjectContext` |
| Remove button | Enabled | Employees AC | `canRemove` | |
| "First" column | Value | Employees AC | `arrangedObjects` | `firstName` |
| "Last" column | Value | Employees AC | `arrangedObjects` | `lastName` |
| "Dept" column | Content | DeptPopUp AC | `arrangedObjects` | |
| "Dept" column | Content values | DeptPopUp AC | `arrangedObjects` | `deptName` |
| "Dept" column | Selected object | Employees AC | `arrangedObjects` | `department` |

Build and run your app. You should now be able to add and remove employees. You should be able to set the manager of a department as well.

# Events and nextResponder

The event methods (such as **mouseDown:** and **keyDown:**) defined in **NSResponder** typically just forward the event on to the nextResponder. Thus, unhandled events flow up the responder chain.

So, for example, when someone selects a row in a table view and presses the Delete key, that flows up the responder chain until it is handled. Let's handle this case for the **EmployeeView** of the **Departments** project. The **NSViewController** is a subclass of **NSResponder**, so we can put it in the responder chain and it can handle unhandled keyboard events. Add these lines to the end of **displayView-Controller:** in MyDocument.m:

```
    [box setContentView:v];
    // Put the view controller in the responder chain
    [v setNextResponder:vc];
    [vc setNextResponder:box];
}
```

Add these two methods to EmployeeViewController.m:

```
// Accept key events
- (void)keyDown:(NSEvent *)e
{
    [self interpretKeyEvents:[NSArray arrayWithObject:e]];
}

// Take care of the delete key
- (void)deleteBackward:(id)sender
{
    [employeeController remove:nil];
}
```

Now, if it gets a **keyDown:** event, the view controller will ask that the event be interpreted. If the key event was a Delete key press, **deleteBackward:** will be called, in which we send the **remove:** message to the array controller.

Now you need an outlet named employeeController. Add it in EmployeeView-Controller.h:

**IBOutlet NSArrayController *employeeController;**

Open EmployeeView.xib. Control-click on the File's Owner. Drag from the employeeController outlet to the Employees array controller.

Build and run the application. Select an employee and press the Delete key. The employee should disappear.

# Chapter 33

# CORE ANIMATION

As Mac OS X has evolved, it has used OpenGL more and more to utilize the power of modern graphics processors. To make some of these capabilities convenient for all programmers, Apple created Core Animation in Mac OS X 10.5. Core Animation is extremely versatile, being useful not only for animating UI components but also as a tool for creating custom UI elements from scratch.

The central class in Core Animation is **CALayer**, which you can think of as a building block. Its appearance can be configured in numerous ways through its properties. Among them are position, size, image contents, background color, border, shadow, and corner radius. It's also possible to mask a layer with another, as well apply a 3D transform. Most properties can be animated simply by setting a new value.

Layers are similar to views in some ways. Like views, layers are arranged in a hierarchy. A view can be covered with a layer, and that layer can have sublayers. You can also draw into a **CALayer**, not unlike a custom view. Unlike views, however, layers do not receive user input events (mouse, keyboard) and are not part of the responder chain.

Manipulating a layer's properties will animate it, but we sometimes need more control. **CAAnimation** and its subclasses let us fine-tune animations. **CATransaction** can be used to group and synchronize multiple animations, as well as to disable animations temporarily.

## Scattered

Let's create an application that uses Core Animation to drive the interface. This particular application will load all the images it finds in a folder and display them using **CALayer** objects (Figure 33.1). For this exercise, we'll use dot notation for setting properties on Core Animation objects.

**Figure 33.1**   Completed Application

In Xcode, create a new project called `Scattered` with a Class Prefix of
`Scattered`. Set it to not be document based. Since we will be using Core
Animation, add the QuartzCore framework. Switch to the project navigator
and select the Scattered project item. In the project editor, select the Scattered
target and click the button below Linked Frameworks and Libraries. Select
`QuartzCore.framework`.

Next, open `ScatteredAppDelegate.h`. Import `QuartzCore.h` and add the
following instance variables:

```
#import <Cocoa/Cocoa.h>
#import <QuartzCore/QuartzCore.h>

@interface ScatteredAppDelegate : NSObject <NSApplicationDelegate> {
    IBOutlet NSView *view;
    CATextLayer *textLayer;
}
@property (assign) IBOutlet NSWindow *window;

@end
```

Open `MainMenu.xib`. Select the window in the Interface Builder dock to show the
window, then drag a Custom View onto it. Size it to fill the window. Make sure that it
is reasonably large, at least 500 × 500.

Right-click on the Scattered App Delegate in the dock to show its Connections
panel. Drag a connection from the `view` outlet to the custom view you created
(Figure 33.2).

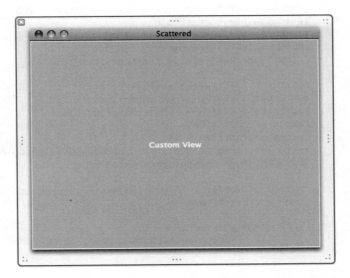

**Figure 33.2**    Custom View in Window

Open ScatteredAppDelegate.m and make the following additions:

```
#import "ScatteredAppDelegate.h"

@interface ScatteredAppDelegate ()
- (void)addImagesFromFolderURL:(NSURL *)url;
- (NSImage *)thumbImageFromImage:(NSImage *)image;
- (void)presentImage:(NSImage *)image;
- (void)setText:(NSString *)text;
@end

@implementation ScatteredAppDelegate

@synthesize window;

- (void)applicationDidFinishLaunching:(NSNotification *)aNotification
{
    srandom((unsigned)time(NULL));

    // Set view to be layer-hosting:
    view.layer = [CALayer layer];
    [view setWantsLayer:YES];

    CALayer *textContainer = [CALayer layer];
    textContainer.anchorPoint = CGPointZero;
    textContainer.position = CGPointMake(10, 10);
    textContainer.zPosition = 100;
    textContainer.backgroundColor =
                        CGColorGetConstantColor(kCGColorBlack);
```

```
textContainer.borderColor = CGColorGetConstantColor(kCGColorWhite);
textContainer.borderWidth = 2;
textContainer.cornerRadius = 15;
textContainer.shadowOpacity = 0.5f;
[view.layer addSublayer:textContainer];

textLayer = [CATextLayer layer];
textLayer.anchorPoint = CGPointZero;
textLayer.position = CGPointMake(10, 6);
textLayer.zPosition = 100;
textLayer.fontSize = 24;
textLayer.foregroundColor = CGColorGetConstantColor(kCGColorWhite);
[textContainer addSublayer:textLayer];

// Rely on setText: to set the above layers' bounds:
[self setText:@"Loading..."];

[self addImagesFromFolderURL:
        [NSURL fileURLWithPath:@"/Library/Desktop Pictures"]];
}

@end
```

Before we continue, let's discuss what we've done so far. When the application launches, we will seed the random number generator. Then we configure the view to be layer-hosting by first assigning its layer property and then calling **setWantsLayer:** with YES. The order of these calls is important. If we had not assigned the layer first, the view would have been configured as layer-backed, which is designed for animating views rather than Core Animation layer hierarchies.

Next, we configure two layers: textContainer and textLayer. The first layer, textContainer, is an instance of **CALayer** (the most basic layer type) and will create a rounded rectangle filled black with a white border and a shadow. The second layer, textLayer, is a **CATextLayer**, which not surprisingly can be used to display text. (Note how properties are used extensively in Core Animation to configure the various graphical elements.)

The first layer, textContainer is added to the view's layer, and textLayer is added to the textContainer (Figure 33.3) . Note that the anchorPoint for each layer is set to (0, 0), which equates to the lower-left corner. The default anchorPoint for a layer is (0.5, 0.5), which is the center of the layer. The anchorPoint governs the position of the layer relative to its position property.

Next, **setText:** is called, which sets the bounds of the layers. The bounds describe the size of the layer; by default, layers have bounds of (0, 0, 0, 0). Layers do have a frame property, like views, but it is more common to set the position and bounds independently.

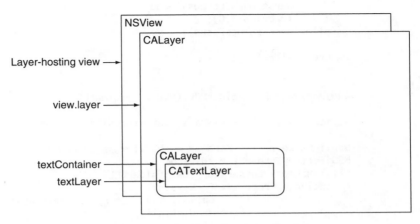

**Figure 33.3**  Completed Application

Next, implement **setText:**, **thumbImageFromImage:**, and **addImagesFrom-FolderURL:**. While you may not be familiar with the specific APIs being used, you should have a general idea of what they are doing.

```
- (void)setText:(NSString *)text
{
    NSFont *font = [NSFont systemFontOfSize:textLayer.fontSize];
    NSDictionary *attrs = [NSDictionary dictionaryWithObjectsAndKeys:
                            font, NSFontAttributeName, nil];
    NSSize size = [text sizeWithAttributes:attrs];
    // Ensure that the size is in whole numbers:
    size.width = ceilf(size.width);
    size.height = ceilf(size.height);
    textLayer.bounds = CGRectMake(0, 0, size.width, size.height);
    textLayer.superlayer.bounds = CGRectMake(0, 0, size.width + 16,
                                                    size.height + 20);

    textLayer.string = text;
}

- (NSImage *)thumbImageFromImage:(NSImage *)image
{
    const CGFloat targetHeight = 200.0f;
    NSSize imageSize = [image size];
    NSSize smallerSize = NSMakeSize(targetHeight * imageSize.width /
                                imageSize.height,
                                targetHeight);

    NSImage *smallerImage = [[NSImage alloc] initWithSize:smallerSize];

    [smallerImage lockFocus];
    [image drawInRect:NSMakeRect(0, 0, smallerSize.width,
                                smallerSize.height)
            fromRect:NSZeroRect
```

```
                    operation:NSCompositeCopy
                      fraction:1.0];
        [smallerImage unlockFocus];

        return smallerImage;
    }

    - (void)addImagesFromFolderURL:(NSURL *)folderURL
    {
        NSTimeInterval t0 = [NSDate timeIntervalSinceReferenceDate];

        NSFileManager *fileManager = [NSFileManager new];
        NSDirectoryEnumerator *dirEnum =
         [fileManager enumeratorAtURL:folderURL
            includingPropertiesForKeys:nil
                              options:NSDirectoryEnumerationSkipsHiddenFiles
                         errorHandler:nil];

        int allowedFiles = 10;

        for (NSURL *url in dirEnum)
        {
            // Skip directories:
            NSNumber *isDirectory = nil;
            [url getResourceValue:&isDirectory
                           forKey:NSURLIsDirectoryKey
                            error:nil];
            if ([isDirectory boolValue])
                continue;

            NSImage *image = [[NSImage alloc] initWithContentsOfURL:url];
            if (!image)
                return;

            allowedFiles--;
            if (allowedFiles < 0)
                break;

            NSImage *thumbImage = [self thumbImageFromImage:image];

            [self presentImage:thumbImage];
            [self setText:[NSString stringWithFormat:@"%0.1fs",
                          [NSDate timeIntervalSinceReferenceDate] - t0]];
        }
    }
```

Finally, implement **presentImage:** in **ScatteredAppDelegate** to animate the
supplied image onto the view, starting from a tiny speck in the middle and
expanding out to a thumbnail version at a random point on the view:

```
- (void)presentImage:(NSImage *)image
{
    CGRect superlayerBounds = view.layer.bounds;
```

```
    NSPoint center = NSMakePoint(CGRectGetMidX(superlayerBounds),
                                 CGRectGetMidY(superlayerBounds));

    NSRect imageBounds = NSMakeRect(0, 0, image.size.width,
                                    image.size.height);

    CGPoint randomPoint = CGPointMake(
                          CGRectGetMaxX(superlayerBounds) *
                            (double)random() / (double)RAND_MAX,
                          CGRectGetMaxY(superlayerBounds) *
                            (double)random() / (double)RAND_MAX);

    CAMediaTimingFunction *tf = [CAMediaTimingFunction
                functionWithName:kCAMediaTimingFunctionEaseInEaseOut];

    CABasicAnimation *posAnim = [CABasicAnimation animation];
    posAnim.fromValue = [NSValue valueWithPoint:center];
    posAnim.duration = 1.5;
    posAnim.timingFunction = tf;

    CABasicAnimation *bdsAnim = [CABasicAnimation animation];
    bdsAnim.fromValue = [NSValue valueWithRect:NSZeroRect];
    bdsAnim.duration = 1.5;
    bdsAnim.timingFunction = tf;

    CALayer *layer = [CALayer layer];
    layer.contents = image;
    layer.actions = [NSDictionary dictionaryWithObjectsAndKeys:
                     posAnim, @"position",
                     bdsAnim, @"bounds", nil];

    [CATransaction begin];
    [view.layer addSublayer:layer];
    layer.position = randomPoint;
    layer.bounds = NSRectToCGRect(imageBounds);
    [CATransaction commit];
}
```

That's it! Run the application. You should see ten images animate out from the center of the window.

# Implicit Animation and Actions

Before we talk about what's going on in **presentImage:**, let's look at how the most basic animation is done with Core Animation. Imagine that you have a **CALayer** called layer that is displayed on the screen. Suppose that you set its position:

```
layer.position = CGPointMake(50, 50);
```

This simple action animates the layer from its current position to the new position: implicit animation. Many properties of layers can be animated by simply setting them. The **setText:** method uses implicit animation to change the size of the black status bubble.

What if we want to customize these animations? As it turns out, there are several styles for achieving customization, which can make Core Animation rather confusing. The most straightforward method is by means of **CALayer**'s actions property, which takes a dictionary. The actions dictionary associates properties (string keys) with the animation (**CAAnimation** subclass) to be used when animating that property. The actions dictionary is used by Core Animation to determine what to do *when a property is assigned.*

**CABasicAnimation** is, well, the most basic animation class. It has two important properties: fromValue and toValue. By setting one or both of these, you will influence the start and end values of the property you are animating. In **presentImage:**, you will note that we set only the fromValue. Thus, later in the method when we assign property and bounds, Core Animation can look in the actions dictionary to determine what animation to use for those properties. Because only fromValue is set, the properties will be animated from fromValue to the value that we assigned. Specifically, we animate the position from the center to a random point and the bounds from zero to the size of the thumbnail, simultaneously.

Note that to have the layer display the image, we simply assign it to the contents property. The contentsGravity property affects how contents is scaled (or not scaled). In this application, we have sized our layers to match the size of the image, so no scaling is necessary.

Last, our use of **CATransaction** is notable. **CATransaction** enables us to group several changes to be executed at once by surrounding them in calls to [CATransaction begin] and [CATransaction commit]. Try commenting out the surrounding **begin/commit** calls. You may notice some flickering in the display as the layers are shown before the animation begins.

**CATransaction** has methods to affect changes on the actions within the current transaction, such as changing the duration, timing functions, or perhaps most useful, disabling all actions, which turns off animations:

```
[CATransaction setDisableActions:YES];
```

You may have noticed that Scattered presently limits the number of files loaded to ten. If you comment out that limit, you'll see why. We'll address that in the next chapter.

## More on CALayer

**CALayer** allows you to control quite a bit about its appearance through its properties. But what if that wasn't enough: What if you wanted to do custom drawing in a **CALayer**? The **CALayerDelegate** method **drawLayer:inContext:** allows you to do just that with Core Graphics/Quartz.

However, much of the time, you will simply want to control a few common things:

- An image
- The background color
- Whether the corners are rounded and, if so, how much
- An image filter to run the contents of the layer through

Subclasses of **CALayer** make particular kinds of drawing easier.

- As we saw, drawing text on a layer is easier if the layer is an instance of **CATextLayer**.
- **CAShapeLayer** makes drawing a stroked and/or filled path simple.
- **CAGradientLayer** displays a configurable gradient.
- Getting OpenGL calls onto a layer is easier if the layer is a subclass of **CAOpenGLLayer**
- The base layer of a view is an instance of **_NSViewBackingLayer** (not a public class!) that knows to draw the contents of the view upon itself.

# Challenge 1

Add a text layer to each image layer to show the filename of that image. You will need to supply an additional parameter to **presentImage:**. Experiment with adding shadows and borders to the layers.

# Challenge 2

Add a button and a text field to the window. When clicked, the button should reposition all the image layers but not the rounded black text container layer! Use the numeric value from the text field to set the duration of this repositioning animation.

# Chapter 34

# CONCURRENCY

Until now, all the applications we've written in this book have been single-threaded. In simplistic terms, this means that only one thing is happening in the application at any given time, such as responding to a button click, updating the display, or counting the number of objects in an array.

Of course, in some cases, it's very useful to be able to do many things at once. In a modern operating system, each application is running in its own process; this division gives each application its own memory space, but it also allows the task scheduler to create the illusion that many applications are running at once.

## Multithreading

Threads give this same power to individual processes. Each thread in a process has its own stack, meaning that each thread can be executing its own code path and has its own stack variables. The heap, however, where objects are allocated, is shared among all threads, as are global variables. Each process starts with one thread, referred to as the main thread. Additional threads, called background threads, can be created at any time and will be scheduled to run concurrently with the other threads in the process. This is called multithreading.

In Cocoa, the display is always updated by the main thread, which is also responsible for handling events from the window manager. Thus, if your application's main thread is busy calculating the value of pi to 6 trillion digits when the user tries to resize the window, the window will appear to ignore the mouse input until the main thread gets back around to processing events. Calculating pi is a great use for background threads. Hardware I/O is an even better candidate, as hard disks are notoriously slower than processors and RAM. If your application calls for synchronous network communication (asynchronous will not do), a background thread will allow life to go on in your application's other threads even amidst network hiccups. By using multithreading, your application can remain responsive to the user even while it is deep in thought.

The emphasis on multicore processors over the past several years has led to a number of Mac OS X improvements, namely **NSOperationQueue** and Grand Central Dispatch, that make multithreading much more accessible to developers. In this chapter, we will look at **NSOperationQueue** and some other methods for creating background threads.

## A Deep Chasm Opens Before You

While multithreading can be essential in certain applications, it also opens up an entirely new category of bugs that are notoriously difficult to fix: race conditions. It is for this reason that we suggest that you carefully weigh the benefits of multithreading against the significant costs.

Race conditions occur when code is modifying the same data in two or more threads. Consider the classic case of two threads incrementing a global variable (Figure 34.1). Here is the global integer variable:

```
int globalCount = 0;
```

Now imagine the two threads executing this code concurrently:

```
for (int i = 0; i < 1000; i++) {
    globalCount = globalCount + 1;
}
```

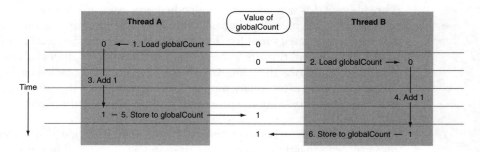

**Figure 34.1**   A Classic Race Condition

It looks like the programmer's expectation is that `globalCount` will be equal to 2,000 when both threads have completed. Depending on how the threads are scheduled, however, the final value of `globalCount` may be much less. Why is this? The reason is that the thread scheduler may interrupt any thread at any time in order to run another thread, or it may even run multiple threads simultaneously on the cores of a multicore system. So it becomes somewhat dangerous that the statement

```
globalCount = globalCount + 1;
```

is actually several instructions:

i. Load the value of `globalCount` into a CPU register.

ii. Add 1 to this value.

iii. Store the result back to `globalCount`.

Consider the effects of two threads running these instructions over and over. The incremented value of `globalCount` by one thread runs a very high risk of being clobbered by the other thread. Worse, the results of such code can be inconsistent between runs on different systems or even the same system.

This is a rather low-level example of a race condition, but it illustrates the general problem with multithreading: You cannot make any assumptions about when a thread will be scheduled, how long it will execute before being interrupted, what other threads might be running at the same time, or exclusivity as far as access to data. Usually, a race-condition bug will have much more serious implications than a not fully incremented integer.

Fortunately, Cocoa provides some tools for dealing with these problems. They won't be solved magically, and you will need to use the tools with care, as they can create their own set of problems, such as deadlocks. We will examine one of these tools at the end of the chapter.

If you plan to use multithreading in your application, take some time early on to consider how your data structures will be used, and try to minimize any sharing of data structures. Careful design will save you a lot of headaches down the road when it comes time to debug.

## Simple Cocoa Background Threads

Now that you are sufficiently wary of multithreading, let's look at one way to create a background thread in Cocoa. `NSThread.h` has a very handy **NSObject** category with the following method:

```
- (void)performSelectorInBackground:(SEL)aSelector withObject:(id)arg;
```

We can use this category method to create a background thread with just a selector:

```
- (void)buttonClicked:(id)sender
{
    [self performSelectorInBackground:@selector(backgroundOperation:)
                           withObject:nil];
}
```

```
- (void)backgroundOperation:(id)unused
{
    // do background work ...
    // the thread will end once this method returns.
}
```

Easy, right? Behind the scenes, an **NSThread** instance is created that runs the selector on the receiver object (in this case, self).

Typically, it's not much fun to do something in the background. More often than not, we would like to update the UI with the results of our background work. Remember, any updates to the UI must be made on the main thread; we can use another **NSObject** category method, **performSelectorOnMainThread:withObject:waitUntilDone:**, for that. Let's flesh out our **backgroundOperation:** method a bit more:

```
- (void)buttonClicked:(id)sender
{
    [self performSelectorInBackground:@selector(backgroundOperation:)
                          withObject:nil];
}

- (void)backgroundOperation:(id)unused
{
    @autoreleasepool {
        NSArray *results = nil;
        // do background work ...
        // the thread will end once this method returns,
        // so let's report our results:
        [self performSelectorOnMainThread:@selector(updateWithResults:)
                               withObject:results
                            waitUntilDone:NO];
    }
}

- (void)updateWithResults:(NSArray *)theResults
{
    [self setResults:theResults];
    [tableView reloadData];
}
```

The method **performSelectorOnMainThread:withObject:waitUntilDone:** is very similar to **performSelectorInBackground:withObject:** in form but has an interesting additional argument: waitUntilDone. The waitUntilDone argument optionally makes this method block until the selector on the main thread has completed. In this case, it is not needed; the withObject: parameter (results) is retained by this method until after the selector is performed.

Note that we added an autorelease pool to our thread body by using `@autorelease pool`. Whenever you create a background thread, you must supply your own autorelease pool.

# Improving Scattered: Time Profiling in Instruments

Open the `Scattered` project from the previous chapter and find **addImages-FromFolderURL:** in **ScatteredAppDelegate**. Find the `allowedFiles` variable, which is used to limit the number of files opened to ten. Remove all traces of `allowedFiles` and run the application.

You should see an unresponsive window for several seconds, followed by the images appearing and animating. It looks like loading the images is blocking the main thread, which is a poor user experience. We have a pretty good idea that the problem is related to loading images, since we just removed the limit, but let's prove it to ourselves.

## Introducing Instruments

Instruments is a tool for analyzing a running program. The tool has many different plug-ins, called instruments, that enable you to look at various aspects, usually performance related, of the running application.

In Xcode, open the Product menu and select Profile. Xcode will use the Release build configuration (configurable in the Scheme Editor) to rebuild the project and will then start Instruments. Under Mac OS X, CPU in the template chooser, select Time Profiler and click Profile (Figure 34.2). Instruments will then run `Scattered`. Once the images have animated, click the red Stop button in Instruments to stop profiling.

The Instruments interface has several parts. The key ones are the Instruments list at the upper left; in this case, only one instrument, Time Profiler, is being run. To the right is the track pane, which displays graphical data over time related to each of the instruments being run. Looking at the graph for the Time Profiler, we can see that there was a fair burst of activity, probably related to loading the images. Below the track is the detail pane, which displays tabular data related to the selected instrument (Figure 34.3).

Time Profiler works by taking snapshots of the application's call stack repeatedly while it is running. This enables us to tell where the application is spending its

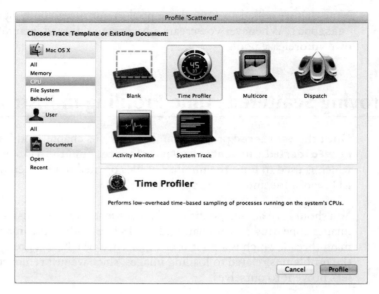

**Figure 34.2**   Choose the Time Profiler in Instruments

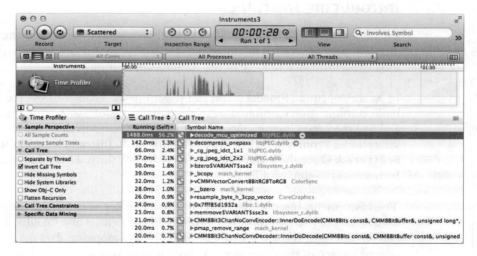

**Figure 34.3**   Running Scattered under the Time Profiler

time but does not, however, tell us how many times a particular method has been called, as it has only been taking snapshots and does not know when methods are entered and exited.

In the detail pane, we see the symbols sorted by time spent. Note the disclosure triangles in the Symbol Name column. Try clicking through them to navigate the stack, or use the keyboard arrow keys to explore the tree if you prefer. Note that Invert Call Tree is checked by default; this means that we are seeing the deepest functions where the CPU spent most of its time. You can toggle Invert Call Tree off to see the individual entry points to the application. Sometimes, this will make it faster to find the information you need.

If you dig down far enough, you'll see that all this time is being spent in **thumbImageFromImage:** (a quick way to find this is to enable Hide System Libraries). If you show the Extended Detail pane (using the View segments in the toolbar), you can see another view of the stack; this tends to be very useful when using memory-related instruments (Figure 34.4).

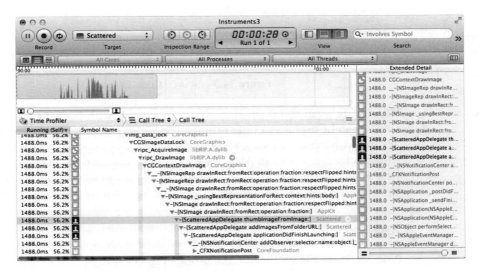

**Figure 34.4**    Show the Extended Detail pane

At this point, it's pretty clear that quite a bit of time is being spent creating the thumbnails. Try double-clicking on the stack frame for **thumbImageFromImage:**. The detail pane will change to show the source code of that method, with highlighting to show how much time is spent on each line (Figure 34.5). Use the jump bar control above the detail view to return to the Call Stack.

Another useful feature of Instruments is constraining the Inspection Range. You can set the range by using the toolbar buttons, but it's much faster to hold down the Option key, click, and drag over the timeline. The information in the detail view will be limited to the selected range of time. This is helpful when focusing on a specific performance problem.

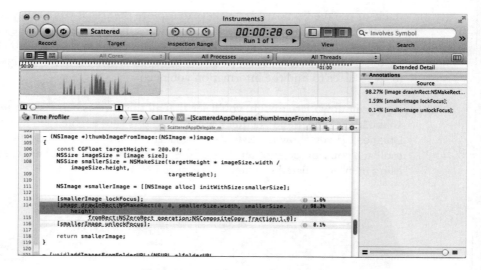

**Figure 34.5**   Source Code Display

We've only scratched the surface of what's possible with Instruments. As we've seen, it can be useful as a time profiler, but it also has a number of tools for dealing with memory issues, including tracking usage and detecting leaks and strong reference cycles in ARC. As you work to improve the performance of your applications, you will want to read Apple's documentation for Instruments. WWDC videos can also be a great resource for learning to use Instruments.

## Analysis

Now we know for sure where the problem is: generating thumbnails is time-consuming; even worse, we're doing that work in `applicationDidFinish-Launching:`, which ties up the main thread while the directory tree is traversed and each thumbnail is created.

There are generally two categories of blocking problems like this: CPU-bound and I/O-bound. I/O-bound problems revolve around waiting for slower hardware to do its thing and return control to us. In a CPU-bound problem, the CPU is the bottleneck; decompressing dozens of JPEG images relies heavily on the CPU. As we saw in Chapter 28, I/O-bound problems can sometimes be solved using asynchronous I/O, but doing so in this case could be complicated.

In this case, we appear to have a mixture of both problems: It is disk-intensive to load many megabytes of data and CPU-intensive to decompress and draw scaled-down thumbnails. One hint that this is the case is that the CPU is not

100% utilized (if it were, the Time Profiler's graph would be straight across the top). The simplest solution in cases like this is to put the work on a background thread.

We could do that by using **performSelectorInBackground:withObject:**, but that's just one thread, so we wouldn't be taking any advantage of a multicore machine. Creating multiple threads in this fashion would get complicated very quickly. We need something more sophisticated.

# NSOperationQueue

Frequently, multithreading is used for processing chunks of information in the background. In such cases, Cocoa's **NSOperationQueue** provides a much more mature framework for organizing the processing, compared to the rather informal **performSelectorInBackground:withObject:** and even creating threads manually using **NSThread**.

**NSOperationQueue** represents a collection of operations (encapsulated by **NSOperation**) and manages the execution of those operations on one or more threads. Every application has a main queue that represents the main thread; it is accessed by [NSOperationQueue mainQueue]. If the application needs additional queues, it can create and configure them simply by allocating and initializing a new **NSOperationQueue**.

By default, **NSOperationQueue** objects are configured to run several operations concurrently; the exact number is determined automatically by the system. You can override this configuration by calling **setMaxConcurrentOperationCount:**. A maximum concurrent operation count of 1 results in a serial queue. The main queue is always serial.

## Multithreaded Scattered

Let's modify Scattered to use **NSOperationQueue** and try to improve it.

Open ScatteredAppDelegate.h and add an instance variable for the **NSOperationQueue**:

```
#import <Cocoa/Cocoa.h>
#import <QuartzCore/QuartzCore.h>
```

```objc
@interface ScatteredAppDelegate : NSObject <NSApplicationDelegate> {
    IBOutlet NSView *view;
    CATextLayer *textLayer;

    NSOperationQueue *processingQueue;
}

@property (assign) IBOutlet NSWindow *window;

@end
```

Switch to ScatteredAppDelegate.m. We'll start by adding an **init** method:

```objc
- (id)init {
    self = [super init];
    if (self) {
        processingQueue = [[NSOperationQueue alloc] init];
        [processingQueue setMaxConcurrentOperationCount:4];
    }
    return self;
}
```

Now we'll make use of the **NSOperationQueue** in **addImagesFromFolderURL:**. Add six lines. Be careful to balance the blocks' braces and the message sends' brackets:

```objc
- (void)addImagesFromFolderURL:(NSURL *)folderURL
{
    [processingQueue addOperationWithBlock:^(void) {
        NSTimeInterval t0 = [NSDate timeIntervalSinceReferenceDate];

        NSFileManager *fileManager = [[NSFileManager alloc] init];
        NSDirectoryEnumerator *dirEnum =
    [fileManager enumeratorAtURL:folderURL
        includingPropertiesForKeys:nil
                        options:NSDirectoryEnumerationSkipsHiddenFiles
                   errorHandler:nil];

        for (NSURL *url in dirEnum)
        {
            // Skip directories:
            NSNumber *isDirectory = nil;
            [url getResourceValue:&isDirectory
                        forKey:NSURLIsDirectoryKey
                          error:nil];
            if ([isDirectory boolValue])
                continue;

            [processingQueue addOperationWithBlock:^(void) {
                NSLog(@"-- processing %@", [url lastPathComponent]);
```

```
NSImage *image = [[NSImage alloc]
                            initWithContentsOfURL:url];
if (!image)
    return;

NSImage *thumbImage = [self thumbImageFromImage:image];

[[NSOperationQueue mainQueue]
                    addOperationWithBlock:^(void) {
    [self presentImage:thumbImage];
    [self setText:
        [NSString stringWithFormat:@"%0.1fs",
        [NSDate timeIntervalSinceReferenceDate] - t0]];
}];
            }];
        }
    }];
}
```

That's it! Run the application and marvel at the new and improved user experience. You should notice a significant speed increase as well, depending on your hardware.

Instead of explicitly creating **NSOperation** objects, we use **NSOperationQueue**'s **addOperationWithBlock:**, which creates an **NSBlockOperation** for us and adds it to the queue. Note how minimal our changes were; the general flow of the application is practically unchanged. It won't always be this clean to add multithreading to an application, but you are seeing more of how blocks allow you to avoid a lot of boilerplate code by enabling you to reference variables that are in scope.

## Thread Synchronization

We didn't appear to worry about race conditions in our exercise. The reason is that the design of the application specifically avoided using any shared data structures from within the background thread. Work in the background threads was limited to enumerating the folder, opening images, and creating thumbnails. The only shared data in this case, the Core Animation layers, were modified from the main thread only. Multithreading is easiest when you can avoid race conditions altogether.

Not all multithreading problems will be solvable using this approach, however. Oftentimes, you will need to protect a section of code (or multiple sections of code) such that only one thread can be running it at a time. This is usually done with a mutex lock (mutually exclusive lock). Objective-C provides a simple way—the @synchronized directive—to employ a mutex lock:

```
- (void)addImage:(NSImage *)image
{
    @synchronized (images) {
        [images addObject:image];
    }
}
```

The @synchronized directive uses a mutex that is unique to the object that is passed to it. In this case, we are locking on images, an **NSMutableArray**. Because **NSMutableArray** is not thread-safe (meaning that it has not been written to be modified from multiple threads), it is recommended to use a mutex lock when modifying one in a multithreaded environment. The use of @synchronized guarantees that, for all @synchronized directives on a certain object, only one thread will be able to execute the enclosed block at a time. So if two threads were attempting to call **addImage:** at the same time, the first would obtain the lock and add the object and the other would block and wait for the lock to be released.

You may be wondering why **NSMutableArray** is not thread-safe. One reason is that mutex locks have overhead associated with them, and thread safety would make **NSMutableArrays** significantly slower. Another reason is that it is often more useful (and common) to lock a section of code, not just a single method call, such as if you were moving objects from one data structure to another.

Cocoa provides a number of other tools for thread synchronization, such as **NSLock** and **NSCondition**. These tools, a more involved look at **NSOperation-Queue**, and Grand Central Dispatch are discussed in detail in *Advanced Mac OS X Programming*.

# For the More Curious: Faster Scattered

Our goal in this chapter was to make Scattered a better-behaved application by moving heavy lifting off the main thread. We didn't, however, fully address the performance issues with this application. If you were watching closely, you may have noticed that in **init**, we limited the number of concurrent operations in processingQueue to four. If you remove that constraint (by commenting out the line), you may find that Scattered runs somewhat faster, or you may find that it runs even slower. What's going on here?

One of the most useful features of Grand Central Dispatch (GCD), which **NSOperationQueue** is built upon, is that GCD manages the number of running operations (threads) based on the system's hardware (number of cores) and the current system load. In higher-level terms, GCD will create as many threads as it thinks the system can handle in order to process the operations in a queue as quickly as possible. If every queued operation is uniform as far as its required resources, this works very well.

Consider how **Scattered** works, however: Each operation starts by reading data (an image) from disk. Disk I/O puts very little demand on the CPU, so GCD sees that that the CPU isn't being utilized and starts another operation, which starts by reading data from the disk, and so forth. Perhaps you can see how GCD would very quickly start a large number of threads to handle the operations in the queue.

When the image data for the first operation is fully read in, the image is decompressed, and a thumbnail is created, which is somewhat CPU-intensive work. While this work is being done, the second thread finishes reading from disk and starts decompressing, and so on. Suddenly, the CPU is being asked to do quite a bit of work!

In the exercise, we avoided this pile up by limiting the number of concurrent operations, but this approach is not ideal, because we are frequently wasting CPU time while waiting on the disk: recall how hilly the CPU graph in Instruments was. The proper solution to this problem is to use two queues: one queue to load image data from the disk, limited in the number of concurrent operations it can conduct (because disks are slow), and another queue to do the work of creating the thumbnail. This is, however, quite a bit more complicated to do properly.

# Challenge

Adapt **Scattered** to use the proper solution outlined in the previous section. Because **NSImage** avoids doing disk I/O until absolutely necessary, you will need to read the data in manually and then create the image using that data. **NSData** will read the image data. Check the documentation or header file for **NSImage** to find a way to create an image from an **NSData** object.

# Chapter 35
# COCOA AND OPENGL

This chapter is not designed to teach you OpenGL. If you want to learn OpenGL, read *The OpenGL Programming Guide*. Rather, this chapter is intended to show you how to do drawing with OpenGL in an application that is written using Cocoa. Like all other drawing in Cocoa, OpenGL rendering will be done in a view. Until now, all your views have used an **NSGraphicsContext** to do drawing with Quartz (via **NSImage**, **NSBezierPath**, and **NSAttributedString**).

**NSOpenGLView** is an **NSView** subclass that has an OpenGL drawing context. Just as you needed the focus locked on a view to do drawing with Quartz, so the OpenGL drawing context must be active for any OpenGL drawing commands to have an effect.

Here are some important methods in **NSOpenGLView**:

```
- (id)initWithFrame:(NSRect)frameRect
        pixelFormat:(NSOpenGLPixelFormat *)format
```

The designated initializer.

```
- (NSOpenGLContext*)openGLContext
```

Returns the views in the OpenGL context.

```
- (void)reshape
```

Called when the view is resized. The OpenGL context is active when this method is called.

```
- (void)drawRect:(NSRect)r
```

Called when the view needs to be redrawn. The OpenGL context is active when this method is called.

# A Simple Cocoa/OpenGL Application

Figure 35.1 shows the application that you will create.

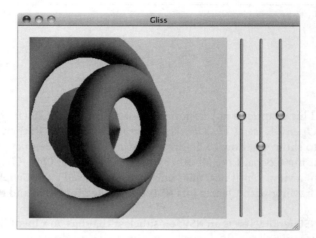

**Figure 35.1** Completed Application

Create a new Cocoa Application project and call it Gliss (short for "GL Bliss"). Set the Class Prefix to Gliss. This will not be a document-based application. Open the project editor by clicking on the project in the project navigator. Use the + button under Linked Frameworks and Libraries to add the frameworks OpenGL.framework and GLUT.framework to the project. You will not be using the GLUT event model—just a couple of convenience functions.

Create a new Objective-C class subclassing **NSOpenGLView**, and name it **GlissView**. In GlissView.h, declare an outlet and an action:

```
#import <Cocoa/Cocoa.h>

@interface GlissView : NSOpenGLView {
    IBOutlet NSMatrix *sliderMatrix;
}
- (IBAction)changeParameter:(id)sender;
@end
```

## Lay Out the Interface

Open MainMenu.xib.

Drag an **NSOpenGLView** onto the window as shown in Figure 35.2.

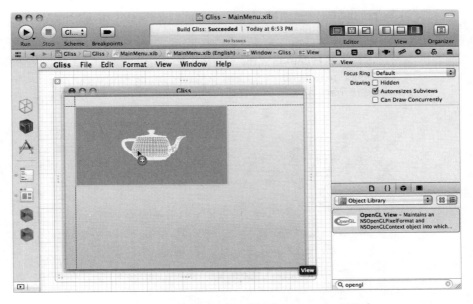

**Figure 35.2**    Drop an NSOpenGLView onto the Window

In the Identity Inspector, set the class of the view to be **GlissView** (Figure 35.3).

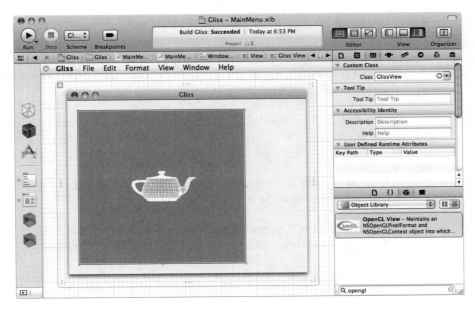

**Figure 35.3**    Set the Class

Select the Gliss window. In the Attributes Inspector, under the Memory section, uncheck One Shot.

Drop an **NSSlider** onto the window. Configure the slider to be continuous. In the Editor menu, choose Embed -> Matrix. In the Attributes Inspector, set the matrix mode to Tracking and give it three columns (Figure 35.4).

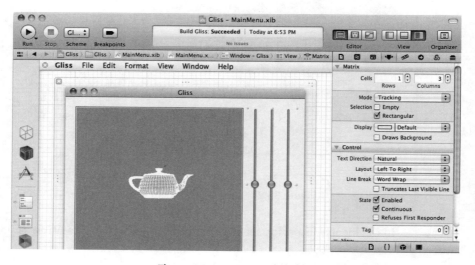

**Figure 35.4**    Matrix of Sliders

Set the target of the matrix to be the **GlissView,** and set the action to be **changeParameter:**. Set the sliderMatrix outlet of the **GlissView** to point to the matrix. (Be sure to create connections in both directions.)

The first slider will control the X-coordinate of the light. Set its range from –4 to 4, and give it an initial value of 1. It should have a tag of 0. The Inspector should look like Figure 35.5.

The second slider will control the angle from which the scene is viewed. Set its range from –4 to 4, and give it an initial value of 0. It should have a tag of 1.

The third slider will control from how far the scene is viewed. Set its range from 0.3 to 5, and give it an initial value of 4. It should have a tag of 2.

Select the **GlissView.** In the Attributes Inspector, set the view to have a 16-bit depth buffer, as shown in Figure 35.6.

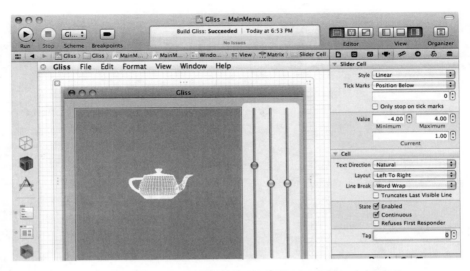

**Figure 35.5**     Set Limit, Initial Value, and Tag for First Slider Cell

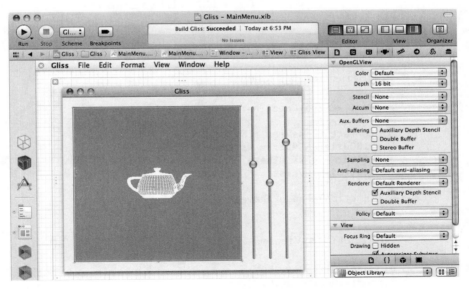

**Figure 35.6**     Create a 16-Bit Depth Buffer

Also, in the Size Inspector, make the **GlissView** resize with the window.

Inspect the **NSMatrix**. Set it to autosize its cells. In the Size Inspector, make the matrix cling to the right edge of the window, as shown in Figure 35.7.

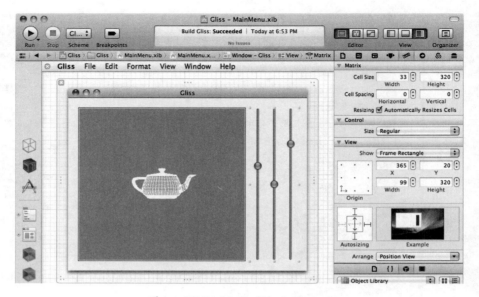

**Figure 35.7**    Matrix Size Inspector

## Write Code

Edit GlissView.h as follows:

```
#import <Cocoa/Cocoa.h>

@interface GlissView : NSOpenGLView {
    IBOutlet NSMatrix *sliderMatrix;
    float lightX, theta, radius;
    int displayList;
}
- (IBAction)changeParameter:(id)sender;
@end
```

Next, edit GlissView.m:

```
#import "GlissView.h"
#import <GLUT/glut.h>

#define LIGHT_X_TAG 0
#define THETA_TAG 1
#define RADIUS_TAG 2
```

```objc
@implementation GlissView

- (void)prepare
{
    NSLog(@"prepare");

    // The GL context must be active for these functions to have an effect
    NSOpenGLContext *glcontext = [self openGLContext];
    [glcontext makeCurrentContext];

    // Configure the view
    glShadeModel(GL_SMOOTH);
    glEnable(GL_LIGHTING);
    glEnable(GL_DEPTH_TEST);

    // Add some ambient lighting
    GLfloat ambient[] = {0.2, 0.2, 0.2, 1.0};
    glLightModelfv(GL_LIGHT_MODEL_AMBIENT, ambient);

    // Initialize the light
    GLfloat diffuse[] = {1.0, 1.0, 1.0, 1.0};
    glLightfv(GL_LIGHT0, GL_DIFFUSE, diffuse);
    // and switch it on.
    glEnable(GL_LIGHT0);

    // Set the properties of the material under ambient light
    GLfloat mat[] = {0.1, 0.1, 0.7, 1.0};
    glMaterialfv(GL_FRONT, GL_AMBIENT, mat);

    // Set the properties of the material under diffuse light
    glMaterialfv(GL_FRONT, GL_DIFFUSE, mat);
}


- (id)initWithCoder:(NSCoder *)c
{
    self = [super initWithCoder:c];
    if (self) {
        [self prepare];
    }
    return self;
}

// Called when the view resizes
- (void)reshape
{
    NSLog(@"reshaping");
    // Convert up to window space, which is in pixel units.
    NSRect baseRect = [self convertRectToBase:[self bounds]];
    // Now the result is glViewport()-compatible.
    glViewport(0, 0, baseRect.size.width, baseRect.size.height);
    glMatrixMode(GL_PROJECTION);
```

```
    glLoadIdentity();
    gluPerspective(60.0, baseRect.size.width/baseRect.size.height,
                   0.2, 7);
}

- (void)awakeFromNib
{
    [self changeParameter:self];
}

- (IBAction)changeParameter:(id)sender
{
    lightX = [[sliderMatrix cellWithTag:LIGHT_X_TAG] floatValue];
    theta = [[sliderMatrix cellWithTag:THETA_TAG] floatValue];
    radius = [[sliderMatrix cellWithTag:RADIUS_TAG] floatValue];
    [self setNeedsDisplay:YES];
}

- (void)drawRect:(NSRect)r
{
    // Clear the background
    glClearColor (0.2, 0.4, 0.1, 0.0);
    glClear(GL_COLOR_BUFFER_BIT |
            GL_DEPTH_BUFFER_BIT);

    // Set the view point
    glMatrixMode(GL_MODELVIEW);
    glLoadIdentity();
    gluLookAt(radius * sin(theta), 0,  radius * cos(theta),
              0, 0, 0,
              0, 1, 0);

    // Put the light in place
    GLfloat lightPosition[] = {lightX, 1, 3, 0.0};
    glLightfv(GL_LIGHT0, GL_POSITION, lightPosition);

    if (!displayList)
    {
        displayList = glGenLists(1);
        glNewList(displayList, GL_COMPILE_AND_EXECUTE);

        // Draw the stuff
        glTranslatef(0, 0, 0);
        glutSolidTorus(0.3, 0.9, 35, 31);
        glTranslatef(0, 0, -1.2);
        glutSolidCone(1, 1, 17, 17);
        glTranslatef(0, 0, 0.6);
        glutSolidTorus(0.3, 1.8, 35, 31);

        glEndList();
    } else {
        glCallList(displayList);
    }
```

```
    // Flush to screen
    glFinish();
}
```

@end

Note that the OpenGL calls are broken into three parts: **prepare**, all the calls to be sent initially; **reshape**, all the calls to be sent when the view resizes; and **drawRect**, all the calls to be sent each time the view needs to be redrawn. Build and run the app.

# Chapter 36
# NSTask

Each application that you have created is a directory, and somewhere down in that directory is an executable file. To run an executable on a Unix machine, like your Mac, a process is forked, and the new process executes the code in that file. Many executables are command-line tools, and some are quite handy. This chapter, then, will be showing you how to run command-line tools from your Cocoa application by using the class **NSTask**.

**NSTask** is an easy-to-use wrapper for the Unix functions **fork()** and **exec()**. You give **NSTask** a path to an executable and launch it. Many processes read data from standard-in and write to standard-out and standard-error. Your application can use **NSTask** to attach pipes to carry data to and from the external process. Pipes are represented by the class **NSPipe**.

# ZIPspector

The tool /usr/bin/zipinfo looks at the contents of a zip file. Find a zip file on your machine and try running zipinfo in the Terminal like this (-1 is dash-one, not dash-el):

```
# /usr/bin/zipinfo -1 /Users/aaron/myfile.zip
greatfile.txt
swellfile.rtf
magnificent.pdf
```

You are going to create an application that uses zipinfo. Note that it will have to send some arguments and read from the process's standard-out (Figure 36.1).

In Xcode, create a new Cocoa Application named ZIPspector, and enable Create Document-Based Application. Set the Class Prefix to My. This program will only view zip files, not edit them. In the Info panel for the target, set ZIPspector to be a viewer for files with the UTI com.pkware.zip-archive (Figure 36.2) (This is a system-defined UTI, so it will know the extension, icon, and so on, for zip files.)

451

**Figure 36.1**   Completed Application

**Figure 36.2**   Setting the UTI

In MyDocument.h, create outlets for an **NSTableView** and an **NSArray** for holding the filenames in the zip file:

```
@interface MyDocument : NSDocument
{
    IBOutlet NSTableView *tableView;
    NSArray *filenames;
}
@end
```

Open MyDocument.xib. Add a table view to the window, and set it to have one uneditable column with the title Filenames. Control-click on the table view to bring up its Connection panel. Make the dataSource outlet point to File's Owner (Figure 36.3).

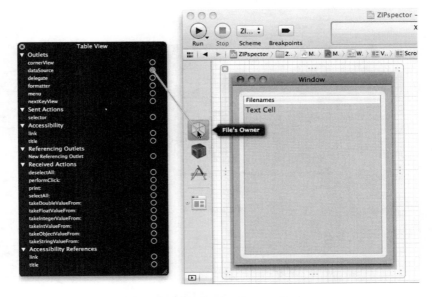

**Figure 36.3**   Set dataSource Outlet

Control-click on File's Owner to bring up its connection window. Drag to set the tableView outlet (Figure 36.4).

In MyDocument.m, remove the default **readFromData:ofType:error:** and override **readFromURL:ofType:error:** to create an **NSTask** that executes zipinfo. Also, create an **NSPipe** and connect it to the standardOut of the **NSTask** (Figure 36.5)

Here is the code:

```
- (BOOL)readFromURL:(NSURL *)absoluteURL
            ofType:(NSString *)typeName
             error:(NSError **)outError
{
    // Which file are we getting the zipinfo for?
    NSString *filename = [absoluteURL path];

    // Prepare a task object
```

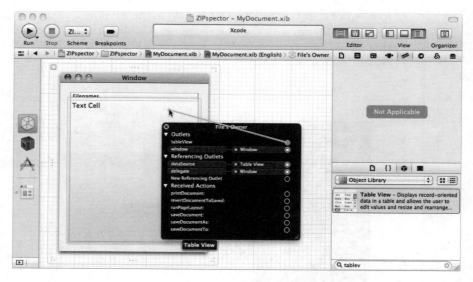

**Figure 36.4**  Set tableView Outlet

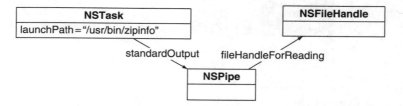

**Figure 36.5**  Object Diagram

```
NSTask *task = [[NSTask alloc] init];
[task setLaunchPath:@"/usr/bin/zipinfo"];
NSArray *args = [NSArray arrayWithObjects:@"-1", filename, nil];
[task setArguments:args];

// Create the pipe to read from
NSPipe *outPipe = [[NSPipe alloc] init];
[task setStandardOutput:outPipe];

// Start the process
[task launch];

// Read the output
NSData *data = [[outPipe fileHandleForReading]
                           readDataToEndOfFile];

// Make sure the task terminates normally
```

```
[task waitUntilExit];
int status = [task terminationStatus];

// Check status
if (status != 0) {
    if (outError) {
        NSDictionary *eDict =
                [NSDictionary dictionaryWithObject:@"zipinfo failed"
                              forKey:NSLocalizedFailureReasonErrorKey];
        *outError = [NSError errorWithDomain:NSOSStatusErrorDomain
                                         code:0
                                     userInfo:eDict];
    }
    return NO;
}

// Convert to a string
NSString *aString = [[NSString alloc] initWithData:data
                                          encoding:NSUTF8StringEncoding];

// Break the string into lines
filenames = [aString componentsSeparatedByString:@"\n"];
NSLog(@"filenames = %@", filenames);

// In case of revert
[tableView reloadData];

return YES;
}
```

Now you need table view data source methods:

```
- (NSInteger)numberOfRowsInTableView:(NSTableView *)v
{
    return [filenames count];
}

- (id)tableView:(NSTableView *)tv
 objectValueForTableColumn:(NSTableColumn *)tc
                       row:(NSInteger)row
{
    return [filenames objectAtIndex:row];
}
```

Your application doesn't save, so you can delete the method **dataOfType:error:** if you wish. Also, you can open up the MainMenu.xib file and delete any menu items that are concerned with saving.

Build and run your application. You should be able to see the contents of any zip file. (No Untitled document will appear (this is a viewer) so you must open an existing .zip file.)

## Asynchronous Reads

As mentioned in Chapter 24, the run loop is the object that waits for events, which may be keyboard, mouse, or timer events. These are all run loop data sources. You can also make a file handle a run loop data source.

In this section, we are going to fork off a process that burps up data occasionally. We will attach a pipe to standardOut, but instead of trying to read all the data from the file handle immediately, we will ask the file handle to read in the background and send a notification when data is ready.

You can use /sbin/ping to check whether you can make an IP connection to another machine. Try running it in Terminal:

```
$ /sbin/ping -c10 www.bignerdranch.com
PING www.bignerdranch.com (69.39.89.150): 56 data bytes
64 bytes from 69.39.89.150: icmp_seq=0 ttl=50 time=35.579 ms
64 bytes from 69.39.89.150: icmp_seq=1 ttl=50 time=35.099 ms
64 bytes from 69.39.89.150: icmp_seq=2 ttl=50 time=34.546 ms
64 bytes from 69.39.89.150: icmp_seq=3 ttl=50 time=35.495 ms
64 bytes from 69.39.89.150: icmp_seq=4 ttl=50 time=35.685 ms
64 bytes from 69.39.89.150: icmp_seq=5 ttl=50 time=35.667 ms
64 bytes from 69.39.89.150: icmp_seq=6 ttl=50 time=36.435 ms
64 bytes from 69.39.89.150: icmp_seq=7 ttl=50 time=52.296 ms
64 bytes from 69.39.89.150: icmp_seq=8 ttl=50 time=36.142 ms
64 bytes from 69.39.89.150: icmp_seq=9 ttl=50 time=36.188 ms

--- www.bignerdranch.com ping statistics ---
10 packets transmitted, 10 packets received, 0% packet loss
round-trip min/avg/max/stddev = 34.546/37.313/52.296/5.021 ms
```

If you want to end the program prematurely, press Control-C to send it a sigint signal. This will cause it to write out the stats and terminate.

## iPing

Now you are going to write a Cocoa app that uses **NSTask** to run ping (Figure 36.6).

In Xcode, create a new project, iPing, of type Cocoa Application. Set the Class Prefix to iPing. Uncheck Create Document-Based Application. In **iPingAppDelegate**, add two outlets, pointers to the **NSTask** and the **NSPipe**, and an action:

```
@interface iPingAppDelegate : NSObject <NSApplicationDelegate> {
    IBOutlet NSTextView *outputView;
```

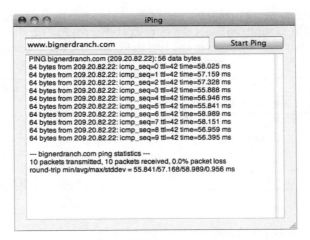

**Figure 36.6**  Completed Application

```
    IBOutlet NSTextField *hostField;
    IBOutlet NSButton *startButton;
    NSTask *task;
    NSPipe *pipe;
}
@property (assign) IBOutlet NSWindow *window;
- (IBAction)startStopPing:(id)sender;
@end
```

Open MainMenu.xib and drop a text view, a text field, and a button onto the window. The button should be put in Toggle mode. The title should be Start Ping (Figure 36.7), and the alternate title should be Stop Ping. Set the state to Off.

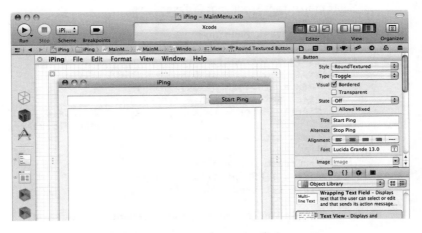

**Figure 36.7**  Button Attributes

Make the **iPingAppDelegate** the target of the button; its action should be **startStopPing:**. Set the outputView, hostField, and startButton outlets to point to the text view, the text field, and the button, respectively (Figure 36.8).

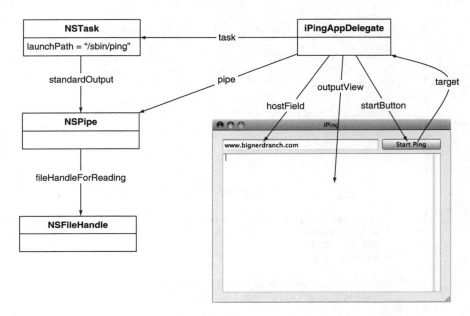

**Figure 36.8**    Object Diagram

In iPingAppDelegate.m, implement **startStopPing:**

```
- (IBAction)startStopPing:(id)sender
{
    // Is the task running?
    if (task) {
        [task interrupt];
    } else {
        task = [[NSTask alloc] init];
        [task setLaunchPath:@"/sbin/ping"];
        NSArray *args = [NSArray arrayWithObjects:@"-c10",
                                        [hostField stringValue], nil];
        [task setArguments:args];

        // Create a new pipe
        pipe = [[NSPipe alloc] init];
        [task setStandardOutput:pipe];

        NSFileHandle *fh = [pipe fileHandleForReading];

        NSNotificationCenter *nc;
```

```
            nc = [NSNotificationCenter defaultCenter];
            [nc removeObserver:self];
            [nc addObserver:self
                    selector:@selector(dataReady:)
                        name:NSFileHandleReadCompletionNotification
                      object:fh];
            [nc addObserver:self
                    selector:@selector(taskTerminated:)
                        name:NSTaskDidTerminateNotification
                      object:task];
            [task launch];
            [outputView setString:@""];

            [fh readInBackgroundAndNotify];
        }
}
```

While the task is running, the file handle will be posting notifications when data is ready. Implement the method that will get called:

```
- (void)appendData:(NSData *)d
{
    NSString *s = [[NSString alloc] initWithData:d
                                        encoding:NSUTF8StringEncoding];
    NSTextStorage *ts = [outputView textStorage];
    [ts replaceCharactersInRange:NSMakeRange([ts length], 0)
                      withString:s];
}

- (void)dataReady:(NSNotification *)n
{
    NSData *d;
    d = [[n userInfo] valueForKey:NSFileHandleNotificationDataItem];

    NSLog(@"dataReady:%ld bytes", [d length]);

    if ([d length]) {
        [self appendData:d];
    }
    // If the task is running, start reading again
    if (task)
        [[pipe fileHandleForReading] readInBackgroundAndNotify];
}
```

When the process is done, we should do some cleanup:

```
- (void)taskTerminated:(NSNotification *)note
{
    NSLog(@"taskTerminated:");
```

```
    task = nil;

    [startButton setState:0];

}
```

Build and run the application.

# Challenge: .tar and .tgz files

A listing of files in a zip file is given by *zipinfo*. You can get a similar listing for tar files by using the command-line tool `tar`:

```
# /usr/bin/tar tf MyFiles.tar
```

If the `tar` file is also compressed, just add a `z` to the flags:

```
# /usr/bin/tar tzf MyFiles.tgz
```

Extend ZIPspector to deal with `.tar` and `.tgz` files also.

## Chapter 37

# DISTRIBUTING YOUR APP

The time will come when you are ready for your app to leave its nest. You've crushed all the bugs you can find and tested for leaks in Instruments. It's high time your app see the world! In this chapter, we'll talk about how to use Xcode to prepare your app for life outside the debugger.

# Build Configurations

Up until now, we've been using debug builds for all our testing. Debug builds contain additional information that enables the debugger to show detailed stack information. Debug builds are generally built with optimization disabled; if you're building for multiple architectures (32- and 64-bit), the debug build is created only for the development system's architecture.

These are all great settings for development. They make the debugger more useful, and builds are generated more quickly, but they're the opposite of what you want in a build that you would release to customers: a release build. In a release build, optimizations are turned up, debugging symbols are stripped (to reduce size and make inspecting the code more difficult), and all the architectures are built.

There is nothing particularly special about the debug and release build configurations. They are simply a convention, and all the settings for these configurations are modifiable within Xcode. You can find the existing build configurations in the project editor, on the Info pane. You can also add new build configurations there.

Xcode has several actions available: run, profile, analyze, and archive. A build configuration is associated with each of these actions. You can configure this using the Scheme Editor to associate a build configuration with a particular action (Figure 37.1). That build configuration will be used when building the target for that particular action.

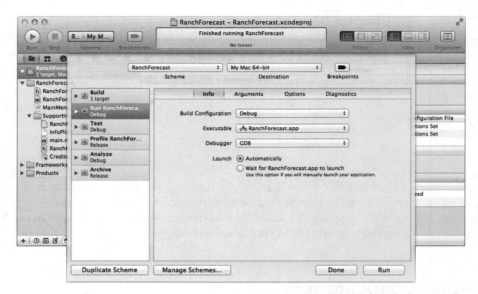

**Figure 37.1**    The Scheme Editor with the Debug Build Configuration Selected for Run

## Preprocessor Macros and Using Build Configurations to Change Behavior

One common use of build configurations is as a means for hardcoding behavioral settings in your application. This is done using preprocessor macros.

In Chapter 3, we saw how to use the NS_BLOCK_ASSERTIONS macro to disable **NSAssert**. Open a project and click on the project in the project browser. Select the target, and under Build Settings find the Preprocessor Macros line (Figure 37.2).

Note that Preprocessor Macros can be expanded to show Debug and Release. This allows you to define unique sets of preprocessor macros for debug and release builds. In this example, the only macro defined is DEBUG=1 in the debug configuration. This sets the DEBUG macro's value to 1. To check the value of DEBUG in code, we can do something like this:

```
#if DEBUG
    [self printOutEverything];
#else
    [self printOnlyWhatsNeeded];
#endif
```

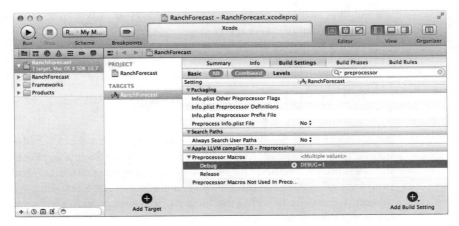

**Figure 37.2**  Preprocessor Macros

If you're not familiar with preprocessor macros, the concept is fairly simple: Before your source code is compiled, it is run through the preprocessor, which processes your source code on a line-by-line basis. In our case, the code sent to the compiler in a debug build would be:

```
[self printOutEverything];
```

Note that the other code is completely omitted: There isn't even a branch to be evaluated when the program runs. You can, however, use macros in branches if you wish. For example:

```
if (DEBUG) {
    NSLog(@"Debug is %d", DEBUG);
}
```

One last note about preprocessor macros: They can be used to do a lot more than simply defining functions. You might want to log only certain statements in your debug build. Our first thought might be something like this:

```
#if DEBUG
    NSLog(@"This happened.");
#endif
```

But it would be much less obtrusive to simply use:

```
    DebugLog(@"This happened.");
```

We could implement this by defining a DebugLog function. A preprocessor macro allows us to erase the logging code completely, however. The following macro gives us a `DebugLog` macro, which looks just like a function but evaluates to nothing when `DEBUG` is zero:

```
#if DEBUG
    #define DebugLog(...) NSLog(__VA_ARGS__)
#lse
    #define DebugLog(...) do { } while(0)
#endif
```

An excellent place for such a macro is your precompiled header file, usually named *ProjectName*-Prefix.pch and found in the Supporting Files group. This file is essentially included by every file in your project. Because modifying the precompiled header file (or any file it includes) triggers rebuilding the entire project, we usually include only files that will change very rarely, such as framework headers.

# Creating a Release Build

Now that you know about build configurations—enough to know that when you're distributing your app, you will want a release build—how do you create one? The simplest way to do this in Xcode is by archiving your target. Note that in the Scheme Editor the Release build configuration is selected for the Archive action. Select Archive in the Product menu. Your target will rebuild.

Xcode's archiving feature is intended to assist with cataloging an application's various release builds, as well as with maintaining its debug symbols for use later on with any crash logs you might gather in the future.

Once your target is archived, it will appear in the Organizer on the Archives tab (Figure 37.3).

You can then extract the app bundle from the archive by using the Share button. You will be prompted for the format to share it in. Choose Application to share only the app bundle (Figure 37.4).

Once Xcode has exported the app bundle, you can compress it in a ZIP archive and post it on your Web site, or send it to your beta testing team.

## A Few Words on Installers

If you are new to Mac, you may be wondering how you are going to create an installer for your application. Our advice is: Don't. Application installation on a

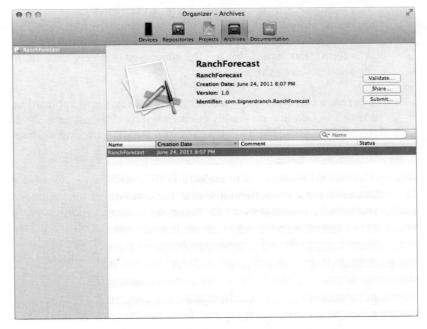

**Figure 37.3**    Archives in the Organizer

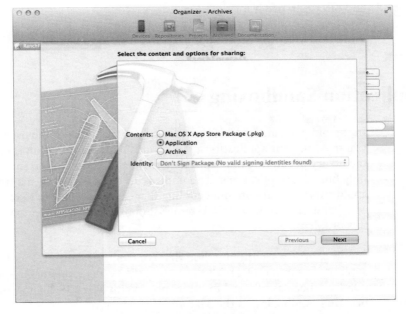

**Figure 37.4**    Sharing Your Application

Mac is different from other platforms, and in most cases an installer adds unneeded complexity, and also hides its actions from the user. Most applications are installed by simply having the user drag them from their downloads folder into /Applications. This has the advantage of a very clear uninstallation: Drag the application to the trash.

There are two common approaches for packaging an application for download. Many app bundles are simply compressed in a ZIP archive. By default, Safari unarchives ZIP archives containing app bundles, making drag installation very easy for the user.

The second approach is to create a DMG (disk image), which has the advantage of displaying a Finder window with the contents of the image when it is opened (mounted). This allows for the inclusion of files in addition to the app bundle itself, such as a readme, a symbolic link to /Applications (to make drag installation even more convenient), and an optional custom background. Configuring such a DMG is complicated enough that there are third-party tools to help with the process.

Both approaches are not without their pitfalls. For example, users sometimes forget to drag the application to their /Applications folder, leaving it in their downloads folder or, worse, running it from the DMG. One solution some developers have implemented is to detect the app bundle's location on startup and offer to move it for the user.

Note that Mac App Store apps cannot use an installer.

# Application Sandboxing

In the old days, an application had all the same rights of the user running it. If you trust all your applications, this sounds fine. However, most users don't have the luxury of running only apps they trust, and, more important, no user can run only bug-free applications. The unpleasant truth is that even a trustworthy application can have an innocent bug that causes damage to a system or allows an attacker access to the user's system. Sandboxing is a big step toward mitigating this problem.

Sandboxing is a security method that constrains the means by which an application can interact with the system (filesystem, network). Applications on iOS have been sandboxed for years now. With Mac OS X Lion, Apple is bringing sandboxing to the Mac and, furthermore, requires that all applications in the Mac App Store be sandboxed.

# Entitlements

Sandboxing requires a bit more thought on the part of the developer than simply turning on an **Enable Sandboxing** flag. The developer must specify the application's entitlements, a list of things it is allowed to do. The OS will then constrain the application to performing only those actions. You can think of the entitlements as a contract between the application and the operating system: The application promises to perform only the listed actions.

For example, consider the requirements of the RanchForecast project. It needs to create outgoing network connections and not much more. It doesn't need to read or write files on disk or use the camera or microphone or open a port for incoming network connections. By setting RanchForecast's entitlements to creating only outgoing network connections, we have severely limited any opportunities for mischief on the part of this application.

To specify an application's entitlements, the plist can be edited, or you can use Xcode's project editor (Figure 37.5).

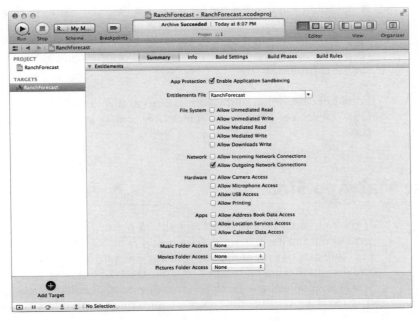

**Figure 37.5**   Application Entitlements

Sandboxed applications are provided with a container: a folder on disk in which they can store caches, preference files, and other resources. Mac OS X changes the home directory reported to via AppKit API calls to return this container folder, which resides within the user's Library.

## Mediated File Access and Powerbox

Mediated read and write access is the preferred means of file access to applications. Mediated access includes access to temporary files, such as those in the application's container, and also read or read/write access to files that are explicitly opened by the user using a Mac OS X file-open dialog or files dragged to the application. That is, when the user chooses a file via an **NSOpenPanel** or **NSSavePanel**, the application's sandbox is automatically expanded to include the selected file or directory.

This functionality is provided by a system daemon called Powerbox. When the developer uses **NSOpenPanel** or **NSSavePanel**, the sheets are rendered by the system daemon, providing a trusted means for file selection that is transparent to the developer—no code changes are necessary.

If an application that has the mediated read or read/write entitlement is terminated and restarted, the sandbox is again expanded to include previously open documents when Lion restores the prior state of the application by reopening those documents. The standard AppKit **Open Recent** menu provides similar capabilities.

For a full description of the entitlements available to applications, see the Mac OS X Developer Library document *Code Signing and Application Sandboxing Guide*.

# The Mac App Store

If you're writing a commercial app, there's quite a bit of work to do beyond the writing the app itself, in order to release it. The Mac App Store has the advantage of taking care of a lot of these aspects for you: purchasing, installation/packaging, and distribution are all handled for you. Much of licensing is addressed, also. If you're an independent developer, working on such tasks can feel as though they're taking valuable time away from making your product better.

The Mac App Store isn't for every app, however. If your application cannot operate in a sandboxed environment or doesn't conform to the review guidelines, you will want to use more traditional means of distribution.

Most aspects of distribution in the Mac App Store are fairly straightforward and similar to the iOS App Store. You will need to use Xcode to sign your application binary, provide a description of your application and screenshots, and, finally, submit the app by using Xcode's Organizer.

## Receipt Validation

Mac App Store apps differ from iOS apps in one key area, however: There is no operating system support for license checking. That is, without special effort on your part, there is no copy protection. If copy protection is important to you, you will need to implement receipt validation.

When purchased from the Mac App Store, an application is downloaded to the user's system. A file containing the application receipt will be placed in the application bundle. The receipt contains the application's bundle identifier, its version string, and a hash of the computer's GUID. Receipts are cryptographically signed by Apple.

By verifying the information in this receipt, your application can determine whether it is authorized to run on this system. The verification steps are:

1. Verify that the receipt is present.

2. Verify that the receipt is properly signed by Apple.

3. Verify that the bundle identifier in the receipt matches.

4. Verify that the version identifier matches.

5. Verify that the hash contained in the receipt matches this computer's GUID hash.

A few notes: although the bundle and version identifiers can be obtained from the Info.plistfile (CFBundleIdentifier and CFBundleShortVersionString keys, respectively), it is strongly recommended that these values be duplicated as constants within the application itself. The reason is that the application's Info.plistfile is easily modified by users; by trusting this information, the application could be tricked into accepting a valid receipt for another application on that system.

If validation fails, the application should terminate with a status of 173:

```
if (!validated)
    exit(173);
```

This instructs the system that validation has failed for this application.

The code for performing this verification process is, frankly, unpleasant for most developers. Low-level C programmers will feel right at home, although working with cryptographic APIs can be daunting to most developers. You may be asking, "Why doesn't Apple provide a reference implementation?"

The reason is that if Apple did provide a reference implementation, the vast majority of developers would use it, and a cracking tool could then be used to disarm the protection in all applications that use this code. By asking developers to concoct their own methods for verifying this information, the problem of cracking copy protection is made more difficult.

Apple has provided code snippets for performing parts of this process, as well as a sample receipt for testing purposes. This is an excellent use of build configurations: Use the debug build configuration, or create a new one that directs your code to use the sample receipt for its validation process.

The aforementioned code snippets can be found in the Mac OS X Developer Library article "Validating App Store Receipts." Be creative in your receipt validation, and remember to use varying patterns between your applications.

# Chapter 38
# THE END

When we teach a class, it always ends with the "Feel-Good Talk," which delivers the following messages:

- The knowledge you have received from this experience never comes easy. You have learned a lot of stuff. Be proud.

- The only way to solidify what you have learned is to write applications. The sooner you start, the easier it will be.

- There is still much more to learn, but you have crossed the hump in the learning curve. Matters will be easier from here. Once again, the only way to progress is to write applications.

- As a speaker, Aaron is available for weddings, parties, bar mitzvahs, and other events. We also offer five- and seven-day classes at the Big Nerd Ranch. For a schedule, please see the Big Nerd Ranch Web site (www.bignerdranch.com/). Or use the RanchForecast exercise.

The final part of the "Feel-Good Talk" is a listing of resources that will help answer your questions as they arise. As with any programming topic, your answers will be found in a hodgepodge of online documentation, Web sites, and mailing lists.

- If you have a question about Cocoa, the first place to check is in the reference documentation. All the classes, protocols, functions, and constants are listed there.

- If you have a question about Objective-C, the first place to check is in the online Objective-C reference documentation.

- If you have a question about Xcode or Interface Builder, the first place to check is in the developer tools reference documentation.

- Mark Dalrymple wrote a book on the plumbing of Mac OS X from a developer's point of view. If your code is going to do anything with the operating system (such as multithreading or networking), we strongly recommend that you pick up a copy of *Advanced Mac OS X Programming*.

- Don't be afraid to experiment—most questions can be answered by creating a tiny application. Creating this application will probably take you less than 15 minutes.

- The Web site for this book (www.bignerdranch.com/books) has the answers to many questions and several fun examples.

- Stack Overflow (www.stackoverflow.com/) is an excellent place to find the answers to your questions, and has a strong Cocoa and iOS presence. Chances are somebody has faced the same challenge you are facing.

- The CocoaDev Wiki (www.cocoadev.com/) is a good place to learn new tricks.

- Apple also has a mailing list for Cocoa developers. You can join the cocoa-dev mailing list at Apple's list server (http: //lists.apple.com/). The list is archived at www.cocoabuilder.com/.

- If you have exhausted all other possibilities, Apple's Developer Technical Support will answer your questions for a fee. The folks there have answered lots of questions for us, and we find them to be consistently knowledgeable and helpful.

- Join the Apple Developer Connection. It will give you access to the latest developer tools and documentation, as well as prior years' WWDC videos. The ADC Web site is http: //developer.apple.com/.

- When you're ready to learn more about Cocoa, the forthcoming *More Cocoa Programming for Mac OS X* will help you take your Mac applications to the next level, with an emphasis on more advanced topics such as custom controls and making your application scriptable using AppleScript.

Finally, try to be nice. Help beginners. Give away useful applications and their source code. Answer questions in a kind manner. It is a relatively small community, and few good deeds go forever unrewarded.

Thanks for reading our book!

# INDEX

## Symbols

: (colon), method name with arguments, 36
@"..." construct, 47
@ symbol
  C strings vs. `NSStrings`, 40–41
  Objective-C keywords, 27
^operator, blocks, 372, 374

## A

abstract class
  defined, 160
  `NSCoder` as, 160
  `NSController` as, 129–130
`acceptsFirstResponder` method, keyboard
  events, 272–275, 280, 282
accessor methods
  declaring for new class, 50–51
  defined, 50
  implementing, 123–125
actions
  implicit animation and, 423–424
  targets and. *See* target/action
actions dictionary, 423
`addObject` method
  add objects to end of array, 36
  `NSMutableArray`, 46
`addObjectsFromArray:` method,
  `NSMutableArray`, 46
`addOperationWithBlock:` method,
  `NSOperationQueue`, 436–437
Alert panel
  as modal window, 336–337
  overview of, 229–230
  using string table, 241
`alloc` method
  coupling with `init` message, 43–44
  retain-count rules for ownership, 76
  retain count using, 69

AppKit framework.
  classes with delegates in, 112
  defined, 6
  UIKit vs. *See* iOS development
applications
  debugging hints, 98
  as directories, 172
  distributing your. *See* distributing your
    application
ARC (automatic reference counting)
  benefits and limitations, 68–69
  defined, 68
  disabling, 63–64
  overview of, 80–81
  strong references, 81
  weak references, 81–82
archiving
  automatic document saving, 174
  document architecture, 163–167
  loading and `NSKeyedArchiver`, 168–169
  `NSCoder` and `NSCoding`, 160–163
  overview of, 159–160
  preventing infinite loops, 172–173
  saving and `NSKeyedArchiver`, 167–168
arguments
  initializers with, 56–58
  methods taking, 36–37
`arrangedObjects` controller key, array
  controller, 136
array controllers
  `NSArrayController`. *See* `NSArrayController`
arrays
  methods implemented by `NSArray`, 45
  methods implemented by
    `NSMutableArray`, 46
asserts, debugging with, 61–62
`assign` attribute, properties, 125
Assistant Editor
  editing implementation file, 27

# ABOUT US

## THE BIG NERD STORY

Big Nerd Ranch exists to broaden the minds of our students and the businesses of our clients. Whether we are training talented individuals or developing a company's mobile strategy, our core philosophy is integral to everything we do.

The brainchild of CEO Aaron Hillegass, Big Nerd Ranch has hosted more than 2,000 students at the Ranch since its inception in 2001. Over the past ten years, we have had the opportunity to work with some of the biggest companies in the world such as Apple, Samsung, Nokia, Google, AOL, Los Alamos National Laboratory and Adobe, helping them realize their programming goals. Our team of software engineers are among the brightest in the business and it shows in our work. We have developed dozens of innovative and flexible solutions for our clients.

## The Story Behind the Hat

*Back in 2001, Big Nerd Ranch founder, Aaron Hillegass, showed up at WWDC (World Wide Developers Conference) to promote the Big Nerd Ranch brand. Without the money to buy an expensive booth, Aaron donned a ten-gallon cowboy hat to draw attention while passing out Big Nerd literature to prospective students and clients. A week later, we landed our first big client and the cowboy hat has been synonymous with the Big Nerd brand ever since. Already easily recognizable at 6'5, Aaron can be spotted wearing his cowboy hat at speaking engagements and conferences all over the world.*

## The New Ranch – Opening 2012

*In the continuing effort to perfect the student experience, Big Nerd Ranch is building its own facility. Located just 20 minutes from the Atlanta airport, the new Ranch will be a monastic learning center that encompasses Aaron Hillegass' vision for technical education featuring a state-of-the-art classroom, fine dining and exercise facilities.*

# TRAINING

## ACHIEVE NERDVANA

Since 2001, Big Nerd Ranch has offered intensive computer programming courses taught by our expert instructors in a retreat environment. It is at our Ranch where we think our students flourish. Classes, accommodations and dining all take place within the same building, freeing you to learn, code and discuss with your programming peers and instructors. At Big Nerd Ranch, we take care of the details; your only job is to learn.

### Our Teachers

Our teachers are leaders in their respective fields. They offer deep understanding of the technologies they teach, as well as a broad spectrum of development experience, allowing them to address the concerns you encounter as a developer. Big Nerd Ranch instructors provide the necessary combination of knowledge and outstanding teaching experience, enabling our students to leave the Ranch with a vastly improved set of skills.

### The Big Nerd Way

We have developed "The Big Nerd Ranch Way". This methodology guides the development and presentation of our classes. The style is casual but focused, with brief lectures followed by hands-on exercises designed to give you immediate, relevant understanding of each piece of the technology you are learning.

### Your Stay At The Ranch

One fee covers tuition, meals, lodging and transportation to and from the airport. At the Big Nerd Ranch, we remove the distractions inherent in standard corporate training by offering classes in quiet, comfortable settings in Atlanta, Georgia and Frankfurt, Germany.

## Available Classes

*Advanced Mac OS X*
*Android*
*Beginning Cocoa*
*Beginning iOS (iPhone/iPad)*
*Beginning Ruby on Rails*
*Cocoa Commuter Class in Spanish*
*Cocoa I*
*Cocoa II*
*Commuter iOS Class*
*Django*
*iOS (iPhone/iPad)*
*OpenGL*
*Python Mastery*
*Ruby on Rails I*
*Ruby on Rails II*

## Interested in a class?

Register online at www.bignerdranch.com or call 404.478.9005 for more information.
Full class schedule, pricing and availability also online.

## OUR NERDS, YOUR LOCATION

Through our on-site training program you can affordably and conveniently have our renowned classes come to you. Our expert instructors will help your team advance through nerd-based instructional support that is fresh, engaging and allows for unencumbered hands-on learning.

Clients around the globe have praised our on-site instruction for some of the following reasons:

### Flexibility

- Classes can be booked when the timing is right for your team.
- We can tailor our existing syllabi to ensure our training meets your organization's unique needs.
- Post-class mentorship is available to support your team as they work on especially challenging projects.

### Affordability

- No need for planes, trains and automobiles for all of your staff; our Nerds come to you.
- Train up to 22 students at a significant discount over open-enrollment training.

### Nerd Know-how

- Our instructors are highly practiced in both teaching and programming. They move beyond theory by bringing their real-life experiences to your team.
- On-site training includes post-class access to our Nerds, our extensive Alumni Network, and our Big Nerd Ranch Forums. Learning support doesn't end just because your class does.

For your on-site training, we provide an instructor, all Big Nerd Ranch copyrighted class materials, gifts, certificates of completion and access to our extensive Alumni Network. You'll provide the classroom set up, computers and related devices for all students, a projector and a screen.

### Ready to book an on-site training course?

For a free Big Nerd Ranch on-site proposal, please contact us at 404.478.9005.

# CONSULTING

BiG nerd ranch

## ACHIEVE NERDVANA IN-HOUSE & ON-SITE

When you contract with Big Nerd Ranch, we'll work directly with you to turn your needs into a full-fledged desktop and/or mobile solution. Our developers and designers have consistently created some of the iPhone App Store's most intriguing applications.

### Management Philosophy

Big Nerd Ranch holistically manages every client relationship. Our goal is to communicate and educate our clients from project initiation to completion, while ultimately helping them gain a competitive advantage in their niche marketplace.

### Project Strategy

We take a detail-oriented approach to all of our project estimations. We'll work with you to define a strategy, specify product offerings and then build them into software that stands alone.

### Our Process

Our consulting process is broken down into three distinct phases: Requirements, Execution and Monitoring/Controlling. Bring your business case to us and we'll develop a plan for a user interface and database design. From there, we'll develop a quote and begin the design and implementation process. Our Nerds will perform many tests, including debugging and performance tuning, ensuring the app does what you want it to do. Finally, we'll beta test your app and get it ready for submission and deployment in the iTunes store and/or the Android Market. Once your app is finished, the Nerds will work with you on subsequent version updates and can even help with the marketing of your app.

## Testimonials

*"tops has worked closely with Big Nerd Ranch for over eight years. Consistently they have delivered high-quality code for our projects; clean and poetic. Thanks to their contributions, we have become a leader in our field."*

**Dr. Mark Sanchez**
President/Founder
tops Software
topsortho.com

*"From the simplest GUI design gig to jobs that plumb the darkest corners of the OS, Big Nerd Ranch should be the first contact in your virtual Rolodex under Mac/iPhone consulting. It's no exaggeration to say that Aaron Hillegass literally wrote the book on Cocoa programming, and you couldn't possibly do better than to bring his and his team's expertise to bear on your application. I've yet to work with a consulting firm that is as competent and communicative as Big Nerd Ranch. Simply put, these guys deliver."*

**Glenn Zelniker**
CEO
Z-Systems Audio Engineering
www.z-sys.com

*"We turned to Big Nerd Ranch to develop the Teavana concept into an iPhone app. More than just a developer, they partnered with us to make the app better than we could have imagined alone. The final app was bug-free and functioned exactly as expected. I would definitely recommend Big Nerd Ranch and can't speak highly enough about their work."*

**Jay Allen**
VP of Ecommerce
Teavana Corporation
www.teavana.com

## We'd love to talk to you about your project.

Contact our consulting team today for a free consultation at consult@bignerdranch.com or visit www.bignerdranch.com/consulting for more information.

## FINELY-CRAFTED APPLICATIONS

Big Nerd Ranch is a leading developer of downloadable mobile and desktop Mac applications. Several of our most intriguing iPhone and desktop apps are available for purchase in the iTunes store.

### Mobile Applications

Smartphones have started to take over the mobile phone market. Since the inception of the iPhone, we have created dozens of apps for our clients and now have a roster of our own applications including games, utilities, music and educational apps. As an ever-evolving frontier of technology, Big Nerd Ranch is committed to staying ahead of the curve.

### Desktop Applications

Big Nerd Ranch leverages the best of our technologies to develop powerful and user-friendly desktop applications. We recently released our first set of utility applications designed to make your workspace more efficient.

## Mobile Apps

*The world has gone mobile. If your company doesn't have a mobile application, you are behind the curve. As of early 2011, the iTunes app store has grown to nearly 400,000 apps and the Android market has climbed to more than 250,000 applications. Google has unveiled its Android platform with an app store of its own and dozens of smartphone manufacturers have announced Android-powered devices. RIM has launched App World, Palm has its Palm Store, Nokia launched Ovi (its online store) and Microsoft has unveiled Windows Marketplace.*

*While still leading the way, the iOS market has put up some staggering statistics:*

- *Total iOS app store downloads: 10.3 billion*
- *iPhone apps are being downloaded at a rate of 30 million per day.*
- *As of early 2011, when the app store hit 10 billion downloads, it did so in half the time (31 months versus 67 months) that it took for songs in the iTunes store to hit the same mark.*
- *The average number of apps downloaded for iPhone/iPad/iPod touch is currently at more than 60.*

### Need an App?

Visit us online at www.bignerdranch.com/software to see all our latest apps.
Many Big Nerd apps are also available for sale at the iTunes store.

# FREE Online Edition

Your purchase of *Cocoa® Programming for Mac® OS X, Fourth Edition,* includes access to a free online edition for 45 days through the Safari Books Online subscription service. Nearly every Addison-Wesley Professional book is available online through Safari Books Online, along with more than 5,000 other technical books and videos from publishers such as Cisco Press, Exam Cram, IBM Press, O'Reilly, Prentice Hall, Que, and Sams.

**SAFARI BOOKS ONLINE** allows you to search for a specific answer, cut and paste code, download chapters, and stay current with emerging technologies.

## Activate your FREE Online Edition at www.informit.com/safarifree

> **STEP 1:** Enter the coupon code: YCMPXAA.

> **STEP 2:** New Safari users, complete the brief registration form. Safari subscribers, just log in.

If you have difficulty registering on Safari or accessing the online edition, please e-mail customer-service@safaribooksonline.com